VOL. X
Founded 1984

The Yearbook of Experts®

The Yearbook of Experts, Authorities & Spokespersons®

An Encyclopedia of Sources®

www.ExpertClick.com

Yearbook of Experts®,
Volume XXXVIII, Number I

The Yearbook of Experts®

An Encyclopedia of Sources®

Broadcast Interview Source, Inc.
Washington, D.C.

Web site: www.ExpertClick.com

Telephone: (202) 333-5000
Fax: (202) 342-5411
E-mail: ExpertClick@Gmail.com

Mitchell P. Davis, Editor & Publisher

Editor's Note: The purpose of the Yearbook of Experts® is to provide bona fide interview sources to working members of the news media. Great care is taken in the review and selection of sources for inclusion. Although all contacts have expressed interest in being available for interview, we do not guarantee the availability of any given participant for any given interview, nor is a warranty offered that every listed contact will be appropriate for a reader's particular purpose. Quotes are provided to show acceptance of the Yearbook of Experts by individuals who work in the news media, but should not be interpreted as endorsements by the named organizations. "America's Favorite Newsroom Resource" is based on tens of thousands of Yearbooks requested by journalists.

ISBN: 0-934333-81-5   ISSN: 1051-4058

Broadcast Interview Source, Inc.
Washington, D.C.

Phone: (202) 333-5000
Toll-free: 1-800-955-0311
Fax: (202) 342-5411
E-mail: ExpertClick@Gmail.com
Web site: www.ExpertClick.com

June 14, 2012

Welcome to the First issue of the 38th volume of the Yearbook of Experts® -- now in a printed version to accompany the online version, ExpertClick.com. This book is based on the live information provided by our member experts and groups, directly from the online database. Each expert has the ability to log in and update their information instantly, 24 hours a day.

You can always search the database at ExpertClick.com for the most up-to-date information, but this book puts the information at your fingertips. Also, you can download new and revised Adobe PDF editions as they become available.

You may be reading this online from the Adobe PDF version, or you may be reading a printed edition. The content is the same, but when you read the book as the Adobe PDF from a Web enabled computer, you can click on links to take you directly to the experts' Web pages and see enhanced content.

Bonus for registered journalists: Contact our experts via e-mail with our InterviewNet.com system.

This Yearbook has five sections:
1) Introduction;
2) Topic Index, when viewed on your computer, these link directly to the profiles;
3) Profile Section, with descriptions of experts linked to their Yearbook.com sites;
4) Geographic Index, so you can find sources in your area;
5) Participant Index, to quickly find Participants.

Questions? Please contact us at (202) 333-5000 or ExpertClick@Gmail.com.

Sincerely,

Mitchell P. Davis, Editor & Publisher

How does the Yearbook of Experts work for JOURNALISTS?

Journalists can access and use the ExpertClick.com Web site free of charge, which includes the download of the Adobe PDF and other features. Also, they can create a profile in our News Media Yearbook. Journalists who choose to create a public profile in our News Media Yearbook also have free access to the News Media Yearbook for networking.

We print and mail copies of the Yearbook of Experts to thousands of leading journalists twice a year.

Journalists -- You can visit Expertclick.com without registration, but some features require free registration.

Here's how to get all of our Journalist benefits:

FREE REGISTRATION: Go to ExpertClick.com, and click on "JOURNALISTS."

Simply fill out the registration form.
This gives you greater access to our news sources.

How does the Yearbook of Experts work for NEWS SOURCES?

The annual membership cost of $995includes:

1) A listing in print and the Adobe PDF with 75 words of print text, indexing to nine topics and your contact information.

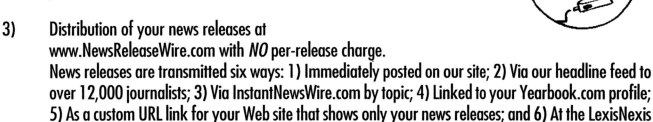

2) A complete profile at the www.ExpertClick.com site with unlimited text, HTML, links to your audio -- *and the profile is also available via LexisNexis.*

3) Distribution of your news releases at www.NewsReleaseWire.com with *NO* per-release charge.
News releases are transmitted six ways: 1) Immediately posted on our site; 2) Via our headline feed to over 12,000 journalists; 3) Via InstantNewsWire.com by topic; 4) Linked to your Yearbook.com profile; 5) As a custom URL link for your Web site that shows only your news releases; and 6) At the LexisNexis database.

4) Your event postings at www.Daybook.com, The Public Record of Today's Events®.

5) Talking News Releases on your profile page, on your news releases, and links from your Web site.

Here's how to be included as a News Source Expert:

Go to **ExpertClick.com,** and click on the "Sign Up" button on the lower left. You can view and print a PDF of our brochure. Then scroll down to the application form to sign up online.

Or call us at (202) 333-5000, and *we will instantly create your profile.*

Visit all the Yearbook of Expert's Web sites:

ExpertClick.com
our main site

NewsReleaseWire.com
*read news from our experts and use the advanced features
to segment geographically or by topic*

Daybook.com
*for The Public Record of Today's Events® -- a
future file of news and events -- perfect for print
journalists who are working several months ahead*

InterviewNet.com
journalists can ask questions via e-mail and send them "one-to-one" or "one-to-many" to reach news sources

ReviewBook.com
registered journalists can request books for review

NewsMediaYearbook.com
our directory of journalists available to news sources and journalists who register for networking in four ways: 1) on the Web; 2) Excel database for download; 3) Adobe PDF for download; and 4) Word document for press-on labels

Broadcast Interview Source, Inc., was founded in July 1984.

1984 -- Broadcast Interview Source publishes first edition of the Yearbook, mailing 750 copies of a 64-page booklet to talk radio shows. Talk Show Yearbook first released with contact information for the nation's talk shows.

1985 -- Broadcast publishes the second edition of the Yearbook with 20 paid listings from The Ad Council. The Associated Press requests 1,000 copies.

1986 -- The New York Times dubs the Yearbook, "Dial-An-Expert."

1987 -- Leading news/talk radio stations, "60 Minutes" and "Donahue" purchase copies of the Yearbook.

1988 -- Media circulation grows to 4,000 copies. The Wall Street Journal and The Washington Post publish reviews. The Associated Press calls it, "An Encyclopedia of Sources."

1989 -- Power Media Yearbook of top print journalists becomes another Broadcast Interview Source publication.

1992 -- Yearbook circulation grows to 12,000 copies a year.

1994 -- The White House, IRS and CIA place listings. 100,000 total copies in print.

1995 -- Newsweek and The New York Times Magazine run features on the Yearbook. Journalists request 9,000 print copies.

1996 -- Our Web site goes online and serves as the interactive companion to the printed Yearbook.

1997 -- Broadcast launches Daybook.com, an online calendar of the day's media events.

1998 -- LexisNexis includes the Yearbook in its extensive search engine.

1999 -- Free Library/BIS Publishing, Inc., now has 5 titles in print: Yearbook of Experts (Annual), Power Media Yearbook (Annual), Talk Show Yearbook (Annual), Baseball Goes to War (History), Family Words (Humor).

2001 -- NewsReleaseWire.com debuts, offering a secure way to send news releases. NewsMediaYearbook.com launches with live listings of journalists.

2002 -- InterviewNet.com comes alive to offer direct e-mail contact, one-to-one or one-to-many.

2003 -- The Yearbook of Experts publishes as an Adobe PDF and printed editions.

---

innovation & leadership for two decades.

Topic Index

B

Burnout
Dr. Gaby Cora -- Leadership & Well-Being Consultant & Speaker, 334
Dr. Patricia A. Farrell -- Psychologist, 352
Tim Ferriss - Productivity,Digital Lifestyles and Entrepreneurship, 213
Overcoming Job Burnout, 225
Vicki Rackner MD FACS -- Doctor Caregiver, 339

Bus Accidents
Baum, Hedlund, Aristei and Goldman, PC, 115

Business
Association for Strategic Planning, 273
Mohammad Bahareth, 206
Professor Bob Boyd -- Home-Based Business, 235
Angela Dingle -- Ex Nihilo Management, LLC, 274
Tim Ferriss - Productivity,Digital Lifestyles and Entrepreneurship, 213
Melvin J. Gravely II Ph.D. - Institute For Entrepreneurial Thinking, LTD., 270
Maggie Holben -- Public Relations Expert Resource, 186
Scott Hunter -- Leadership Expert, 288
Chas Klivans -- The CEO's Navigator, 266
Judi Moreo -- A Speaker with Substance and Style, 273
National Speakers Association, 197
Loreen Sherman, MBA - Business Consultant & Leadership Speaker, 274
Society for Advancement of Consulting, LLC, 258
Stefan Swanepoel -- Surviving Your Serengeti, 197
Sam Waltz, 188
Dan Weedin -- Crisis Leadership and Insurance Consultant, 224
Wharton School Club of Washington, 100

Business Alliances
Ed Rigsbee -- Strategic Alliance and Business Relationship Expert, 272

Business Analytics
Othniel Denis, MBA -- Microsoft Excel Expert, 308

Business and Investing
Mark LeBlanc -- Small Business Success, 278

Business Author
Robin Jay -- Las Vegas Keynote Speaker, 196

Business Aviation
121five.com -- Aviation Industry News, Tim Kern, 153

Business Backgrounds
Michelle Pyan -- Commercial Investigations LLC, 123

Business Blogging
Debbie Weil -- Corporate Blogging Expert, 210

Business Bootstrapping
Julie Austin - Creativity -- Innovation -- Entrepreneur -- Expert, 88

Business Buying
John Martinka -- Partner On-Call Network, 262

Business Card
International Society of Protocol and Etiquette Professionals, 297

Business Change
Wharton School Club of Washington, 100

Business Coach
Global Strategic Management Solutions, 265
Roberta Guise, MBA -- Small Business Marketing Expert, 276
Larry LaRose -- Performance Coach, 266
Lethia Owens - Personal Branding and Social Media Strategist, 234
Gary W. Patterson -- Enterprise Risk Management Expert, 267
David Rohlander - The CEO's Coach, 252

Business Coaching
Don Benton -- Marketing Expert, 286
Voss W. Graham -- InnerActive Consulting, 230
Al Lautenslager -- Certified Guerrilla Marketing Coach, 232
Mark LeBlanc -- Small Business Success, 278

Business Communication
Katie Schwartz -- Business Speech Improvement, 187

Business Communications
Granville Toogood Associates, Inc., 299

Business Consultant
Mark LeBlanc -- Small Business Success, 278

Business Consultants
Bill Wagner -- Accord Management Systems, 240

Business Consulting
Lisa Anderson M.B.A. - - Business and Management Expert, 244
Glen Boyls -- Risk Management - Business Continuity Expert, 258
Shawn Casemore - Operational Performance and Leadership Development, 265
Marvin H. Doniger -- Financial Security Expert, 215

Business Continuity
Glen Boyls -- Risk Management - Business Continuity Expert, 258
Marvin H. Doniger -- Financial Security Expert, 215
Edward Poll, J.D., M.B.A., CMC -- Law Firm Management Expert, 110

Business Crime
Michael G. Kessler, President and CEO of Kessler International, 122

Business Development
Stuart Cross -- Morgan Cross Consulting, 286
Mark LeBlanc -- Small Business Success, 278

Business Entertaining
Robin Jay -- Las Vegas Keynote Speaker, 196

Business Ethics
Christopher Bauer, Ph.D. -- Business Ethics Training, 100
Shel Horowitz, Marketing Consultant - Green And Profitable, 230
Institute of Management Consultants USA. Inc., 260
Jack Marshall -- ProEthics, Ltd., 100

Business Etiquette
Deborah Boland -- Image -- Etiquette -- Communications, 322
Heba Al Fazari -- Executive Image - Etiquette and Communication Coach, 322
The Lett Group -- Business Etiquette, 297
Barbara Pachter - Business Etiquette Expert, 298
Gloria Starr -- Image Etiquette -- Communication and Leadership, 298
Jan Yager, Ph.D. -- Speaker, Author and Consultant, 310

Business Evolution
Phyllis Ezop --- Growth Strategy Expert, 248

Business Flying
Aircraft Owners and Pilots Association -- AOPA, 154

Business Franchise
OneCoach, Inc -- Small Business Growth Experts, 278

Business Growth
Bob Bare--Entrepreneurial Expert, 349
Stephanie Diamond -- Marketing Message Expert, 213
Phyllis Ezop --- Growth Strategy Expert, 248
Anne Graham -- Inspiring Tomorrow's Legendary Companies, 288
Al Lautenslager -- Certified Guerrilla Marketing Coach, 232
John Martinka -- Partner On-Call Network, 262
OneCoach, Inc -- Small Business Growth Experts, 278
Ford Saeks - Business Growth - Internet Marketing - Marketing, 214
Wharton School Club of Washington, 100

Business Image
Deborah Boland -- Image -- Etiquette -- Communications, 322

Business Innovation
Daniel Burrus -- Professional Speaker - Bestselling Author, 189
Dr. Howard Rasheed -- Idea Accelerator Technologies, 249

Business Issues
Michael J. Mayer -- Licensed Psychologist - Consultant, 364

Business Leaders
John Di Frances, 254
Wharton School Club of Washington, 100

O

LISTINGS

JEFF COBB -- LIFELONG LEARNING
Carrboro, NC United States
www.tagoras.com

Jeff Cobb is a recognized authority on lifelong learning and the market for continuing education and professional development. As an expert on the learning economy he has helped a long list of organizations maximize the reach, revenue, and impact of their knowledge and learning assets through embracing emerging technologies and new mindsets. Jeff 's books include Shift Ed: A Call to Action for Transforming K-12 Education (Corwin, 2011) and Leading the Learning Revolution (AMACOM, 2012).

Jeff Cobb
Managing Director
Tagoras
Carrboro, NC United States
Contact Phone: 919-201-7460
Contact Main Phone: 919-201-7460
Click to Contact from Web Site

KANSAS STATE UNIVERSITY
Manhattan, KS United States
www.k-state.edu/media

Kansas State University is on its way to becoming a top 50 public research university by 2025. Founded in 1863 as a land-grant institution, the university has campuses in Manhattan, Olathe and Salina, Kan. A leader in food safety and animal health, the university boasts the Biosecurity Research Institute, a biosafety level-3 laboratory, and is the future home of the National Bio and Agro-Defense Facility. Additional university sites include four agricultural experiment stations and an 8,600-acre native tallgrass prairie, Konza Prairie Biological Station.

Erinn Barcomb-Peterson
Director, News & Editorial Services
Kansas State University Media Relations
Manhattan, KS United States
Contact Phone: 785-532-1543
Click to Contact from Web Site

NCTM President Mike Shaughnessy

NATIONAL COUNCIL OF TEACHERS OF MATHEMATICS
Reston, VA United States
http://www.nctm.org

The National Council of Teachers of Mathematics (NCTM) is a public voice of mathematics education, supporting teachers to ensure equitable mathematics learning of the highest quality for all students through vision, leadership, professional development, and research. NCTM is the world's largest mathematics education organization, with 90,000 members. NCTM's "Principles and Standards for School Mathematics" includes guidelines for teachers and its "Focus in High School Mathematics: Reasoning and Sense Making" advocates practical changes to the high school mathematics curriculum to refocus learning on reasoning and sense making.

Gay Dillin
Media Relations Manager
National Council of Teachers of Mathematics
Reston, VA United States
Contact Phone: 703-620-9840
Contact Main Phone: 703-620-9840
Click to Contact from Web Site

THE ART AND CREATIVE MATERIALS INSTITUTE, INC.
Hanson, MA United States
http://www.acminet.org

ACMI certifies that art materials are nontoxic or properly labeled with any needed health warnings. ACMI creates a positive environment for art and creative materials usage, promotes safe use of these materials, and serves as an information and service resource. Look for the ACMI seals on art and creative materials.

Deborah M. Fanning, CAE
Executive Vice President
The Art and Creative Materials Institute, Inc.
Hanson, MA United States
Contact Phone: 781-293-4100
Click to Contact from Web Site

DR. HENRY BORENSON -- ALGEBRA PROBLEMS EXPERT
Allentown, PA United States
http://www.borenson.com

Dr. Henry Borenson is the inventor of Hands-On Equations®, a system of instruction which uses pawns and numbered cubes to enable grade school students to be successful with basic algebra. His system demystifies the learning of algebra, so that even 4th graders can solve algebraic linear equations such as $4x + 3 = 3x + 9$. He and his colleagues have now provided the Making Algebra Child's Play workshops to more than 25,000 teachers.

Dr. Henry Borenson
President
Borenson and Associates, Inc.
Allentown, PA United States
Contact Phone: 800-993-6284
Click to Contact from Web Site

GLOBAL ACADEMY ONLINE, INC.
Washington, DC United States
http://www.GlobalAcademyOnline.com

Global Academy Online, Inc., (known as The Academy), is an international online education university builder. Developed and created by the Executive Director of the Center for Ethics in Free Enterprise in 2002 to service colleges and universities worldwide, The Academy has become a premier supplier of global private label online degree programs, curriculum, and instruction. These specialized private academic services are available exclusively to organizations, associations and individuals desiring to create eLearning and distance online education institutions. To further understanding of the value of online education, The Academy publishes annually a free eBook, the BEST/WORST ONLINE DEGREE PROGRAM PROVIDERS.

LaFonda Oliver-Bowen
Sr. VP, Director of Communications
Global Academy Online , Inc
UpMarketing.com
Washington, DC United States
Contact Phone: 432-847-4040
Contact Main Phone: 202 827 7376
Click to Contact from Web Site

JERRY MINTZ -- ALTERNATIVE EDUCATION RESOURCE ORGANIZATION
New York, NY United States
www.educationrevolution.org

Jerry Mintz is the founder of the Alternative Education Resource Organization (AERO). He has been fighting for learner-centered, empowering education for his whole working life. AERO has the answers for many people struggling to discover what really works in education. It networks educational alternatives around the world, including homeschooling, democratic schools, Montessori, Waldorf and higher education alternatives. AERO helps people find and start learner-centered schools that empower students, parents, and teachers. Jerry's been on network TV, PBS, and has written several books.

Jerry Mintz
Director
AERO
Roslyn Hts, NY United States
Contact Phone: 516 621 2195
Click to Contact from Web Site

The **Landmark** Forum
Our powerful flagship program

- Experience a positive, permanent shift in the quality of your life.
- Redefine the very nature of what's possible.
- Create a future of your own design.

LANDMARK EDUCATION
San Francisco, CA United States
http://www.landmarkeducation.com/

DR. JOYCE WILLARD TEAL
Dallas, TX United States
http://untealthen.com/

Joyce Willard Teal is a retired educator. She is a graduate of Prairie View A&M University. She began her teaching career in Texas, but her career path took her through New Jersey, Maryland, Pennsylvania, Georgia and Virginia before ending in Texas where she and her husband returned following his retirement. During the thirty-plus years that she was an educator, she taught at the college, elementary, middle and high school levels. She says, 'The middle school level is my level of choice, and the level at which I spent the bulk of my career teaching language arts to boys and girls.'

Dr. Joyce Willard Teal
Dallas, TX United States
Contact Phone: 214-349-7361
Contact Main Phone: 2143497361
Cell: 2143497361
Click to Contact from Web Site

DAVID FARROW -- MEMORY EXPERT
Toronto, Ontario Canada
www.millionairememory.com

Dave Farrow is an author, speaker, current world record holder for greatest memory and today's foremost expert on memory training. Guinness Record: He memorized the order of 59 decks of cards. That's 3,068 cards! Head of three companies. Clients: Citi-group, Bank of America, Bombardier, US ARMY, CFL Terry Evershan, & academy award winning actor Forest Whitaker. Seen: CNN, CBS, Fox news, The Discovery Channel, CW, CBC, City TV, and over 1000 radio and television interviews.

David Farrow
Wizard Tech Inc
Toronto, ON Canada
Contact Phone: 416-530-4941
Click to Contact from Web Site

Landmark Education is a global educational enterprise offering The Landmark Forum and graduate courses that are innovative, effective, and immediately relevant. Landmark's leading-edge educational methodology enables people to produce extraordinary results and enhance the quality of their lives. Landmark Education's courses and seminars are offered in more than 125 cities via 51 major offices around the world. More than 160,000 people participate in Landmark's courses each year. A fundamental principle of Landmark Education's work is that people — and the communities, organizations, and institutions with which they are engaged — have the possibility not only of success, but also of fulfillment and greatness. The ideas, insights, and distinctions on which Landmark's programs are based make Landmark a leader and innovator in the field of training and development.

Deborah Beroset
Director of Corporate Communications
Landmark Education
Chicago, IL United States
Contact Phone: 312-204-6111
Click to Contact from Web Site

THE COUNCIL OF INDEPENDENT COLLEGES
Washington, DC United States
www.cic.edu/

Founded in 1956, the Council of Independent Colleges (CIC) is an association of independent colleges and universities working together to: support college and university leadership, advance institutional excellence, and enhance private higher education's contributions to society. CIC is the major national service organization for all small and mid-sized, independent, liberal arts colleges and universities in the U.S. CIC is not a lobbying organization, but rather focuses on providing services to campus leaders as well as seminars, workshops, and programs that assist institutions in improving educational programs, administrative and financial performance, and institutional visibility.

Laura Wilcox
The Council of Independent Colleges
Washington, DC United States
Contact Phone: 202-466-7230
Click to Contact from Web Site

ANN DOLIN -- EDUCATIONAL CONSULTANT
Washington, DC United States
www.AnnDolin.com

Ann Dolin M.Ed. is a recognized expert in education and learning disability issues. A former teacher with over 20 years of teaching and tutoring experience, Ann is an accomplished public speaker having delivered hundreds of presentations focused on academic achievement and parenting issues. Dolin's book Homework Made Simple: Tips, Tools, and Solutions for Stress-Free Homework is the recipient of the Benjamin Franklin Award, Moms Choice Award, and Forward Book Review Award. Dolin has a B.A. degree in child psychology and a M.Ed. from Boston College. Dolin resides in Northern Virginia with her husband and two children.

Judi Campbell
Educational Connections, Inc.
Fairfax, VA United States
Contact Phone: 703-934-8282
Click to Contact from Web Site

MARC GARFINKLE -- LAW SCHOOL JOB AND CAREER EXPERT
Maplewood, NJ United States
www.solocontendere.com

Thousands of law school students, some saddled with enormous debt from school loans, will graduate this year with no place to land. The firms and agencies that traditionally hire new lawyers are just not doing so anymore. Some are even downsizing. The new attorneys are disillusioned, frustrated and scared by the absence of jobs. "But the fact is that law school grads do not need jobs - they need work!" stresses attorney and law professor Marc Garfinkle, author of $olo Contendere: How to Go Directly From Law School Into the Practice of Law Without Getting a Job.

Scott Lorenz
Publicist
Westwind Communications
Plymouth, MI United States
Contact Phone: 734-667-2090
Contact Main Phone: 7346672090
Cell: 7346672090
Click to Contact from Web Site

STEVEN ROY GOODMAN, M.S., J.D. -- COLLEGE ADMISSIONS EXPERT
Washington, DC United States
http://www.topcolleges.com

College Admissions Consultant: Selective Colleges, Graduate Programs, Business, Law Schools and Medical Schools, Educational Planning and Career Strategies. He is an Admissions Commentator/Expert Witness: Applicant Pool Generation, Recruiting Strategies, Interview Process, Socioeconomic Diversity, Evaluation of Applicants, College Rankings. As one of the foremost education consultants in the United States, Steve Goodman lectures about the college admissions process and privately consults with applicants to selective colleges and universities, graduate programs and professional schools. His new book, College Admissions Together: It Takes a Family, shares Mr. Goodman's 18 years' professional experience with family dynamics that can stand in the way of a successful college search.

Steven Roy Goodman, M.S., J.D.
3554 Appleton Street, N.W.
Washington, DC United States
Contact Phone: 202-986-9431
Click to Contact from Web Site

NATIONAL SCHOOL CHOICE WEEK
Miramar Beach, FL United States
www.schoolchoiceweek.com

Andrew R. Campanella is one of the education reform movement's leading policy and communications strategists. He is the vice president of public affairs for National School Choice Week (www.schoolchoiceweek.com), responsible for planning and promoting hundreds of education reform-related events to shine an unprecedented spotlight on the need for educational choice. A recognized author, commentator, and public speaker, Andrew worked for nearly five years as national director of communications at the American Federation for Children, the school choice movement's largest lobbying and political organization. He was also a senior advisor for the Federation's nonprofit affiliate, the Alliance for School Choice.

Andrew R. Campanella
Vice President
National School Choice Week
Alexandria, VA United States
Contact Phone: 202-276-1303
Cell: 202-276-1303
Click to Contact from Web Site

NATIONAL ADOPTION CENTER
Philadelphia, PA United States
http://www.Adopt.org

Expands adoption opportunities for children throughout the United States, particularly for children who now live in foster care. Has a Web site and access to adoptive parents, adopted children and adoption professionals and can address important adoption and child welfare issues. Has facilitated the adoption of more than 23,000 children since 1972.

Gloria Hochman
Dir., Communications & Marketing
National Adoption Center
Philadelphia, PA United States
Contact Phone: 215-875-0324
Contact Main Phone: 215-735-9988
Click to Contact from Web Site

WE SHARE THE SECRET -- LITERACY ADVOCATES

Las Vegas, NV United States
www.wesharethesecret.com

First, a child must learn the primary sound of each letter. Share the Secret Alphabet Books have lowercase tactile letters in two textures with letter writing prompts. Second, a child must understand that a group of letters make up a word. Share the Secret Alphabet Books use large print with extra spacing between words and parent prompts so you know what to say and do.

Tamara Lemmon
We Share the Secret
St. George, UT United States
Contact Phone: 435-275-5980
Click to Contact from Web Site

ATEBA CROCKER -- SHOE REVOLT

Beaverton, OR United States
www.shoerevolt.com

Sex slavery is real in the United States. You can see it thriving in any community across our country. Sex Slavery transactions happen daily in strip clubs, shady massage parlors, websites, and even newspapers that sell sex services. Unlike drugs and weapon, human beings can be sold over and over again making them a commodity to predators. We have an immense problem that requires an even bigger solution. The symbol of our American flag declares that modern day slavery is not welcome; and freedom is every human being's right.

Ateba Crocker
CEO
Shoe Revolt
Beaverton, OR United States
Contact Phone: 971 217 1822
Click to Contact from Web Site

"I believe the most beneficial and fulfilling thing we can do, personally and professionally, is help one another."

ANDREW HORN-- DREAMS FOR KIDS - WASH DC

Washington, DC United States
www.dreamsforkids.org/DC

Andrew Horn, Executive Director of Dreams for Kids D.C., is based in Washington, D.C., and is available for TV, radio and print interviews. He is an experienced media guest who has been interviewed by Fox News, the Washington Post, ABC News and many other media outlets. He speaks in smart sound-bites. You can trust him to share fresh, provocative insights that will engage your viewers, readers and listeners.

Andrew Horn
Executive Director
Dreams for Kids - Wash DC
Washington, DC United States
Contact Phone: 703 475-9322
Cell: 703-475-9322
Click to Contact from Web Site

Millennial Spokesperson and Social Entrepreneur
Andrew Horn

Are you looking for an articulate Millennial spokesperson and social entrepreneur who can address the following issues?

■ **Recruiting and motivating Gen Y's** so they are inspired to perform their best. (Andrew writes columns about this for GenJuice.)

■ **Teen self esteem:** surprising ways to help teens respect themselves and their life. (Andrew spoke at TEDx-NASA on this topic.)

■ **Careers for students and college grads:** innovative ways to turn your passion into a profession. (Andrew gives inspiring presentations at schools, colleges and youth conventions on this.)

■ **20-Something social entrepreneurs** (As a member of Summit Series and Renaissance weekends, Andrew is connected with some of the most influential and innovative groups of young entrepreneurs around the globe.)

■ **Youth empowerment** (Andrew's non-profit organization, www.DreamsForKids.org/dc, has helped thousands of disadvantaged and disabled youth realize their dreams and become young leaders who pay it forward and help other children who are less fortunate.)

■ **Giving back** (Andrew founded a national movement to turn Black Friday into GiveBack Friday.)

■ **Adaptive activities for kids with disabilities** (Andrew is Executive Director of Dreams for Kids, Washington, D.C., which hosts clinics with pro sports teams, such as the Washington Nationals and the Washington Capitals.)

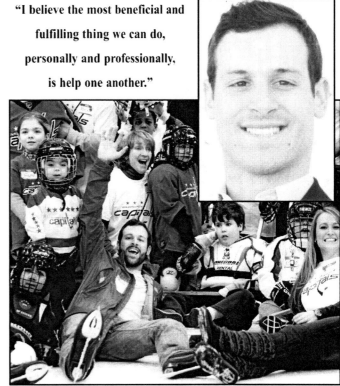

"I believe the most beneficial and fulfilling thing we can do, personally and professionally, is help one another."

"Miracles on Ice - circa 2011" Andrew Horn (center) at Dreams For Kids-DC event with Washington Capitals.

Andrew Horn, Executive Director of Dreams for Kids D.C., is based in Washington, D.C., and is available for TV, radio and print interviews.

He is an experienced media guest who has been interviewed by Fox News, the Washington Post, ABC News and many other media outlets. He speaks in smart sound-bites.

You can trust him to share fresh, provocative insights that will engage your viewers, readers and listeners.

Dreams for Kids
Changing Lives...One Kid at a Time

Andrew Horn
20-Something Social Entrepreneur
www.DreamsForKids.org/DC
AHorn@DreamsForKids.org/DC
703-475-9322

JOAN JOHNSON, B. S., - DOMESTIC VIOLENCE EXPERT
Scottsdale, AZ United States
http://www.joanjohnson.tv

Joan formerly hosted a radio talk show in Atlanta, Georgia. She has appeared on numerous TV and radio talk shows in America. She has ghost authored two books, conducts keynotes for The SHARE Committee for The Arizona Coalition Against Domestic Violence. Expert and authority on dynamics of Domestic Violence and recovery. Currently writing her book - a 31 day spiritual recovery guide after domestic abuse. Coaching, keynotes, and workshops available.

Joan Johnson
Bachelor of Science
Scottsdale, AZ United States
Contact Phone: 602-377-3004
Click to Contact from Web Site

JO ANN LORDAHL
Kalaheo, HI United States
http://www.JoAnnLordahl.com

Jo Ann Lordahl's most recent novel is Princess Ruth: Love and Tragedy in Hawaii. She has published over 20 books in many genres. Entranced by the peace and beauty of the islands, she has lived in Hawaii for the past eleven years and enjoys the beach and gardening in her free time. Princess Ruth: Love and Tragedy in Hawaii features a map of Hawaii, many factual endnotes, a book list of resources, and a chronology of Hawaiian royalty from antiquity, including Princess Ruth dates.

Jo Ann Lordahl
Kalaheo, HI United States
Contact Phone: 808-332-5717
Click to Contact from Web Site

NATIONAL CHILD ABUSE DEFENSE AND RESOURCE CENTER
Toledo, OH United States
http://www.falseallegation.org

False allegations child abuse/neglect--mistaken, mischievous, malicious--continue dismembering innocent families. 'Shaken Baby' and 'Munchausen Syndrome by Proxy' theories lack scientific validity. Faulty interviewing techniques, too rarely taped, inspire molestation 'disclosures' devastating the guiltless, traumatizing unabused children for life. Internationally recognized strategist Kimberly Hart adds science to suspicions of crimes. Former investigative reporter Barbara Bryan exposes law, policy, practice and family courts. Educational resource NCADRC supplies 'victims,' objective experts for programs/panels seeking 'whole' or hidden truth.

Kimberly Hart
Executive Director
National Child Abuse Defense & Resource Center
Holland, OH United States
Contact Phone: 419-865-0513
Click to Contact from Web Site

Kathryn Seifert, Ph.D.
Trauma Expert

contributing to the greater good—a few pennies at a time

WORLDPENNYJAR
Chicago, IL United States
www.worldpennyjar.com

EDIE RAETHER ENTERPRISES AND WINGS FOR WISHES INSTITUTE
Charlotte, NC United States
www.stopbullyingwithedie.com

Known as the Bully Buster, Edie Raether is an international keynote speaker, bestselling author and character coach. She has integrated over 40 years of experience in human potential development, motivation, and behavioral psychology into a revolutionary character building program, I Believe I Can Fly!. As president of Performance PLUS, a speaking, corporate training and consulting firm, Edie has empowered over 3,500 professional associations, educational organizations, and Fortune 500 companies on five continents. Edie is an authority on the neuropsychology of achievement and brain-based performance, including emotional and intuitive intelligence.

Edie Raether, MS, CSP
CEO
Edie Raether Enterprises and Wings for Wishes Institute
Charlotte, NC United States
Contact Phone: (704)658-8997
Click to Contact from Web Site

KATHRYN SEIFERT, PH.D., TRAUMA AND VIOLENCE EXPERT
Baltimore, MD United States
http://www.drkathyseifert.com/

Kathryn Seifert, Ph.D. is a psychotherapist, author, speaker, and researcher with over 30 years of experience. An expert in family violence and trauma, her award winning book, 'How Children Become Violent: Keeping Your Kids out of Gangs, Terrorist Organizations, and Cults,' (Acanthus Publishing) is quickly becoming a definitive guide for preventing violence. She also developed the CARE2 Assessment which aids professionals in providing interventions for high risk youth. Now available online at http://care2systems.com. Dr. Seifert is a regular Speaker for PESI.com and has appeared on CNN, Ebru TV, Fox News Radio, and Discovery ID. Dr. Kathy's new book, Youth Violence: Theory, Prevention, and Intervention, has been released from Springer Publishers. The book addresses the latest research on what works in prevention and treatment. Get her free newsletter at http://drkathyseifert.com or visit her bullying website at http://preventbullyingnow.info. Dr. Kathy is also a Crime & Law blogger for Psychology Today at http://www.psychologytoday.com/blog/stop-the-cycle

Kathryn Seifert, Ph.D.
CEO
ESPS, LLC
Sailsbury, MD United States
Contact Phone: 410-334-6961
Contact Main Phone: 410-334-6961
Cell: 410-726-9065
Click to Contact from Web Site

In response to an increase in natural and man-made disasters around the world—and as our world and its people become increasingly interconnected, we wanted to find a quick, convenient, and efficient way to allow people to make small 'micro donations' during the course of their normal, everyday activity. Our solution: WorldPennyJar. In simple terms, the WorldPennyJar concept allows consumers to electronically round up the price of their purchases to the nearest dollar (online, in store, or on a monthly bill). That 'extra change' from each transaction will then be directed to help fund disaster relief efforts and other non-disaster humanitarian efforts.

Michael J. Greene
Founder & CEO
WorldPennyJar
Chicago, IL United States
Contact Phone: 773.234.1350
Click to Contact from Web Site

JULIE AUSTIN - CREATIVITY -- INNOVATION -- ENTREPRENEUR -- EXPERT

Los Angeles, CA United States
www.creativeinnovationgroup.com

Julie Austin is an award-winning author, inventor, and multiple business owner. Her patented product, swiggies, wrist water bottles, have been a NASDAQ product of the year semi finalist and are currently sold in 24 countries. She's appeared on ABC, CBS, NBC, and FOX News, along with dozens of TV shows, magazines and radio shows around the world. She's a go-to media expert in the fields of innovation & creativity, and is featured in the books Patently Female and Girls Think of Everything. Author of The Money Garden: How to Plant the Seeds for a Lifetime of Income.

Julie Austin
owner
Creative Innovation
Job Security for Life
Los Angeles, CA United States
Contact Phone: 310-444-7788
Contact Main Phone: 310-44-7788
Cell: 310-444-7788
Click to Contact from Web Site

KRISTA FABREGAS -- KIDSMARTLIVING.COM

Houston, TX United States
www.KidSmartLiving.com

In 1999, Krista Fabregas was a working mother with a toddler and a vision -- that parents should be able to combine safety, livability and style in a home that's welcoming to family members of all ages. This belief led Krista to found KidSmartLiving.com, a resource for busy parents seeking ways to make the most of their homes. Through KidSmartLiving.com, Krista delivers a unique blend of family-friendly products, ideas and strategies that help parents combine easy-care function with fashion. From child safety how-to's to DIY decor videos to product trends, Krista continues to bring families home solutions, with style.

Krista Fabregas
Founder
SmartLiving Companies, Inc
Stafford, TX United States
Contact Phone: 832-476-5482
Cell: 281-435-5422
Click to Contact from Web Site

Barbara J. Feldman

BARBARA J. FELDMAN -- SURFNETKIDS.COM

San Diego, CA United States
www.surfnetkids.com

Barbara J. Feldman is owner and founder of Surfnetkids.com, an online publishing company that creates content sites for families, parents, teachers and kids. Her more than sixty sites include Surfnetkids.com (an educational site based on her nationally syndicated newspaper column 'Surfing the Net with Kids'), FreeKidsColoring.com and JokesByKids.com. Barbara is an expert in building audiences for advertising-supported content sites, and an evangelist for educational uses of the Internet.

Barbara J. Feldman
Surfnetkids.com
Solana Beach, CA United States
Contact Phone: 858-793-8300
Click to Contact from Web Site

Kathryn Seifert, Ph.D.
Trauma Expert

Kathryn Seifert, Ph.D., is a psychotherapist, author, speaker and researcher who specializes in family violence, trauma and stress management and has more than 30 years of experience in mental health, addictions and criminal justice work. She is the founder and CEO of Eastern Shore Psychological Services (www.ESPSMD.com), a private practice with three public mental health clinics and a healthy families prevention program. The agency focuses on serving children, adolescents, and at-risk youth and their families.

Dr. Seifert is the author of the award winning book, *How Children Become Violent: Keeping Your Kids out of Gangs, Terrorist Organizations, and Cults* (Acanthus Publishing), and her articles on violence, trauma and risk have appeared in The Journal of Psychiatry and Law, Paradigm Magazine, Reaching Today's Youth, Self-Help and Psychology Magazine, The Maryland Psychologist, Hot Psychology Magazine and the Forensic Examiner. She is also the author of *CARE2 (Chronic Violent Behavior Risk and Needs Assessment)*, a manual and assessment that allows mental health professionals to understand the risk of potential violence in youths and how to prevent and treat it. The kit is widely used and trusted as a premier youth risk assessment in the industry.

Dr. Seifert lectures nationally and internationally on youth and family violence.

Kathryn Seifert, Ph.D.
Salisbury, Maryland
410-334-6961
k.seifert@ESPSMD.com

For media inquiries and bookings: Derek McIver,
The Ictus Initiative -- 617-717-8294
derek@ictusinitiative.com

www.DrKathySeifert.com

DEBRA HOLTZMAN. J.D.. M.A. -- CHILD SAFETY EXPERT
Hollywood, FL United States
http://www.thesafetyexpert.com

Debra Holtzman, JD, MA, is an internationally acclaimed child safety and health expert and award-winning parenting author. Frequently appears on regional and national television and radio, she has been featured on The Today Show, Weekend Today, Dateline, ABC World News, The Associated Press Radio, Martha Stewart Living Radio, and in USA Weekend Magazine. She was the official on-air safety expert for the popular weekly Discovery Health series, Make Room for Baby. She was named an 'Everyday Hero' by Reader's Digest and a 'Woman Making a Difference' by Family Circle Magazine. Debra has a law degree, an M.A. in occupational health and safety, a B.A. in communications, and is the mother of two children. She teaches infant and toddler safety, CPR, and sibling classes at Memorial Regional Hospital. Her latest book, 'The Safe Baby: A Do-it Yourself Guide to Home Safety and Healthy Living' (Sentient Publications, 2009) is in bookstores everywhere.

Debra Holtzman, J.D., M.A.
Hollywood, FL United States
Contact Phone: 954-963-7702
Click to Contact from Web Site

EITAN D. SCHWARZ MD -- ZILLYDILLY FOR IPAD
Chicago, IL United States
www.mydigitalfamily.org

MyDigitalFamily, Ltd. announces the release of the ZillyDilly curated iPad browser for children. Based on parenting guidance by a leading American child and adolescent psychiatrist Eitan Schwarz, MD DLFAPA FA ACAP('Dr. S®'), ZillyDilly reinvents the internet for parents and children alike. Dr. S states, 'Technology can be very positive, but parents must pay attention and make it so. Otherwise, unless a digital device enhances family life and child development, it does not belong in the home.' To align the use of technology with positive benefits to kids and families, ZillyDilly encourages a healthy balance of online growth in a childproof browser.

Dr.S
Founder/CEO
MyDigitalFamily, Ltd.
ZillyDilly for iPad
CHICAGO, IL United States
Contact Phone:
Contact Main Phone: 847.675.5393
Cell: 847.507.9185
Click to Contact from Web Site

TEAMCHILDREN -YOUTH CHARITY
Philadelphia, PA United States
www.TeamChildren.com

Teamchildren is on the leading edge of transforming early childhood growth and development. We have through extraordinary teamwork distributed over 10,000 low cost refurbished computers to families and organizations around the world. Teamchildren believes that every baby/child should grow up with the benefits of massage and Rolfing. We are working in Partnership with AS-PIRA of PA on a project to teach extrodinary literacy skills to 3 and 4 year old low income Hispanic children living in North Philadelphia. This area has some of the worst poverty and failing schools in the nation. We are transforming that.

Robert Toporek
President/founder
TeamChildren
Audobon, PA United States
Contact Phone: 610-666-1795
Cell: 484-744-1868
Click to Contact from Web Site

Debra Holtzman
Child Safety Expert
Health, Safety and Lifestyle Consultant

Debra Holtzman, J.D., M.A., is an internationally acclaimed child safety and health expert as well as an award-winning parenting author.

A proven specialist on the subjects of injury prevention, healthy living, toxic chemicals, child passenger safety, parenting issues, consumer issues, lifestyle, travel, food safety and pet safety, Holtzman has been helping families for nearly two decades.

Frequently appearing on regional and national television and radio, she has been featured on The Today Show, Dateline, ABC World News, CNBC, MSNBC, and The Associated Press Radio -- and in USA Weekend Magazine. Holtzman served as the official safety expert on the Discovery Health Channel's popular TV series, "Make Room for Baby." She was named an "Everyday Hero" by Reader's Digest.

Her latest book, "The Safe Baby: A Do-it Yourself Guide to Home Safety and Healthy Living," is in bookstores everywhere.

Holding a master's degree in occupational health and safety, Holtzman is a lawyer and mother of two children. She also teaches infant safety and CPR classes at Memorial Regional Hospital.

Debra Smiley Holtzman, J.D., M.A.
Child Safety Expert -- Health, Safety and Lifestyle Consultant
Hollywood, Florida

954-963-7702 ■ TheSafetyExpert@gmail.com

CONGRESS OF RACIAL EQUALITY -- CORE

New York, NY United States
http://www.core-online.org

Founded in 1942, CORE is the third oldest and one of the 'Big Four' civil rights groups in the United States. From the protests against 'Jim Crow' laws of the 40's to the 'Sit-ins' of the 50's and the 'Freedom Rides' of the 60's; through the cries for 'Self-Determination' in the 70's and 'Equal Opportunity' in the 80's to the struggle for community development in the 90's, CORE has championed true equality for all people. As the 'shock troops' and pioneers of the civil rights movement, CORE has paved the way for the nation to follow. As we approach the end of the 20th century, CORE has turned its focus to preparing minorities for the technical and skills demands of the new millennium.

Brian McLaughlin
Publicist
Congress of Racial Equality -- CORE
New York, NY United States
Contact Phone: 212-598-4000
Click to Contact from Web Site

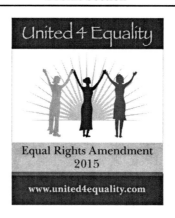

CAROLYN A. COOK -- UNITED 4 EQUALITY, LLC

Washington, DC United States
www.united4equality.com

When our country was founded in 1776, women were considered the property of white men.

Carolyn A. Cook
Washington, DC United States
Contact Phone: 202-309-1963
Click to Contact from Web Site

OMEKONGO DIBINGA -- THE UPSTANDER

Washington, DC United States
www.upstanderinternational.com

Om [e96b6f]ngo Dibinga is the UPstander. In this capacity he serves as a diversity educator, CNN contributor, and trilingual recording artist. He is the Director of UPstander International and host of the cable TV talk show 'Real Talk.' Internationally, he has performed in 8 countries. His work has appeared on TV & radio in over 150 countries. He is the winner of the 'CNN iReport Spirit Award' and the 'Urban Music Award'. He provides educational empowerment for organizations, associations, corporations, and educational institutions. He is the author of the motivational book & CD entitled 'G.R.O.W. Towards Your Greatness!'

Omekongo Dibinga
Director
UPstander International
Washington, DC United States
Contact Phone: 202-251-7746
Cell: 202-251-7746
Click to Contact from Web Site

CAROL M. SWAIN -- VANDERBILT UNIVERSITY LAW SCHOOL
Nashville, TN United States
http://www.carolmswain.com

Carol M. Swain is professor of political science and of law at Vanderbilt University. Her media appearances include ABC News, Fox News Live, Fox News' Hannity, CNN's News from the Headlines, CNN's Lou Dobbs Tonight, C-SPAN's Washington Journal, PBS's Lehrer News Hour, NPR's Morning Edition, and Daybreak USA Today. Her books include Be the People: A Call to Reclaim America's Faith and Promise (Forthcoming, 2011); Debating Immigration (2007), New White Nationalism in America: Its Challenge to Integration (2002) and Contemporary Voices of White Nationalism (2003); Black Faces, Black Interests: The Representation of African Americans (1993, 95).

Carol M. Swain
Prof: Political Science and Law
Vanderbilt University Law School
Nashville, TN United States
Contact Phone: 615-322-1001
Contact Main Phone: 615-322-2615
Cell: 615-310-8617
Click to Contact from Web Site

GOODWILL INDUSTRIES INTERNATIONAL, INC.
Rockville, MD United States
http://www.goodwill.org

Goodwill Industries International is a network of 165 community-based agencies in the U.S. and Canada with 14 affiliates in 13 other countries. Goodwill agencies are innovative and sustainable social enterprises that fund job training programs, employment placement services and other community-based programs by selling donated clothing and household items in more than 2,400 retail stores and online at shopgoodwill.com. In 2009, nearly 2 million people in the U.S. and Canada benefited from Goodwill's career services. Goodwill channels 83 percent of its revenues directly into its programs and services. To find your nearest Goodwill, go to www.goodwill.org, or call (800) 741-0186.

Media Relations Department
Goodwill Industries International, Inc.
Rockville, MD United States
Contact Phone: 240-333-5266
Cell: 240-388-8309
Click to Contact from Web Site

SKILLS USA-VICA
Leesburg, VA United States
www.skillsusa.org

SkillsUSA is a partnership of students, teachers and industry working together to ensure America has a skilled workforce. SkillsUSA helps each student excel. SkillsUSA is a national nonprofit organization serving teachers and high school and college students who are preparing for careers in trade, technical and skilled service occupations, including health occupations. It was formerly known as VICA (Vocational Industrial Clubs of America

Thomas W. Holdsworth
Dir. of Comm. & Gov't Relations
Skills USA-VICA
Leesburg, VA United States
Contact Phone: 703-777-8810
Click to Contact from Web Site

BE AN ELF
Los Angeles, CA United States
www.BeAnElf.org

At 75 postal branches across the US, you can read real letters to Santa from needy kids, take home one or more that move you and send your gift. There's no middle man or charity. It's microphilanthropy, direct from you to a child, when you volunteer in this way. You'll catch the true spirit of the holidays, and put smiles on the faces of needy kids on Christmas morning. Stop by a participating postal branch. Come alone, or bring your kids!

Patrick Reynolds
Be An Elf
Playa del Rey, CA United States
Contact Phone: 310-577-9828
Click to Contact from Web Site

BENJAMIN Y. CLARK, PHD -- PUBLIC BUDGETING EXPERT
Cleveland, OH United States
http://about.me/benyclark

I am an Assistant Professor (Public Budgeting, Finance, and Administration) in the Levin College of Urban Affairs at Cleveland State University. I came to the Levin College after earning my PhD in Public Administration in 2009 from the University of Georgia and a career in public service. Prior to my appointment at the Levin College of Urban Affairs, I worked as a budget analyst for the Unified Government of Athens-Clarke County (Athens, Georgia). I also previously worked in a Washington, DC based public health consulting firm (Futures Group International) to assist foreign governments, multilateral organizations, and NGOs in the development and implementation of HIV/AIDS and reproductive health programs. I am also a former Peace Corps Volunteer in the West African nation of Senegal.

Benjamin Y. Clark, PhD
College of Urban Affairs --Cleveland State University
Cleveland, OH United States
Contact Phone: 216-687-2497
Click to Contact from Web Site

 LINCOLN INSTITUTE
OF LAND POLICY

LINCOLN INSTITUTE OF LAND POLICY
Boston, MA United States
www.lincolninst.edu

Experts available on housing and the economy, land use and climate change, land conservation, conservation easements, property rights, urban planning and urban design, land use in the Intermountain West, property tax, land value tax, municipal finance, informal settlement (slums), global urban expansion, urbanization in China. The Lincoln Institute of Land Policy is a leading resource for key issues concerning the use, regulation, and taxation of land. Providing high quality education and research, the Institute strives to improve public dialogue and decisions about land policy. As a private operating foundation, whose origins date to 1946, we seek to inform decision-making through education, research, policy evaluation, demonstration projects, and the dissemination of information, policy analysis, and data through publications, our Web site, and other media. By bringing together scholars, practitioners, public officials, policymakers, journalists and involved citizens, the Lincoln Institute integrates theory and practice and provides a nonpartisan forum for multidisciplinary perspectives on public policy concerning land, both in the U.S. and internationally.

Anthony Flint
Lincoln Institute of Land Policy
Cambridge, MA United States
Contact Phone: 617-661-3016, #116
Click to Contact from Web Site

LINCOLN INSTITUTE
OF LAND POLICY

The Lincoln Institute of Land Policy is a think tank based in Cambridge, Mass., that conducts research, evaluation and analysis, publishes books, a quarterly journal and documentary films, and holds conferences and seminars on the use, regulation, and taxation of land. Founded in 1974, the Lincoln Institute covers tax policy including tax limitations and the property tax; housing, community land trusts and the role of universities in urban development; land use planning and climate change, regional planning, smart growth, land conservation, property rights, and density; and international land policy, with a special emphasis on China and Latin America.

Anthony Flint
Lincoln Institute of Land Policy
Cambridge, Massachusetts

Contact Phone: 617-661-3016, #116

anthony.flint@lincolninst.edu

www.LincolnInst.edu

NATIONAL TAXPAYERS UNION

Alexandria, VA United States
http://www.ntu.org

The National Taxpayers Union is the nation's largest non-profit, non-partisan organization representing American taxpayers. Its spokespeople often appear on national television and radio news programs on issues of importance to the nation's taxpayers. Their expertise includes: state and federal tax policies, state and federal budget policies, Social Security and Medicare programs and citizen activism as well as many other areas of concern.

Pete Sepp
Vice President, Policy & Communications
National Taxpayers Union
Alexandria, VA United States
Contact Phone: 703-683-5700
Click to Contact from Web Site

ROB O'DELL -- EXPERT ON GOVERNMENT SPENDING

Tucson, AZ United States

Rob O'Dell is a reporter for the Arizona Daily Star who specializes in public records investigations. He is an expert in government spending and government waste. His investigations into waste and mismanagement of $200 million by Tucson's downtown redevelopment agency caused changes in Arizona state law. He was a 2009 finalist for the prestigious Gerald Loeb awards, which honor the nation's top business journalism. He was named Arizona Journalist of the Year by the Arizona Newspapers Association and the Associated Press in 2009. He is the author of the upcoming book on government waste called Other People's Money.

Rob O'Dell
Author - Other People's Money, Reporter - Arizona Daily Star
Tucson, AZ United States
Contact Phone: 520-609-7799
Click to Contact from Web Site

ELLIE LUCAS -- HUNGER-FREE MINNNESOTA

Minneapolis, MN United States
hungerfreemn.org

Ellie Lucas joined Hunger-Free Minnesota in November 2010 as Chief Campaign Officer. She is responsible for overall campaign leadership. Ellie has 25 years' experience in public affairs, corporate relations and strategic marketing. Ellie serves on the board of directors of The Center for Victims of Torture, a leading international human rights organization; the Children's Defense Fund scholarship program nomination committee and the Edina Education Fund.

Christine Tsang
Henry Schafer Partners
Minneapolis, MN United States
Contact Phone: 612-843-2142
Click to Contact from Web Site

RICHARD WAGNER, PH.D., ACS
Seattle, WA United States
GayCatholicPriests.org

Many clergy in the Catholic Church are homosexual. Richard Wagner is a gay priest. The media firestorm that erupted after he went public and the backlash within his religious community because of this publicity eventually destroyed his public priesthood. The story of his 13-year battle with the Church to save his ministry exemplifies the spiritual isolation, emotional distress and ecclesiastical reprisals every gay priest most fears. Secrecy, Sophistry And Gay Sex In The Catholic Church provides an intimate and disturbing look into the inner-workings of the Catholic Church. It details the Church's take-no-prisoners attitude toward dissent in its midst.

Rev. Richard Wagner, Ph.D.
Clinical Sexologist
Seattle, WA United States
Contact Phone: 206-709-8813
Click to Contact from Web Site

NINA AMIR - HUMAN POTENTIAL SPEAKER
San Jose, CA United States
www.PureSpiritCreations.com

Nina Amir, Inspiration-to-Creation Coach, inspires people to combine their purpose and passion so they Achieve More Inspired Results. She motivates her clients and audiences to achieve their goals, fulfill their purpose and live inspired lives. Nina is an author, speaker, blog-to-book coach, author and book coach as well a Kabbalistic conscious creation coach and change agent. She holds a BA in magazine journalism from Syracuse University with a concentration in psychology, is a life coach, rebirther, and Voice Dialogue facilitator. The author of ten self-published books and workbooks, her most recent book is How to Blog a Book (Writer's Digest Books). Nina's work spans religious lines and is pertinent to people of all faiths and spiritual traditions. In all she does, Amir focuses on helping people live their lives fully and manifest their desires -- whether those desires look like written products or something entirely different.

Nina Amir
Los Gatos, CA United States
Contact Phone: 408-353-1943
Click to Contact from Web Site

RABBI YITZHAK MILLER - SPIRITUALITY RELIGION THEOLOGY JUDAISM
San Francisco, CA United States
www.RabbiYitzhakMiller.org

Mainstream Ordained Rabbi - Executive Director CyberJudaism.org - Provides 'CyberRabbi' Services to 4 continents - 10+ Years as Congregational Rabbi and Education Director - Rabbi Yitzhak Miller brings experience as a Congregational Rabbi plus years of experience in the US and International business world following a degree in Technology Management from Stanford University. With a family background that spans the gamut from ultra-Reform to ultra-Orthodox, Rabbi Yitzi reflects a love for both the breadth and depth of Judaism, and his 'FaithBridging' efforts demonstrate extraordinary ability to bridge religious and cultural differences. Rabbi Miller has won both a House of Representatives award for Community Service and 3 consecutive National Outreach Awards.

Rabbi Yitzhak Miller
Rabbi
RabbiYitzhakMiller.org
CyberJudaism.org
Santa Cruz, CA United States
Contact Phone: 831-594-9489
Cell: 831-594-9489
Click to Contact from Web Site

STAN WEISLEDER -- TUSKEGEE AIRMEN EXPERT

Los Angeles, CA United States
www.StanWeisleder.com

Stan Weisleder is author of the just released novel, The Trees, which is the definitive novel about Jews and Italians growing up in Brooklyn after World War II who seek money and power in a never before seen Las Vegas revealed from an insider's point of view. His second book, A Killer of Lions, will come out in October 2011. A Killer of Lions is about the famed Tuskegee Airmen of World War II who fought racism in the Army Air Corps for the right to fight the Nazis in Europe.

Brad Butler
Promotion in Motion
Hollywwood, CA United States
Contact Phone: 323-461-3921
Click to Contact from Web Site

JACKIE CARPENTER - GEORGIA JUSTICE - BRIDGE TO A MIRACLE

Atlanta, GA United States
http://www.BridgeToAMiracle.com
www.book-marketing-expert.com

A native of Georgia, author Jackie Carpenter is a church organist, assistant Sunday School teacher, social director of a senior adult Bible Class, wife, mother and grandmother. She knows God inspired her to write Georgia Justice and The Bridge and followed His leading throughout the writing process. "I am God's Secretary. He dictated and I typed." Georgia Justice is a story of faith-building - a how to story of what it takes to escape from doubt, depression, and torment to faith, hope, and victory. The author appears regularly as a speaker at ladies' retreats and Christian conferences.

Scott Lorenz
Book Publicist
Westwind Communications
Plymouth, MI United States
Contact Phone: 734-667-2090
Contact Main Phone: 248-705-2214
Cell: 248-705-2214
Click to Contact from Web Site

THE CHURCH OF THE LATTER-DAY DUDE

Los Angeles, CA United States
http://dudeism.com

The Church of the Latter-Day Dude is a religious organization with over 100,000 ordained 'Dudeist Priests' worldwide (as of 2010). The religion of Dudeism is essentially an updated form of Chinese Taoism which takes its inspiration from modern sources like American Transcendentalism and -- most obviously -- the 1998 Coen Brothers film 'The Big Lebowski.' Dudeism aims to promote a worldview in which relaxation and simple pleasures can be esteemed as much as hard work and materialism are currently. The Church believes that Dudeism has existed throughout history, as a corrective to the imperatives of civilization.

Rev. Oliver Benjamin
The Dudely Lama
The Church of the Latter-Day Dude
Sherman Oaks, CA United States
Contact Phone: (818) 350 3833
Click to Contact from Web Site

AMY JO GARNER MINISTRIES
Oklahoma City, OK United States
http://www.amyjogarner.com

'Promoting grace and simplicity in the Christian life' Rev. Amy Jo Garner is a graduate of Northwest Nazarene University with a Master of Arts degree in Religion with a concentration in Pastoral Ministry. Amy Jo is a member of Christians for Biblical Equality, the American Academy of Religion and Christian Women United in Business. She works as freelance writer/editor and adjunct instructor. Rev. Garner is available as a speaker for women's retreats, seminars and workshops. She can participate in live events, teleseminars, and webinars. Her areas of specialty are Christian Spiritual Practices and Christian Simplicity.

Rev. Amy Jo Garner
Amy Jo Garner Ministries
Midwest City, OK United States
Contact Phone: 405-633-2549
Click to Contact from Web Site

DORIS WISE MONTROSE
Los Angeles, CA United States
http://www.cjhsla.org/

For three years I have been imploring you, Jews of Poland, the crown of world Jewry, appealing to you, warning you unceasingly that the catastrophe is nigh. My hair has turned white and I have grown old over these years, for my heart is bleeding that you, dear brothers and sisters, do not see the volcano which will soon begin to spew forth its fires of destruction. I see a horrible vision. Time is growing short for you to be spared. I know you cannot see it, for you are troubled and confused by everyday concerns. . .

Brad Butler
Hollywood, CA United States
Contact Phone: 323-461-3921
Click to Contact from Web Site

NETTIE REYNOLDS
Austin, TX United States
www.nettieink.com

Enlightenment is defined as education that results in understanding and the spread of knowledge. In Buddhism, enlightenment (orthodoxy Bodhi in Sanskrit) refers to a unique experience which wholly transforms the individual from their previous state in samsara. Let's now look at the term bloglightenment, which I define in this way - using your blog to enrich [...]

Nettie Reynolds
NettieInk
Austin, TX United States
Contact Phone: 512-753-9984
Click to Contact from Web Site

TRINITY FOUNDATION, INC --
RELIGION FRAUD DETECTIVES
Dallas, TX United States
http://www.trinityfi.org/

The foundation regularly provides assistance to print and electronic journalists investigating suspected fraud or other abuses of the public trust by members of the religious media. The foundation maintains a private investigative license with the State of Texas and frequently provides undercover operatives to news programs like PrimeTime Live, 60 Minutes, Dateline, CNN Special Reports, 20/20, British Broadcasting Corporation, Canadian Broadcasting Corporation, and Inside Edition, among many others. Check out their religious satire magazine at http://www.TheDoorMagazine.com

Ole Anthony
President/Publisher
Trinity Foundation, Inc./The Door Magazine
Dallas, TX United States
Contact Phone: 214-827-2625
Contact Main Phone: 214-827-2625
Click to Contact from Web Site

JACK MARSHALL -- PROETHICS, LTD.
Alexandria, VA United States
www.ProEthics.com

Speaker, teacher, writer, and innovator in ethics training and ethics consulting, in law, accounting, business; national, state, and local governments; non-profits and associations, entertainment, sports, and the workplace. President of ProEthics, an ethics and compliance firm dedicated to helping organizations and professions build ethical cultures; former Adjunct Professor of Legal Ethics at Washington College of Law, American University in Washington, D.C. A Harvard- and Georgetown-educated attorney, Jack Marshall's ethics commentary has appeared in 'O' and 'The Hardball Times Annual,' heard on NPR's 'Tell Me More!' and 'Religion and Ethics Weekly.' He writes about the ethics of current events on his ethics commentary blog, Ethics Alarms.

Jack Marshall
President
ProEthics, Ltd.
Alexandria, VA United States
Contact Phone: 703-548-5229
Contact Main Phone: 703-548-5229
Click to Contact from Web Site

CHRISTOPHER BAUER, PH.D. -- BUSINESS ETHICS TRAINING
Nashville, TN United States
http://www.Bauerethicsseminars.com

Ethics expert Dr. Christopher Bauer's training as a clinical psychologist gives him a unique perspective on how individuals manage matters of ethics. It also allows him to provide equally unique commentary and analysis. As a speaker, seminar leader and consultant, he helps individuals and organizations make more ethically-informed decisions while maximizing their bottom line. Bauer Ethics Seminars provides keynotes, breakouts, seminars, retreats, and consultation. Each helps individuals, teams and organizations take effective responsibility for 'walking the talk' of ethical behavior as well as improving their bottom line through improved leadership and management skills.

Christopher Bauer, Ph.D.
Bauer Ethics Seminars
Nashville, TN United States
Contact Phone: 615-385-3523
Cell: 615-268-8726
Click to Contact from Web Site

 the Wharton Club *of* DC

WHARTON SCHOOL CLUB OF WASHINGTON
Washington, DC United States
www.whartondc.com

Outstanding varied programs, 150-200 per year, such as our Embassy Receptions & Briefings, VIP luncheons, green business & other roundtables, Annual Conference and Joseph Wharton Gala Dinner that honors area business and public sector leaders, offer sponsors, members and attendees the opportunity to develop valuable business opportunities and expand critical knowledge.

Alan N. Schlaifer
President & CEO
Wharton School Club of Washington
Bethesda, MD United States
Contact Phone: 301-365-8999
Click to Contact from Web Site

RALPH J. BLOCH -- ASSOCIATION MANAGEMENT EXPERT
Sarasota, FL United States
http://www.ralphjbloch.com/

Our company is dedicated to helping trade and professional associations become more effective and more relevant to their members. We accomplish this by consulting in critical performance areas, and by providing development, management and marketing of association programs. Our approach to consulting is practical, personal and results-oriented. Our clients appreciate the way we work with their volunteer leaders and management staffs in the areas of strategic planning, leadership development, program assessment, organizational development and issues resolution. Our Association Programs division excels in membership development, trade show management, exhibit sales, advertising sales, sponsorship program development and sales, and affinity programs.

Ralph J. Bloch
President
Ralph J. Bloch & Associates, Inc.
Bradenton, FL United States
Contact Phone: 941-306-5222
Cell: 312-371-6673
Click to Contact from Web Site

SEARCH FOR COMMON GROUND
Washington, DC United States
http://www.sfcg.org

SFCG is an international nongovernmental organization dedicated to changing the way the world deals with conflict: away from adversarial approaches, toward cooperative solutions. With projects in 26 countries, our 'toolbox' includes mediation/facilitation training, community organizing, radio/TV, journalism, sports, , and music.

Susan Koscis
Director of Communications
Search for Common Ground
Washington, DC United States
Contact Phone: 202-777-2215
Contact Main Phone: (202) 265-4300
Click to Contact from Web Site

FOREIGN-TRADE ZONE CORPORATION
Mobile, AL United States
www.ftzcorp.com

The Foreign-Trade Zone Corporation is the only nationally recognized consulting firm that limits its practice to FTZ consulting, software systems, and management. Its range of consulting work in the FTZ program is all-encompassing, with services extending from cost-benefit analysis, Board applications, activations with CBP, to the operation and management of nine FTZ projects. With involvement in over 200 projects located in more than 40 states and Puerto Rico, the Foreign-Trade Zone Corporation has in-depth experience in virtually every industry imaginable.

Craig M. Pool
President
Foreign-Trade Zone Corporation
Mobile, AL United States
Contact Phone: 251-471-6725
Click to Contact from Web Site

VERNON JACOBS, CPA -- PRESIDENT, OFFSHORE PRESS, INC.
Kansas City, KS United States
http://www.offshorepress.com

International Tax Law: How to Go Offshore Without Getting in Trouble with the IRS. Foreign trusts, foreign corporations, foreign partnerships and foreign investments. Vernon Jacobs is a CPA and author with a focus on international tax law.

Vernon K. Jacobs, CPA
President
Offshore Press, Inc.
Prairie Village, KS United States
Contact Phone: 913-362-9667
Contact Main Phone: 913-362-9667
Cell: 913-481-3480
Click to Contact from Web Site

JIM LYNCH -- AUTHOR 'THE 2020 PLAYERS'

Newark, MI United States
http://www.facebook.com/
JimLynchAuthor2020Players

Political Novelist Starts Petition for National One Day Primary. While Mitt Romney, the presumed Republican nominee for President is already looking for a Vice Presidential running mate, there are 14 states that have yet to vote in the Republican primary. As a result millions of Americans have absolutely no voice in the process. Let's face it; the primary system is broken.

Scott Lorenz
Westwind Communications
Plymouth, MI United States
Contact Phone: 734-667-2090
Click to Contact from Web Site

NORDLINGER ASSOCIATES, INC. -- POLITICS AND PUBLIC AFFAIRS

Washington, DC United States

For the inside story on politics and public affairs, talk with Gary Nordlinger. Ranked as one of the nation's top four Democratic media consultants by Campaigns & Elections Magazine, he's been a key player in hundreds of elections in 34 countries on six continents. Despite some real long shots, Mr. Nordlinger's record in Congressional campaigns is 81-7. His media have won 120+ awards for excellence. Mr. Nordlinger is an expert on politics, Congress, advertising, PACs and fundraising. Gary Nordlinger founded Nordlinger Associates in 1976. His clients include leading political candidates, associations, labor unions and corporations.

Gary Nordlinger
President
Nordlinger Associates, Inc.
Arlington, VA United States
Contact Phone: 202-225-2434
Click to Contact from Web Site

SENATOR DON BENTON -- POLITICAL EXPERT

Portland, OR United States
www.donbenton.com

Elective Office: Served as state GOP Chairman in 2000 and set a fundraising record that still stands today. Elected to state Senate, 1996, 2000, 2004 and 2008; Washington State House of Representatives, 1994. Community Involvement: Clark County American Red Cross, 20-year volunteer; Republican precinct committeeman; Vancouver Moose Lodge, life member; College of the Canyons, past president, board of trustees; The Jaycees, SCV Chapter, past president; Assistant Scout Master, Boy Scouts of America and Member, Financial Literacy Public-Private Partnership.

Don Benton
Vancouver, WA United States
Contact Phone: 360-754-7369
Click to Contact from Web Site

FOREIGN-TRADE ZONE
C O R P O R A T I O N

A Foreign-Trade Zone is a specially designated area in, or adjacent to, a U.S. Customs Port Of Entry, which is considered to be outside the Customs Territory of the U.S.

The following is a partial list of the many benefits you can attain when using Foreign-Trade Zones or Foreign-Trade Zone Subzones:

- ❑ No duty is ever paid on merchandise re-exported from a Foreign-Trade Zone;
- ❑ If the merchandise is sold domestically, no duty is paid until it leaves the Zone or Zones;
- ❑ Generally, no duty is paid on waste or yield loss in a Foreign-Trade Zone or Subzone;
- ❑ Duty on scrap is eliminated or reduced in a Foreign-Trade Zone;
- ❑ Generally, if foreign merchandise is manufactured within a Foreign-Trade Zone or Subzone into a product with a lower duty rate, then the lower duty rate applies on the foreign content when duty is paid;
- ❑ Merchandise in a Foreign-Trade Zone may be stored, repackaged, manipulated, manufactured, destroyed or otherwise altered and changed.

The Foreign-Trade Zone Corporation is the only nationally recognized consulting firm that limits its practice to Foreign-Trade Zone consulting, FTZ software systems and management.

Its range of consulting work in the FTZ Program is all-encompassing, with services extending from Foreign-Trade Zones cost-benefit analysis, Board applications, activations with Customs and Border Protection, to the operation and management of nine U.S. Foreign-Trade Zone projects.

With involvement in more than 150 FTZ projects located in more than 35 states and Puerto Rico, the FTZ Corporation has in-depth experience in virtually every industry imaginable.

SmartZone® is the complete FTZ inventory control solution offered by the FTZ Corporation. It is the only software package designed by FTZ experts and experienced operators. With more than 250 companies currently using SmartZone®, and with the SmartZone® team's hands-on experience operating both manufacturing and distribution Zones, the company has developed a reputation as the experts in this field.

Foreign-Trade Zone Corporation: 2062 Old Shell Road, Mobile, Alabama 36607

Tele: (251) 471-6725
Fax: (251) 471-6727
E-mail: ftzconsultinginfo@ftzcorp.com
Web site: ftzcorp.com

WILLIAM S. BIKE -- POLITICAL COMMENTATOR
Chicago, IL United States
www.CentralParkCommunications.com

As a political commentator, William S. Bike, senior vice president of public relations, writing and political consulting firm Central Park Communication, uses his encyclopedic knowledge of history to add an unusual depth to discussions of current events. Bike has made frequent radio and television appearances and literally wrote the book on politics: Winning Political Campaigns, a how-to handbook on political campaigning. Reviews of Political Books (http://www.ficoa.biz/reviews_of_political_books.htm) said, 'from a practical political standpoint, it is the best book out--yet.'

William S. Bike
Senior Vice President
Central Park Communications
Chicago, IL United States
Contact Phone: 773-229-0024
Cell: 312-996-8495
Click to Contact from Web Site

 National Association of Government Communicators

NATIONAL ASSOCIATION OF GOVERNMENT COMMUNICATORS
Falls Church, VA United States
www.nagconline.org

The National Association of Government Communicators (NAGC) is a national not-for-profit professional network of federal, state and local government employees who disseminate information within and outside government. Its members are editors, writers, graphic artists, video professionals, broadcasters, photographers, information specialists and agency spokespersons.

Dawn Shiley
National Association of Government Communicators
Falls Church, VA United States
Contact Phone: 703-538-1787
Click to Contact from Web Site

MARK DANKOF'S AMERICA
San Antonio, TX United States
http://www.MarkDankof.com

Areas of Interest/Expertise: The American Right; Paleo-Conservatism; Libertarianism; Constitutionalism; Christianity; Lutheranism; Dispensationalism; the Israeli Lobby; Iran; the Mujahedeen-e-Khalq (MEK-MKO-PMOI); U. S. Congressional Roll-Call analysis. Profile: Paleo-conservative political writer, consultant, and broadcaster; Christian clergyman; ex-U.S. Senate candidate (Delaware); ex-Republican Party District Chairman (Seattle). Agencies: Breaking All the Rules News (BATR); The Ugly Truth with Mark Glenn; Mark Dankof's America on The Voice of Reason Radio Network; Press TV/Iran.

Mark Dankof
Investigative Journalist
Mark Dankof's America
San Antonio, TX United States
Contact Phone:
Click to Contact from Web Site

JUDITH LEE BERG -- HUMAN RESOURCE COMMUNICATION
Denver, CO United States

Judith dissects and analyzes the anatomy and disease of hate, hate groups and hate crimes. She confronts the sociopathic nature of choosing to hate, as the pathological background noise of the 1984 assassination of her husband, Alan Berg. Alan was a criminal trial attorney and talk radio personality. Judith relates the Turner Diaries, the Aryan Nation's militia mentality and neo-nazi pathology to the hateful terrorism that is threatening the destrction of America. Judith is an educator, public speaker and journalist. She has covered the Oklahoma Bombing Trial, and has been interviewed by international journalists, as well as having appeared on major radio and television shows.

Judith Lee Berg
Human Resource Communication
Denver, CO United States
Contact Phone: 303-322-6229
Pager: 303-207-8566
Click to Contact from Web Site

CAROLYN LONG -- ANGELS OVER AMERICA
Columbia, MD United States
www.AngelsOverAmerica.org

Angels Over America, 9/11 Memorial DVD, celebrates victims and heroes. A spectacular tribute to 9/11 victims and heroes, Carolyn Long's video, 'Angels Over America,' brings an entirely new perspective to this pivotal moment in our nation's history. 'It is dedicated to an America that lost its innocence on this day—but never its hope,' says Long, poet and executive producer of this stirring memorial DVD. 'The events of 9/11 will be a part of the American consciousness forever. How they are held there will shape our future,' says Long. 'Angels Over America' celebrates the courage and resilience that are the hallmarks

Carolyn Long
Author, Executive Producer
Angels Over America
Columbia, MD United States
Contact Phone: 410-730-1440
Contact Main Phone: 410-730-2345
Cell: 443-250-0222
Click to Contact from Web Site

JOSEPH AND JOHN TRIMBACH -- AMERICAN INDIAN MOVEMENT MYTH BUSTERS
Atlanta, GA United States
americanindianmafia.com

Former FBI Special Agent in Charge Joseph Trimbach and his son John have published the long-awaited correction to the historical record of the Pine Ridge Reservation and the American Indian Movement (AIM) of the 1970s. American Indian Mafia blows away prevailing myths about convicted-killer-turned-political-activist Leonard Peltier, the occupation and destruction of Wounded Knee village in 1973, and the Anna Mae Aquash murder in 1975. Trimbach's first-person account promotes genuine Pine Ridge healing with present-day solutions to Indian Country's most pressing issues.

John M. Trimbach
Trimbach & Associates, Inc.
Atlanta, United States
Contact Phone: 770-883-5086
Click to Contact from Web Site

Standing in front of the Agency seal is
Jason R. Hanson
who wants to share with
you personal protection secrets
99% of Americans will _never_ know about.

JASON R. HANSON -- CONCEALED CARRY ACADEMY
Fairfax, VA United States
http://www.ConcealedCarryAcademy.com

Jason R. Hanson is a former CIA Officer, Eagle Scout and NRA Certified Instructor (Instructor # 179627296.) He is the author of The Covert Guide to Concealed Carry: Confessions of a Former CIA Officer. He is also a contributing writer to Concealed Carry Magazine, Personal and Home Defense Magazine, and Combat Handguns Magazine, to name a few. He is the founder and president of the Concealed Carry Academy, a firearms training firm in Fairfax, VA. Jason specializes in teaching civilians personal protection secrets that 99% of Americans will never know about.

Jason R. Hanson
Concealed Carry Academy
Fairfax, VA United States
Contact Phone: 703-942-9292
Click to Contact from Web Site

JOHN M. SNYDER -- GUN LAW EXPERT
Washington, DC United States
www.gunrightspolicies.org

Noted as the Gun Dean by Human Events and the 'dean of gun lobbyists' by The Washington Post and The New York Times, gun law expert John Snyder is the author of the book GUN SAINT, which gives an account of a canonized Catholic saint who used handguns in 1860 to rescue Italian villagers from a gang of terrorists. Snyder has worked for 45 years on behalf of Second Amendment rights as a National Rifle Association editor, Citizens Committee for the Right to Keep and Bear Arms director, Second Amendment Foundation trustee, National Association of Chiefs of Police board member, and www.GunRightsPolicies.org founder

John M. Snyder
Manager
Telum Associates, LLC
Arlington, VA United States
Contact Phone: 202-239-8005
Contact Main Phone: 202-239-8005
Cell: 202-629-8425 .
Click to Contact from Web Site

WARREN D. WOESSNER -- SCHWEGMAN LUNDBERG AND WOESSNER
Minneapolis, MN United States
www.slwip.com

Warren D. Woessner is a leading biotechnology patent attorney and a founding partner of Schwegman, Lundberg, Woessner and Kluth, a sixty attorney intellectual property law firm in Minneapolis, Minnesota. He holds a Ph.D. in chemistry and a law degree from the University of Wisconsin-Madison. Woessner obtained the patents that cover Bt-corn and the anti-HIV drug Ziagen®.

Warren D. Woessner
Founding Shareholder
Schwegman Lundberg and Woessner
Minneapolis, MN United States
Contact Phone: 612-373-6903
Click to Contact from Web Site

JOHN M. SNYDER, GUN LAW EXPERT

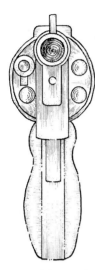

John M. Snyder is the Gun Dean, according to Human Events. Named "dean of gun lobbyists" by The Washington Post and The New York Times, "the senior rights activist in Washington" by Shotgun News, and a "champion of the right to self-defense" by The Washington Times, John M. Snyder has spent 45 years as a proponent of the individual Second Amendment civil right to keep and bear arms as a National Rifle Association editor, Citizens Committee for the Right to Keep and Bear Arms public affairs director, Second Amendment Foundation treasurer, and www.GunRightsPolicies.org founder.

A former Jesuit seminarian, Snyder is founder/manager of Telum Associates, LL.C., founder/chairman of the St. Gabriel Possenti Society, Inc., a director of Council for America, and serves on the boards of the National Association of Chiefs of Police and the American Federation of Police & Concerned Citizens.

He is author of the book, "Gun Saint."

He has been quoted extensively by national and local media, testified before Congress and state legislatures in defense of firearms carry by law-abiding citizens, and written about the social and personal merits of ordinary, responsible citizens bearing arms to protect themselves and their communities. He makes for a thoughtful and provocative interview.

John M. Snyder
Telum Associates, LLC
Arlington, Virginia, U.S.A.
Contact Phone: 202-239-8005
Cell #: 202-744-3111

info@possentisociety.com
GunDean@aol.com

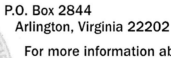

P.O. Box 2844
Arlington, Virginia 22202

For more information about the St. Gabriel Possenti Society and the right to armed self-defense, write or e-mail Possenti Society founder John M. Snyder at the address above.

THE JOHN MARSHALL LAW SCHOOL
Chicago, IL United States
http://www.jmls.edu

The John Marshall Law School is forging a future of unparalleled achievement, offering J.D., LL. M., joint J.D./LL.M. and M.S. degrees, including specialty focuses in Employee Benefits, Global Legal Studies (for foreign lawyers), Information Technology and Privacy Law, Intellectual Property Law, International Business and Trade Law, Real Estate Law and Tax Law. The staffs at Fair Housing Legal Clinic and Veterans Legal Support Center & Clinic, as well as legal faculty regularly provide commentary for print, radio and TV.

Marilyn Thomas
Director of Public Relations
The John Marshall Law School
Chicago, IL United States
Contact Phone: 312-360-2661
Click to Contact from Web Site

ALAN GOLDBERGER -- REFEREE LAW EXPERT
Millburn, NJ United States
http://www.RefLaw.com

Attorney: New Jersey -- New York -- Maryland Bars Speaker: Sports Law -- Sports Officials' Training -- Risk Management/Liability -- Association Law Basketball Referee Football Official Baseball Umpire Author: Sports Officiating: A Legal Guide Co-Author: Sport, Physical Activity and the Law Past President: North Jersey Board of Approved Basketball Officials, Inc. Former three sport college and high school official.

Alan Goldberger
Partner
Brown Moskowitz & Kallen, P.C.
Millburn, NJ United States
Contact Phone: 973-376-0909
Contact Main Phone: 973-376-0909
Click to Contact from Web Site

JUDGE MONTY AHALT (RET)
VIRTUALCOURTHOUSE ONLINE
MEDIATION EXPERT
Annapolis, MD United States
www.virtualcourthouse.com

VirtualCourthouse.com is an Internet-based service that enables mediators and arbitrators to list and market their services and manage their business of dispute resolution. VCH enables the parties to submit disputed claims, responses and supporting material in digital form for resolution by a neutral provider of Alternative Dispute Resolution (ADR) services such as a mediator or arbitrator.

Judge Monty Ahalt (Ret.)
CEO
VirtualCourthouse.com
Annapolis, MD United States
Contact Phone: 410-881-0137
Click to Contact from Web Site

Offering the Midwest's Largest Selection of Law Specialty Programs

In addition to the JD program, our professors and adjunct professors in the Centers for Excellence can offer legal expertise in these areas.

Employee Benefits
- ERISA, Cobra and HIPAA Regulation
- Executive Compensation Issues

Information Technology and Privacy Law
- Identity Theft
- SPAM
- Social Networking

Intellectual Property Law
- Patent, Copyright, Trademark, Trade Secret and Unfair Competition

International Business and Trade Law
- International Corporate and Finance Law
- International Trade Law
- International Customs Law

Real Estate Law
- Fair Housing Issues
- Commercial Real Estate

Tax Law
- Corporate, Individual and Foreign Taxation
- Estate Planning

For information on these specialties, visit our website at *www.jmls.edu*
To arrange an interview, call the Office of Public Information.

Contact: Marilyn Thomas, Director of Public Relations, 312.360.2661 or *6thomas@jmls.edu*

JOHN MARSHALL LAW SCHOOL
CENTERS FOR EXCELLENCE
312.360.2661   *www.jmls.edu*   **jmls.**

EDWARD POLL, J.D., M.B.A., CMC -- LAW FIRM MANAGEMENT EXPERT
Los Angeles, CA United States
http://www.LawBiz.com

Ed Poll, J.D., M.B.A., CMC, is a nationally-recognized expert in law practice management. He coaches attorneys to increased profitability, consulting with them on issues of internal operations, business development, and financial matters. Ed brings his clients a solid background in both law and business. He has 25 years experience as a practicing attorney and has also served as CEO and COO for several manufacturing businesses. Poll is the author of numerous publications that have become the definitive works in the field and is a syndicated columnist for the Dolan Press; he also writes for the Association of Legal Administrators. He publishes a weekly LawBiz®Tips and blogs regularly at www.LawBizBlog.com. His latest effort appears at www.lawbizforum.com. He's a Fellow of the College of Law Practice Management & a charter member of the Million Dollar Consulting Hall of Fame. No one knows more about running a law practice than Ed does.

Edward Poll, J.D., M.B.A.., CMC
Principal
LawBiz Management Company
Venice, CA United States
Contact Phone: 800-837-5880
Click to Contact from Web Site

DR. IRA WILLIAMS, A BETTER HEALTH CARE DELIVERY SYSTEM EXPERT
Greenville, SC United States
misdiagnosed.tatepublishing.net/

Adverse medical events (never events) are the patient safety aspects of the quality of health care that continue to plague our health care system because every state has failed to create an organized health care delivery system. All medical care is local and states license doctors, therefore states are where improvement of the quality of patient care must begin. I know why every state's health care delivery system is broken and I know how to completely reorganize any state's health care system and allowed those states to harness their medical expertise. States are where one must cross the Quality Chasm.

Dr. Ira Williams
Greenville, SC United States
Contact Phone: 864-676-1420
Click to Contact from Web Site

IAN LYNGKLIP -- CONSUMER LAW FIRM
Detriot, MI United States
www.sue4abuse.com

Ian Lyngklip is an experienced lawyer representing consumers in disputes with debt collectors, car dealers, banks, credit reporting agencies and bad corporate actors. He specializes in representing victims of collection abuse, credit reporting errors, and car dealer fraud. He is senior partner of Lyngklip & Associates Consumer Law Center, PLC which offers free consultations and does not collect a fee unless a recovery is made.

Scott Lorenz
Westwind Communications
Plymouth, MI United States
Contact Phone: 248-705-2214
Click to Contact from Web Site

Law Firm Management Expert

Ed Poll, J.D., MBA, CMC, is a nationally recognized expert in law practice management.

He helps attorneys and law firms increase revenues, enhance profits and reduce stress by more effectively managing the Business of Law® — allowing them to spend less time on the business and more on the practice of law.

Ed Poll's services include:

* Coaching
* Consulting
* Buying and Selling a Law Practice
* Speaking Engagements
* Books and Practical Guides
* LawBiz®Tips eNewsletter
* Blawg, www.LawBizBlog.com*

*Named top 100 blawg in 2007 by ABA Journal

Winner of the 2002 Law Practice Management Magazine (ABA) Edge Award for best article

Member of the Million Dollar Consultant® Hall of Fame and the College of Law Practice Management

Poll has practiced law on all sides of the table for 25 years and has also served as CEO and COO for several manufacturing businesses. He founded LawBiz® Management Company in 1990 and now focuses on coaching, consulting, and advising attorneys and law firms on internal operations, business development, and financial matters, as well as speaking and training for bar associations and at universities.

800.837.5880

Edward Poll & Associates, Inc. • 421 Howland Canal, Venice, California 90291-4619 • edpoll@lawbiz.com
www.LawBiz.com • www.LawBizBlog.com • www.lawbizforum.com

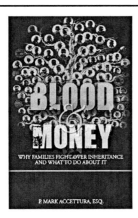

MARK ACCETTURA --- INHERITANCE EXPERT
Detroit, MI United States
www.bloodandmoneybook.com

Why do families fight over inheritance and what can be done about it? Answers to both questions are given in Blood & Money: Why Families Fight Over Inheritance and What to Do About It by Elder Law attorney Mark Accettura. In clear, concise language he explains why squabbles between siblings can reach blood-letting levels once Mom and Dad leave this earth and are no longer around to deal with jealousy and misunderstandings. In 'Blood & Money' -- Mark Accettura discusses what it is that so often drives people to wage war against their own flesh and blood.

Scott Lorenz
Plymouth, MI United States
Contact Phone: 734-667-2090
Click to Contact from Web Site

JUSTICE ON TRIAL -- CRIMINAL JUSTICE SYSTEM EXPERT
Reno, NV United States
www.JusticeOnTrial.org

Justice On Trial, a Nevada Non-Profit corporation, formed in April of 2002, is a defense-of-innocence advocacy organization whose motto is 'Organized Opposition to the Declaration of Guilt.' The company's website, www.JusticeOn-Trial.org, its affiliation with mainstream media and a planned television series are devoted to accomplishing: Review of cases for prosecutorial and/or law enforcement improprieties; Dramatic presentation of cases to national broadcast audiences; Publicize cases nationally and locally in other media; Assist in the defense of those wrongly accused/imprisoned; Collect leads/clues on selected cases and investigate where applicable; Reduce the number of innocent people in; or going to; jail/prison; Reduce crime through public education about the justice system; Lobby for reason and national equity in sentencing; Help create more humane conditions & rehabilitation for all prisoners; Establish acceptable standards for those incarcerated but not convicted; Offer suggestions as to how to improve or help repair the system. Justice On Trial is actively seeking cases to review. Contributions can be made by contacting John Bradley at 1-888-833-9463 or JJB@JusticeOnTrial.org.

John J. Bradley
Managing Director
Justice on Trial
Glenbrook, NV United States
Contact Phone: 775-749-5522
Click to Contact from Web Site

KEVIN KLESERT
Los Angeles, CA United States
TheOtherSideOfLight.com

Kevin Klesert, a successful independent businessman, has experienced first hand how small businesses all over the country carried a disproportionate amount of the burden to meet their legal obligations. The steady erosion of Main Street USA under mountains of onerous regulations, licenses, taxes, and fees from Federal, State, and Local Governments have all but destroyed their ability to succeed and turn a reasonable profit. His intense study of historical trends brought to him the correlation between the down fall of dominant societies of the past and the current struggle to maintain the most noble and ambitious political experiment in human

Brad Butler
Hollywood, CA United States
Contact Phone: 323-461-3921
Click to Contact from Web Site

RUFUS & JENNY TRIPLETT,
PRISONWORLD, PRISON-PRISONER
EXPERTS
Powder Springs, GA United States
www.linkedin.com/in/jennytriplett

GRANT LANGDON -- LAND OWNERSHIP
EXPERT HISTORY
Penfield, NY United States
www.GrantLangdon.com

LOUISA MORITZ -- ACTRESS AND
LAWYER
Los Angeles, CA United States
http://www.promotioninmotion.net/
louisamoritzcontactinfo.html

Rufus & Jenny Triplett, co-editors-in-chief of Prisonworld Magazine, are passionate about family and detouring young men and women from the criminal justice system. They take the non-judgmental and forgiveness approach with their work. Dealing with educating inmates and their families brings great satisfaction to the couple knowing they are a part of improving someone's life. When asked the question what would make you start a magazine like this, the owners respond intelligently 'We hope to bring new and different ideas to the multimedia game as well as enlighten views and perceptions of an uninformed and forgotten society.'

Jenny Triplett
Owner
Dawah International, LLC
Powder Springs, GA United States
Contact Phone: 678-233-8286
Click to Contact from Web Site

Grant Langdon,bS,ISU, grew up in house built in 1687. A serial arsonist burned three of his barns. A crooked Sheriff arrested his 19-year-old son for arson. It was a malicious prosicution and was covered up by the DA. He lost everything and moved to Ohio with just $200 in his pocket. It lead to his first book, Scandal in the Courtroom. His second book, Rebels of the North is about the Anti-Rent Movement that proposed the Homestead Act and led to the election of Lincoln and the start of the Civil War. The Homstead act becamea law 150 year ago

Grant Langdon
Penfield, NY United States
Contact Phone: 585-388-4303
Cell: 513-227-5287
Click to Contact from Web Site

A native of Cuba, Louisa Moritz came to the United States and lived the American dream of a foreigner by finding success first in show business and now as an attorney practicing in Southern California. She arrived in the United States from Cuba with the rather infamous last name of Castro, however, upon established herself in the entertainment business as a performer in movies, on television shows and in the theatre. She has appeared in a number of very famous movies, including co-starring with Jack Nicholson and Danny Devito in One Flew Over the Cuckoo's Nest.

Brad Butler
Promotion In Motion Public Relations
Hollywood, CA United States
Contact Phone: 323-461-3921
Click to Contact from Web Site

BRIAN H. DAVIS -- CLEANBIZ HORIZONS LLC
Minneapolis, MN United States
www.cleanbizhorizons.com

Brian H. Davis is CEO of CleanBiz Horizons LLC, which consults and advocates for Cleantech, supports entry into the U.S. market from Israel, and provides professional services. Brian's experience includes 30 years in sustainable environmental law at 3M, US EPA and Ecolab, with service on government, environmental and emergency response boards. He now serves as Vice-Chair of the Environmental Technologies Trade Advisory Committee of the U.S. Department of Commerce. As Adjunct Assistant Professor at the University of Minnesota Law School since 1997, international speaker, and President of the American-Israel Chamber of Commerce of Minnesota, Brian is active in international cleantech.

Brian H. Davis
CEO
CleanBiz Horizons LLC
Lino Lakes, MN United States
Contact Phone: 651-731-0101
Cell: 651-308-7141
Click to Contact from Web Site

EVAN T. SUSSMAN -- BEVERLY HILLS DIVORCE LAWYER
Beverly Hills, CA United States
www.SussmanLawFirm.com

Since 1994, Evan T. Sussman has been exclusively devoted to protecting clients with respect to prenuptial agreements, separation, divorce-related issues and equitable distribution of the marital estate: such as custody over children, child support, and spousal support. Mr. Sussman knows these are among the most important and stressful issues anyone faces in their lives, and he is committed to providing you with the guidance and expertise you need to navigate what can be treacherous waters.

Evan T. Sussman
Sussman & Associates
Beverly Hills, CA United States
Contact Phone: 310-288-1990
Click to Contact from Web Site

DIANA P. ZITSER --- DIVORCE ATTORNEY
Los Angeles, CA United States
http://zitserlaw.com

Ms. Zitser is the founder of the law firm of Law Offices of Diana P. Zitser, APC, a highly respected and well-known LA firm in the family law arena. The firm has successfully represented a large number of high net worth and entertainment industry clients. Ms. Zitser is certified as a Legal Specialist in Family Law by the State Bar of CA Board of Legal Specialization. She is licensed to practice before all of the Courts of the CA State, the US Court of Appeals for the 9th Circuit, and the US Dist Court for the Central Dist of CA.

Diana P. Zitser
Law Offices of Diana P. Zitser, APC
Universal City, CA United States
Contact Phone: 818 763-5274
Click to Contact from Web Site

BAUM, HEDLUND, ARISTEI AND GOLDMAN, PC
Los Angeles, CA United States
http://www.baumhedlundlaw.com

Expert Media Sources on Accident Aftermath and Mass Tort Litigation. Mass disaster attorneys, pilots and engineers, providing knowledgeable, articulate, technical analysis of accident investigations and litigation. They have represented thousands in aviation, bus, train, truck and structural disasters as well as defective pharmaceutical products. Over 2,500 media appearances on TV, radio and documentaries; and in newspapers, books and magazines, including, Wall St. Journal, USA Today, Fox News, CNN, MSNBC, CNBC, ABC, CBS, NBC, BBC, NY Times and Newsweek. Staff include three law professors, aviation accident law professor, fmr. airline capt., mech. engineer and a bioengineer. Several attorneys have testified before state, federal and foreign governments concerning product safety. Baum Hedlund is a national preeminent plaintiffs law firm representing victims across the nation of catastrophic injury and wrongful death. They are authorities in air safety, airline procedures, aviation crashes and commercial transportation accidents.

Robin McCall
Media Relations Director
Baum, Hedlund, Aristei & Goldman, PC
Los Angeles, CA United States
Contact Phone: 310-207-3233
Click to Contact from Web Site

CALIFORNIA SCHOOL OF FORENSIC STUDIES AT ALLIANT
Los Angeles, CA United States
ForensicStudies.alliant.edu

Calfornia School of Forensic Studies faculty experts are able to provide insight on motives for criminal behavior as well as how this behavior can be identified before any criminal action occurs. Faculty are criminologists (with expertise in predators and serial killers), forensic psychologists, police psychologists, expert in terrorism and risk assessment as well as death penalty, domestic violence and custody cases. Our experts can provide clarity on how U.S., military, and international courts may handle certain cases. CSFS runs doctoral programs in Forensic Psychology at five California campuses: Fresno, Irvine, Los Angeles, Sacramento,and San Diego.

Erica Nogueira
Outreach and Communications Coordinator
Alliant International University
California School of Forensic Studies
San Diego, CA United States
Contact Phone: (858) 635-4428
Contact Main Phone: (858) 635-4772
Cell: (508) 802-8131
Click to Contact from Web Site

COCHRAN, FOLEY AND ASSOCIATES PERSONAL INJURY LAWYERS
Detroit, MI United States
www.cochranfoley.com

Cochran, Foley & Associates, a Michigan law firm, is dedicated to representing individuals and families who have suffered catastrophic losses as a result of injuries, disabilities and death. Cochran, Foley lawyers specialize in personal liability, workman's compensation, Social Security disability, medical malpractice and auto and truck accidents. Cochran, Foley won a $15.8 million verdict, the largest in Michigan for 2006, in a birth injury lawsuit.

Scott Lorenz
President
Westwind Communications
Plymouth, MI United States
Contact Phone: 734-667-2090
Cell: 248-705-2214
Click to Contact from Web Site

JON MITCHELL JACKSON- 2009 TRIAL LAWYER OF THE YEAR.
Orange County, CA United States
www.TrialLawyerExpert.com

Outside the Box legal analysis, commentary, and opinion by 2009 Orange County Trial Lawyer of the Year, Jon Mitchell Jackson. With more than 24 years of battle tested trial experience, Mitch has obtained multiple million dollar settlements, judgments and verdicts for his clients. Since 1986, Mitch has been the Senior Litigation Partner of Jackson and Wilson, Inc., a top AV rated firm (ethics and ability) by Martindale-Hubbell. The firm is also listed in the Bar Register of Preeminent Lawyers, an exclusive listing reserved for only the most respected lawyers.

Jon Mitchell Jackson
Senior Litigation Partner
Jackson & Wilson, Inc.
Laguna Hills, CA United States
Contact Phone: 949-855-8751
Click to Contact from Web Site

SUSAN FILAN -- MSNBC SENIOR LEGAL ANALYST
Westport, CT United States
www.SusanFilan.com
4

I am a litigator and a mediator. My areas of practice are Criminal Defense, Family Law, and General Practice. I am a skilled and powerful advocate, a compassionate avenger. Whether you have been arrested, or your family life is changing, or you have a problem in general, I can help you. I know how the courts work, and I understand people. I am an experienced trial lawyer, a former Connecticut state prosecutor, a professional mediator, and a sought after legal analyst for cable and television news. I appear frequently on NBC's "The Today Show" and am MSNBC's Senior Legal Analyst.

Rick Thomas
MediaRich Marketing
Los Angeles, CA United States
Contact Phone:
Contact Main Phone: 213-382-0500
Cell: 310-595-5800
Click to Contact from Web Site

WILLIAM C. HEAD -- TOP-RATED TRIAL AND LITIGATION ATTORNEY
Atlanta, GA United States
www.trial-attorneys-usa.com

William C. Head has litigated over 30 types of criminal & civil cases for over 34 years. Today, he balances his time acting OF COUNSEL to his Atlanta-based law firm, while pursuing catastrophic civil cases involving personal injury, medical/dental malpractice, products liability, pharmaceutical errors as well as complex alcohol and drug related criminal cases. Mr. Head has also developed a national reputation for teaching attorneys multi-platform media marketing of their legal services. The Internet is the central platform for providing full media exposure to his affiliated lawyers who are the top-rated legal counsel in their respective fields of legal practice.

William C. Head
Senior Partner
William C. Head
Atlanta, GA United States
Contact Phone: 404-835-5563
Contact Main Phone: 404-250-1113
Cell: 404-316-6324
Click to Contact from Web Site

TRANSPORTATION DISASTER ATTORNEYS

AIRLINES • SMALL PLANES • HELICOPTERS
TRUCKS • TRAINS • BUSES • STRUCTURES

Baum, Hedlund, Aristei & Goldman, P.C.
Handling mass disasters since 1985.

Attorney Paul Hedlund on the steps of the U.S. Supreme Court, immediately after arguing a wrongful death case.

Attorney Michael Baum has over 20 years experience handling transportation disasters and pharmaceutical injuries.

For many years the media has turned to Baum Hedlund attorneys who have appeared more than 2,500 times on TV, radio and documentaries; and in newspapers, books and magazines. Baum Hedlund is a national preeminent plaintiffs law firm representing victims of catastrophic injury and wrongful death. They have represented thousands of victims in airline, general aviation, bus, train, trucking and structural accidents as well as defective pharmaceutical products.

Appearances:

New York Times • Wall Street Journal • Newsweek
U.S. News & World Report • USA Today • Chicago Tribune
Washington Post • Boston Globe • Los Angeles Times
San Francisco Chronicle • St. Paul Pioneer Press
San Jose Mercury News • Newsday • Baltimore Sun
Fox News • Larry King Live • CNN • CNBC • MSNBC
PrimeTime Live with Sam Donaldson • Dateline
ABC World News Tonight • Good Morning America
Court TV • People • Associated Press • Reuters • Forbes
Dow Jones News • Bloomberg News • Airline Industry News
National Law Journal • American Lawyer Magazine • TRIAL
Aviation Litigation Reporter • Mealey's Emerging Drugs & Devices
Pharmaceutical Litigation Reporter • NPR
The Guardian • The Times (London) • Radio Europe

Attorney Ronald L. M. Goldman
Pilot & Certified Civil Trial Advocate
Frmr. Adj. Aviation Accident Law Prof.

Attorney John Greaves
Airline Transport Pilot
Former Captain for Comair

525+ Aviation Cases

American Airlines Flt. 587, NY

9-11 Hijacked Airliners

Alaska Airlines Flt. 261, Pt. Mugu, CA

TWA Flt. 800 Explosion, NY

ValuJet Flt. 592, Everglades, FL

United Airlines Flt. 232, Sioux City, IA

160+ small plane, helicopter & balloon

60+ Train Cases

Metrolink Derailment, Glendale, CA

Amtrak/MARC Collision, Silver Spring, MD

Amtrak Train Derailment, Saraland, AL

Amtrak/Conrail Train, Chase, MD

Expert Media Sources on Accident Aftermath and Mass Tort Litigation

Articulate technical analysis of accident investigations and litigation. Authorities in air safety, airline procedures, aviation crashes and commercial transportation accidents.

Contact:
Robin McCall, Media Relations
(800) 827-0087
rmccall@baumhedlundlaw.com
(Los Angeles • DC • Philadelphia)
www.baumhedlundlaw.com

150+ Truck Cases

Recent $7M Verdict

80+ Bus Cases

British Tour Bus, Faversham, England

Mexico Tour Bus, Cancun, Mexico

Girl Scouts Bus, Palm Springs, CA

Ford Motor Co. School Bus, Carrollton, KY

Structural Accidents

Hatchie River Bridge Collapse, TN

Northridge Meadows Apts. Collapse, CA

Train Trestle Bridge Collapse, AL

Gap Building Facade Collapse, CA

PETER J. KILLEEN -- POLICE PSYCHOTHERAPIST - MEDIATOR
Manahawkin, NJ United States
www.myserenlife.com

TIMOTHY A. DIMOFF -- HIGH RISK SECURITY EXPERT
Akron, OH United States
http://www.timothydimoff.com/

ROBERT A. GARDNER, CPP -- SECURITY, CRIME PREVENTION ADVISOR
Santa Paula, CA United States
www.crimewise.com

Former Police Officer. Police Psychotherapist, 9/11 Trauma Expert, Former Franciscan Friar, Peter Killeen has a unique and extensive background in the law enforcement field and spirituality world. Peter Killeen holds masters degrees in both Counseling Psychology and Theology, and is a former police officer for the Port Authority of New York and New Jersey. He has done extensive trauma work with the Port Authority of NY and NJ following the September 11 attacks. He is a recognized expert on PTSD. Peter also works with the Bureau of Alcohol, Tobacco and Firesrams, as well as The Drug Enforcement Administration. In addition, he presents, on a national stage, a workshop entitled: 'Search for Serenity.' He uses the famous 'Serenity Prayer' as the core for his message. It has been met with wonderful success. When speaking with Peter, you feel he practices and lives a true centered spiritual life.

Peter Killeen, MS, MTS, LCADC
Director
Peter J. Killeen
Manahawkin, NJ United States
Contact Phone: 973-819-8537
Cell: 973-819-8537
Click to Contact from Web Site

Timothy A. Dimoff, CPP, high-risk security expert is President/Founder of SACS Consulting, Inc. (www.sacsconsulting.com), a risk mitigation firm providing preventative measures and response for substance abuse, workplace violence, harassment, crime, and policy development/enforcement problems for the security and human resources fields. Tim has appeared on NBC Dateline, Court TV, CNN, on radio shows and in major newspapers and magazines including The Wall Street Journal, The New York Times, the Chicago Tribune, Inc. and Entrepeneur. Tim is the author of numerous articles and training programs, and of the book Life Rage, an in-depth look at the rages terrorizing society.

Carol Saferin
Mart Saferin & Assoc.
Cleveland, OH United States
Contact Phone: 440-461-6753
Click to Contact from Web Site

Robert A. Gardner, is a 'board-certified' security management professional with multi-state security consultant, private patrol and private investigator 'Qualified Manager' licenses. His background includes more than 40 years of training and experience in evaluating, developing, and managing security and crime prevention programs. For 25 of those years, he served as both a private sector security consultant and a public-sector peace officer. He is a former corporate security manager, police crime prevention specialist, detective supervisor and police training manager. Gardner provides security consulting and expert witness services from offices in Santa Paula, Calif., Las Vegas, Nev., and Scottsdale, Ariz.

Robert A. Gardner, CPP
Santa Paula, CA United States
Contact Phone: 805-659-4294
Click to Contact from Web Site

NATIONAL SCHOOL SAFETY AND SECURITY SERVICES -- KEN TRUMP
Cleveland, OH United States
http://www.SchoolSecurity.org

National School Safety and Security Services is a Cleveland-based, national consulting firm specializing in K-12 school security and emergency preparedness issues. Kenneth S. Trump, President, has over 25 years school safety experience with school and public safety officials from all 50 states and Canada. Ken is one of the most widely quoted school safety experts and has appeared on all cable and network news.

Kenneth S. Trump, M.P.A.
President
National School Safety and Security Services
Cleveland, OH United States
Contact Phone: 216-251-3067
Click to Contact from Web Site

KLUEGER AND STEIN, LLP --- ASSET PROTECTION EXPERTS
Encino, CA United States
www.maximumassetprotection.com

We are asset protection. With over 30 years of real-life experience and over 3,000 clients, we are the nation's leading and most respected asset protection law firm. Every year we set up hundreds of structures to protect residences, rental real estate, investments and retirement plans. We have represented Fortune 100 executives, prominent real estate developers, business owners and professionals. Our partners, Jacob Stein and Robert Klueger, teach over 50 seminars and write numerous articles on asset protection each year. They are also authors of published books and technical manuals on asset protection. Visit www.maximumassetprotection.com for more information on asset protection.

Jacob Stein
Klueger & Stein, LLP
Encino, CA United States
Contact Phone: 818-933-3838
Click to Contact from Web Site

DAVID NANCE -- PERSONAL SAFETY EXPERT
Chicago, IL United States
www.personalsafetyexpert.com

The simple and affordable solution to keep you and your family safe, the SABRE Personal Safety Academy (PSA) teaches protection without throwing a punch. PSA is the first and only nationwide program providing risk reduction techniques to discourage threats and protection at a safe distance if an attack occurs. Students learn awareness and avoidance, how to use pepper spray effectively and responsibly, and the best self defense technique to escape and attacker. Taught by police officers and personal safety experts, PSA supports the charity RAINN (www.rainn.org). PSA is proud to introduce the SABRE College Safety Program, fall 2011.

David Nance
Chicago, IL United States
Contact Phone: 312-765-6767
Cell: 314-422-5152
Click to Contact from Web Site

ROBERT SICILIANO -- IDENTITY THEFT EXPERT
Boston, MA United States
http://www.IDTheftSecurity.com

STING ALARM
Henderson, NV United States
http://www.stingalarm.com

Sting Alarm, Inc., which works with homeowners and small businesses, including retailers, he sees thieves constantly coming up with new ways to steal. The best way to minimize that, he says, is technology and surveillance.

Ruth Furman
ImageWords
Las Vegas, NV United States
Contact Phone: 702-255-8288
Click to Contact from Web Site

JOHN CRUZ -- WORLD BANKING WORLD FRAUD
New York, NY United States
www.worldbankingworldfraud.com

Bank Vice President reveals Money Laundering, Identity Theft, Bank Fraud in new book: World Banking World Fraud, Using Your Identity, Available now at Amazon.com. Whistleblower Lawsuit. NEW YORK - John Cruz just released his book claiming he was terminated from HSBC after discovering and subsequently refusing to ignore repeated instances of fraud, money laundering and identity theft. He is now coming forward with documented findings in, 'World Banking World Fraud, Using Your Identity.' (ISBN 146378659X) Cruz first became aware of the fraud when he was named VP & senior business relationship manager over some of HSBC's highest producing branches on Long Island.

John Cruz
Longmont, CO United States
Contact Phone: 631-504-9510
Click to Contact from Web Site

Identity Theft Expert, Author and Television News Correspondent. ROBERT SICILIANO, CEO of IDTheftSecurity.com is fiercely committed to informing, educating, and empowering Americans so they can be protected from violence and crime in the physical and virtual worlds. His "tell it like it is" style is sought after by major media outlets, executives in the C-Suite of leading corporations, meeting planners, and community leaders to get the straight talk they need to stay safe in a world in which physical and virtual crime is commonplace. Siciliano is accessible, real, professional, and ready to weigh in and comment at a moment's notice

Robert Siciliano
Personal Security and Identity Theft Expert
Identity Theft Expert and Speaker
Boston, MA United States
Contact Phone: (617) 329-1182
Click to Contact from Web Site

School Security Consultant: Kenneth S. Trump

K ENNETH S. TRUMP, M.P.A., is President of National School Safety and Security Services, a Cleveland-based national consulting firm specializing in school security and emergency preparedness training, school security assessments and related school safety and crisis consulting services. Ken is one of the nation's leading school safety experts with more than 20 years of school security experience working with education and public safety officials in 45 states.

Ken is author of the 1998 best-selling book, "Practical School Security: Basic Guidelines for Safe and Secure Schools" (Corwin Press), and more than 45 articles on school security and crisis issues. His book, "Classroom Killers? Hallway Hostages? How Schools Can Prevent and Manage School Crises," was released in July 2000. In May 1999, he testified before the U.S. Senate Committee on Health, Education, Labor and Pensions on school safety.

Ken is one of the most widely quoted national expert consultants on school security and crisis issues. He has been interviewed by all network and cable news outlets, top 50 U.S. daily print newspapers and radio stations nationwide.

Kenneth S. Trump, M.P.A.
President
National School Safety
and Security Services
Cleveland, Ohio

(216) 251-3067

kentrump@aol.com
www.schoolsecurity.org

MARK S. GOTTLIEB -- CPA, PC

Great Neck, NY United States
http://www.msgcpa.com/

Mark S. Gottlieb, CPA PC (MSG) is distinguished as one of the Tri-State's premier business valuation and litigation support firms. Our practice is devoted exclusively to providing attorneys and their clients with a diverse continuum of forensic accounting, business valuation and litigation support services.

Melissa Lefcort
Marketing & Communications Coordinator
Mark S. Gottlieb, CPA, PC
Great Neck, NY United States
Contact Phone: 516-829-4936
Click to Contact from Web Site

MICHAEL G. KESSLER, PRESIDENT AND CEO OF KESSLER INTERNATIONAL

New York, NY United States
www.Investigation.com

Michael G. Kessler is the President and CEO of Kessler International, a corporate investigation and forensic accounting firm headquartered in New York with offices worldwide. A graduate of St. John's University, Mr. Kessler has held a number of distinguished government positions throughout his notable career, including Chief of Investigations for the New York State Department of Taxation and Finance, and Assistant Chief Auditor for the NYS Attorney General. Since founding Kessler International in 1988, Mr. Kessler has become globally recognized as one of the foremost experts in the field of forensic accounting.

Michael G. Kessler
President and CEO
Kessler International
New York, NY United States
Contact Phone: 212-286-9100
Contact Main Phone: 212 286-9100
Click to Contact from Web Site

FIDELIFACTS -- BACKGROUND INVESTIGATIONS

New York, NY United States
www.Fidelifacts.com

With over 50 years of experience in providing accurate, reliable information to our clients, Fidelifacts stands out as a leader in the field of pre-employment screening and due-diligence background investigative services. Employment screening and background checks; credit, driving and criminal history checks. Due Diligence investigations. Educational and employment verifications and interviews of former supervisors. Caregiver, nanny, home companion, health aide and tenant background checks.

Thomas W. Norton
President
Fidelifacts/Metropolitan NY Inc.
New York, NY United States
Contact Phone: 800-678-0007
Click to Contact from Web Site

0

MIKE MCCARTY -- SAFE HIRING SOLUTIONS
indianapolis, IN United States
www.safehiringsolutions.com

Mike McCarty is the CEO of Safe Hiring Solutions LLC a global background screening firm with clients that range from large corporations to small not-for-profit organizations. Prior to founding Safe Hiring Solutions, Mike was a violent crime detective with the Metropolitan Police Department in Nashville, TN where he was instrumental in the development and implementation of one of the largest community-based family violence investigative units in the United States. The program was labeled a model program by the U.S. Department of Justice and former President Bill Clinton. Mike has facilitated violence prevention training and consulting nationally and internationally to organizations such

Mike McCarty
Safe Hiring Solutions LLC
Danville, IN United States
Contact Phone: 888-215-8296
Click to Contact from Web Site

MICHELLE PYAN -- COMMERCIAL INVESTIGATIONS LLC
Troy, NY United States
www.commercialinvestigationsllc.com

COMMERCIAL INVESTIGATIONS LLC (CI), a woman-owned licensed private investigative agency, offers thorough and affordable BACKGROUND INVESTIGATIONS. CI provides accurate, timely, cost effective and fully compliant reports supported by high standards of customer service. CI provides the PROACTIVE TRUTH regarding applicants, thereby reducing turnover and limiting exposure to civil liability. CI also offers CIchecked an electronic trust mark that is displayed on your social networking profiles, web pages, blogs, auctions and e-mail signatures. Visitors can click to verify your Certified Identification and view your certificate (www.cichecked.com).

Michelle Pyan
President
Commercial Investigations LLC
Troy, NY United States
Contact Phone: 800-284-0906
Contact Main Phone: 800-284-0906
Cell: 518-470-6813
Click to Contact from Web Site

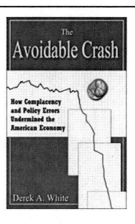

DEREK A. WHITE -- THE AVOIDABLE CRASH
Ottawa, Ontario Canada
http://www.buddgraphics.com/itoolkit.asp?pg=products&specific=jnmolqq8

A critical take on why the American economy is in trouble, how it could have been avoided, and how to regain sound growth. It is vitally important that the underlying causes of the collapse be fully understood in order that appropriate measures can be taken to bring about a sustainable U.S. recovery and prevent recurrence. This book provides compelling evidence that, from 1980 on, the following led inexorably to the U.S. financial meltdown.

Evelyn Budd, R.G.D.
Budd Publishing
Ottawa, ON Canada
Contact Phone: 613-824-9707
Click to Contact from Web Site

ROSE COLOMBO

Long Beach, CA United States
http://fightbacklegalabuse.com

Rose Colombo was a young housewife and mother with four small children. She said, 'I never gave a thought until 1984 about the legal system. I was taught that people who worked in the legal system were 100% protecting the citizens.' She remarked, 'I was just a mom at home baking cookies.' But as fate would have it, her abusive husband led her to file for a simple divorce with substantial assets. Rose found herself in a state of shock and confusion when injustices reared its ugly head and knocked on her back door. She said, 'I was thrust into the dark side of justice where I felt isolated and scared with no where to go for help.'

Rose Colombo
Hollywood, CA United States
Contact Phone: 323-461-3921
Click to Contact from Web Site

AUDRI G. LANFORD, PH.D. -- GOING PAPERLESS -- PRODUCTIVITY EXPERT

Charlotte, NC United States
www.paperitis.com

Dr. Audri Lanford is an internationally recognized expert on going paperless and productivity. In 1985, she started one of the fastest growing private US companies (an Inc. 500 company) that helped businesses save millions of dollars by going paperless. Her websites and products now help experts and entrepreneurs cure 'Paperitis' to save money, time and a few trees.

Audri G. Lanford, Ph.D.
CEO
Lanford Inc.
NC United States
Contact Phone: 815-642-0460
Click to Contact from Web Site

NATIONAL ASSOCIATION OF MILITARY MOMS AND SPOUSES

Washington, DC United States
www.nammas.org

National Association of Military Moms and Spouses (NAMMAS) is the premier online support network for moms of service members and spouses, serving every military branch and Guard and Reserve families. Thousands of women count on NAMMAS to provide an ear to listen, a heart for good advice, and a shoulder to lean on when things get too hard. At NAMMAS, members function like a great 'support bra', because as they say, 'when life gets tough, we hold you up and together!' Lori Bell, Air Force wife and mom of 3, founded NAMMAS after her husband deployed with 3 week's notice.

Lori R. Bell
Founder/CEO
National Association of Military Moms and Spouses
National Harbor, MD United States
Contact Phone: 1-888-964-8222
Contact Main Phone: 1-888-964-8222
Click to Contact from Web Site

MAJ. BRIAN HAMPTON, PUBLISHER, VETERANS VISION
Washington, DC United States
www.theveteransvision.com

As the president of three nationwide veterans' organizations, MAJ Brian Hampton, USAR (ret) has developed a reputation for being a forceful, intrepid and controversial national advocate for veterans' causes. In city rallies around the country, Hampton has challenged federal elected officials for spending $70 billion on benefits for illegal aliens, while investing 1/10 of 1% of that to help 300,000 homeless veterans. A Vietnam Veteran, Hampton earned a Masters' Degree from Michigan State University.

Brian Hampton
Founder and Publisher
VETERANS' VISION
Falls Church, VA United States
Contact Phone: 703-237-8980
Contact Main Phone: 800-528-5385
Click to Contact from Web Site

YOUNG MARINES OF THE MARINE CORPS LEAGUE
Washington, DC United States
http://www.YoungMarines.com

The Young Marines is a non-profit youth education and service program for boys and girls, ages 8 through completion of high school. The Young Marines strengthens the lives of America's youth by teaching self-confidence, academic achievement, honoring our nation's veterans, responsible citizenship, community service and the importance living a healthy, drug-free lifestyle. The program focuses on character building and leadership and promotes a lifestyle that is conducive to being productive members of society.

Mike Kessler
National Executive Director
Young Marines of the Marine Corps League
Washington, DC United States
Contact Phone: 800-717-0060
Click to Contact from Web Site

AMERICAN FOREIGN SERVICE ASSOCIATION
Washington, DC United States
http://www.afsa.org

AFSA speaks for the 25,000 Foreign Service professionals about the importance of vigorous American leadership in international affairs; international trade facilitation and American prosperity; dangers of isolationism; role of diplomacy in ensuring national security; safety of Americans abroad; political ambassadorial appointments; budget allocations for diplomacy, foreign aid, and other foreign affairs activities.

Tom Switzer
Director of Communications
American Foreign Service Association
Washington, DC United States
Contact Phone: 202-944-5501
Click to Contact from Web Site

CIRCLE OF FRIENDS FOR AMERICAN VETERANS
Falls Church, VA United States
www.vetsvision.org

The Circle of Friends for American Veterans is a 501-c(3) designated non-profit organization dedicated to raising awareness about veterans issues, particularly homeless veterans, by influencing public opinion to shape public policy. Since 1993, The Circle of Friends for American Veterans, and its allied publication, the VETERANS' VISION, have provided and continues to provide advocacy for those who deserve it the most and have it the least by conducting nationwide rallies, holding receptions with policymakers and providing direct financial support to transitional facilities that assist homeless veterans.

Brian A. Hampton
President
Circle of Friends for American Veterans
Falls Church, VA United States
Contact Phone: 703-237-8980
Click to Contact from Web Site

FIDELIS -- MILITARY TO CIVILIAN CAREER TRANSITION.
San Francisco, CA United States
www.fideliseducation.com

Fidelis is an early stage technology company that's partnering with the University of California, top colleges, and hiring partners to provide an end-to-end solution to the military to civilian career transition. For our main program, students find us while on active duty and begin completing their general education requirements through us, from the University of California system online. Once our students leave the military, we help get them into traditional universities that align with their academic goals, coach them through to graduation, and then place them into careers at top companies.

Heidi Hudson
Fidelis
San Francisco, CA United States
Contact Phone: (800) 379-3004
Click to Contact from Web Site

U.S. ARMY WAR COLLEGE
Carlisle, PA United States
http://www.carlisle.army.mil

The U.S. Army War College is the senior education center of the Army. College expertise emphasizes strategic leadership and the landpower. See military security studies at www.carlisle.army.mil, or contact these experts: regional military assessments, strategic issues of leadership and management and ethics, defense strategy analysis, campaign planning, Homeland defense, Peace keeping and stability operations, Strategic logistics, Force development, Strategic communications, Military History, Executive [over 40] Health and Fitness.

Carol Kerr
Public Information Officer
U.S. Army War College
Carlisle, PA United States
Contact Phone: 717-245-4389
Click to Contact from Web Site

GINA ELISE -- PIN-UPS FOR VETS
Redlands, CA United States
www.PinUpsForVets.com

In 2006, in response to the expanding numbers of ill and injured Veterans entering VA and military hospitals, a granddaughter of a WWII Veteran, Gina Elise, created a unique project called, Pin-Ups For Vets, to serve hospitalized Veterans and to support deployed troops. Pin-Ups For Vets produces a yearly 1940's-style pin-up calendar that helps to raise much-needed funding to improve rehabilitation programs in VA and military hospitals. The organization's Founder and volunteers personally deliver the popular calendars to the bedsides of hospitalized Vets in all 50 states. These calendar gifts are also shipped to the combat zones to boost morale.

Gina Elise
Pin-Ups For Vets
Redlands, CA United States
Contact Phone: (909) 792-6055
Click to Contact from Web Site

M. SALAHUDDIN KHAN--- AFGHANISTAN EXPERT -- AUTHOR SIKANDER
Chicago, IL United States
www.sikanderbook.com
IL

M. Salahuddin Khan of Lake Forest, IL, is author of SIKANDER a 586 page novel which follows the coming of age and maturing of a young Pakistani who befriends and joins Afghan mujahideen warriors in their fight against Soviet occupation in the mid 1980's. It examines America's rollercoaster relationship with the people of the region and with Islam in general, from thirty years ago into the present day post-9/11 era. SIKANDER took top honors at the Los Angeles Book Festival in 2010. Visit: http://www.sikanderbook.com

Scott Lorenz
Book Publicist
Westwind Communications
Plymouth, MI United States
Contact Phone: 734-667-2090
Click to Contact from Web Site

CHIKA ONYEANI -- AFRICA AFFAIRS EXPERT
New York, NY United States
www.africansuntimes.com

The African Sun Times, published by Dr. Chika Onyeani is the largest African weekly in the United States. This comprehensive newspaper, accompanied by an online edition, brings readers into the issues of the world from the perspective of the African continent. A native of Nigeria, Dr. Onyeani is the author of best selling books and participates in major conferences on African issues all the time. Onyeani also founded and runs the Celebrate Africa Foundation, which seeks to bring attention to positive contributions to Africa through its Country of the Year Award.

Brad Butler
Promotion in Motion
Hollywood, CA United States
Contact Phone: 323-461-3921
Click to Contact from Web Site

ZOE RASTEGAR -- TALK SHOW HOST
Washington, DC United States
accentproductions.org

Zohreh 'Zoe' Rastegar is the host of Accent, a groundbreaking talk show promoting education and cultural understanding of the Middle East during these increasingly volatile political times. Accent offers a positive message encouraging assimilation of Iranian-Americans, Iraqi-Americans, and other foreign nationals into American culture without losing touch with their proud, magnificent heritage.

Zoe Rastegar
Washington, DC United States
Contact Phone: 202-841-8733
Click to Contact from Web Site

GAIL WINSTON -- WINSTON MID EAST ANALYSIS AND COMMENTARY
Chicago, IL United States

Mid-East regional conflicts, weapons, war, technology and oil. Forecasts of probable scenarios: relations between Washington & Jerusalem. Radio & TV interviews - good with live call-ins. 150 interviews during the Gulf War. Have published over 3,500 related articles in USA Today, Washington Post, U.S. Defense News, Boston Globe and Chicago Tribune. Articles available via e-mail.

Gail Winston
Winston Mid-East Commentary
Highland Park, IL United States
Contact Phone: 847-432-1735
Click to Contact from Web Site

INSTITUTE FOR GILGIT BALTISTAN STUDIES
Washington, DC United States
www.gilgitbaltistan.us

IGBS works primarily on socio-economic, political and environmental issues of a region called Gilgit-Baltistan, which remains under Pakistani occupation since 1947. The region has gained importance due to China's growing role, three cups of tea, Pakistan's war with India over Kashmir and terrorism in Afghanistan. The region borders China, Tajikistan, Afghanistan, India and Pakistan and is rich in uranium, copper, water, gold and precious stones. It is claimed by India and remains a constitutional limbo. Senge Sering has Masters in Development Studies from UK and works with think tanks and academia to promote the issue of Gilgit Baltistan

Senge Sering
Mr.
Institute for Gilgit Baltistan Studies
Washington DC, DC United States
Contact Phone: 202 689 0647
Click to Contact from Web Site

WORLD GOVERNMENT OF WORLD CITIZENS --WORLD CITIZEN GOVERNMENT

Washington, DC United States
http://www.worldservice.org

World Peace: The Most Important Subject of the 21st Century. GARRY DAVIS is a former B'way actor and B-17 bomber pilot in WWII. At age 26, he renounced his US nationality and declared himself a 'citizen of the world.' Supported by Albert Einstein, Albert Camus and Albert Schweitzer, based on human rights, he founded the World Government of World Citizens in 1953. Now the foremost authority on world law, world citizenship and human rights, he travels with a World Passport issued by the new government. His books are My Country is the World, Passport to Freedom. World Government, Ready or Not!, Dear World, A Global Odyssey, Letters to World Citizens, Views From My Space, A World Citizen in the Holy Land, World Peace Is You! (ebook), World Citizen Garry Davis Goes to Court.

Garry Davis
Founder/President
World Government Of World Citizens
World Government House
Washington, DC United States
Contact Phone: 802-864-6818
Contact Main Phone: (202) 638-2662
Cell: 802 598-3211
Click to Contact from Web Site

NATIONAL IMMIGRATION FORUM

Washington, DC United States
http://www.immigrationforum.org

The leading pro-immigration organization in the country. Quoted by every major U.S. newspaper and on national radio and television shows. Expert spokespeople in English and Spanish, immigrants and refugees who can put a human face on your story. Clear and concise written materials on legal and illegal immigration, the impact of recent laws on immigrant communities, citizenship, and public benefits. Publications on the fiscal impact of immigration and how immigrants are assimilating into American society.

Katherine Vargas
Press Secretary
National Immigration Forum
Washington, DC United States
Contact Phone: 202-383-5987
Click to Contact from Web Site

AMERICANS FOR IMMIGRATION CONTROL, INC.

Monterey, VA United States
http://www.immigrationcontrol.com

Americans for Immigration Control, Inc. is the nation's largest grassroots lobby for immigration reform. With more than 250,000 members, AIC is leading the fight to reduce overall immigration levels, end welfare and affirmative action benefits for aliens, and protect America's borders from illegal entry by foreign populations. Besides lobbying for immigration control, AIC conducts public education campaigns through direct mail, paid advertisements, opinion surveys, and public appearances by its spokesmen on radio and television.

Robert Goldsborough
President
Americans for Immigration Control, Inc.
Monterey, VA United States
Contact Phone: 540-468-2023
Click to Contact from Web Site

DANNY QUINTANA
Salt Lake City, UT United States
http://www.promotioninmotion.net/
dannyquintanaesq.html

Author of the just released Caught in the Middle: Stories Of Hispanic Migration And Solutions To America's Immigration Dilemma, Utah-based Danny Quintana is a tireless supporter advocating on behalf of the world's disabled and immigration reform. Danny was a top high school wrestler and walked on to the University of Utah's college team. Two weeks later at the age of 21, he became afflicted with transverse myelites. He has been in a wheelchair since and has shifted his athletic skills to wheelchair tennis. He successfully competes in national and international wheelchair tennis tournaments. He graduated from the University of Utah in 1980 and from their College of Law where he received his J.D degree in 1983. After a successful legal career, he retired from full time practice in 2000. He is the author of several books: Hunting and Gathering, An Urban Youth Survival Guide; Martian Peace, Why We Must Explore.

Brad Butler
Promotion in Motion Public Relations
Hollywood, CA United States
Contact Phone: 323-461-3921
Click to Contact from Web Site

LARRY EIDELMAN - EMERGENCY MANAGEMENT EXPERT
Yorktown Heights, NY United States
www.altarisgroup.com

Larry Eidelman is a Managing Partner of Altaris Consulting Group, LLC, a firm specializing in emergency planning and preparedness in K-12 schools. Altaris works with schools to develop their capacity to prevent and when necessary, successfully respond to virtually any crisis. Journalists from various media outlets utilize Larry as a source for insights on prominent crises in our nation's educational institutions and communities. From commentary on incidents of school violence, intruders on school campuses, natural disasters and emergency management in schools, Larry provides expert analysis and the type of insightful commentary journalist desire.

Larry Eidelman
Managing Partner
Altaris Consulting Group
Yorktown Heights, NY United States
Contact Phone: 866-960-8739
Contact Main Phone: 866-960-8739
Click to Contact from Web Site

ANDREW P. JOHNSON -- IMMIGRATION AUTHOR -- EXPERT -- ATTORNEY
New York, NY United States
www.lawapj.com

Andrew P. Johnson, Esq. was quoted in the New York Daily News as an Immigration Expert, was featured in a New York Times article on immigration law, and has been interviewed by CBS News. (see www.lawapj.com) He is the co-founder of a nonprofit think tank that presents recommendations to Congress to reduce costs and streamline US CIS and the Immigration Courts. Andrew P. Johnson is a former government prosecutor who has litigated over 1,000 deportation cases and argued several high profile asylum cases. In addition, Mr. Johnson has given lectures on Business immigration in both Europe and Asia, and has advocated for a bipartisan passage of a restricted version of the Dream Act.

Andrew P. Johnson, PC
Law Offices of Andrew P. Johnson, PC
New York, NY United States
Contact Phone: (212) 693-3355
Click to Contact from Web Site

www.lifesaving.com

LIFESAVING RESOURCES, LLC
Kennebunkport, ME United States
www.lifesaving.com

Lifesaving Resources, LLC is dedicated to drowning and aquatic injury prevention and emergency management. The company develops Aquatics Safety (drowning prevention), Lifeguarding, Water Rescue, Swiftwater Rescue, and Ice Rescue training curriculums and conducts this training throughout North America for the Public Safety and Rescue Sector; the Lifeguard and Aquatic Recreation Sector; and, the General Public. Gerald Dworkin serves as the technical consultant, and is a leading author and educator in his field. Dworkin has over 35 years of professional experience as a Firefighter, EMT, Lifeguard, Water Rescue and Ice Rescue Technician and has published numerous articles and several textbooks.

Gerald M. Dworkin
Consultant, Aquatics Safety and Water Rescue
Lifesaving Resources, LLC
Water and Ice Rescue Specialists
Kennebunkport, ME United States
Contact Phone: 207-967-8614
Contact Main Phone: 207/967-8614
Cell: 207/604-4240
Click to Contact from Web Site

LOIS CLARK MCCOY -- NATIONAL INSTITUTE FOR URBAN SEARCH AND RESCUE
Santa Barbara, CA United States
http://www.niusr.org/

NIUSR is a collection of intelligent and committed folks of disparate backgrounds. They have come together by invitation. We call them the 'Eagles'. This is because they are so varied and eagles don't flock. You find them one at a time.

Barbara Gaughen
Gaughen Global PR
Santa Barbara, CA United States
Contact Phone: 805 968 8567
Click to Contact from Web Site

SURVIVAL CENTER -- FAMILY PREPAREDNESS, HEALTH AND SURVIVAL SUPPLIES
Seattle, WA United States
http://www.survivalcenter.com

Richard Mankamyer 'Uncle Richard' Author, Preparedness Trainer and General Manager of The Survival Center ™ has over 35 years experience helping people prepare for most any emergency that may come their way. We have helped thousands of families to prepare. We have worked with Federal Reserve Bank locations, nuclear power plants, various businesses and governmental agencies as consultants and suppliers. The Survival Center™, America's Premier Preparedness Center, is helping Americans prepare to be on their own for extended periods of time. "We have the knowledge and experience to help you prepare" said 'Uncle Richard'. Our "Basic Preparedness" book and 3 DVD Home Study Course along with our catalog is a great training and resource guide. The Survival Center™ is a complete one stop shop for survival supplies, emergency kits, disaster kits and supplies, along with long term food storage, MRE's, water filters, medical kits, and Under Ground Shelters.

Richard Mankamyer
Director of Preparedness and Emergency Planning
Survival Center
Preparedness/Emergency Supplies
McKenna, WA United States
Contact Phone: 1-360-458-6778
Click to Contact from Web Site

CENTER FOR WILDLIFE INFORMATION

Missoula, MT United States
http://www.BeBearAware.org

General H. Norman Schwarzkopf, is a national spokesperson for this group which is involved with grizzly bear conservation and education and the wildlife stewardship campaign. They are concerned with hiking and camping in bear, mountain lion and rattlesnake country and with urban wildlife-bears, mountain lions and coyotes returning to the city. Some topics include: Saving the Grizzly Bear, What to Do if Attacked by a Wild Animal and Bear Pepper Spray-Does it Work? Their professional speakers include bear management specialists and forest and park rangers.

Chuck Bartlebaugh
Executive Director
Center for Wildlife Information
Missoula, MT United States
Contact Phone: 406-721-8985
Contact Main Phone: 406-523-7750
Click to Contact from Web Site

THE NATIONAL ANXIETY CENTER

South Orange, NJ United States
nationalanxietycenter.blogspot.com/

Global Warming? Urban Sprawl? Endangered Species? Pesticides? Ozone 'Holes'? Are these and other issues real or just 'scare campaigns'? Since 1990, the Center has been a clearinghouse for information about scare campaigns that create widespread anxiety and drive public policy, generating countless new laws, regulations, and international treaties, affecting all aspects of life in America. Talkers Magazine calls this veteran science and business writer, 'one of the great guests of talk radio.' Print journalists value his expertise.

Alan Caruba
Founder
The National Anxiety Center
South Orange, NJ United States
Contact Phone: 973-763-6392
Click to Contact from Web Site

CRUSADE AGAINST FIRE DEATHS -- RICHARD M PATTON

Citrus Heights, CA United States
www.firecrusade.com

Richard M. Patton, Fire Protection Engineer, realized years ago that fire codes and 'certifications' for fire related products and systems were often oriented to benefit those who profited from fire at the expense of the consumer. For example, fire sprinkler systems are regulated by code to be priced at two to four times as much as a properly engineered system would cost. To create a market for smoke detectors costing one dollar to manufacture and selling for ten dollars up, 'certification tests' were falsified and codes were rigged to hide an excess of a 50 percent failure rate.

Richard M Patton
President
Crusade Against Fire Deaths
Citrus Heights, CA United States
Contact Phone: 916-721-7700
Click to Contact from Web Site

PHIGENICS LLC -- WATER MANAGEMENT - EFFICIENCY - SAFETY

Chicago, IL United States
www.phigenics.com

Phigenics is a water management company that partners with facility owners and suppliers to improve the efficiency, effectiveness and overall safety of all water systems. We help our clients remediate problems associated with waterborne pathogens, including Legionella. We specialize in bringing technical solutions and new innovations to the water industry

Dr. William McCoy, Ph.D
Phigenics LLC
Naperville, IL United States
Contact Phone: 630-717-7546
Click to Contact from Web Site

ALLIANCE TO SAVE ENERGY

Washington, DC United States
http://www.ase.org

The Alliance to Save Energy is a coalition of prominent business, government, environmental, and consumer leaders who promote the efficient use of energy worldwide to benefit consumers, environment, the economy, and national security. The Alliance offers expertise on: Energy, Energy Efficiency, Energy Policy, Environment, Climate Change/Global Warming, Consumer Money-Saving Tips, Utility Restructuring, Energy Prices, Pollution, Disasters—Rebuilding Efficiently, 'Green Schools' - Energy Efficiency in School Buildings and Curricula. Alliance President Kateri Callahan brings 20 years of experience in policy advocacy, fundraising, coalition building, and organizational management.

Ms. Ronnie J. Kweller
Deputy Director of Communications
Alliance to Save Energy
Washington, DC United States
Contact Phone: 202-530-2203
Contact Main Phone: 202-857-0666
Cell: 202-276-9327
Click to Contact from Web Site

Are You Ready?
It Is About the Future — Yours.

*The Survival Center now offers
a DVD series to help you be prepared*

It is obvious to many that some serious and life style-altering things are happening politically, economically, geologically and environmentally. How you prepare for these changes will determine your future well-being. Yes, it is about the future — yours. Are you ready?

It is our individual responsibility to get ready and be prepared to be on our own for extended periods of time. We have already seen that no group is standing by to come and "save" us. Look outside the box.

Since the early 1970s, Richard Mankamyer — "Uncle Richard" — author, preparedness trainer, general manager and regular talk show guest from The Survival Center, of McKenna, Washington, has been helping people prepare for most any emergency that may come their way.

"We have the knowledge and experience to help you prepare." Mankamyer says.

The Survival Center, America's Premier Preparedness Center, carries a complete selection of emergency supplies including survival kits, disaster preparedness supplies, MRE's, long term storage food, medical kits, water filters and underground shelters, to name a few. The Survival Center's Web site — www.SurvivalCenter.com — is a wealth of information and offers thousands of products to help you prepare.

Based on decades of experience, the Survival Center has written what has come to be recognized as the industry standard book, "Basic Preparedness," and has now produced a 6-hour (3-DVD) Home Study Course around the extensive subject of preparedness. Whether you are a beginner or expert, this Home Study Course has something for you.

As Mankamyer says, "Preparedness is a lot like insurance, you have to have it before the need arises."

ENERGY EDUCATION COUNCIL
Springfield, IL United States
http://energyedcouncil.org

The Energy Education Council (EEC) is committed to the education and empowerment of energy consumers, with the goal of enhancing lives by promoting the safe and efficient use of energy. We value collaboration, relationships, and partner input in the continuing effort to create broad safety and efficiency knowledge. EEC's award-winning Safe Electricity program (SafeElectricity.org) has grown to include over 400 utility partners and sponsors reaching millions of consumers in 27 states.

Molly Hall
Executive Director
Energy Education Council/Safe Electricity
Springfield, IL United States
Contact Phone: 217.546.6815
Contact Main Phone: 217.546.6815
Click to Contact from Web Site

MATTHEW FREIJE - WATERBORNE PATHOGENS EXPERT
San Diego, CA United States
www.hcinfo.com

Matt Freije earned an engineering degree from Purdue University a graduate certificate in epidemiology and biostatistics at Drexel University. He is president of HC Info, which provides HACCP water plans, online training courses, and consulting. Freije has served as an expert in more than 50 lawsuits, spoken to groups about waterborne pathogens and bottled water, and been interviewed on radio and TV. His book, Legionellae Control in Health Care Facilities: A Guide for Minimizing Risk, has sold in more than 30 countries. His latest book is Protect Yourself from Legionnaires' Disease: The waterborne illness that continues to kill and harm.

Matt Freije
President
HC Info
San Diego, CA United States
Contact Phone: 619-821-8184
Click to Contact from Web Site

INTEGRITY RESEARCH INSTITUTE -- RESEARCHING SCIENTIFIC INTEGRITY
Washington, DC United States
www.IntegrityResearchInstitute.org

Integrity Research Institute (IRI) is a non-profit 501(c)3 charitable organization dedicated to helping establish integrity in scientific research, primarily regarding the physics of energy whether it is in the technical, human health, or environmental area. The exciting mission challenge of IRI positions us to address the crucial aspect of emerging energy sciences, force production for transportation, and bioenergetics for energy medicine, with a concern for the future.

Thomas Valone
President
Integrity Research Institute
Beltsville, MD United States
Contact Phone: 301-220-0440
Contact Main Phone: 888-802-5243
Cell: 301-318-1071
Click to Contact from Web Site

DR. ROB MOIR -- OCEAN RIVER INSTITUTE
Cambridge, MA United States
www.OceanRiver.org

The Ocean River Institute, a 501(c)(3) nonprofit corp, helps people and groups make a difference where they live through environmental stewardship and science. Many environmental issues are best addressed by people taking action in their own communities and regions, not by large, national entities. However, localized or newly formed groups often need help to achieve their goals. Thats where ORI comes in. We maintain a network of ORI Partners, connecting them with resources and services to help them maximize their impact, expand their capacity and weather unanticipated setbacks. ORI Actions and Events offer opportunities to make a difference for environments

Rob Moir
Director
Ocean River Institute
Massachusetts Environmental League of Voters
Cambridge, MA United States
Contact Phone: 617-661-6647
Contact Main Phone: 617 661-6647
Cell: 978 621-6657
Click to Contact from Web Site

NATIONAL RURAL ELECTRIC COOPERATIVE ASSOCIATION
Arlington, VA United States
http://www.nreca.coop

NRECA is the national trade organization representing the nation's more than 900 private customer-owned electric cooperatives providing electric service to 39 million people in 47 states. Electric cooperatives own and maintain nearly half the nation's power lines, spanning three quarters of the United States. Electric co-op consumers live in 2,600 of the nation's 3,136 counties. NRECA provides programs and services to ensure that electric cooperatives remain a vital segment of the electric utility industry.

Patrick Lavigne
Director of Media & Public Affairs
National Rural Electric Cooperative Association
Arlington, VA United States
Contact Phone:
Click to Contact from Web Site

MICHAEL D. SHAW -- AIR QUALITY EXPERT
Washington, DC United States
www.gasdetection.com

Michael D. Shaw has extensive experience in all aspects of air quality monitoring, encompassing both chemical and biological toxins. Renowned in the industry for his applications knowledge and his pursuit of evidence-based rational approaches to potential environmental hazards, Michael has developed an international reputation as a straight-talking, scientifically-grounded commentator. Be prepared to hear some contrarian thoughts!

Michael D. Shaw
Executive VP/Director of Marketing
Interscan Corporation
Reston, VA United States
Contact Phone: 703-796-6063
Contact Main Phone: 1 800 458-6153
Click to Contact from Web Site

LINDA JESCHOFNIG - SCIENCE LAB KIT - ONLINE LAB KIT- BIOLOGY LAB

Denver, CO United States
www.LabPaq.com

Linda and Peter Jeschofnig are the founders of Hands-On Labs, Inc., and are co-authors of Teaching Lab Science Courses Online: Resources for Best Practices, Tools and Technology. The book, which promises to be a partner in developing a new consensus on teaching science, is a must-read for university leaders and college science professors. Hands-On-Lab sells over 30,000 LabPaqs a year as lab kits for online science courses. Of the students who purchase LabPaqs,, 75 percent are working adults and 70 percent are female. More than 200 universities are using LabPaqs and 1,000 Lab-Paqs a year are used by military personnel.

Scott Lorenz
Westwind Communications
Plymouth, MI United States
Contact Phone: 734-667-2090
Contact Main Phone: 248-705-2214
Cell: 248-705-2214
Click to Contact from Web Site

INTERNATIONAL ASSOCIATION OF CANINE PROFESSIONALS

Orlando, FL United States
www.CanineProfessionals.com

The International Association of Canine Professionals is an organization of dog trainers, behavior experts, groomers, dog walkers, veterinarians and others dedicated to the well being of dogs. IACP was established to maintain the highest standards of professional and business practice among dog professionals. The IACP commitment is to develop professional recognition, communication, education, understanding and co-operation. With over 1500 members worldwide it has an extensive knowledge and related experience on all dog matters. Information can be obtained from www. canineprofessionals.com or by calling 407 469 2008

Martin Deeley
Exec Director
International Association of Canine Professionals
Montverde, FL United States
Contact Phone: 407 469 5583
Cell: 407 469 5583
Click to Contact from Web Site

AMI MOORE -- CHICAGO DOG TRAINING EXPERT

Chicago, IL United States
www.chicagodogcoach.com

Ami Moore, The Chicago Dog Expert, dog behaviorist, dog trainer, has devoted her life to discover the most humane, most dog-friendly dog training and behavior rehabilitation methods. Ami Moore is an educator, a speaker, a coach and an expert in the rehabilitation of aggressive and fearful dogs. Ami Moore is sought after guest on radio and television programs all over America.

Ami Moore The Chicago Dog Expe
Director of Training
The Chicago Dog Coach
Chicago, IL United States
Contact Phone: 847-284-7760
Click to Contact from Web Site

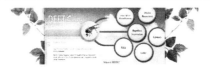

TAMIRA CI THAYNE -- HUMANE TREATMENT FOR DOGS
Altoona, PA United States
www.DogsDeserveBetter.org

Tamira Ci Thayne, 'Peaceful Dog Warrior', fights for dogs who live chained. A finalist for Animal Planet's 'Hero of the Year', she is founder of Dogs Deserve Better, a nonprofit boasting 100 reps. Legislation is a growing trend, California passing in September 2006, Texas passing legislation in 2007, and Nevada passing legislation in 2009. Parents Against Dog Chaining logged 336 children killed/injured by chained dogs since October 2003. Thayne faced charges for helping a dying dog; survived a dog attack.

Tamira Ci Thayne
Executive Director
Dogs Deserve Better
Tipton, PA United States
Contact Phone: 814.941.7447
Cell: 814.207.4586
Click to Contact from Web Site

DEET EDUCATION PROGRAM
Washington, DC United States
http://deetonline.org/

DEET is the active ingredient in most insect repellents available in the United States that are applied to the skin. The most commonly used chemical name for DEET is N,N-diethyl-m toluamide, though DEET also is expressed often as N,N-diethyl-meta-toluamide and N,N-diethyl-3-methylbenzamide. 'DEET is one of the safest, most reliable products on the market. Researchers are constantly searching for new repellents and during the past 40 years, nothing has come close to DEET in terms of repellent efficacy against biting arthropods (insects and ticks).' Jonathan F. Day, Professor of Medical Entomology, University of Florida, Florida Medical Entomology Laboratory. Enjoy outdoor activity with fewer bug bites and reduced risk of insect-borne disease through proper use of insect repellents and other simple steps.

Judi Anderson
Kroeger Associates
Chapel Hill, NC United States
Contact Phone: 919-942-8847
Click to Contact from Web Site

NEW JERSEY PEST MANAGEMENT ASSOCIATION
Livingston, NJ United States
http://www.njpma.com/

The New Jersey Pest Management Association was founded in 1941 and is one of the oldest trade associations representing the industry. Members of NJPMA are also dual members of the National Pest Management Association. The insect and rodent pest problems, as well as others, that occur in New Jersey are common to other States. . Journalists are encouraged to contact Alan Caruba at (973) 763-6392, the Association's longtime public relations counselor for any assistance.

Leonard Douglen
Executive Director
New Jersey Pest Management Association
Livingston, NJ United States
Contact Phone: 1-800-524-9942
Click to Contact from Web Site

DAN STOCKDALE -- ADVENTURES IN LEADERSHIP

Knoxville, TN United States
www.TigerGuy.com

Dan is a leadership keynote speaker, author and tiger trainer who has appeared on CNN, Fox News, Fox Business Channel, New York Times and many others. As a leadership speaker Dan speaks to audiences across the country with his leadership secrets from the wild. His leadership experience includes running organizations of more than 1,000 employees. As the Host of Fox News Channels Fox & Friends 'Wild America!' Dan spotlights zoos, wildlife sanctuaries, and national parks across America bringing mother nature into the living room of viewers around the globe. Dan is a conservationist, motivational speaker, and is the Founder of Adventures in Leadership and the non-profit, Washington DC based World Nature Coalition.

Dan Stockdale
Founder
Adventures in Leadership
Harriman, TN United States
Contact Phone: (865) 300-3232
Cell: (865) 300-3232
Click to Contact from Web Site

PET FOOD INSTITUTE

Washington, DC United States
http://www.petfoodinstitute.org

The Pet Food Institute has been the voice of U.S. pet food manufacturers since 1958. PFI is dedicated to supporting initiatives to advance the quality of dog and cat food, educating the public on proper pet feeding and care, representing the pet food industry to government officials and promoting the overall care and well being of pets.

Kurt Gallagher
Communications Director
Pet Food Institute
Washington, DC United States
Contact Phone: 202-367-1120
Click to Contact from Web Site

BUDDY BEDS -- ORTHOPEDIC MEMORY FOAM DOG BEDS

Denver, CO United States
http://www.BuddyBeds.com/

Voted 'Best Pet Bed' by Pet Age Magazine. Our orthopedic memory foam eliminates all painful pressure points which cut off circulation. Perfect for animals with painful arthritis, hip & elbow dysplasia and joint issues. Don't forget our younger dogs: Start them early on an orthopedic dog bed to assist in the aging of their joints. Our unique waterproof, yet breathable, liner protects the memory foam from liquids, stains and odors, keeping the memory foam clean and dry, anti-bacterial, anti-microbial, anti-dust mite and hypoallergenic. Animal Wellness Seal of Approval. Memory foam provides the comfort and support our beloved pet deserve.

Debra Holte
Buddy Beds, LLC
Denver, CO United States
Contact Phone: 303-744-0424
Click to Contact from Web Site

COOL PET HOLISTIC REMEDIES
St. Petersburg, FL United States
www.yourcoolpet.com

No More Pills! COOL PET develops holistic remedies for dogs, birds, cats, and horses that offer an alternative to high dollar drugs, costly veterinary visits and hard to feed supplement pills. All COOL PET Holistic Remedies: Taste like a treat!, Are easier to feed than pills, Act faster and are better digested than any pill or powder, Have no side effects like many prescription drug products, Are made in the USA with human pharma grade materials. All this for an average of less than .63 cents per day! COOL PET Holistic Remedies provide what normal treats and normal supplements cannot!

Jonathan Lewis
COOL PET Holistic Remedies
St. Petersburg, FL United States
Contact Phone: 727-641-6175
Cell: 727-641-6175
Click to Contact from Web Site

TOBI KOSANKE -- CRAZY K FARM PET AND POULTRY PRODUCTS, LLC
Hempstead, TX United States
www.crazykfarm.com/tobi-kosanke.html

Tobi Kosanke, Ph.D., President of Crazy K Farm Pet and Poultry Products, is a multi-faceted expert source and speaker. She has used her long experience in teaching, lecturing and curriculum development to create engaging presentations on such varied subjects as: starting a home-based business; becoming a stay-at-home Momtrepreneur; reinventing yourself; maintaining a work life balance for entrepreneurs; backyard and pet chicken ownership; and off-the-job safety.

Tobi Kosanke, Ph.D.
President
Crazy K Farm Pet and Poultry Products
Hempstead, TX United States
Contact Phone: 800-980-4165
Cell: 281-380-4450
Click to Contact from Web Site

ANDY LOPEZ - THE INVISIBLE GARDENER
Malibu, CA United States
www.organicdatabank.info

ANDREW LOPEZ, 'The Invisible Gardener'. Is one of the world's most respected Organic Gardeners/Organic Horticulturist and is considered by many as an environmental leader. Declared an Environmental Pioneer, Mr. Lopez has been featured on PBS, and in many journals and publications and runs several websites: www.invisiblegardener.com and his newest www.organicdatabank.info He started a worldwide club called ClubIG. He has written and published over 30 Ebooks, some of his book are 'Natural Pest Control, Alternatives to Chemicals for the Home and Garden', 'Dances with ants-Natural Ant Control Secrets', 'Organic Vegetable Growers Guide', 'The Natural Lawn', and more! Dont Panic Its Organic!

Invisible Gardener
The Invisible Gardener
Malibu, CA United States
Contact Phone: 310-457-4438
Cell: 310-457-4438
Click to Contact from Web Site

VICTORIA BOWMANN
Phoenix, AZ United States
http://myrealhealth.com

Victoria Bowmann is a health care professional, author and speaker with more than 30 years of expertise in cleansing, detoxification, digestive and gastro-intestinal (GI) health. Growing up with allergies and a predisposition to arthritis and other genetic ailments, Bowmann began in earnest at a young age to research alternative treatments to invasive conventional approaches. Bowmann honed in on the importance of cleansing and detoxification as a major factor in optimizing health. She created a widely used manual on reflorastation, a technique used to reintroduce healthy bacteria into the bowel following a colon hydrotherapy.

Brad Butler
Promotion In Motion
Hollywood, CA United States
Contact Phone: 323-461-3921
Click to Contact from Web Site

PATRICIA BRAGG -- VEGATARIAN HEALTH RECIPIES
Santa Barbara, CA United States
www.bragg.com

Paul, and his daughter, Patricia, have been health pioneers for decades. When the 'engineered fast food' products of science and industry had captured the attention of most Americans, Paul Bragg campaigned for a diet and lifestyle that focused on natural live foods and a healthy regime for a vital and long life. These ideas, based around natural and organic foods, are gaining praise and acceptance world-wide.

Brad Butler
Promotion in Motion
Hollywood, CA United States
Contact Phone: 323-461-3921
Click to Contact from Web Site

FOOD ALLERGY INITIATIVE
New York, NY United States
http://www.FoodAllergyInitiative.org

Founded in 1998, the Food Allergy Initiative (FAI) is a 501(c)(3) nonprofit organization whose mission is to support research to find a cure for life-threatening food allergies; clinical programs to effectively diagnose and treat people at risk; and public policy initiatives and educational programs to make their world safer. It is estimated that more than 11 million Americans suffer from food allergies, which cause some 30,000 emergency room visits and 150 deaths annually.

[ad]Barbara Rosenstein
Director of Communications
Food Allergy Initiative
New York, NY United States
Contact Phone: 212-207-1974
Click to Contact from Web Site

SCOTT ANTHONY - PIZZA MARKETING EXPERT

Punxsutawney, PA United States
www.foxspizzapunxsy.com/consulting.shtml

Scott Anthony, owner of Fox's Pizza Den in Punxsutawney, Pennsylvania, is a 14-year pizza veteran. Scott is rapidly becoming an industry expert in the art of working with the media and gaining FREE publicity. Scott sought a change of careers in 1994, he looked into the pizza business and has never looked back. Applying basic business principles to his den in Punxsutawney, Pennsylvania, he now operates one of the most successful stores in the company.

Scott Anthony
Fox's Pizza Den
Punxsutawney, PA United States
Contact Phone: 814-591-1489
Click to Contact from Web Site

CULINARY VISIONS PANEL

Chicago, IL United States
www.culinaryvisions.org

Culinary Visions Panel program, led by Chicago-based Olson Communications, shows consumers are continuing to enjoy eating out but ordering differently to satisfy pocketbooks and palates. The online survey polled 210 consumers who identified themselves as frequent patrons of casual-dining restaurants, and their responses reflect a 'New frugality' mindset. More than half of participants reported changing their dining choices in the past 12 months as a result of the economy; another 81 percent are paying closer attention to menu prices.

Sharon M. Olson
Olson Communications, Inc.
Chicago, IL United States
Contact Phone: 312-280-9203
Contact Main Phone: 312-2804573
Click to Contact from Web Site

OLSON COMMUNICATIONS, INC. -- FOOD INDUSTRY COMMUNICATIONS STRATE

Chicago, IL United States
www.OlsonCom.com

Olson Communications is a full service marketing communications company specializing in the foodservice industry, the business that feeds America away from home. Olson Communications concentrates on foodservice markets, trends, issues, and communication strategy. They are expert in tracking trends in many industry segments, including: supermarket deli, school and college foodservice and senior dining.

Sharon M. Olson
President
Olson Communications, Inc.
Chicago, IL United States
Contact Phone: 312-280-4573
Click to Contact from Web Site

MELISSA MURPHY -- SPOKANE REALTOR
Spokane, WA United States
melissamurphysells.com

With a strong understanding of the Spokane community and a vision for its future, Melissa Murphy has emerged as a shining star in the Inland Northwest real estate community. From the time she started her graduate work to present day, Melissa has listed and sold more than 200 homes throughout Spokane, with a special focus on the neighborhood where she grew up and lives today: Spokane's South Hill. In addition, she has helped dozens of buyers find the right house at the best price.

Melissa Murphy
Owner/Designated Broker
Prime Real Estate Group
Spokane, WA United States
Contact Phone: (509) 218-4663
Cell: (509) 220-0128
Click to Contact from Web Site

BUILDING OWNERS AND MANAGERS ASSOCIATION (BOMA) INTERNATIONAL
Washington, DC United States
http://www.boma.org

Founded in 1907, BOMA International is an international federation of more than 100 local associations. The 18,000 members own or manage over 8.5 billion square feet of downtown and suburban properties worldwide. BOMA International's mission is to advance the performance of commercial real estate through advocacy, professional competency, standards and research.

Lisa Prats
VP, Communications, Marketing & Meetings
Building Owners and Managers Association (BOMA) International
Washington, DC United States
Contact Phone: 202-326-6333
Contact Main Phone: 202-408-2662
Click to Contact from Web Site

BRIAN FOLB -- HOLLYWOOD OFFICE BUILDINGS
Hollywood, CA United States
www.HollywoodOffices.com

Paramount Developers and Contractors is a leading property management and real estate developer in Hollywood. Located in the heart of the entertainment industry, we specialize in providing you with the highest quality of service by offering the most competitive prices. With over fifty years of business experience, our highly trained technicians and support personnel provide an exceptional level of expertise, versatility, and responsiveness. Our staff is here to quickly respond and accommodate all of your office requirements. Whether you need office space, retail space or specialty office occupancy, we can satisfy all of your leasing and rental requirements. Our architectural design team is equipped to customize your office environment. Our uniquely friendly and inviting atmosphere guarantees an exceptional working experience. Paramount, it's where YOU want to be.

Brian Folb
Paramount
Hollywood, CA United States
Contact Phone: 323-462-6727
Click to Contact from Web Site

GATSKI COMMERCIAL REAL ESTATE SERVICES
Las Vegas, NV United States
http://www.gatskicommercial.com

With an extensive Las Vegas history, Gatski Commercial delivers in-depth market knowledge and perspective. Whether you're looking for traditional services, such as property management and investment sales and leasing, or innovative new offerings, such as landscape and building maintenance services, cost segregation and property tax appeals, Gatski offers it all under one roof. The company has under contract a portfolio of approximately 8 million square feet comprised of about 475 commercial buildings, occupying in excess of 1,700 tenants. For four years, Gatski Commercial Real Estate Services has been included on the Inc. 5000 list of the fastest-growing companies in the United States. Sign up for our services today and learn why.

Ruth Furman
ImageWords
Las Vegas, NV United States
Contact Phone: 702-255-8288
Click to Contact from Web Site

DEBRA GOULD - THE STAGING DIVA
Toronto, Ontario Canada
www.stagingdiva.com

Internationally recognized home staging expert Debra Gould is President of Six Elements Inc. and creator of The Staging Diva® Home Staging Business Training Program. Gould has staged hundreds of real estate properties priced from $170,000 to $1.7 million in addition to 8 of her own homes. She has trained over 4000 home stagers in the US, Canada, and 20 other countries. She is the only home staging trainer with an MBA in marketing, 20 years experience as an entrepreneur, and a track record of growing her own successful home staging business. Visit Debra Gould's Online Media Room at http://www.debragould.com

Debra Gould, The Staging Diva
President
Six Elements, Inc.
Toronto, ON Canada
Contact Phone: 416-691-6615
Click to Contact from Web Site

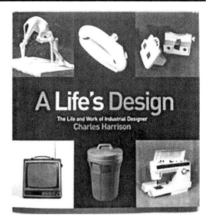

CHARLES HARRISON -- INDUSTRIAL DESIGN
Richmond, VA United States
http://alifesdesign.com/

Chuck Harrison, industrial designer and educator was the first Black design executive to work for a major corporation, Harrison improved the quality of life of millions through the breadth and innovation of his designs for more than three decades. During his career, he has designed more than 750 products including the iconic View-Master. Harrison is the 2008 recipient of the Cooper-Hewitt National Design Award for Lifetime Achievement among numerous other awards and recognitions for his contribution to design and industry. Read an account of his remarkable career in 'A Life's Design' available at www.alifesdesign.com.

Joeffrey Trimmingham
Philip Reese, LLC
Richmond, VA United States
Contact Phone: 888-445-6111
Click to Contact from Web Site

MARGARET INNIS -- HOME STAGING & COLOR EXPERT

Boston, MA United States
http://www.DecToSell.com

Creating environments that encourage success for businesses & entrepeneurs, homeowners & students since 1994. We proudly serve many repeat clients who look to us for great quality, incredible service & professionalism. We try to deliver on these expectations every day.

Margaret Ann Innis
Staging - Color - Redesign - Training
Decorate To Sell
Billerica, MA United States
Contact Phone: 508-572-8225
Click to Contact from Web Site

MAHAFFEY FABRIC STRUCTURES

Memphis, TN United States
http://www.FabricStructures.com/

Since 1924, Mahaffey Fabric Structures has been a leading manufacturer and provider of portable shelter in North America and the Caribbean. Our turnkey service, speed, and efficiency has continued to set us apart. Whether you're in need of a temporary or semi-permanent structure for industrial applications, a special event gala, an upcoming military exercise, or disaster relief shelter, Mahaffey's got you covered! We look forward to providing a solution for your tent and fabric structure needs.

Beth Wilson
Marketing Manager
Mahaffey Fabric Structures
Memphis, TN United States
Contact Phone: 901-541-6956
Click to Contact from Web Site

MAHAFFEY TENT AND PARTY RENTALS

Memphis, TN United States
www.MahaffeyTent.com

Since 1924, Mahaffey has been a leading provider of tent and party rentals in the Mid-South. Whether it's brainstorming innovative d [e9636f]r ideas, creating a CAD layout of your space, or coordinating your event, one of Mahaffey's special event consultants will be there every step of the way. Mahaffey Tent and Party Rentals...Turning Ordinary Places into Extraordinary Spaces!

Beth Wilson
Mahaffey Tent and Party Rentals
Memphis, TN United States
Contact Phone: 901-541-6956
Click to Contact from Web Site

CAPITOL LIGHTING -- 1800LIGHTING.COM

East Hanover, FL United States
www.1800lighting.com
33487-1900

Light Up Your Life! Whether you're seeking the ultimate chandelier, new fixtures for a kitchen remodel, stunning nighttime landscape effects or a complete lighting package to showcase your new home, Capitol Lighting stands ready to serve. Capitol's eight stores are the offspring of a family retailing tradition that dates back to 1924, when Max Lebersfeld, an electrical contractor and recent immigrant from Austria-Hungary, opened a light fixture store in Newark, N.J. Four generations later, Capitol Lighting has expanded up and down the east coast and with a leading website 1-800LIGHTING.com.

Eric Lebersfeld
President
Capitol Lighting
Boca Raton, FL United States
Contact Phone: 5615364334
Contact Main Phone: 5619949570
Click to Contact from Web Site

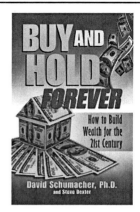

MOBILEHOMEUNIVERSITY.COM
Denver, CO United States
www.mobilehomeuniversity.com

EUGENIA FOXWORTH, CIPS, NYRS,
BROKER FOXWORTH REALTY
New York, NY United States
www.FoxworthRealtyOnline.com

Dave Reynolds earned a bachelor's degree in Accounting from Mesa State College and also went to CSU for a master's in Accounting and Taxation. He was introduced to the mobile home park business early on as his parents owned a couple of parks. He became involved in the mobile home park industry in 1995 by purchasing his first park. Since that time, he has purchased and operated nearly 50 mobile home parks across the country and has been involved as a real estate broker for several more.

STEVE DEXTER - REAL ESTATE AND
FORECLOSURE EXPERT
Hollywood, CA United States
www.schumacherenterprises.com

Eugenia Foxworth is a unique real estate Broker 'without borders', specializing in exceptional Properties in New York City, Riverdale, NY and internationally. She has acquired a reputation with both buyers and sellers as someone who can make a deal happen through her tenacity, knowledge of the market, professionalism and personality. She is licensed by the New York State Department of State and and is a member of the Real Estate Board of New York (REBNY) and the NYC Local Council of FIABCI-USA (International Federation of Real Estate). She has been chosen as a member of Elite 2003, 2004, 2005, 2006,

Dave Reynolds
Member
Mobile Home Park Store . com LLC
OutdoorBillboard.com
Cedaredge, CO United States
Contact Phone: 800-937-6151
Click to Contact from Web Site

Steve Dexter, author of two books on real estate, is promoting a revised edition of the bestseller, Buy and Hold Forever: How to Build Wealth for the 21st Century by David Schumacher. Dexter updated all the laws and tips based on current market conditions, thus adding a nice touch to book that has been praised as one of the best how to real estate books ever written.

Brad Butler
Promotion In Motion
Hollywood, CA United States
Contact Phone: 323-461-3921
Click to Contact from Web Site

Eugenia Foxworth, CIPS, NYRS
Owner/Broker
Foxworth Realty
New York, NY United States
Contact Phone: 212-368-4902
Click to Contact from Web Site

GLENN PLANTONE -- REAL ESTATE INVESTMENT EXPERT
Las Vegas, NV United States
www.viewpointequity.com

Glenn has been a full time real estate investor for almost ten years. In the last two years, he and his team have purchased and renovated over 80 distressed properties in Las Vegas, NV. Glenn then places a high quality, long-term renter or lease option tenant in the home and sells it to his investor clients as a turn-key investment with great cash flow and strong appreciation potential. Glenn closely follows current market trends and his predictions and analysis have been featured regularly in such well respected publications as the LV Review Journal, LV Sun Business Journal, and CNN Money.

Glenn Plantone
Director
Las Vegas, NV United States
Contact Phone: (702) 656-3264
Contact Main Phone: (702) 656-3264
Cell: 702-769-9872
Click to Contact from Web Site

PLATINUM PROPERTIES INVESTOR NETWORK
Costa Mesa, CA United States
http://www.JasonHartman.com

Real estate investment is the most accessible route to wealth for the average American family. According to the National Association of Realtors, more people are buying residential investment property than ever before. Many people enjoy financial independence by investing in rental real estate and you could, too. We can help you identify the best investment real estate markets and our experienced professionals can guide you toward your goal of financial independence through real estate. We have access to good Realtors, mortgage lenders, lawyers, accountants, property management companies, escrow and title companies to get the job done right for you.

Brittney McKaig
Public Relations Coordinator
Platinum Properties Investor Network
Costa Mesa, CA United States
Contact Phone: 714-820-4200
Click to Contact from Web Site

PROGRESSIVE REAL ESTATE INVESTMENTS, LLC
Las Vegas, NV United States
www.progressive-rei.com/

Progressive REI is an expert in the foreclosure market. We specialize in the purchase of investment properties from the Trustee Sales Auctions. Utilizing our years of industry experience and knowledge of the market we have designed a targeted investment strategy and business model along with the development of our custom research software program. To take advantage of the growing foreclosure market. Since the housing crash, using our customized tools and investment strategies, we have successfully purchased and sold over 100 properties at an annualized return of over 30%.

Joey Paulos / Mickey Griffin
Managing Partner
Progressive Real Estate Investments, LLC
Las Vegas, NV United States
Contact Phone: (702) 938-9033
Cell: (702) 499-7303
Click to Contact from Web Site

JEAN LOUIS RACINE - COMMERCIAL LEASE EXPERT

Montreal, Quebec Canada
www.commercialeasexpert.com
Quebec

Jean Louis Racine. His 4 Books: 'Don't Sign This Lease', 'Rent Reduction', '250 Comments For Your Lease', 'Exercises', are a Guide, showing commercial tenants, realtors, and bankers: 1: How to negotiate cash-free Rent and bonuses from strangled landlords. 2. Field 92 = What your landlord's weaknesses are. 3. How to pit landlords against each other, earning more cash-free rent, bonuses, and money from landlords. 4. 57 Stories+50 Examples. The author has worked as a lawyer, a real estate broker and a tenant representative since 1978, negotiating over 130 million square feet of office and industrial space for a total value of over $302,000,000.00.

Commercial Lease Expert
Groupe Racine, Real Estate Broker inc.
Quebec, QC Canada
Contact Phone: 1-418-683-0003
Click to Contact from Web Site

PATRICK SKIFFINGTON -- FLORIDA REAL ESTATE EXPERT

Orlando, FL United States
http://www.patskiffington.com

Pat Skiffington has spent over 10 years as one of Orlando, Florida's most respected Real Estate Professionals. Pat leads his own sales team of professionals and is Broker/Owner of Three Keller Williams Real Estate Franchise Offices in Central Florida. He is Supervising Broker for over 300 Real Estate Agents in Orlando. Pat also serves as a TASA Registered Expert Witness and is licensed as a Florida Real Estate Instructor and teaches Salesperson and Broker Licensing Classes throughout the State of Florida. Pat is also a highly sought-after Instructor and Coach working with Realtors on their Sales Skills.

Patrick Skiffington
Broker/Owner
Keller Williams Realty
Orlando, FL United States
Contact Phone: 407-924-3313
Cell: (407) 924-3313
Click to Contact from Web Site

DAVID STONE --- NEVADA ASSOCIATION SERVICES, INC.

Las Vegas, NV United States
nas-inc.com

Nevada Association Services, Inc., has more than a decade of experience specializing in assessment collection. As Nevada's largest assessment collection company, NAS provides its community association clients with the most efficient and cost-effective services available.

ImageWords
Las Vegas, NV United States
Contact Phone: 702-255-8288
Click to Contact from Web Site

INSTITUTE FOR BUSINESS AND HOME SAFETY

Tampa, FL United States
www.disastersafety.org

Mission -- The Institute for Business & Home Safety's mission is to reduce the social and economic effects of natural disasters and other property losses by conducting research and advocating improved construction, maintenance and preparation practices. Vision -- The Institute for Business & Home Safety envisions a nation that promotes resiliency from natural disasters and other property losses by developing an infrastructure that is damage-resistant and through personal and corporate action that helps minimize disruption to normal life and work patterns.

Joseph King
Institute for Business & Home Safety
Tampa, FL United States
Contact Phone: 813-442-2845
Click to Contact from Web Site

THE AMERICAN WATERWAYS OPERATORS

Arlington, VA United States
http://www.americanwaterways.com

AWO is the national association representing the inland and coastal tugboat, towboat and barge industry. Comprised of nearly 4,000 tugboats and towboats and over 27,000 barges, the industry safely and efficiently moves over 800 million tons of cargo each year, including over half of America's export grain, energy sources such as coal and petroleum, including most of New England's home heating oil and gasoline, and other bulk commodities that are the building blocks of the U.S. economy. Recognized leaders in marine safety, all AWO members must participate, as a condition of membership, in The Responsible Carrier Program, an award-winning, third-party audited safety and environmental protection regime. AWO provides expert information on issues affecting this vital economical and environmentally-friendly segment of America's commercial transportation system.

Anne Burns
Vice President - Public Affairs
The American Waterways Operators
Arlington, VA United States
Contact Phone: 703-841-9300
Click to Contact from Web Site

AMERICAN PUBLIC TRANSPORTATION ASSOCIATION

Washington, DC United States
http://www.apta.com/

APTA is a nonprofit international association of more than 1,500 member organizations including public transportation systems; planning, design, construction and finance firms; product and service providers; academic institutions; and state associations and departments of transportation. APTA members serve the public interest by providing safe, efficient and economical public transportation services and products. APTA members serve more than 90 percent of persons using public transportation in the United States and Canada.

Virginia Miller
Senior Manager-Media Relations
American Public Transportation Association
Washington, DC United States
Contact Phone: 202-496-4816
Click to Contact from Web Site

LAUREN FIX -- AUTOMOTIVE EXPERT -- CONSULTANT
Buffalo, NY United States
http://www.laurenfix.com

Lauren Fix, the Car Coach®, is a nationally recognized automotive expert, speaker and journalist. Founder of Automotive Aspects and author of numerous books and articles, including the award-winning Lauren Fix's Guide to Loving Your Car (St. Martins Press, June 2008), Lauren provides solid information and an auto industry insider's perspective on a wide range of automotive topics, including car care, repair, safety, driving skills and industry trends. In addition to being a leader in positive consumer awareness of the automotive world for over 20 years, Lauren is often solicited for her expertise in marketing, entrepreneurship, parenting and other lifestyle topics. Lauren was recently named Time Warner's new national automotive correspondent. Her extensive broadcast experience includes Oprah, The View, Regis and Kelly, TODAY, 20/20, The Early Show, CNN, FOX News, MSNBC, Headline News, TBS Makeover and a Movie, Inside Edition, ESPN, TBS, Discovery, Speed, and NPR.

Lauren J. Fix
Automotive Consultant/Expert
Lancaster, NY United States
Contact Phone: 716-440-3888
Contact Main Phone: 646-475-4357
Cell: 716-440-3888
Click to Contact from Web Site

SHELBY FIX -- TEEN CAR COACH
Buffalo, NY United States
http://www.laurenfix.com/site/?site=2&d=11&dt=7

Shelby Fix, the Teen Car Coach,® is the daughter of The Car Coach,® Lauren Fix, a nationally recognized automotive expert. Shelby inherited her family's passion for cars and has partnered with Midas, Skip-Barber New Driver Program and national news networks to educate teens and young drivers. Shelby contributes her talents to radio, television, magazines and web content, including Fox News, CNN International, Channel One News and regional stations across the nation. She is the youngest registered member of the International Motor Press Association, an esteemed organization comprised of top automotive journalists and industry luminaries. Shelby's passion drives teen audiences everywhere.

Shelby Fix
Lauren Fix, The Car Coach
Lancaster, NY United States
Contact Phone: 646-475-4357
Click to Contact from Web Site

NATIONAL AUTOMOBILE DEALERS ASSOCIATION
McLean, VA United States
http://www.nada.org

The National Automobile Dealers Association, founded in 1917 represents 17,000 new-car and -truck dealers with 37,500 separate franchises. NADA represents dealers on Capitol Hill, to automobile manufacturers and to the public. The association offers a variety of products and services, including educational training, to help dealers improve their businesses. NADA also publishes the N.A.D.A. Official Used Car Guide.

David Hyatt
Vice President and Chief Public Affairs Officer
National Automobile Dealers Association
McLean, VA United States
Contact Phone: 703-821-7120
Click to Contact from Web Site

Lauren Fix: *Automotive Expert,*
The Car Coach® / Car Smarts®

A highly credible automotive and lifestyle expert, Lauren Fix provides solid information on safety and a wide range of automotive topics and issues. Her motivational speeches, such as the "Carma Coach," will help you find the "vehicle" that gets you "where you want to go." Fix toured with O Magazine for "Oprah's 2005 Live Your Best Life Tour," presenting motivational inspiration, consumer information and automotive advice.

TV & Radio

■ Oprah, Today, The View, CNN, Fox News, Headlines News, MSNBC, Inside Edition, The Early Show, NBC, ABC, CBS, WB, UPN, The Weather Channel, ESPN, Discovery, Speed, B. Smith Style, National Public Radio.

■ Host, auto expert for Talk 2 DIY Automotive on Scripps Do-It-Yourself Network (DIY); 65 one-hour shows.

■ Syndicated segments: The Car Coach® (car care tips) and His Turn–Her Turn™ (car reviews from a male and female perspective).

Print & Internet

■ Automotive editor for YourLifeMagazine.com; contributing to USA Today; Good Housekeeping; Woman's World; Redbook; Self; InTouch Weekly; Essence; Marie Claire; Prevention; Intellichoice; Motor Trend; Truck Trend; Hot Rod; Car Craft; TheCarConnection.com; familycar.com; and more.

Books

■ "Driving Ambitions: A Complete Guide to Amateur Auto Racing" and "The Performance Tire and Wheel Handbook."

■ Soon: "The Carma Coach" and "Just Drive It!"

Promotions

■ Spokesperson for the "Be Car Care Aware" program.

Lauren J. Fix
80 Rotech Drive,
Lancaster, N.Y. 14086

646-475-4357
Fax: 501-639-9360

thecarcoach
@laurenfix.com
www.laurenfix.com

IN-MOTION COURIER SERVICE
New York, NY United States
http://www.inmotioncouriers.com/

We offer a broad range of services including: New York Metro area - Same-day messenger service via bikes, vans or trucks - Daily, weekly or monthly scheduled mail pick-ups or drop-offs - Flexible timetables to suit your needs - Out of town deliveries available within 100 miles of New York City - Our Guarantee - We promise to take excellent care of your deliveries. That means we cover and securely wrap things we move in and out of our trucks. We want you to be totally satisfied with our messenger services. Please give us your feedback - good or bad.

Marino Frost
Stardust Studio
Astoria, NY United States
Contact Phone: (212) 234 - 5828
Click to Contact from Web Site

DRIVELAB
Washington, DC United States
www.MiriamShottland.com/

Miriam Schottland is an instructor in accident avoidance, car control techniques, high performance driving and counter terrorism techniques, with 16 years experience in working with the most highly recognized advanced driver training school in the country. She is chief instructor for the BMW Club, the Audi Club and senior instructor for the Ferrari Club as well as many other organizations. Driving is the most dangerous and complicated thing we will ever do, and yet we know so little about it. There are many myths regarding driving, and a little knowledge of applied physics can go long way in explaining why cars do what they do when we drive them. This is why the Driving Company has been created. Infamous in her outspoken criticism of the poor quality of drivers and the training they receive, she is a frequent guest lecturer on nation wide radio and TV talk shows as well as an expert witness and consultant in the area of driving.

Miriam Schottland
Washington, DC United States
Contact Phone: 202-265-3438
Click to Contact from Web Site

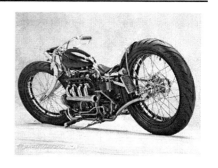

GIANT MOTORCYCLE SWAP MEET
Detroit, MI United States
www.MotorcycleSwap.com/

Giant Motorcycle Swap Meets, headquartered in Traverse City, MI, is the Midwest's largest promoter of motorcycle swap meets. The company promotes several one-day events in multiple locations each year: The Lansing Center, The Delta-Plex in Grand Rapids, The Birch Run Expo Center, The Suburban Collection Showplace in Novi, the I-X Center in Cleveland and the Wisconsin Expo Center in Milwaukee. All events are held indoors from 11 a.m. to 4 p.m. on Sundays. For more information and a calendar of events visit www. motorcycleswap.com or call 800-968-4242.

Scott Lorenz
Westwind Communications
Plymouth, MI United States
Contact Phone: 734-667-2090
Click to Contact from Web Site

EXPERIMENTAL AIRCRAFT ASSOCIATION (EAA)
Oshkosh, WI United States
www.eaa.org

International 175,000-member aviation organization dedicated to recreational flying and aviation participation. Members include pilots and non-pilots, designers, builders, restorers and enthusiasts of vintage, experimental amateur-built, ultra-light, rotorcraft and warbird aircraft. Hosts annual EAA AirVenture fly-in at Oshkosh, Wisconsin, with 500,000 attendees and 10,000 aircraft. Nearly 1,000 chapters worldwide.

Dick Knapinski
Director of Communications
Experimental Aircraft Association (EAA)
Oshkosh, WI United States
Contact Phone: 920-426-6523
Contact Main Phone: 920-426-4800
Click to Contact from Web Site

MARK N. LEWELLEN -- UNMANNED AIRCRAFT SYSTEMS (UAS) INSTRUCTOR
Washington, DC United States
www.linkedin.com/in/marknlewellen

Mr. Mark N. Lewellen is an instructor for a course designed for engineers, aviation experts and project managers who wish to enhance their understanding of unmanned Aircraft Systems (UAS). He has authored several consulting reports on UAS, has over twenty-five years of experience and has actively participated in over forty international meetings where he successfully advocated various technical and regulatory issues. Mr. Lewellen also teaches GPS Workshops in conjunction with several Universities. He is an active member of Toastmasters International and an excellent speaker who knows how to take command of an audience.

Mark N. Lewellen
RMT Spectrum Associates, Inc.
Bowie, MD United States
Contact Phone: 240-882-1234
Click to Contact from Web Site

121five.com
Where Everybody's Tuned In

121FIVE.COM -- AVIATION INDUSTRY NEWS, TIM KERN
Indianapolis, IN United States
http://121five.com/

Successful ideas become successful because they fill needs. www.121five.com is unabashedly structured to deliver General Aviation's messages directly to the interested public, without comment, editing, or change. The Contributing Sponsors have their own logins and passwords, and enter their own News Stories directly into the site. There is no middleman. Features include original work and the best of pre-published aviation information - valuable information that is lost to the individual publications' archives. Aviation organizations and marque clubs contribute tips and articles to wider audiences through 121five. All participants benefit from their exposure in "a giant shopping mall of aviation information." 121five navigates byzantine websites at FAA and NTSB to make N-Number and accident database searches one-click easy. 121five is international, including translation, for non-English-speaking readers.

Tim Kern
Director
Tim Kern INK
Anderson, IN United States
Contact Phone: 863-651-6095
Click to Contact from Web Site

AIRCRAFT OWNERS AND PILOTS ASSOCIATION -- AOPA
Frederick, MD United States
http://www.aopa.org

As the world's largest civil aviation organization, AOPA represents more than 400,000 U.S. pilots and aircraft owners. Information and policy perspective on General Aviation, safety, airspace regulations, airports, air traffic control and air navigation.

Kristen L. Seaman
Communications Coordinator
Aircraft Owners and Pilots Association
Frederick, MD United States
Contact Phone: 301-695-2222
Contact Main Phone: 301-695-2000
Click to Contact from Web Site

CHUCK GUMBERT -- AEROSPACE AND AVIATION CONSULTANT
Wichita, KS United States
www.tomcat-group.com

A dynamic, driven and visionary leader, Chuck Gumbert has acquired almost 40 years of Aerospace business expertise with demonstrated achievements in the handling of undermanaged assets (turnarounds) and Accelerating Business Performance in both the Aerospace aftermarket (MRO) and manufacturing (OEM) segments. Mr. Gumbert is adept at creating synergies and business strategies that gain organizational alignment while enabling accelerated business growth through enhanced operational performance, business development and new product development in both stable and unstable markets. He recently published a book titled 'George S. Patton on Accelerating Performance in Today's Business World.'

Chuck Gumbert
Founder & CEO
The Tomcat Group
Goddard, KS United States
Contact Phone: 210-262-5880
Cell: 210-262-5880
Click to Contact from Web Site

JIM JENKINS - APPLIED TECHNOLOGY INSTITUTE
Annapolis, MD United States
www.aticourses.com/
21140

Jim Jenkins is the founder and executive director of ATI. He maintains close contact with the classes and training personnel to ensure that you the client are completely satisfied. Mr. Jenkins continues to teach several classes and attends the majority of public seminars in order to maintain the high standard of excellence for which ATI is known. He has been organizing and presenting professional development training programs since 1977. He is a senior physicist with degrees from Gettysburg College (physics and mathematics) and the University of Wisconsin (physics). Please feel free to call him to personally discuss your requirements and objectives. Mr. Jenkins will be glad to explain in detail what ATI can do for you, what it will cost, and what you can expect in results and future performance.

Jim Jenkins
President
Applied Technology Institute
21140
Annapolis, MD United States
Contact Phone:
Contact Main Phone: 410-956-8805
Cell: 410-956-8805
Click to Contact from Web Site

COSTA RICA LUXURY RENTALS AND TOURS
Playa Jaco, Costa Rica
http://www.crluxury.com/

CR Luxury, the official Costa Rica vacation rental company for Los Sue [f16f7320]Resort and Marina, offers an exclusive portfolio of privately owned Costa Rica vacation properties. CR Luxury's guests enjoy access to the resort's world-class amenities including a 200 slip international marina; championship golf; private beach club; casino; spa; meeting facilities; shopping and fine dining restaurants. CR Luxury's condominiums and villas offer the perfect base to explore the riches of Costa Rica's Central Pacific Coast.

Marcela Laborde
President
Costa Rica Luxury Rentals and Tours
Playa Jaco, Puntarenas, Costa Rica
Contact Phone: 1-866-525-2188
Click to Contact from Web Site

SCOTT LORENZ - BALLOONIST - HOT AIR BALLOON RIDE MICHIGAN
Detroit, MI United States
www.westwindcos.com/balloon
www.westwindcos.com

Take a Hot Air Balloon Flight Over Michigan! Westwind Balloon Company flies over the woods and streams of Kensington Park and Island Lake State Park in Brighton, Michigan. On most flights passengers see hundreds of birds, deer and other wildlife as the balloon basket gently touches the tree tops. It's a spectacular view you can ONLY experience in a hot air balloon. Chief Pilot and owner Scott Lorenz has been a commercial balloon pilot since 1982 logging 1,450 + hours as pilot. Call 734-667-2098 or visit www.westwindcos.com/balloon to schedule your flight.

Scott Lorenz
Chief Pilot
Westwind Balloon Company
www.westwindcos.com
Plymouth, MI United States
Contact Phone: 734-667-2090
Cell: 248-705-2214
Click to Contact from Web Site

JIMMY MURPHY -- RIVER CRUISING - TRAVEL EXPERT
Los Angeles, CA United States
www.amawaterways.com

AmaWaterways, the premier river cruise line in the travel industry, will be launching the most luxurious river cruise ship in the industry, the MS AmaCerto, that will join the 12 other state of the art ships operating all over Europe, in Russia and along with Mekong River in Cambodia and Vietnam. Jimmy Murphy, Chairman and co-owner of AmaWaterways, has been a major factor is shaping the modern travel industry since founded Brendan Tours in 1968. In 2002 Murphy joined up with Rudi Schreiner and Kristin Karst to found AmaWaterways, which has since become the leader in River Cruising.

Brad Butler
Promotion in Motion
Hollywood, CA United States
Contact Phone: 323-461-3921
Click to Contact from Web Site

CAROL MARGOLIS -- SMART WOMEN TRAVELERS INC.
Lake Mary, FL United States
http://www.smartwomentravelers.com

Carol Margolis, author of Business Travel Success . . . How to Reduce Stress, Be More Productive and Travel with Confidence (Morgan James 2012) and 70 Secrets to Safe Travel (ebook), is a powerful speaker and a highly sought-after trainer and consultant, the voice of authority when it comes to how to travel smart and safe - and how to live life on the road as a successful business traveler. Carol consults to corporations who employ frequent travelers and with organizations in the travel industry.

Carol Margolis
CEO
Smart Women Travelers, Inc.
Lake Mary, FL United States
Contact Phone: 877-212-7364
Contact Main Phone: 877-212-7364
Cell: 407-758-4322
Click to Contact from Web Site

BILL HINCHBERGER - BRAZIL EXPERT
Paris, France
www.BrazilMax.com

Bill Hinchberger is the founding editor of the award-winning online travel guide BrazilMax. He returned to consulting after spearheading the unprecedented media coverage of the 2009 World Water Forum as director of external relations and communications for the World Water Council. He worked in Brazil for over two decades as a foreign correspondent - for The FT, ARTnews, Business Week, etc. - and media consultant. Hinchberger holds an M.A. in Latin American Studies and a B.A. in Political Science, both from the University of California, Berkeley. He is the former president of the Sao Paulo Foreign Press Club.

Bill Hinchberger - BrazilMax
Founding Editor
BrazilMax
Paris, France
Contact Phone:
Contact Main Phone: +33 6 2991-7594
Click to Contact from Web Site

AROUNDTHERINGS.COM -- OLYMPIC GAMES EXPERTS
Atlanta, GA United States
http://www.aroundtherings.com

AroundTheRings.com (ATR) For 20 years Around the Rings has been 'the most influential internet presence on the Olympics.' (The Guardian, Feb. 4, 2010). On-the-scene coverage of every bid and Games since 1992 means unparalleled access to decision-makers. Regular features include bidding for the Games, host city preparations, sponsorship, doping, federations and Olympic committee news delivered via Internet, Twitter, Facebook, special edition magazines and publications.

Sheila S. Hula
Publisher
Around the Rings.com
Atlanta, GA United States
Contact Phone: 404-874-1603
Click to Contact from Web Site

BRAD BUTLER -- TRAVEL EXPERT
Hollywood, CA United States
http://www.MooreaTahiti.com

Brad Butler is Vice President of Promotion in Motion, which is a full service corporate and book publicity firm that has been representing travel companies such as AmaWaterways, the premier river cruise line in the travel industry, Brendan Vacations and destinations such as the Tahitian Islands, Ireland, Europe and many others for over six years. Author of A World Flight Over Russia, Brad Butler has been working in publicity ever since he began promotin in own book in 1998. Located in Hollywood, Promotion in Motion also represents an extensive line of authors and experts in a wide-variety of fields.

Brad Butler
Promotion in Motion
Hollywood, CA United States
Contact Phone: 323-461-3921
Click to Contact from Web Site

FORT LAUDERDALE YACHT CHARTER, INTERCOASTAL YACHT TOUR, POMPANO
Fort Lauderdale, FL United States
www.aquaportllc.com

Fort Lauderdale Yacht Charter provides a fantastic, enjoyable and close-up view of the most exclusive homes in the world owned by billionaires, rock stars, and Hollywood's elite aboard a luxury yacht sailing along the beautiful, sunny Florida coast. The Greater Fort Lauderdale area has become known as the 'Venice of America' with its more than 300 miles of navigable waterways and an average air temperature of 77 degrees. That's another reason Hollywood's most elite escape to the Fort Lauderdale area for fun and relaxation. Aqua Port offers guided private tours on the intercoastal waterways from Deerfield Beach to Ft. Lauderdale.

Scott Lorenz
Publicist
Westwind Communications
Plymouth, MI United States
Contact Phone: 734-667-2090
Click to Contact from Web Site

JEANNE HESS - AUTHOR OF SPORTUALITY -- FINDING JOY IN THE GAMES
Kalamazoo, MI United States
www.sportualitybook.com

Sportuality is an examination of sports at all levels from a Western perspective, focusing on how it reflects our cultural belief in separation and dualistic thinking, as well as how sports can grow peace, understanding, and joy. Sportuality crosses disciplines of sports and spirituality to help readers—athletes, coaches, parents, and fans—evolve a higher consciousness within sports and competition. Using a journal and questions for self-reflection—called a 'box score' and 'time-out'—readers can reflect upon and create their own sportual stories. By examining words traditionally used within sports, Sportuality helps the reader think critically about competition, community, communication, spirit, humor, enthusiasm, education,

Scott Lorenz
Westwind Communications Book Marketing
Plymouth, MI United States
Contact Phone: 724-667-2090
Click to Contact from Web Site

TRAVEL GOODS ASSOCIATION
Princeton, NJ United States
www.travel-goods.org

PRIDE TRAVEL - GAY TRAVEL, CRUISE AND VACATION OWNERSHIP EXPERTS
Los Angeles, CA United States
www.pride.travel

MIKE THIEL -- HIDEAWAYS INTERNATIONAL, INC.
Portsmouth, NH United States
http://www.hideaways.com

The Travel Goods Association is the world's largest trade association for travel goods, representing manufacturers, distributors and retailers of luggage and travel products, casual bags, business cases and travel accessories which in 2010 was an $18.6 billion market in the United States alone. TGA sponsors The Travel Goods Show, the world's largest trade show devoted to travel products, and publishes Travel Goods Showcase, the voice of the travel goods industry.

Experts in gay travel, cruise, vacation ownership, and travel insurance. Award-winning executives possess diverse backgrounds including consulting, real-estate and travel/leisure. Multiple certification and award recipients. Executives Marc Kassouf and Nathan Depetris are very active in the global travel industry, speaking at trade shows and writing articles for the travel trade. They have sat on committees or boards of American Society of Travel Agents, the International Gay & Lesbian Travel Association, and local LGBT non-profits. Past media collaboration includes magazine and newspaper articles, events, and television in expertise areas. We welcome inquiries regarding all media opportunities.

First as the son of a U.S. diplomat, then an international oil and gas industry consultant, and now president of Hideaways International, Mike Thiel has spent his life living and traveling around the globe. Professionally, he has focused on luxury, out-of-the-ordinary, and experiential travel. Mike is the president of Hideaways and is the editor-in-chief of Hideaways Life™ newsletter, several electronic newsletters, and Villa Vacations Made Easy. Contact Mike for a lively exchange and insider's insight on: The world's most alluring getaways, from villas to boutique hotels, barge vacations, and luxury cruises, Travel tips and anecdotes, Exceptional international destinations, and Current

Kate Ryan
Travel Goods Association
Princeton, NJ United States
Contact Phone: 774-929-5223
Click to Contact from Web Site

Marc R Kassouf
CEO
PRIDE Travel
San Pedro, CA United States
Contact Phone: +1 562 432 3888
Contact Main Phone: 888-748-9876
Click to Contact from Web Site

Gail Richard
Press Contact for Hideaways International, Inc.
Hideaways International
Portsmouth, NH United States
Contact Phone: 603-430-4433
Contact Main Phone: 603-430-4433
Click to Contact from Web Site

ELLYNANNE GEISEL -- APRON EXPERT
Pueblo, CO United States
www.apronmemories.com

STEVANNE AUERBACH -- DR TOY'S GUIDE
San Francisco, CA United States
http://www.drtoy.com

Dr. Stevanne Auerbach, Director, a popular media contributor. Dr. Auerbach/Dr. Toy™ was founder/director of the world's first museum to promote play and appreciation of toys, The San Francisco International Toy Museum. 15 Books include Dr. Toy's Smart Play/Smart Toys: How to Raise a Child with a High P.Q. (Play Quotient), Toys for a Lifetime: Enhancing Childhood Through Play, The Toy Chest, Choosing Child Care. Produces annual reports, 'Dr. Toy's 100 Best Children's Products', 'Best Vacation Products', 'Best Classic Products' 'Best Green Products' on www.drtoy.com. She writes Dr. Toy, articles online and in publications. 'Smart Play Smart Toys' published internationally. First novel-'The Contest.'

Stevanne Auerbach, Ph.D. /Dr. Toy
Consultant/Author/Speaker
Dr Toy's Guide
San Francisco, CA United States
Contact Phone: 510-540-0111
Click to Contact from Web Site

Apron archaeologist EllynAnne Geisel is the author of THE APRON BOOK: MAKING, WEARING AND SHARING A BIT OF CLOTH AND COMFORT, APRONISMS: POCKET WISDOM FOR EVERY DAY and THE KITCHEN LINENS BOOK: USING, SHARING AND CHERISHING THE FABRICS OF OUR DAILY LIVES; the writer of her exhibition APRON CHRONICLES: A Patchwork of American Recollections (managed by The Women's Museum in Dallas); creator of National Tie One On Day, and the owner/designer of APRON MEMORIES®, a collection of aprons as worn by Desperate Housewife Bree and showcased in Vogue. EllynAnne has appeared on CBS Sunday Morning and NPR's All Things Considered.

EllynAnne Geisel
Apron Memories
Pueblo, CO United States
Contact Phone: 1-877-9-APRONS
Click to Contact from Web Site

RICHARD GOTTLIEB -- TOY INDUSTRY EXPERT
New York, NY United States
http://www.richardgottliebassoc.com

Richard Gottlieb is a well known toy industry commentator and President of Richard Gottlieb's USA Toy Experts, a toy industry consultancy. Richard is frequently interviewed by media worldwide, and has been called on by CNN, PBS, ABC and other media outlets. He is also a Contributing Editor to Playthings magazine in the US, Toys n' Playthings in the UK, Juguetes in Spain and other European toy magazines. Richard writes a popular blog, "Out of the Toy Box," and a book, Ambassador to the Kingdom of Wal-Mart. Richard is a voting member of the National Toy Hall of Fame.

Richard Gottlieb
President
Richard Gottlieb and Associates, LLC
New York, NY United States
Contact Phone:
Cell: 646-675-3019
Click to Contact from Web Site

CORINNE INNIS -- ARTIST
New York, NY United States
www.corinneinnis.com

Corinne Innis gets her inspiration from the fluid streams of communication that is fostered by street art. She has created a series of paintings on canvas that play with the notion of a cat as a wise and mysterious creature. Corinne has a BA in sociocultural anthropology from SUNY Purchase. Her work has been shown at the African American Museum in Texas and has appeared in the International Review of African American Art.

Corinne Innis
corinneinnis.com
New York, NY United States
Contact Phone: (516) 902-5640
Click to Contact from Web Site

ARNIE WEXLER -- ARNIE AND SHEILA WEXLER ASSOCIATES
Lake Worth, FL United States
http://www.aswexler.com

Work with all aspects of compulsive gambling: counseling, referrals, public awareness, education, treatment, court cases, colleges, employee assistance programs, judicial systems, legislators and gaming organizations. They have presented workshops and training seminars internationally. Wexler is the most quoted expert on compulsive gambling and is writing a book on gambling in America. They have authored many articles on compulsive gambling and sell a video tape on compulsive gambling. They have trained over 35,000 casino workers.

Arnie Wexler
Arnie & Sheila Wexler Associates
Lake Worth, FL United States
Contact Phone: 561-249-0922
Cell: 954-501-5270
Click to Contact from Web Site

GAIL HOWARD -- LOTTERY EXPERT
Las Vegas, NV United States
www.gailhoward.com

Gail Howard, author of Lottery Master Guide, has a solid background in lotteries and the lottery industry since 1983. In her capacity as lottery expert, Gail Howard has written articles for numerous magazines, including Family Circle; is former lottery editor of Gambling Times magazine, publisher of Lottery Advantage, and for 26 years a weekly columnist for New York Lottery News. Gail Howard's lottery books are sold all over the world, including foreign language editions translated into Spanish, French, German, Norwegian, Latvian, Korean, Japanese and Chinese. Gail Howard has been featured or quoted in Newsweek, U.S. News & World Report, Playboy, Real Simple, The Wall Street Journal, The New York Times, Washington Post, Shanghai Evening Post and more. Gail Howard's remarkable track record in helping people win big money in lotto has led to appearances on hundreds of radio and TV shows, including The Today Show and Good Morning America.

Gail Howard
Las Vegas, NV United States
Contact Phone: 800-945-4245
Contact Main Phone: 702-365-9270
Click to Contact from Web Site

Gail Howard
The World's Best Known
Lottery Expert

Lottery Expert Gail Howard is internationally recognized as the creator of the most highly acclaimed and successful lottery systems used in the world today. She is America's original lottery expert -- the pioneer of scientific lottery strategy. Since she created her lottery systems in 1982, she has turned thousands of lottery losers into winners, and she has made dozens of people rich. Her ability to turn people into millionaires has made lottery history!

Gail Howard's lottery systems are the *only* lottery systems that have been credited with winning dozens of first-prize lottery jackpots. To date, 101 documented first-prize Lotto jackpot winners have won a combined total of more than $102 million dollars with her systems. Documentation consists of more than 400 pages of letters from her jackpot winners, copies of their jackpot winning tickets, checks and/or congratulatory letters from the lottery, lottery press releases, newspaper articles, etc.

MEDIA EXPOSURE: Gail's remarkable track record in helping people win big money in Lotto has led to appearances on hundreds of radio and TV shows, including *The Today Show* and *Good Morning America*. She has also been featured or quoted in *Newsweek, U.S. News &*
World Report, Real Simple magazine, Playboy, Family Circle, The Wall Street Journal, Los Angeles Times, New York Daily News, Chicago Tribune, New York Times, Washington Post, Shanghai Evening Post and many more.

WRITER/EDITOR: *Family Circle; Gambling Times; Lottery Advantage; Lottery Buster*; Gail Howard's Special Report, State Lotteries: How to Get In It and How to Win It (first edition published in 1985; more than two million copies sold); a weekly columnist for 25 years for *New York Lotto News.*

Gail Howard's books are sold all over the world; these include foreign language editions in Spanish, French, German, Norwegian, Latvian, Korean, Japanese, Mao Chinese and traditional Chinese.

BOOKS IN PRINT:
Lotto Winning Wheels for Powerball & MEGA Millions
Lotto How to Wheel a Fortune
Lotto Wheel Five to Win
Lottery Master Guide
Lottery Winning Systems

Gail Howard
P.O. Box 81770
Las Vegas, Nevada
89180-1770

702-365-9270
800-945-4245

www.SmartLuck.com
www.GailHoward.com
books@SmartLuck.com

**SANDY MALONE -- OWNER OF
WEDDINGS IN VIEQUES - CULEBRA**
Vieques Island, PR United States
http://www.weddingsinvieques.com/

Let the experienced, professional wedding planners from Weddings in Vieques plan your stress-free Caribbean destination wedding, whether it's just the two of you, or a group of your friends and family. Our clients are the Guests of Honor, let us do the hard work of the hosts. We handle all the little details behind the scenes so you can relax and enjoy your special weekend. And, let Sandy Malone, the owner of the company, give your audiences the best advice and perspective she can.

Rita Rich
Weddings in Vieques & Culebra
Vieques Island, PR United States
Contact Phone: 301-404-9609
Click to Contact from Web Site

DAVE KLIVANS -- FIREPIT CERAMICS
Austin, TX United States
firepitceramics.com

Potato chips are great -- but so is clay! Play with clay all day with FirePit Ceramics in Austin, TX. We currently have one location, but we're looking to expand nationwide and offer the benefits and joys of pottery to the masses. We have a small competent staff, top-of-the-line equipment, and attention to detail that's won us commissions with top retailers and restaurants.

Dave Klivans
FirePit Ceramics
Austin, TX United States
Contact Phone:
Click to Contact from Web Site

**ANTOINETTE MATLINS --
PROFESSIONAL GEMOLOGIST**
Woodstock, VT United States
http://www.gemstonepress.com

Antoinette Matlins, P.G. (Professional Gemologist) is an internationally respected gemologist and jewelry expert and leading consumer advocate. She is available for interviews and to answer questions about diamonds, colored gems, consumer fraud, pearls and jewelry in general. An independent expert, former gemology editor for National Jeweler Magazine and noted columnist, Matlins has been featured on ABC, CBS, NBC, CNBC and CNN, as well as in USA Today, US News & World Report and many national and international consumer and trade publications. She is author of seven leading books in the field, including Jewelry & Gems: The Buying Guide; Diamonds: The Antoinette Matlins Buying Guide; and The Pearl Book: The Definitive Buying Guide. Unaffiliated with any jewelry industry organization, Matlins' qualifications are unsurpassed. Her unique background has given her a vast knowledge of all aspects of the field and a keen understanding of what people really don't know, what they want to know and, perhaps most important, what they need to know—both good and bad. Whether the story is fashion, glamour, bridal, investment or consumer affairs—whether you're looking for a sparking newsmaker or a startling expose—Matlins' input can provide the brilliant angle you are searching for.

Antoinette Matlins, P.G.
Author
Gemstone Press
Woodstock, VT United States
Contact Phone: 802-457-5145
Click to Contact from Web Site

RESTOCKIT.COM -- OFFICE SUPPLIES AND CLEANING SUPPLIES
Miami, FL United States
www.ReStockIt.com

RestockIt.com is here to offer restaurant supplies, cleaning supplies and office supplies to small businesses at the lowest prices, the most competitive shipping, the largest selection and the fastest delivery online. We've been around for over 5 years and have satisfied well over 400,000 customers to date. We offer the most competitive prices on bakery supplies, bar supplies, cleaning supplies, glassware and so much more for every small business restaurant in the United States. We also pride ourselves on offering 100,000s of items in office supplies including office furniture, office chairs, printers, ink and toner, paper supplies, and office accessories.

Jennifer DiMotta
ReStockIt.com
Hollywood, FL United States
Contact Phone: 954-967-1150 ext 224
Click to Contact from Web Site

SHOPLET.COM -- DISCOUNT OFFICE SUPPLIES
New York, NY United States
www.shoplet.com

Since its launch in 1994, Shoplet.com has positioned itself as a leading e-marketplace in the office/business products sector, by providing its customers with better product selection, superior customer service, free shipping on most orders over $45, competitive pricing, and an efficient eProcurement platform to streamline the purchasing process. 'In an effort to provide our customers with everything they need for the office, Shoplet provides an award-winning website that functions as one of the world's largest online office and business supply superstores, with over 2.5 million customers, and over 400,000 products and equipment for the office,' states founder Tony Ellison.

Leslie Scharf
Senior Vice-President
Shoplet.com
New York, NY United States
Contact Phone: 212-619-3353 x-218
Click to Contact from Web Site

Leopard Bikini, Blue Leopard $74.00	Navy Bikini, White Navy Bikini $89.00	Wonderbra Bikini, Wonderbra $84.00

Sexy Orange Bikini, Hot $88.00	Surf Bikini, Surf Bikinis, Surfer $72.00	Camo Bikini Swimsuit, Pink $79.00

SWIM KITTEN
San Francisco, CA United States
SwimKitten.com

New Bikinis - Most Popular Bikinis - Little Black Bikinis - Bikini Bargains - Romantic Bikinis - Sexy Bikinis - Glamorous Bikinis - Athletic Bikinis - Solid - Bikinis - Neon Bikinis - Wild Print Bikinis - Floral Bikinis - Polka Dot Bikinis - Stripe Bikinis - Metallic Bikinis - See Through Bikinis - Crochet Bikinis - Retro Bikinis - Bust Support Bikinis - Bust Enhancing Bikinis - Tummy Flattening Bikinis - Hip Slimming Bikinis - Butt Enhancing Bikinis - Leg Lengthening Bikinis - Plus Size Bikinis

United States
Contact Phone: Web Site Preferred
Click to Contact from Web Site

DISCOUNT WATCH STORE
New Haven, CT United States
www.discountwatchstore.com

Zai Zhu is a watch connoisseur and founder of www.DiscountWatchStore.com. Discount Watch Store is a premier retail watch site featuring a collection of over 3000 watches from over 50 different watch brands. Discount Watch Store carries men's watches and ladies watches from well known brands such as Citizen, Seiko, Invicta, Luminox, Casio, Bulova, Orient, Wenger, Tag Heuer, Movado, and from niche brands such as Oniss, H3 Tactical, Mondaine, and more. The website also offers a large selection of watch bands.

Zai Zhu
Milford, CT United States
Contact Phone: 203-874-6888
Click to Contact from Web Site

THE WATCH CO
Appleton, WI United States
www.watchco.com

The Watch Co. is a leading dealer of wrist watches including popular brands such as Seiko, Citizen, Bulova and Swiss Army Watches as well as fashion and specialty brands such as Dolce & Gabbana, Skagen, Reactor, M.H. Bertucci and Suunto totaling more than 40 brands altogether. The Watch Co. operates four retail locations in Wisconsin, Iowa, North Dakota and South Dakota in addition to an e-commerce website at www.Watchco.com. Watchco.com is one of only a few online watch dealers that are authorized dealers for each brand they sell. The Watch Co. was established in 1993.

Dave Gerczak
The Watch Co
Appleton, WI United States
Contact Phone: 920-450-6181
Click to Contact from Web Site

ROBERT FRIPP - SPEAKING ENGAGEMENTS
San Francisco, CA United States
www.robertfrippspeaks.com

Robert Fripp is a legendry guitarist and articulate speaker on the art of craft, how to be a hero for more than one day, and how to go from beginner to mastery. Unlike many guitarists he is an intellectual and exceptionally well-read in multiple areas of study. A founding (and ongoing) member of King Crimson, he has collaborated with David Bowie, Peter Gabriel, and Brian Eno. Rolling Stone magazine named Robert Fripp "42 among the top 100 guitarists of all time." Robert presents with his sister Hall of Fame speaker Patricia Fripp.

Patricia Fripp, CSP, CPAE
fripp.com
San Francisco, CA United States
Contact Phone: 415-753-6556
Cell: 415-637-4281
Click to Contact from Web Site

MENC -- THE NATIONAL ASSOCIATION FOR MUSIC EDUCATION
Reston, VA United States
http://www.menc.org

MENC, among the world's largest arts education organizations, marked its centennial in 2007 as the only association that addresses all aspects of music education. With membership of more than 75,000 active, preservice, and retired music educators, plus 60,000 more honor students and music supporters, MENC represents all levels of teaching from pre-school to graduate. Best resource for information on music education trends, advocacy, research and publications, including National Standards for Arts Education. Advocacy initiatives include The National Anthem Project, Music In Our Schools Month, and the World's Largest Concert.

Elizabeth W. Lasko
Director, Public Relations
MENC: The National Association for Music Education
Reston, VA United States
Contact Phone: 703-860-4000
Click to Contact from Web Site

NAMM (NATIONAL ASSOCIATION OF MUSIC MERCHANTS)
Carlsbad, CA United States
http://www.namm.org

Before there was an industry or an association, there was a belief. . .in music. That belief led to a mission: to unify, lead and strengthen the global music products industry and increase active participation in music making. More than a century later, that mission has attracted a growing, thriving worldwide community of thousands of deeply passionate, talented companies that make, buy and sell the instruments that allow millions of people to play music. That community is called NAMM, the National Association of Music Merchants. NAMM produces two U.S. trade shows and promotes the many proven benefits of playing music.

Scott Robertson, APR
Director of Marketing & Communications
NAMM
Carlsbad, CA United States
Contact Phone: 760-438-8007
Contact Main Phone: 800-767-NAMM
Cell: 949-212-7096
Click to Contact from Web Site

JAMES TAYLOR -- ONLINE MUSIC EDUCATION
San Francisco, CA United States
http://jamestaylor.me/speaking/

James Taylor is CEO of P3 Music and Director of Global Business Development of ArtistWorks, a pioneer in online education and the largest provider of online music schools in the world. James is a frequent guest at conferences, universities, TV and radio on entrepreneurship, startups, online education, edtech, marketing strategy, brand marketing, online marketing, social media, SEO and video marketing. He is an award-winning entrepreneur, drummer and marketer with over 15 years experience in technology, online education and entertainment startups in both the USA and Europe. He has consulted for government development agencies, non-profits, education companies and arts organisations.

James Taylor
Director of Global Business Development
ArtistWorks Inc
Napa, CA United States
Contact Phone: 7072277909
Contact Main Phone: 7072551840
Click to Contact from Web Site

MARCUS TILGMANN -- THE CHANGING MUSIC INDUSTRY EXPERT
Helsinki, Finland
www.hitlantis.com
Finland

HITLANTIS offers an exiting new way to discover music. Featuring the best music from independent artists in all musical genres, Hitlantis is your window to the ongoing battle-of-the-bands where artists compete and music lovers decide who the best is and worth getting points and closer to the breakthrough. Hitlantis unites music lovers and great unsigned music with best content discovery current internet offers.

Marcus Tilgmann
CEO
Hitlantis.com
Helsinki, Finland
Contact Phone: +358400573327
Click to Contact from Web Site

AMERICAN SOCIETY OF JOURNALISTS AND AUTHORS (ASJA)
New York, NY United States
www.asja.org

ASJA, founded in 1948, is the nation's professional association of independent nonfiction writers. ASJA members share inside information via an ongoing confidential survey of magazine payment rates, book advances, contract provisions as well as candid evaluations of individual editors. Support comes from the Contracts Committee, Grievance Committee, and expert advice on professional issues. Contact ASJA to reach the writers America reads.

Alexandra Owens
Executive Director
ASJA (American Society of Journalists and Authors)
New York, NY United States
Contact Phone: 212 997-0947
Click to Contact from Web Site

VALERIE GELLER -- TALK RADIO CONSULTANT
New York, NY United States
www.gellermedia.com

Valerie Geller is an author and expert on talk radio, news radio, and broadcasting. With more than 30 years of experience in the field, Geller is President of Geller Media International, a full service broadcast consulting firm specializing in News, Talk, Information and personality broadcasting. She's the author of three books about radio including the latest from Focal Press - CREATING POWERFUL RADIO: GETTING, KEEPING & GROWING AUDIENCES. A noted workshop and seminar leader, Geller trains and works with on air personalities, talk radio hosts and news journalists in more than 27 countries throughout the world.

Valerie Geller
United States
Contact Phone:
Contact Main Phone: 212-580-3385
Click to Contact from Web Site

CHRIS MURCH -- WORLD SYNDICATED RADIO
San Diego, CA United States
wsradio.com

wsRadio.com started broadcasting on August 15, 2001 with 5 shows. The ws of wsRadio stands for World Syndicated Radio. We have grown to over 120 shows adding additional shows each month. We are proud to claim the title as the largest independent Internet talk radio station in the world. It is important to note that we produce all of the shows on wsRadio using professional broadcast equipment in a turnkey process. We are proud to have a history of partnering and producing shows for some of the most notable entities in America.

Chris Murch
World Syndicated Radio
San Diego, CA United States
Contact Phone: 858-623-0199 Ext 8
Click to Contact from Web Site

CHAPLAIN DR. KEITH ROBINSON -- PTSD MEDIA CONSULTANTS, LLC
Houston, TX United States
www.ptsdmediasolutions.com

PTSD Media Consultants, LLC . . . 'First Responders to the Media.' News media journalists endure a daily emotional battering of real human tragedy that becomes televised, or print/electronic news. Journalists are being attacked, beaten, raped or kidnapped. When tragic mental pictures are retained, the result is often depression, divorce, drug/alcohol abuse, Post Traumatic Stress Disorder or sometimes. . . suicide. PTSD Media Consultants confidentially serve media organizations in two primary ways: 1) acute emergency mental health intervention to overwhelmed staff members; and 2) Media Emotional Resiliency Training (M.E.R.T.)TM to strengthen and help prevent emotional overload. Email: ChapDrKeith@ptsdmediasolutions.com; Cell phone 713-826-3220 24/7/365.

Chaplain Dr. Keith A. Robinson
Lead Media Consultant/Founder
PTSD Media Consultants, LLC
Houston, TX United States
Contact Phone: 713-826-3220 (cell)
Cell: 713-826-3220
Click to Contact from Web Site

SAN FRANCISCO WRITERS CONFERENCE
San Francisco, CA United States
www.sfwriters.org

The San Francisco Writers Conference, one of the finest writers' events in the country, is celebrating its 10th anniversary in 2013 with R.L. Stine (Goosebumps) as one of several keynoters. Best-selling authors, literary agents and respected editors from top publishing houses are presenters at SFWC events. The goal is to help attendees become published authors. The 100 presenter to 300 attendee ratio means optimum interaction. The San Francisco Writers Conference is held over President's Day weekend at the Mark Hopkins Hotel. A second event, the San Francisco Writing for Change Conference is held biannually. SFWC is a 501(c)3 nonprofit

Barbara Santos
Marketing Director
San Francisco Writers Conference
SANTOS!PR
Livermore, CA United States
Contact Phone: 19254206223
Cell: 19258955841
Click to Contact from Web Site

SOCIETY OF PROFESSIONAL JOURNALISTS

Indianapolis, IN United States
http://www.spj.org

The Society of Professional Journalists works to improve and protect journalism. The organization is the nation's largest and most broad-based journalism organization, dedicated to encouraging the free practice of journalism and stimulating high standards of ethical behavior. Founded in 1909 as Sigma Delta Chi, SPJ promotes the free flow of information vital to a well-informed citizenry, works to inspire and educate the next generation of journalists, and protects First Amendment guarantees of freedom of speech and press.

Joe Skeel
Executive Director
Society of Professional Journalists
Indianapolis, IN United States
Contact Phone: 317-927-8000
Click to Contact from Web Site

TALKERS MAGAZINE --- TALK RADIO MAGAZINE

Springfield, MA United States
www.talkers.com

TALKERS magazine is the leading trade publication serving the talk media industries in America. The term 'talk media' includes broadcast talk radio and television, cable news/talk television, as well as the new talk media delivered via the Internet, podcasting and satellite radio. On this site you will find brief opening excerpts from the current stories in each monthly print edition of TALKERS magazine. Plus, you will find free online versions of some of the publication's most popular features including NewsNotes, the Week in Review, the 100 Most Important Radio Talk Show Hosts in America (The Heavy Hundred), the Top Talk

Michael Harrison
TALKERS Magazine
Springfield, MA United States
Contact Phone: 413-565-5413
Click to Contact from Web Site

HOLLAND COOKE

Block Island, RI United States
http://survivalspeech.com

ATTENTION IS CURRENCY, and competition for attention has never been tougher. Does your message cut-through the clutter? Or do you simply blend-into the blah-blah-blah? Media consultant Holland Cooke is a veteran broadcaster, talent coach, and marketing tactician. He helps storytellers of all sorts craft messages for greater impact.

Holland Cooke
Holland Cooke Media
Block Island, RI United States
Contact Phone: 401-330-6868
Click to Contact from Web Site

INFOCOMMERCE GROUP --
SPECIALIZED BUSINESS
INFORMATION PUBLISHING EXPERT
Philadelphia, PA United States
www.infocommercegroup.com/

InfoCommerce Group Inc.(ICG) is the leading consulting, publishing, conference and research company focused on the data publishing industry. Our tagline, 'Defining the possible ... delivering the practical,' reflects our position of thought leadership within the industry, balanced by many years of frontline experience. Our visionary outlook and real-world expertise has been employed by nearly 30 database publishers of all types and sizes in nearly a dozen countries.

Russell Perkins
InfoCommerce Report
United States
Contact Phone: 610.649.1200, ext. 2
Click to Contact from Web Site

DAVID KING -- WIKIPEDIA EXPERT
Raleigh, NC United States
www.ethicalwiki.com

David King improves Wikipedia articles on notable subjects organizations care about in compliance with Wikipedia policy and conflict of interest best practices. Through transparency, community collaboration and adherence to Wikipedia's rules, David supports organizations that want to make genuine improvements in the neutrality and completeness of the encyclopedia.

David King
EthicalWiki
Raleigh, NC United States
Contact Phone: (919) 605-2115
Click to Contact from Web Site

SPECIALIZED INFORMATION
PUBLISHERS ASSOCIATION,
FORMERLY NEPA
Washington, DC United States
http://www.sipaonline.com

SIPA is the international trade association dedicated to advancing the interests of for-profit subscription newsletter publishers and specialized-information services. The mission of the Specialized Information Publishers Association is to serve its member newsletter and other specialized-information publishers worldwide through education, training, networking and advocacy to foster growth, profitability and professional excellence.

Kati Fritz
Specialized Information Publishers Association
Vienna, VA United States
Contact Phone:
Contact Main Phone: 703-992-9339
Click to Contact from Web Site

SUBSCRIPTION SITE INSIDER -- HOW
TO CREATE MEMBERSHIP SITES
Newport, RI United States
http://www.subscriptionsiteinsider.com

Join the Business-building Resource for Paywall, Subscription, & Membership Site Executives ... and gain instant access to 60+ Case Studies, live monthly webinars with experts, and Q&A networking with 250+ of your peers. Drive traffic and improve conversions to sell more online subscriptions Raise retention and reduce churn - keep members longer. Better manage finances, tech & legal Make your job easier with sales calculators, and best practices training videos.

Anne Holland
Anne Holland Ventures Inc
Newport, RI United States
Contact Phone: (401) 354-7555
Click to Contact from Web Site

TW TELECOM INC.
Denver, CO United States
www.twtelecom.com
NASDQ TWTC

tw telecom inc., (NASDAQ: TWTC), headquartered in Littleton, CO, is a leading provider of managed voice, Internet and data networking solutions to a wide array of businesses and organizations throughout the U.S. and globally. As one of the country's premier competitive service providers, tw telecom integrates data, dedicated Internet access, and local and long distance voice services for long distance carriers, wireless communications companies, incumbent local exchange carriers, and enterprise organizations in healthcare, finance, higher education, manufacturing, and hospitality industries, as well as for military, state and local government.

Robert G. Meldrum, APR
Vice President - Corporate Communications
tw telecom inc.
Littleton, CO United States
Contact Phone: 303-566-1354
Click to Contact from Web Site

AD COUNCIL
New York, NY United States
www.AdCouncil.org

The Ad Council has endeavored to improve the lives of all Americans since first creating the category of public service advertising in 1942. From our earliest efforts including 'Loose Lips Sink Ships' to the more recent 'I am an American,' Ad Council PSAs have been raising awareness, inspiring action and saving lives for more than 70 years. Based on our long history of effecting positive change, it's fair to say that Ad Council campaigns have inspired several generations of Americans. Our ultimate goal is to ensure that future generations will reap the benefits of our efforts to date, and continue to be inspired by our public service campaigns in the future.

Lisa Cullen
The Advertising Council
New York, NY United States
Contact Phone: (212) 922-1500
Click to Contact from Web Site

LINDA HUNT -- MEDIA CRITIC
St. Petersburg, FL United States

Provocative commentary on TV news, media ethics, women in television. This former CNN reporter and author of Secret Agenda: The U.S. Government, Nazi Scientists and Project Paperclip (St. Martin's Press) is available on short notice for talk shows or commentary. Recent appearances include ABC's PrimeTime Live, MSNBC, NPR. Current media topics are a specialty.

Linda Hunt
Media Critic
St. Petersburg, FL United States
Contact Phone: 305-731-3264
Click to Contact from Web Site

Providing profitable guidance to specialized information publishers

The Specialized Information Publishers Association, located in Vienna, Virginia, has continued to grow and enjoys strong support from the industry. The Association was born in 1977 with 16 members and today has nearly 500 corporate members (of all sizes), which publish more than 3,500 newsletters.

SIPA offers many services to its members and works at expanding its list of member benefits. SIPA offers the International Newsletter & Specialized-Information Conference, a Fall Conference, Special Publishers Conferences, Listservs, Roundtable Forums, Specialized Information Publishing Days, as well as various specialized workshops and seminars each year.

In addition to SIPA's *Hotline* newsletter and daily *SIPAlert* free e-zine, SIPA publishes an annual Membership Directory & Buyer's Guide.

Specialized Information Publishers Association (SIPA)

8229 Boone Blvd., Suite 260, Vienna, Virginia 22182

Tel: (703) 992-9339 Fax: (703) 992-7512

www.sipaonline.com

ELI JUST -- SUPERNATURAL WRITER
Hollywood, CA United States
www.MannyJonesSeries.com

After spending most of his life in Louisiana riding motorcycles, playing the blues, and traveling around, Eli Just moved to Atlanta where he married again, and later divorced. He then married again (later) and is living in Atlanta, writing novels. He also writes songs in all genres, plays guitar and harmonica, and sings. He has two excellent sons and a charming wife. His Dream is to live in the North Georgia Mountains, where he could continue to write, fish, and ride, while doing anything else involving the enjoyment of life.

Brad Butler
Promotion in Motion
Hollywood, CA United States
Contact Phone: 323-461-3921
Click to Contact from Web Site

THE NEWSEUM
Washington, DC United States
http://www.newseum.org

The Newseum — a 250,000-square-foot museum of news — offers visitors an experience that blends five centuries of news history with up-to-the-second technology and hands-on exhibits. The Newseum is located at the intersection of Pennsylvania Avenue and Sixth Street, N.W., Washington, D.C., on America's Main Street between the White House and the U.S. Capitol and adjacent to the Smithsonian museums on the National Mall. The exterior's unique architectural features include a 74-foot-high marble engraving of the First Amendment and an immense front wall of glass through which passers-by can watch the museum fulfill its mission of providing a forum where the media and the public can gain a better understanding of each other.

Michael Fetters
Director of Marketing and Communications
Newseum
Washington, DC United States
Contact Phone: 202-292-6320
Click to Contact from Web Site

ZIGGY CHAU -- NEXT MEDIA ANIMATION LLC
New York, NY United States
http://newsdirect.nma.com.tw/About.aspx

Liven up your video news with animated graphics and news packages from Next Media Animation News Direct. News Direct provides colorful, eye-catching and informative animated graphics and packages each day for TV news and websites around the world. Our fast, accurate and engaging segments tackle all the top breaking stories - and for a limited time we are providing them for free. Sign up now for access to ready-to-use, broadcast quality news clips and animation

Ziggy Chau
Next Media Animation LLC
New York, NY United States
Contact Phone: 212-278-0189
Click to Contact from Web Site

SOURCES -- CANADIAN EXPERTS FOR INTERVIEW
Toronto, Ontario Canada
http://www.sources.com

Sources is Canada's directory for journalists, writers and researchers. Sources provides 5,000 experts and spokespersons ready to answer questions on thousands of topics, including: Canadian trade with Cuba, universal Medicare coverage, cultural protectionism, U.S.-Canada trade issues, cross-border pollution, wilderness preservation, Arctic air masses, gun control, Quebec separatism, dealing with crime, public broadcasting, agricultural subsidies, and drug smuggling -- plus a selection of links to the best Internet sites for journalists and researchers.

Mr. Ulli Diemer
Sources
Toronto, Ontario Canada
Contact Phone: 416-964-7799
Click to Contact from Web Site

NATIONAL CARTOONISTS SOCIETY
New York, NY United States
http://www.reuben.org

We know cartoonists! Looking for information on comics, cartoons, cartoon history, humorous illustration, greeting cards, and the people who draw and write all that funny stuff? The National Cartoonists Society has it all. We're the oldest, largest organization of cartoonists in the U.S. Contact us if you need a resource for a story, a quote, or just background information about the business and the people in it.

Hilary Price
National Cartoonists Society
Florence, MA United States
Contact Phone: 413-320-2165
Click to Contact from Web Site

NINA AMIR -- NONFICTION WRITING - PUBLISHING CONSULTANT
Los Gatos, CA United States
www.copywrightcommunications.com

Nina Amir, Inspiration-to-Creation Coach, helps writers Achieve More Inspired Results--publishable and published products and careers as writers and authors. The author of How to Blog a Book (Writer's Digest Books), she is a journalist, nonfiction book editor and consultant, blog-to-book coach, and author and book coach with more than 34 years experience in the publishing field. She is also the founder of Write Nonfiction in November, a blog and writing challenge. She serves as the national Jewish Issue Examiner and Self-Improvement Examiner at Examiner.com, writes five blogs and appears weekly as a writing and publishing expert on the popular radio show Dresser After Dark. She has edited or written for 45+ local, national and international publications, produced hundreds of articles, self-published ten books and workbooks, and helped her clients produce books, some of which have sold more than 230,000 copies. Amir holds a BA in magazine journalism from Syracuse University.

Nina Amir
CopyWright Communications
Los Gatos, CA United States
Contact Phone: 408-353-1943
Click to Contact from Web Site

LORRAINE KLEINWAKS -- BOOK WISH FOUNDATION
Reston, VA United States
www.BookWish.org

What You Wish For (ISBN: 9780399254543) is a collection of short stories and poems by 18 top young adult authors with combined sales of more than 600 million books and numerous literary awards, including two Newbery Medals. The 501(c)(3) Book Wish Foundation organized the collection and will donate 100% of its proceeds to the UN Refugee Agency, UNHCR, to build libraries in Darfuri refugee camps in Chad. Release date: September 15, 2011, published by Penguin/G.P. Putnam's Sons.

Lorraine Kleinwaks
Vice President
Book Wish Foundation
Reston, VA United States
Contact Phone: (571) 281-3117
Click to Contact from Web Site

CLAUDIA GERE -- PUBLISHING EXPERT
Boston, MA United States
www.ClaudiaGereCo.com

Claudia Gere, author of Name Your Book: 94 Nonfiction Title Tips, speaker, author consultant, book coach, and literary agent, helps business leaders, consultants, speakers, and other entrepreneurs develop their best writing and publishing strategies to realize their aspirations of becoming an author. Through speaking, webinars, workshops, and individual coaching, she has launched many first-time authors on a path to writing and publishing success.

Claudia Gere
Shutesbury, MA United States
Contact Phone: 413-259-1741
Click to Contact from Web Site

RICK FRISHMAN -- MORGAN JAMES PUBLISHING
Hampton, VA United States
morgan-james-publishing.com/

Morgan James has revolutionized book publishing -- from the author's standpoint. Its 'Entrepreneurial Publishing' model enriches authors as well as the company, which actively works with authors to help them not only maximize revenue from their book royalties but also build new business and increase their revenue substantially through follow-on sales to their readers. One of Morgan James's core values is having strong and mutually beneficial relationships. 'We've spent years developing many of the key business relationships that allows us to get our books in bookstores and the widespread Web coverage we've been able to achieve. We intend to stay constant in our pursuit of positive relationships with people in all facets of our business, and we see that as a strategic advantage,' says David L. Hancock, founder of Morgan James.

Rick Frishman
Morgan James Publishing
Hamton, VA United States
Contact Phone: 757-591-2828
Contact Main Phone: 800-485-4943
Click to Contact from Web Site

RUTH FURMAN -- IMAGE WORDS PUBLICITY AND WRITING SERVICES
Las Vegas, NV United States
www.RuthFurman.com

Image Words Publicity & Writing is a full-service public relations firm, owned by Ruth Furman. The entrepreneurial bug inspired Ruth Furman to leave a high-level corporate communications job in the Chicago area. Furman relocated to fabulous Las Vegas in 1999. Initially building business with a niche as 'the agency's agency,' Image Words now nurtures a diverse mix of clients in construction, convention services, commercial real estate, home improvement and home furnishings. As a virtual agency, she works closely with a cadre of professionals to support client needs.

Ruth Furman
Publicist
Image Words
United States
Contact Phone: 702-615-2244
Contact Main Phone: 702-255-8288
Click to Contact from Web Site

KENT GUSTAVSON, PHD BLOOMING TWIG BOOKS.
New York, NY United States
www.BloomingTwigBooks.com

Blooming Twig, based in New York City, is the publisher of award-winning books that matter, from self-help to children's fiction. We publish between 15 and 20 new titles each year, and are distributed in the United States and internationally by Cardinal Publishers Group, and through our affiliate publisher in New Zealand, Oratia Media. Blooming Twig has two catalogs per year, one in the fall and one in the spring, and we currently have three imprints, "15-Minute Books" for all kinds of electronic devices, "Rag Man Project" books for children of all ages, and "Blooming Twig Anthologies" for readers of all kinds. We are a growing independent publisher that supports an ever-expanding line up of both up-and-coming and well-known authors.

Kent Gustavson
Blooming Twig Books
Setauket, NY United States
Contact Phone: 866-389-1482
Click to Contact from Web Site

PAIGE STOVER HAGUE -- CONTENT DEVELOPMENT EXPERT
Boston, MA United States
http://www.IctusInitiative.com

Paige Stover Hague, a content development expert, is a distinguished public relations expert who specializes in promoting speakers, authors, and business executives. Paige offers the specialized skills, perspectives, and professional leadership experience that make her an invaluable partner, advisor, and consultant in building a client's image. An attorney and a former senior executive for numerous publicly traded and multinational publishing houses, she founded Ictus in 2002 and has enjoyed tremendous success.

Paige Stover Hague
President
The Ictus Initiative
Boston, MA United States
Contact Phone: 508-577-0271
Contact Main Phone: 617-230-2167
Click to Contact from Web Site

SHELLEY HITZ -- SELF PUBLISHING COACH
Findlay, OH United States
http://www.self-publishing-coach.com

Shelley Hitz is a Christian, an entrepreneur, speaker, author and consultant to individuals, organizations and small businesses who want to multiply their impact through self publishing. And she teaches from personal experience. Over a two year span, while working full-time, she published five books, multiple audio CDs, authored two websites that attract thousands of visitors each month, and created multiple products that she sells through her website and at her speaking engagements. www.Self-Publishing-Coach.com also offers free book templates, articles, monthly newsletter, teleclasses, special reports, e-books, webinars, podcasts, videos and other resources to help you get self published!

Shelley Hitz
Self Publishing Coach
Findlay, OH United States
Contact Phone: 419-581-9003
Click to Contact from Web Site

BRIAN JUD -- BOOK MARKETING EXPERT
Hartford, CT United States
http://www.bookmarketingworks.com/

Brian Jud is an author, book-marketing consultant, seminar leader, television host and president of Book Marketing Works, LLC. Brian is active in special-sales marketing. He is the author of the Publishers Weekly title, Beyond the Bookstore and The Marketing Planning CD-ROM that accompanies it. Brian is the editor of the Book Marketing Matters newsletter on special sales topics. Brian developed and introduced the Special-Sales Profit Center, the web-based, targeted-marketing system that helps deliver incremental sales and profits. This system is being used by publishers around the country and by R. R. Bowker to sell books to non-bookstore markets.

Brian Jud
Book Marketing Works, LLC
Avon, CT United States
Contact Phone: (800) 562-4357
Click to Contact from Web Site

SCOTT LORENZ - BOOK MARKETING EXPERT - BOOK PUBLICITY - PUBLICIST
Detroit, MI United States
www.Book-Marketing-Expert.com

Book publicist Scott Lorenz is President of Westwind Communications, a public relations and marketing firm that has a special knack for working with authors to help them get all the publicity they deserve and more. Lorenz works with best-selling authors and self-published authors promoting all types of books, whether it's their first book or their 15th book. He's handled publicity for books by CEOs, Navy SEALS, Homemakers, Fitness Gurus, Doctors, Lawyers and Adventurers. His clients have been featured by Good Morning America, FOX & Friends, CNN, ABC Nightly News, The New York Times, Nightline, TIME, PBS and many more.

Scott Lorenz
President
Westwind Communications Book Marketing
Plymouth, MI United States
Contact Phone: 734-667-2090
Click to Contact from Web Site

LAURA B. POINDEXTER
Washington, DC United States
www.laurabcreative.com

Laura B. Poindexter has had a career focus on low-cost marketing strategies. She employed these techniques in the sporting goods and telecom industries before starting her own firm, laura b creative, in 2000. She is also a professional speaker who presents keynote speeches, convention breakouts, presentations, seminars and workshops on small business marketing topics. If you are searching for an experienced speaker for small business owners, you need look no further. Her topics include social media marketing including individual seminars on Blogging, Facebook, LinkedIn, Twitter, YouTube, SEO, and Email Marketing.

Laura B. Poindexter
queen b
laura b creative
Sterling, VA United States
Contact Phone: 703-609-2200
Click to Contact from Web Site

LEE POUND -- WRITING AND PUBLISHING EXPERT
Orange County, CA United States
http://www.leepound.com

Lee, owner of Solutions Press Publishing and co-producer of the world class Speak Your Way to Wealth seminar, specializes in helping business owners, entrepreneurs and professionals become the recognized experts in their market by speaking to groups and organizations and writing high quality books. Lee has been a newspaper editor, chief financial officer, professional speaker, and a writing coach and consultant. His books include '57 Steps to Better Writing' and 'Coaching for the New Century.'

Lee Pound
President
Lee Pound International
Newport Beach, CA United States
Contact Phone: 949-246-8580
Cell: 949-246-8580
Click to Contact from Web Site

DAN POYNTER -- BOOK PUBLISHING INDUSTRY EXPERT
Santa Barbara, CA United States
http://ParaPublishing.com

Book writing, publishing/self-publishing expert. Dan Poynter: Author (100+ books), Publisher (since 1969), Speaker (CSP). Web site has more than 500 pages of helpful information including statistics on the book publishing industry. History, trends and predictions on printed books and eBooks. Author of Writing Nonfiction, Is There a Book Inside You?, The Self-Publishing Manual, The Skydiver's Handbook, The Parachute Manual, The Expert Witness Handbook and many more.

Dan Poynter
Author-Publisher-Speaker
Para Publishing
Santa Barbara, United States
Contact Phone: 805-968-7277
Cell: 805-448-9009
Click to Contact from Web Site

JAKE FARROW -- HORROR NOVELIST
New York, MI United States
http://www.thechromabook.com/

Author Rides Rails by Day- Writes Horror Novels by Night. Jake Farrow is a native of New York City now residing in Brooklyn. Farrow earned an associate degree in liberal arts from Kingsborough Community College and a Bachelor of Arts degree in English from Brooklyn College. A train operator for the Metropolitan Transit Authority, Farrow is a movie and science fiction enthusiast with a passion for combat aircraft and military history. The Chroma is his first novel. http://www.TheChromaBook.com

Scott Lorenz
Westwind Communications
Plymouth, MI United States
Contact Phone: 2487052214
Click to Contact from Web Site

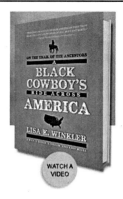

D.E. LAMONT - FICTION AND HEALTH & SELF IMPROVEMENT AUTHOR-WRITER
New York, NY United States
www.TheWayOfTheEagle.com

Author D.E. Lamont's historical Native American novella, The Way of the Eagle: An Early California Journey of Awakening, was published in May 2011 by her independent imprint Cloud River Press. It has earned two national awards awards and been nominated for the 2012 Global Ebook Awards. Ms. Lamont co-authored Becoming a True Champion: Achieving Athletic Excellence from the Inside Out, with Kirk Mango, published in May 2012 by Rowman & Littlefield. In 2008 she coauthored Taking Charge of Your Stroke Recovery: A Personal Recovery Workbook with Roger Maxwell. Her website are www.thewayoftheeagle.com & magicalmysticalyou.com.

D.E. Lamont
Author
Author, Writer and Independent Publisher
Yonkers, NY United States
Contact Phone: 914-376-6892
Click to Contact from Web Site

MARY TERZIAN, AUTHOR, GLOBAL E-BOOK NOMINEE
Los Angeles, CA United States
www.maryterzian.com

Mary Terzian (www.maryterzian.com)is a witty blogger, speaker and nonfiction writer. She has contributed numerous essays, travel articles, reflections and profiles "leavened with humor", in Armenian and in English, to newspapers, magazines, anthologies and online. Some of her articles and excerpts are posted at wwww.authorsden.com/maryterzian or can be traced online with keyword "Mary Terzian." A few chapters from her award-winning book, The Immigrants' Daughter are available at Amazon.com, Kindle and other website or digital bookstores. Links to some articles:
- The Acid Test http://www.back2college.com/bestlesson.htm - The Masala (spicy) Armenians: http://www.reporter.am/go/article/2008-11-30-the-masala-spicy-armenians - A Christmas Offer with Dividends - http://www.absolutewrite.com/freelance_writing/christmas_offer.htm

Mary Terzian
Author, Essayist
Hacienda Heights, CA United States
Contact Phone: 626-333-1610
Click to Contact from Web Site

LISA K. WINKLER -- A BLACK COWBOY'S RIDE ACROSS AMERICA
New York, MI United States
http://www.Lisakwinkler.com

One of the most recent and fascinating Black History memoirs published in 2012 tells the little-known six-month adventure of an African-American cowboy who rode horseback from Manhattan to California. That gripping journey by Miles Dean, filled with stops to recognize sites that were milestones in African-American culture, is shared in detail by author Lisa K. Winkler in On The Trail of the Ancestors: A Black Cowboy's Ride Across America (ISBN 978-1468123920, 2012, Create Space, 148 pages, $12.95 available on Amazon or through http://www.lisakwinkler.com/

Scott Lorenz
Westwind Communications
Plymouth, MI United States
Contact Phone: 248-705-2214
Click to Contact from Web Site

ALAN CARUBA -- PUBLIC RELATIONS EXPERT

South Orange, NJ United States
carubaeditorialservices.blogspot.com/

Alan Caruba's commentaries are posted daily at 'Warning Signs' his popular blog and thereafter on dozens of other websites and blogs. If you love to read, visit his monthly report on new books at Bookviews. Visit The Boring Institute for some laughs and tips on how to avoid boredom. For information on his professional skills, Caruba Editorial Services is the place to go! You can find me on both Facebook and Twitter as well.

Alan Caruba
South Orange, NJ United States
Contact Phone: 973-763-6392
Click to Contact from Web Site

ADAM KARWOSKI -- TAKING THE MYSTERY OUT OF SOCIAL MEDIA

Atlanta, GA United States
www.socialbrandu.net
GA

Adam Karwoski is the founder and CEO of Social Brand U. Social Brand U is a social media strategy, education and consulting company based in Atlanta, GA. Social Brand U partners with businesses to leverage social media to build value for the customer, build a brand for the business and build growth for the company. Learn more about Social Brand U by visiting our website, www. socialbrandu.net or our Facebook page, www. facebook.com/socialbrandu. Let's start building your brand!

Adam Karwoski
Social Brand U, LLC
Woodstock, GA United States
Contact Phone: 770-241-0102
Contact Main Phone: 770-241-0102
Cell: 770-241-0102
Click to Contact from Web Site

MICHAEL LEVINE -- HOLLYWOOD PUBLIC RELATIONS EXPERT

Los Angeles, CA United States
www.LCOonline.com

Levine Communications Office (LCO) is one of the nation's most prominent entertainment PR firms. Established in 1983, by Michael Levine, LCO has represented many hundreds of very well known celebrities including Barbra Streisand, Michael Jackson, Charlton Heston, Nancy Kerrigan, Demi Moore. Michael Levine as an author has written many books including the original best seller 'Guerrilla PR,' now in a totally new edition for the computer age as: 'Guerrilla PR Wired: Waging A Successful Publicity Campaign On-line, Offline, and Everywhere in Between.'

Michael Levine
Levine Communications, Inc.
Beverly Hills, CA United States
Contact Phone: 310-300-0950
Click to Contact from Web Site

JILL LUBLIN -- NETWORKING AND PUBLICITY EXPERT

San Francisco, CA United States
www.JillLublin.com

Jill Lublin is the author of three national best selling books, Guerrilla Publicity (which is often considered the PR bible and is used in university publicity courses) Networking Magic (which went to #1 at Barnes and Noble), and Get Noticed...Get Referrals (recently published by McGraw-Hill). Jill is the founder of GoodNews Media, Inc. and host of the nationally syndicated radio show, Do the Dream, and TV series, Messages of Hope.

Jill Lublin
Promising Promotion
Novato, CA United States
Contact Phone: 415-883-5455
Click to Contact from Web Site

LARRY MANDELBERG -- GROWTH BY DESIGN

Sacramento, CA United States
www.growthbydesign.biz

Noted author, speaker and strategist, Mandelberg was the keynote at Insiders Look at Acquisition Strategies, program chair for Institute of Management Consultants' National convention, and serves as board chair for Innovative Education Management. His published articles include 'Social media is here to stay; it's time to jump in' and 'Executives should know when to seek outside help.' Larry is the principal of Growth by Design, whose philosophy is based on creating strong organizational focus, performance and morale. He helps companies thrive in a changing economy by leading in the development and execution of strategic plans.

Larry Mandelberg
Principal
Growth by Design
Citrus Heights, CA United States
Contact Phone: (916) 798-0600
Contact Main Phone: (916) 798-0600
Cell: (916) 798-0600
Click to Contact from Web Site

PARTYLINE - PUBLIC RELATIONS MEDIA NEWSLETTER

New York, NY United States
http://www.Partylinepublishing.com

PartyLine is the premier media placement newsletter for the public relations trade. Each week, their skilled researchers ferret out what the media need from PR sources. They explain just who has gone online and what types of information are needed. Year after year, the most respected names in public relations, promotion, marketing and management, from top public relations and advertising agencies, corporations, universities, hospitals, associations, publishers, travel bureaus, health and government agencies, hotels, the entertainment industry use their services.

Betty Yarmon
Vice President
PartyLine, Public Relations Media Newsletter
New York, NY United States
Contact Phone: 212-755-3487
Click to Contact from Web Site

Organizational Futurist

Larry Mandelberg
STRATEGIC PLANNING

With more than 30 years experience as CEO and consultant, Larry Mandelberg has been called both an organizational futurist and non-recovering serial entrepreneur. He has launched four start-ups, led a merger and performed a successful turnaround.

Mandelberg has published more than 40 articles and has a monthly column in the Sacramento Business Journal. He is a student of organizational lifecycles and has developed a system to help business owners create sustainable growth. He has been a guest on television and radio programs talking about business and entrepreneurship.

In his consulting practice, Mandelberg provides strategic planning, leadership development, executive coaching and ethics training to mid-sized organizations and their boards in a broad range of industries from television to scientific research.

In addition to his consulting practice, he also serves as the board chair for Innovative Education Management, a $40-million, not-for-profit charter school management firm.

Powerful Topics That Mandelberg Presents:

- 3 secret ingredients for leadership stew . . . and how to cook 'em
- Where are our leaders? Recognizing potential and developing greatness
- Why leaders fail and what to do about it
- 7 steps to effective delegation for managers
- How healthy organizations become ill, and what to do before they become terminal

> "Larry saved me a year's salary… It was a wonderful experience."
> -- *Fritz Durst, board chairman, Reclamation District 108*

Growth by Design   www.GrowthByDesign.biz

twitter@businessincites   blog – http://lm523.wordpress.com   916-798-0600

Larry@Mandelberg.biz

JOAN STEWART -- PUBLICITY EXPERT
Milwaukee, WI United States
www.PublicityHound.com

Publicity expert Joan Stewart shows you how to use free publicity in traditional media, as well as social media strategies, to establish your credibility, enhance your reputation, position yourself as an expert, sell more products and services, promote a favorite cause or issue, and position your company as an employer of choice. She worked as a newspaper editor and reporter for 22 years and accepted and rejected thousands of story ideas, so she knows what the media want.

Joan Stewart
The Publicity Hound
Port Washington, WI United States
Contact Phone: 262-284-7451
Click to Contact from Web Site

IRWIN ZUCKER -- PROMOTION IN MOTION PUBLIC RELATIONS
Los Angeles, CA United States
www.promotioninmotion.net

The IRWIN Award, named for Book Publicists of Southern California founder Irwin Zucker, was introduced in 1995 as a way to formally and publicly recognize BPSC members who conduct the best book sales/promotion campaigns. Honorees share with the BPSC audience the steps they took that led to the success of their book promotion campaigns.

Irwin Zucker
President
Promotion In Motion
Hollywood, CA United States
Contact Phone: 323-461-3921
Click to Contact from Web Site

DAVID ADLER -- BIZBASH.COM -- PARTY PLANNING EXPERTS
New York, NY United States
www.BizBash.com

Since its founding in 2000, BizBash Media has become the event industry's leading source for inspiration, smart marketing strategies, and useful tools, helping to revolutionize the ways event professionals get ideas and connect with each other. BizBash serves six major markets in New York, Los Angeles, Chicago, Toronto, Florida, and Washington, D.C. The BizBash National Venue Guide covers an additional 16 markets. BizBash also hosts event planner expos in New York City, Los Angeles, and Chicago.

David Adler
BizBash, Inc.
New York, NY United States
Contact Phone: 646.638.3600
Click to Contact from Web Site

The Publicity Hound

Tips, tricks and tools for free publicity

Joan Stewart

- ■ I can provide commentary, background and story ideas on the topic of publicity.

- ■ If you are looking for publicity success stories, I can share sources and contact information.

- ■ If you need articles, columns, tip sheets, or other short items, I can meet even the toughest deadlines without fail.

- ■ I can provide more than 50 publicity and media-related articles you can reprint -- and adjust the word count to meet your needs to save you time editing. (See my Free Articles page at Web site).

- ■ I write freelance articles for a variety of publications and have built a reputation for suggesting off-the-wall topics, writing clean and compelling copy, and respecting deadlines.

- ■ I can provide a list of other experts and contact information on the topic you want.

Publicity expert Joan Stewart shows you how to use free publicity to establish your credibility, enhance your reputation, position yourself as an expert, sell more products and services, promote a favorite cause or issue, and position your company as an employer of choice. She worked as a newspaper editor and reporter for 22 years -- she knows what the media want.

As a media relations consultant and professional speaker, Stewart is an author of several books on writing and the media.

She is also the creator of the popular electronic newsletter, "The Publicity Hound's Tips of the Week," which goes to more than 40,000 subscribers worldwide and includes the best publicity tips.

Joan Stewart
262-284-7451
JStewart@PublicityHound.com
www.PublicityHound.com

THE CELEBRITY SOURCE -- ACCESS TO THOUSANDS OF CELEBRITIES
Los Angeles, CA United States
www.CelebritySource.com

Rita Tateel, president of The Celebrity Source, has been matching celebrities with corporate and non-profit public relations & marketing campaigns plus special events for over 20 years. Her international company has access to over 10,000 stars of film, television, music, sports and fashion. Ms. Tateel has been interviewed as a celebrity expert for countless media sources including CNN, Wall Street Journal, People Magazine, Playboy, Hollywood Reporter, LA Times, NY Times, E! Entertainment Television, 'Extra!' and 'Entertainment Tonight,' among many others.

Rita Tateel
President
The Celebrity Source
Los Angeles, CA United States
Contact Phone: 323-651-3300
Click to Contact from Web Site

ROOM 214 - SOCIAL MEDIA AGENCY
Boulder, CO United States
www.room214.com

Room 214 serves organizations desiring to go deep with social media. We help you engage your customers, humanize your brand and build upon what works. If leadership in your market is the goal, this agency should be your agency. Our services include social media strategy and training, blogging, video scribing, video marketing, custom Facebook app development, search engine optimization, pay per click, article marketing, optimized press releases, syndicating press rooms, RSS marketing and customized online reputation monitoring.

James Clark
Room 214, INC
Capture the Conversation
Boulder, CO United States
Contact Phone: 303-444-9214
Cell: 303-886-4259
Click to Contact from Web Site

CRAIG CONROY, CONROY RESEARCH GROUP
Gibsonia, PA United States
www.CraigConroy.com

Animated authority, author and a great guest, two books, numerous trade publication articles. 'A producer's dream, talk show host's ideal guest.' He speaks in soundbites, great source for reporters. Material backed by market research. Book him today for your next sweeps. 'He lights up switchboards like a Christmas tree.'

Terry or Rosa
Marketing
Craig Conroy, Conroy Research Group
Gibsonia, PA United States
Contact Phone: 800-344-1492
Contact Main Phone: 724-443-6876
Click to Contact from Web Site

JOHN FISCHER - STICKERGIANT.COM - STICKER SOCIOLOGIST

Denver, CO United States
www.stickergiant.com/custom_stickers/index.html

StickerGiant.com was founded in 2000 after the contested Al Gore and George W. Bush Presidential Election. StickerGiant serves as a clearinghouse for the first amendment. They carry over 20,000 stickers and related ephemera covering over 1100 categories of topics. StickerGiant carries a complete line of NFL, NBA and MLB stickers.

John Fischer
StickerGiant.com Inc
Hygiene, CO United States
Contact Phone: 303-774-7900 x 101
Click to Contact from Web Site

CORINNE INNIS -- PENN FLEMING PUBLIC RELATIONS

New York, NY United States
http://www.pennflemingpr.com

Clients can depend on personal and individualized attention 24 hours a day, seven days a week. Our services are tailor-made to suit the client's needs. Whatever it takes will be done to find venues and solutions for all our clients. At Penn Fleming, the process of doing business is one that is open-minded, flexible and creative. We serve clients from many industries. Many come from the arts, entertainment, as well as the non-profit sector.

Corinne Innis
Executive Director
Penn Fleming Public Relations
New York, NY United States
Contact Phone: (516)902-5640
Click to Contact from Web Site

SHERYL WOODHOUSE-KEESE -- ECO-FRIENDLY INVITATIONS & CELEBRATIONS

Bloomington, IN United States
www.twistedlimbpaper.com

Twisted Limb® Paperworks, an art studio in Bloomington, Indiana, has been sustainably creating handmade 100% recycled paper, invitations, and greeting cards and advising couples on earth-friendly weddings since 1998. Among the first to produce recycled wedding invitations, they have been pioneers in the green wedding movement, setting high environmental standards for themselves and their successors. Using old colored office paper, and recycled water, the company has created invitations for over 4,000 events. The company also designs memorial stationery under the brand Remembrance Tree® Papers. Twisted Limb donates 22% of profits to environmental and community groups each year.

Sheryl Woodhouse-Keese
Founding Artist/CEO
Twisted Limb Paperworks
Bloomington, IN United States
Contact Phone: 812-606-8304
Contact Main Phone: 812-606-8304
Cell: 812-606-8304
Click to Contact from Web Site

L. AVIVA DIAMOND -- BLUE STREAK - A COMMUNICATIONS COMPANY
Los Angeles, CA United States

L. Aviva Diamond is President of Blue Streak/A Communications Company, a Los Angeles-based executive media and speaker training firm. She is an Emmy-winning former ABC Network News correspondent with more than 20 years of experience in training top executives and has helped thousands of people improve their skills in speaking with reporters, colleagues and the business community. Aviva differs from other trainers in her attention to individual needs. Her trainings are highly personalized and often yield rapid, long-lasting results. Clients have included top executives from: Symantec, Microsoft, Toshiba, Universal Studios, Orbitz, Yahoo!, Kaiser Permanente and Transamerica. She has been quoted by the Wall St. Journal, Associated Press, Los Angeles Times, Investor's Business Daily and Business 2.0. As a correspondent for ABC News, Aviva appeared on Good Morning America, World News Tonight and Nightline. During her years in tv and radio news, she received: the Emmy Award, AP Bay State Award, Tom Phillips/UPI Award, RTNDA Regional Award, Sigma Delta Chi Award and Distinguished Achievement in Journalism from the American Academy of Pediatrics.

L. Aviva Diamond
Blue Streak/A Communications Company
Los Angeles, CA United States
Contact Phone: 323-655-2583
Click to Contact from Web Site

MAGGIE HOLBEN -- PUBLIC RELATIONS EXPERT RESOURCE
Lakewood, CO United States
www.absolutelypr.com

Maggie Chamberlin Holben, APR, owner and founder of Denver's Absolutely Public Relations, specializes in media relations - the strategies and tactics necessary to achieve impactful editorial placements in the national, trade press and local media. Holben is accredited by the Public Relations Society of America and is a member of its Counselors Academy, plus she is certified as an Industry Analyst Relations Practitioner. She brings more than 25 years of experience to both interviewers and clients.

Maggie Holben
Principal
Absolutely Public Relations
Lakewood, CO United States
Contact Phone: 303-984-9801
Click to Contact from Web Site

GAYL MURPHY -- INTERVIEW TACTICS
Los Angeles, CA United States
http://gaylmurphy.com

Gayl Murphy is a Media Expert, veteran Hollywood correspondent, speaker, media and presentational business coach and the author of the best-selling Interview Tactics! How to Survive the Media without Getting Clobbered! As a Hollywood Correspondent, Murphy specializes in interviewing the industry's biggest stars. Based in Hollywood, she has worked with many of the top news outlets including; ABC News, BBC News and SKY News, to name a few. The media-savvy Murphy has been up-close and personal with about 14,000 of the most famous celebrities and newsmakers in the world.

Brad Butler
Hollywood, CA United States
Contact Phone: 323-461-3921
Click to Contact from Web Site

KATIE SCHWARTZ -- BUSINESS SPEECH IMPROVEMENT
Chattanooga, TN United States
www.BusinessSpeechImprovement.com

JULIE SALISBURY - INFLUENCE PUBLISHING
Victoria, British Columbia Canada
www.inspiredauthorscircle.com/influence-publishing-2/

Influence Publishing represents Authors of Influence that are leaders of change. The subject matters range from new ideas on health issues, conscious parenting and social issues such as addiction. New out of the box opinions on human relationships, evolutionary development and medical advancement are thought provoking and often controversial. A unique website hub lists these authors and their area of expertise at inspiredauthorcircle.com All are experienced speakers and have been featured in the media for their controversial opinions on religion, health, social issues, parenting and spiritual perspective. For a fresh exciting interview contact our authors.

Julie Salisbury
PR Director
Influence Publishing
Cowichan Bay, BC Canada
Contact Phone: 250-746-9989
Click to Contact from Web Site

Katie Schwartz, CCC-SLP is the director of Business Speech Improvement in Chattanooga, TN. A corporate speech pathologist, Ms. Schwartz has expertise in communication techniques used in business settings such as public speaking, interpersonal communication techniques, communication techniques for leadership, accent modification, and learning to speak slower. She is also a certified, licensed speech-language pathologist with expertise in working with communication disorders. Ms. Schwartz is the author of 4 books and numerous concise e-books on communication, and has been quoted in many publications.

Katie Schwartz
Business Speech Improvement
Chattanooga, TN United States
Contact Phone: 423-894-8024
Click to Contact from Web Site

WESTWIND COMMUNICATIONS PUBLIC RELATIONS
Plymouth, MI United States
www.westwindcos.com

Scott Lorenz is President of Westwind Communications, a public relations and marketing firm. Lorenz works with doctors, lawyers, inventors, authors, start-ups and entrepreneurs. As a seasoned publicist he is often called upon in the early stages of a company's existence to get them "on the radar." As a book marketing expert Lorenz is consulted by top execs and bestselling authors to promote their books. His clients have been featured by Good Morning America, FOX & Friends, CNN, ABC Nightly News, ESPN, The New York Times, Nightline, TIME, PBS, NPR, USA Today, Woman's World, & Howard Stern to name a few.

Scott Lorenz
President
Westwind Communications
Plymouth, MI United States
Contact Phone: 734-667-2090
Contact Main Phone: 7346672090
Cell: 248-705-2214
Click to Contact from Web Site

DEBRA HOLTZMAN, J.D., M.A. --
CORPORATE CONSULTANT AND
SPOKESPERSON
Hollywood, FL United States
www.thesafetyexpert.com

Debra Holtzman brings integrity, professional credentials, technical expertise and experience to your media campaign. She has a masters degree in occupational health and safety, a B.A. in communications, is an award-winning author and mother of two children. Debra has appeared on hundreds of radio and television shows around the world and was named an 'Everyday Hero' by Reader's Digest. Her Latest book, 'The Safe Baby: A Do-it-Yourself Guide to Home Safety and Healthy Living' (Sentient Publications, 2009) is in bookstores everywhere.

Debra Holtzman
Hollywood, FL United States
Contact Phone: 954-963-7702
Click to Contact from Web Site

DR. RICK KIRSCHNER --
COMMUNICATION SKILLS EXPERT
Ashland, OR United States
http://www.theartofchange.com/

Dr. Rick Kirschner delivers savvy expertise on persuasive communication and dealing with change, to give an interview your audience will love! His message is simple—Change is inevitable, but progress is not. Discover how you make the difference. Respected faculty of the Institute for Management Studies, client organizations include Heineken, NASA, Starbucks, Texas Instruments. Author of "How To Click With People: The Secret To Better Relationships In Business And In Life.' Coauthor of the international bestseller 'Dealing With People You Can't Stand:How To Bring Out The Best In People At Their Worst.

Dr. Rick Kirschner
Author, Speaker, Educator, Coach
The Art of Change LLC
Ashland, OR United States
Contact Phone: 541-488-2992
Cell: 5412100678
Click to Contact from Web Site

SAM WALTZ
Philadelphia, PA United States
www.samwaltz.com

Sam Waltz, APR, Fellow PRSA, a Greenville, DE, neighbor of VP Joe Biden, operates Sam Waltz & Associates LLC Business & Communications Counsel in the greater Philadelphia area, from where he provides senior strategic business, investment banking, and merger & acquisition (M&A) counsel. Waltz, 63, dropped from the University of Illinois at 20 to enlist in the Vietnam-era US Army CounterIntelligence Corps 1967-70. Later he earned BS and MS degrees from Illinois. He was State Capitol Bureau Chief in the mid-1970s covering then-Sen. Joe Biden, now-Sen. Tom Carper, Gov. Pete duPont, and the Delaware General Assembly. Waltz served as elected CEO of the Public Relations Society of America, and he was a senior DuPont Company External Affairs executive.

Samuel L. Waltz Jr.
Counselor to Leaders ™
Sam Waltz & Associates LLC Counsel
Greenville, Wilmington, DE United States
Contact Phone: 302.777.7774
Contact Main Phone: 302.777.7774
Cell: 302.777.7774
Click to Contact from Web Site

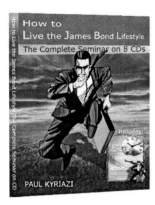

PAUL KYRIAZI -- JAMES BOND LIFESTYLE

Los Angeles, CA United States
http://www.bondlife.com

Live the JAMES BOND Lifestyle. A serious seminar and book. Subjects include: Appearance -- Relationships -- Car -- Hotels -- Casino Gambling -- Upgrading Image -- Avoiding Villains -- The Ultimate Secret of Women.

Paul Kyriazi
James Bond Lifestyle
Los Angeles, CA United States
Contact Phone: 310-826-0222
Click to Contact from Web Site

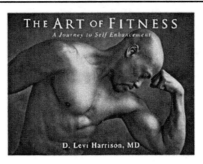

D. LEVI HARRISON, M.D., THE ART OF FITNESS

Glendale, CA United States
www.DrLeviHarrison.com

D. Levi Harrison, MD is the first American physician/Orthopedic surgeon to write and demonstrate all exercises in a comprehensive fitness book. Currently practicing in the Los Angeles area, his diverse education includes a Bachelor of Arts in French /Romance Languages and a Bachelor of Science in Electrical Engineering from the University of Notre Dame, a Master's of Engineering from Howard University and a diploma of French Perfection from the Alliance Fran [e76169]se in Angers, France from the Universit [e92043]atholique de L' Ouest.

Brad Butler
Promotion in Motion
Hollywood, CA United States
Contact Phone: 323-461-3921
Click to Contact from Web Site

DANIEL BURRUS -- PROFESSIONAL SPEAKER - BESTSELLING AUTHOR

San Diego, CA United States
www.burrus.com

Daniel Burrus is considered one of the world's leading technology forecasters and business strategists, and is the founder and CEO of Burrus Research, a research and consulting firm that monitors global advancements in technology driven trends to help clients better understand how technological, social and business forces are converging to create enormous, untapped opportunities. He is the author of six books, including The New York Times and The Wall Street Journal best seller Flash Foresight: How To See the Invisible and Do the Impossible as well as the highly acclaimed Technotrends.

Jennifer Metcalf
V.P. of Marketing
Burrus Research Associates Inc
Hartland, WI United States
Contact Phone: 262-367-0949
Contact Main Phone: 262-367-0949
Cell: 262-354-2029
Click to Contact from Web Site

HARRY J. BURY -- AN EMERGING WORLDVIEW TO THE THIRD MILLENNIUM.
Berea, OH United States
http://homepages.bw.edu/~hbury/
What%27s%20New.htm

Presently, I am working on the book entitled Thinking and Feeling Differently: An Emerging Worldview to the Third Millennium. The purpose of this book is twofold: to explain a new way of looking and feeling about life that is emerging called a worldview and to illustrate how significant areas of our lives (intimacy, health care, work, education, ecology, justice, politics, and spirituality) will appear when the emerging worldview becomes the common view.

Harry J Bury
Baldwin Wallace College
Berea, OH United States
Contact Phone: 440-826-2395
Click to Contact from Web Site

FUTURETAKES.ORG INTERNATIONAL FUTURIST MAGAZINE
Washington, DC United States
www.FutureTakes.org

FUTUREtakes is an independent educational resource serving World Future Society members and the intellectually curious, future-minded public at large. It assembles leading foresight thinkers and others from a diversity of nations, cultures, professions and disciplines to examine the future, with special emphasis on identifying hidden culture-based assumptions that shape how people live, work and think. Articles and program synopses explore alternative futures and the cross-cutting implications of social trends, technology advances and policy options. A nonpartisan, non-advocacy publication, FUTUREtakes is replete with provocative discussion points designed to inspire student and faculty thought, discussion, commentary, articles and research projects. It offers authors visibility and exposure across organizations, professions, demographic and socioeconomic groups, cultures, and nations -- with the possibility to inspire dialogue with other readers worldwide and to influence thinking across the globe. Authors have included educators, diplomats and think tank staff.

David E. Stein
President
Center for Transcultural Foresight, Inc.
Washington, DC United States
Contact Phone: 202-263-1140
Click to Contact from Web Site

THE HERMAN GROUP -- STRATEGIC BUSINESS FUTURISTS
Austin, TX United States
http://www.hermangroup.com

High content thought leaders on workforce and workplace issues, trends, and employee retention. Available 24/7, highly responsive and deadline-sensitive. Articulate Certified Management Consultants, they demystify complicated issues. Upbeat about the future, with realistic focus on employee turnover, labor shortages, corporation of the future and similar current issues. Authors of recent books on management and near-term future, including 'Impending Crisis,' 'How to Become an Employer of Choice,' 'Keeping Good People,' 'Lean & Meaningful,' 'Signs of the Times,' and 'How to Choose Your Next Employer.' The Herman Group helps organizations and their leaders prepare for tomorrow.

Joyce L. Gioia, CMC, CSP
Certified Speaking Professional and Management Consultant
The Herman Group
Austin, TX United States
Contact Phone: 336-210-3548
Contact Main Phone: 800-227-3566
Cell: 336-210-3548
Click to Contact from Web Site

FUTUREtakes is an independent educational resource serving World Future Society members and the intellectually curious, future-minded public at large. It assembles leading foresight thinkers and others from a diversity of nations, cultures, professions, and disciplines to examine the future, with special emphasis on identifying hidden culture-based assumptions that shape how people live, work, and think.

Articles and program synopses explore alternative futures and the cross-cutting implications of social trends, technology advances, and policy options. The myriad of topics include

Healthcare	Governance
Demographics	Geostrategic issues
Living and working patterns	Information technology
Climate change	Education
Social change	Nanotechnology
Transportation	Identity
Energy and other resources	Privacy
Sustainable development	Foresight methodologies

A nonpartisan, non-advocacy publication, FUTUREtakes is replete with provocative discussion points designed to inspire student and faculty thought, discussion, commentary, articles, and research projects.

FUTUREtakes offers authors visibility and exposure across organizations, professions, demographic and socioeconomic groups, cultures, and nations – with the possibility to inspire dialogue with other readers worldwide and to influence thinking across the globe. Authors have included educators, diplomats, and think tank staff.

Articles may be submitted to articles@futuretakes.org.
For more information, contact info@futuretakes.org.

---

www.FUTUREtakes.org
202-263-1140

JOHN RENESCH -- THE SUSTAINABILITY FUTURIST
San Francisco, CA United States
www.renesch.com

John is a businessman-turned-global futurist, humanitarian, writer and keynote speaker on topics that integrate the subjects of business, human consciousness and possible scenarios for the future of humanity. He has also become a social activist, an advocate of social and organizational transformation and awakening what he sees as the latent potentialities of the human race. He offers a variety of services as an international keynote speaker, private mentor and advisor to consultants. His latest of 14 books is 'The Great Growing Up: Being Responsible for Humanity's Future.' He publishes a free monthly newsletter called 'John Renesch's Mini-Keynote.'

John Renesch
Futurist, author, keynote speaker
Renesch Advisory Services
San Francisco, CA United States
Contact Phone: 415-437-6974
Click to Contact from Web Site

WORLD FUTURE SOCIETY
Washington, DC United States
WFS.org

What Is the World Future Society? The World Future Society is a nonprofit, nonpartisan scientific and educational association of people interested in how social and technological developments are shaping the future.

Patrick Tucker
World Future Society
Bethesda, MD United States
Contact Phone: 1-301-656-8274
Click to Contact from Web Site

MICHAEL G. ZEY, PH.D. -- FUTURE TRENDS AND LONGEVITY EXPERT
Mt. Freedom, NJ United States
http://www.zey.com

Dr. Michael Zey, an internationally-recognized sociologist, and future trends/longevity expert, is the author of Ageless Nation (New Horizon Press Books), The Future Factor (McGraw-Hill/Transaction), Seizing the Future (Simon and Schuster) and numerous articles on social, economic and political trends. Dr. Zey has discussed topics such as longevity, energy, the media and communications, space, and technology on ABC, CNN, CNBC, and FoxNews. He is a noted speaker at trade shows and corporate conferences hosted by Sprint, Prudential, IBM and United Technologies.

Michael G. Zey, Ph.D.
Exec. Director
Expansionary Institute
Montclair State University
Mount Freedom, NJ United States
Contact Phone: 973-879-4776
Click to Contact from Web Site

MIKE CERMAK -- TECH SUPPORT GUY

Waynesboro, PA United States
www.techguy.org/

Mike Cermak is 'The Tech Support Guy.' Cermak (pronounced Sir-Mack) holds two degrees in Information Sciences and Technology from Penn State University, and maintains several certifications from the Computer Technology Industry Association (CompTIA) and Microsoft. Cermak put his extensive knowledge to good use; in 1996 he created TechGuy.com, one of the first tech support communities on the web. TechGuy.com hosts over 500,000 registered users and was included by Yahoo! Internet Life Magazine in its 'Top 50 Most Incredibly Useful Sites.' His work has garnered attention in Reader's Digest, Computer Shopper, PC World, NetGuide Magazine, and on the BBC. An expert who makes the obscure accessible, Cermak has provided insight in interviews with Money Magazine, TechTV and CNet Radio.

Michael Cermak
Founder
TechGuy, Inc.
Waynesboro, PA United States
Contact Phone: 1-877-483-2448
Click to Contact from Web Site

CERULEAN ASSOCIATES LLC -- FDA COMPLIANCE EXPERTS

Williamsburg, VA United States
www.ceruleanllc.com

John Avellanet is an internationally syndicated author, award-winning writer and speaker. He's written several books, publishes a monthly newsletter, and serves on industry boards in the pharmaceutical, medical device, and biotech industries. A list of previous interviews and speaking engagements can be found on the site of his most current book, Get to Market Now! Turn FDA Compliance into a Competitive Edge in the Era of Personalized Medicine, at www.Get2MarketNow.com.

John Avellanet
Managing Director
Cerulean Associates LLC
Williamsburg, VA United States
Contact Phone: 757-645-2864
Click to Contact from Web Site

ROXANNE EMMERICH, CPAE, CMC - THE EMMERICH GROUP, INC.

Minneapolis, MN United States
www.thankgoditsmonday.com

Roxanne Emmerich is America's most sought-after workplace transformation expert. She is listed by Sales and Marketing Management magazine as one of the 12 most requested speakers in the country for her ability to transform negative workplace performance and environments into 'bring-it-on,' results-oriented cultures. Emmerich's book, 'Thank God It's Monday,' is a New York Times, Wall Street Journal and Amazon #1 bestseller. As president and CEO of the Emmerich Group, Inc., she has consulted and spoken to most of the financial institutions in the top one percent of performance, as well as clients like Merck, Pfizer, Allianz, Lockheed Martin and hundreds of other leaders in almost every industry. Emmerich was inducted into the National Speaker Hall of Fame for her impact and quantifiable effectiveness.

DIna Simon
Vice President
The Emmerich Group, Inc.
Minneapolis, MN United States
Contact Phone: 952-820-0360
Contact Main Phone: 952-820-0360
Click to Contact from Web Site

CORBIN BALL -- CONVENTION TECHNOLOGY EXPERT
Seattle, WA United States
http://www.corbinball.com

Corbin Ball, CSP, CMP, MS is an international speaker, consultant and writer helping clients worldwide use technology to save time and improve productivity. With 20 years of experience running international technology meetings, he now is a highly acclaimed speaker with the ability to make complex subjects understandable and fun. His articles have appeared in hundreds of national and international publications and he has been quoted in the US and News Report, Wall Street Journal, the New York Times, USA Today, Fast Company, PC Magazine and others. Corbin serves or has served on numerous hotel, corporate, convention bureau and association boards.

Corbin Ball, CMP, CSP
Corbin Ball Associates
Bellingham, WA United States
Contact Phone: 360.734.8756
Click to Contact from Web Site

GAIL KINGSBURY -- SPEAKER RESOURCE CONNECTION
Redmond, OR United States
http://gailkingsbury.com

Gail Kingsbury has played a central role in the US seminar industry since 1988 when she went to work for Brian Tracy in Solana Beach, CA. Her ability to plan and orchestrate the smooth operation of events with hundreds of attendees and dozens of speakers is now well-known among the top seminar hosts in almost every field.

Gail Kingsbury
Speaker Resource Connection
Redmond, OR United States
Contact Phone: Contact from site
Click to Contact from Web Site

GOLD STARS SPEAKERS BUREAU
Tucson, AZ United States
www.GoldStars.com

Gold Stars Speakers Bureau® provides you with excellent keynote speakers, trainers, facilitators, motivational speakers, entertainers, emcees and celebrities for your upcoming meeting or convention. Call us and experience an enjoyable and professional working relationship with integrity, fun and star-quality service. We love special requests. Gold Stars provides speakers and experts for both face-to-face meetings and virtual meetings (including webinars, teleseminars, satellite links). We work with corporations, assocations, education groups and government agencies for meetings and conventions worldwide. Andrea Gold is co-author of 'The Business of Successful Speaking: Proven Secrets to Becoming a Million-Dollar Speaker.'

Andrea Gold
President
Gold Stars Speakers Bureau
Tucson, AZ United States
Contact Phone: 520-742-4384
Contact Main Phone: 520-742-4384
Cell: 520-730-4356
Click to Contact from Web Site

NOEL JAMESON -- FAMOUS QUOTES
Boone, NC United States
http://www.famous-quotes-and-quotations.com/

Whether for a special birthday, anniversary, or wedding celebration we all have need to find that perfect quote. At www.Famous-Quotes-and-Quotations.com we have top 10 lists of the best quotes in all kinds of categories, like love quotes, success quotes, birthday quotes and more. And for an inspirational start to your day, sign up for the FREE newsletter to get a hand-picked inspiring -- and sometimes funny -- quote, an entertaining fact about the day, and an interesting, helpful article to check out. http://www.famous-quotes-and-quotations.com/your-inspirational-quote.html

Dr. Audri G. Lanford
Lanford Inc
Boone, NC United States
Contact Phone: 815-642-0460
Click to Contact from Web Site

Looking for an Expert on Kick-Butt Workplace Cultures?

Roxanne Emmerich

is the most in-demand transformation agent in business today due to her astonishing ability to create profound change in workplace cultures.

"Roxanne helped transform our culture, instill passion into our people and drive up our profits 23 percent! Nobody has ever given us better results."
– *P. Steele, President & CEO, First Volunteer Bank*

"Roxanne took our group to the next level!"
– *V. Thoreson, Sales Director, BlueCross BlueShield*

As one of the most applauded business women in the United States, Roxanne Emmerich is listed by *Sales and Marketing Management* magazine as one of the **12 most requested speakers in the nation** for her unparalleled ability to create immediate, profound and sustainable transformations for her clients.

Having been interviewed by CBS, CNN, the Wall Street Journal and more than 100 radio and television stations, Roxanne offers a unique approach which blends kick-butt marketing and no-excuses leadership development systems that work!

ROBIN JAY -- LAS VEGAS KEYNOTE SPEAKER
Las Vegas, NV United States
www.RobinJay.com

Robin Jay is an award-winning movie writer/ producer, author, and speaker. Her first film is The Keeper of the Keys - the first funny self-help film. It stars Jack Canfield and John Gray. Robin wrote, produced, and costars in the movie. She is also president of the Las Vegas Convention Speakers Bureau, a publisher, and a Business Relationship Expert. Her award-winning book, 'The Art of the Business Lunch', has been published in 12 languages.

Robin Jay
President
Las Vegas Convention Speakers Bureau
Las Vegas, NV United States
Contact Phone: 702-460-1420
Click to Contact from Web Site

JEFF HURT -- VELVET CHAINSAW -- MIDCOURSE CORRECTIONS
Cleveland, OH United States
VelvetChainsaw.com

Midcourse Corrections is the online home and blog of Velvet Chainsaw Consulting, Inc. Jeff, Dave and Donna blog on Midcourse Corrections about annual meeting improvement, association and corporate meetings and education, and the convergence of Web 2.0, social media, meetings, events and education.

Jeff Hurt
Velvet Chainsaw -- Midcourse Corrections
Aurora, OH United States
Contact Phone: 330.474.1047
Click to Contact from Web Site

MARK MIKELAT - SPEAKER LEADS -- BUILDING ASPIRATIONS
Long Beach, CA United States
http://www.buildingaspirations.com/

Mark is the author and founder of the Aspirations Program. From years of research and practice he has created a powerful 3-step plan for achieving what you want for yourself and your life. This excitingly simple recipe for achievement provides greater happiness and fulfillment to your life. By mixing the Aspirations principles with his experience living and working in multiple cultures in Spain, Germany, and Switzerland Mark has demonstrated that the Aspirations idea, because of its simplicity and ease of implementation, has universal appeal.

Mark Mikelat
Building Aspirations
Long Beach, CA United States
Contact Phone: Prefers E-mail
Click to Contact from Web Site

NANCI MCGRAW, FOUNDER-INT-L DO-ERS ORGANIZATION
San Diego, CA United States
http://www.Nanci.org

Make it happen! Get it Done! 'Add Zip to Your Trip!' Speaker/Author/Award-winning Broadcaster Nanci Mcgraw has made 1,000+ presentations: all 50 U.S., Canada, Caribbean, and Asia. Sparkling style won her 100 media awards. Happy clients include: Avis, Boeing, IBM, Marriott, Motorola, NASA, VISA. Motivational, results oriented Books: Organized for Success! Speak Up and Stand Out! I-netRadio-'Life Rewards the DO-ers!' DO-ers Newsletter: 'Ya Gotta Wanna!'

Nanci McGraw
Professional Speaker,
Founder-Int'l DO-ers Organization
Wildomar, CA United States
Contact Phone: 800-578-2278
Contact Main Phone: 951-245-4694
Click to Contact from Web Site

NATIONAL SPEAKERS ASSOCIATION
Tempe, AZ United States
http://www.nsaspeaker.org

National Speakers Association (NSA) members are EXPERTS who speak professionally. NSA's 3,200 members are experts in a variety of fields and are ideal sources for expert commentary and thought-provoking interviews. As a service to media professionals, the NSA marketing team will assist with your media needs and set you up with the perfect source for your story. Or, find your expert online at www.nsaspeaker.org. Click on the Find a Speaker section of NSA's website to search by keyword, name, location or one of 74 main topics. Additionally, NSA's online press room offers quick links to events and news from the speaking profession.

Andrea DiMickele
Marketing Specialist
National Speakers Association
Tempe, AZ United States
Contact Phone: 480-968-2552
Click to Contact from Web Site

STEFAN SWANEPOEL -- SURVIVING YOUR SERENGETI
Los Angeles, CA United States
http://www.serengetibook.com/

Surviving Your Serengeti: 7 Skills to Master Business & Life (Wiley; hardcover; March 1, 2011) will refine how you view and comprehend people. Africa-born, New York Times bestselling author, Stefan Swanepoel shares the different parallels between our concrete jungle and the real jungle. Take the surprisingly accurate 3-minute quiz and discover whether you are an enterprising crocodile, a strategic lion, a risk-taking mongoose or another one of the 'Serengeti Seven.' Learn to develop your own strongest survival skill, identify and understand the strengths of those you work with - all while having fun and developing an extraordinary team.

Stefan Swanepoel
Realsure, Inc.
Laguna Niguel, CA United States
Contact Phone: (949) 681-9409
Click to Contact from Web Site

TOASTMASTERS INTERNATIONAL
Rancho Santa Margarita, CA United States
www.Toastmasters.org

Toastmasters International is a non-profit educational organization that teaches public speaking and leadership skills through a worldwide network of meeting locations. Headquartered in Rancho Santa Margarita, California, the organization has more than 270,000 members in more than 13,000 clubs in 116 countries. Since 1924, Toastmasters International has helped people of all backgrounds become more confident in front of an audience.

Suzanne Frey
Toastmasters International
Mission Viejo, CA United States
Contact Phone: (949) 858-8255
Click to Contact from Web Site

DAVE VANHOSE -- 7 FIGURE SPEAKING EMPIRE
Tampa, FL United States
www.SpeakingEmpire.com

Industry insiders know us as the secret weapon quietly working behind the scenes with some of the world's most sought after speakers, gurus and information marketers. Over the years, we've helped companies and individuals create millions in additional revenue by causing back of the room buying frenzies and floods of server crushing online orders. Combined we have a HUGE amount of experience in the seminar industry, filling rooms for over 2000 live events, delivering over 3000 presentations, selling millions from stages and on the Internet.

Dave VanHose
7 Figure Speaking Empire
Tampa, FL United States
Contact Phone: 813-938-2160
Click to Contact from Web Site

DOTTIE WALTERS -- SHARE AND GROW RICH BIOGRAPHY -MICHAEL MACFARLANE
Gledora, CA United States
http://www.speakandgrowrich.com/

Find out exactly what Dottie Walters told Jack Canfield, Mark Victor Hansen, Tom Antion, David Bach and many others that helped them launch multi-million-dollar speaking and publishing empires. It's all here! The private advice, the breakthrough ideas, and other trade secrets that Dottie Walters developed and generously shared during her phenomenal 50+ year career. Don't miss this official biography of the woman who single-handedly led thousands of entrepreneurs to their greatest success.

Michael MacFarlane
Glendora, CA United States
Contact Phone: Prefers E-mail
Click to Contact from Web Site

We've Got Your Source

National Speakers Association (NSA) members are authorities in a variety of fields and are ideal sources for expert commentary and thought-provoking interviews.

As a free service to media professionals, NSA offers an online membership directory featuring more than 3,500 expert sources. This comprehensive directory at www.nsaspeaker.org is searchable by areas of expertise, geographical locations, key words and names.

Additionally, NSA's online press room offers quick links to events, statistics and news from the speaking profession. Call 480-968-2552 for help finding an expert or to talk with the communication team about your media needs.

www.nsaspeaker.org is searchable by:

- **areas of expertise;**
- **geographical locations;**
- **key words; and**
- **names.**

NSA®

NATIONAL SPEAKERS ASSOCIATION

BRENDON BURCHARD
Portland, OR United States
http://brendonburchard.com/

Brendon Burchard is one of the most in-demand speakers on motivation, high performance, leadership, and marketing in the world. Brendon has shared the stage with the Dalai Lama, Sir Richard Branson, Tony Robbins, Deepak Chopra, Wayne Dyer, Jack Canfield, Keith Ferrazzi, Tony Tsieh from Zappos, and some of the most respected teachers and leaders of our age. His speaking clients have included Alcoa, Accenture, Morgan Stanley, and dozens of the top universities and non-profits in the world.

Brendon Burchard
The Burchard Group
Portland, OR United States
Contact Phone: Prefers E-Mail
Click to Contact from Web Site

CRAIG DUSWALT -- ROCKSTAR SYSTEM FOR SUCCESS
Valencia, CA United States
www.CraigDuswalt.com

Craig Duswalt is the creator of the RockStar System For Success - How to Achieve RockStar Status in Your Industry. Craig's background includes touring with Guns N' Roses, as Axl Rose's personal manager, and Air Supply, as the band's personal assistant. Prior to this Craig was an award-winning Creative Director for a Los Angeles-based ad agency until opening up his own ad agency. Craig combined his backgrounds in both music and marketing, and is now a professional speaker and author, promoting his RockStar System for Success all over the country, teaching entrepreneurs, small businesses, and home-based businesses how to promote themselves and their business by thinking outside the box at his 4 1/2-Day RockStar Marketing BootCamps every March and September in Los Angeles.

Craig Duswalt
RockStar System for Success
Valencia, CA United States
Contact Phone: 661-222-2300
Click to Contact from Web Site

CHRIS HOWARD -- ACADEMY OF WEALTH AND ACHIEVEMENT
Manhattan Beach, CA United States
http://www.wealthandachievement.com/mc-home?

The Academy of Wealth & Achievement™ was conceived to develop and deliver next generation tools and technologies so that all people have the opportunity to create the rich and fulfilling life and lifestyle they most desire and truly deserve. Founded by internationally acclaimed lifestyle and wealth strategist Christopher Howard, The Academy is the culmination of his life's work in the research, creation and teaching of the cutting edge strategies, powerful skills and unstoppable mindset of the most wealthy and successful individuals and businesses on the planet. By bringing together the best mentors, teachers, experts and resources on earth in a forum designed to allow access to as many people as possible (regardless of situation or circumstance) it truly lives up to Christopher Howard's founding vision. To eradicate poverty on a global scale and to help all people become masters of their own wealth and achievement through education and entrepreneurship.

Triscka Mallia
Academy of Wealth and Achievement
Sacramento, CA United States
Contact Phone: (858) 752-2492
Click to Contact from Web Site

Stefan Swanepoel

20 Books | 700 Talks | 500,000 People

Motivational & Inspiring

New York Times bestseller Surviving Your Serengeti: 7 Skills to Master Business and Life will redefine how you view and comprehend people. Book Stefan for your next event today.

For Media Inquiries and Bookings:
Phone: 949.681.9409
Email: dj@serengetibook.com

Building Better Teams By Connecting With The Animal In All Of Us!

 /serengeti   /serengeti   /serengetibook

What Animal Am I?
Discover Your Instinctive Skill

www.SerengetiBook.com

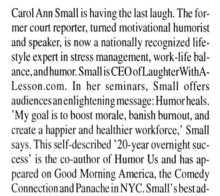

CSP SHERYL NICHOLSON
Tampa, FL United States
www.sheryl.com

Top Rated and Results Oriented Professional Speaker has shared the international platform with celebs and President Ford. CSP Sheryl Nicholson's expertise is published in Inc, Success, Entrepreneur, YM, Parents, Floral Management, Chicken Soup for the Soul, Recruiting Mag and many more. Often a TV and Radio Guest as a People Productivity Expert. Topics include sales, communication, life balance, leadership, and team building. Keynotes, workshops and in-house training. Highly recommended by clients and meeting planners.

CSP Sheryl Nicholson
Speaker Author Coach
Sheryl.com
Tampa, FL United States
Contact Phone: 727-678-6707
Cell: 727 678 6707
Click to Contact from Web Site

CAROL ANN SMALL -- LAUGHTER WITH A LESSON.COM
Boston, MA United States
www.LaughterWithaLesson.com

Carol Ann Small is having the last laugh. The former court reporter, turned motivational humorist and speaker, is now a nationally recognized lifestyle expert in stress management, work-life balance, and humor. Small is CEO of LaughterWithA-Lesson.com. In her seminars, Small offers audiences an enlightening message: Humor heals. 'My goal is to boost morale, banish burnout, and create a happier and healthier workforce,' Small says. This self-described '20-year overnight success' is the co-author of Humor Us and has appeared on Good Morning America, the Comedy Connection and Panache in NYC. Small's best advice for the perpetually stressed? 'Life's short. Buy the shoes!'

Carol Ann Small
Motivational Humorist /Stress Management Expert
Melrose, MA United States
Contact Phone: 781-662-2078
Click to Contact from Web Site

MIKKI WILLIAMS
Chicago, IL United States
www.MikkiWilliams.com

Mikki is the unexpected, a one-of-a-kind talent; eclectic, original, refreshing, outrageous and smart. She has a dynamic ability to communicate to an audience, delivering practical information in a down to earth style. Mikki will not only light a fire of enthusiasm, she helps audiences internalize all the materials so it doesn't wear off. 'Maximum learning occurs when the teaching is heart to heart, not head to head.' Mikki is a catalyst for change. She gets rave reviews and standing ovations for her spectacular presentations.

MIkki Williams
Chicago, IL United States
Contact Phone: 312-664-8477
Click to Contact from Web Site

GAYLE LANTZ - LEADERSHIP DEVELOPMENT EXPERT

Birmingham, AL United States
www.workmatters.com/

Gayle Lantz is an leadership development expert and executive coach who helps organizations improve performance. She provides organizational consulting, executive coaching and speaking services in areas related to leadership and career development, team improvement and cultural change. Clients include such organizations as NASA, Microsoft, Southern Company and BBVA Compass Bank. Her articles have been featured in a variety of business publications around the world. Gayle Lantz is author of 'Take the Bull by the Horns: The Busy Leader's Action Guide to Growing Your Business . . . and Yourself.'

Gayle Lantz
WorkMatters
Birmingham, AL United States
Contact Phone: 205 879-8494
Click to Contact from Web Site

CAROLYN SCHUR -- SLEEP AND FATIGUE MANAGEMENT

Saskatoon, Saskatoon Canada
www.alertatwork.com

Alert@Work Human Resource Services maximizes health, safety and performance through sleep and fatigue management. Carolyn Schur offers expertise about sleep, shiftwork, night owls and sleep disorders to organizations throughout Canada and the US. She has been quoted and interviewed by media around the world including The New York Times. Her publications include 'Birds of A Different Feather: Night Owls and Early Birds' and 'Working 'Round the Clock: Survival Guide for Shift and Night Workers.'

Carolyn Schur
Alert@Work Human Resource Services
Saskatoon, SK Canada
Contact Phone: 306-975-1165
Click to Contact from Web Site

MARY MURCOTT -- CUSTOMER SERVICE EXPERT

Ft. Worth, TX United States
http://www.novo1.com/about-us/management-team/

Mary Murcott, Chief Executive Officer Mary Murcott is the Chief Executive Officer of NOVO 1 and leads the company's efforts to support clients' business goals in building customer relationships and growing their brands. Before being appointed Chief Executive of NOVO 1 in 2010, Murcott was President and founder of her own company Performance Transformations, Inc. Prior to consulting she was SVP American Express and held executive positions at Budget Rent a Car and Ryder Trucks, DHL and Cox Communications. Murcott is an international keynote speaker and author of 'Driving Peak Sales Performance in Call Centers'.

Jack Wilkie
NOVO 1
Ft. Worth, TX United States
Contact Phone:
Click to Contact from Web Site

NANCY FRIEDMAN -- TELEPHONE DOCTOR
St. Louis, MO United States
http://www.telephonedoctor.com

HELL HATH NO FURY LIKE A CUSTOMER SCORNED. When Oprah, Fox News, CNN, The Today Show, Good Morning American, CBS This Morning, KMOX, KCMO, WJAR, WCCO, and a host of other radio & TV shows need an EXPERT on Customer Service & Communication Skills, they call on Nancy Friedman, The Telephone Doctor. YOU SHOULD TOO! Nancy is internationally recognized as a leading authority of customer service, sales and communication skills. She is the author of 6 best-selling books and the featured spokesperson in the popular Telephone Doctor DVD library series. She is a featured speaker at conferences and association meetings around the country. Her latest book -- How to Get Your Customers Swearing BY You and Not AT You -- is now available. Nancy is lively, humorous and always asked back! Pick a topic on customer service, sales or communications and bring Nancy on.

Nancy Friedman
President
Telephone Doctor
St. Louis, MO United States
Contact Phone: 314-291-1012
Click to Contact from Web Site

TERRY BROCK -- ACHIEVEMENT SYSTEMS
Orlando, FL United States
www.TerryBrock.com

Terry Brock is a leading expert in technology as it applies to marketing and growing a business' revenues. Different technologies work best in different industries, and Terry's wide range of experience, from multi-national corporations to one-person startups, and sensitivity to industry-specific needs, gives him the unique ability to precisely, concisely diagnose and deliver exactly what you or your company need most.

Terry Brock
Achievement Systems
Orlando, FL United States
Contact Phone: 407-363-0505
Click to Contact from Web Site

DON CROWTHER -- SOCIAL MEDIA AND INTERNET MARKETING EXPERT
Chicago, IL United States
www.doncrowther.com

Don Crowther helps companies make money online through social media and Internet marketing. Don is the author of the world's most successful social media training program, and is a popular speaker at marketing events. Don is regularly quoted by media in the areas of social media, Internet marketing, pay-per-click advertising, business blogging, search engines, internet success stories, marketing, public relations, branding, positioning, and advertising. Call Don, he'll help!

Don Crowther
President
DonCrowther.com
101PublicRelations.com
Racine, WI United States
Contact Phone: 262-639-2270
Contact Main Phone: 262-639-2270
Cell: 262-880-1362
Click to Contact from Web Site

HELL HATH NO FURY LIKE A CUSTOMER SCORNED

When Oprah, Fox News, CNN, The Today Show, ABC's Good Morning America, CBS This Morning, KMOX, KCMO, WJAR, WCCO and a host of other radio and TV shows need an expert on customer service and communication skills, they call on Nancy Friedman, The Telephone Doctor® .

YOU SHOULD, TOO!

Nancy is internationally recognized as a leading authority of customer service and communication skills. She is the author of five best-selling books and the featured spokesperson in the popular Telephone Doctor DVD library series.

She is a featured speaker at conferences and association meetings around the country.

Her latest book, *The Good The Bad & The Ugly* (With

Apologies to Clint Eastwood) is now available.

Nancy is lively, humorous and always asked back! Pick a topic on customer service or communications and bring Nancy on. Cell phones, email, voice mail, automated attendants, telemarketers, pet peeves . . . and more.

For an interview, call her in St. Louis -- 314-291-1012.

Nancy Friedman, The Telephone Doctor®

www.TelephoneDoctor.com   Nancy@TelephoneDoctor.com

314-291-1012

JENNIFER ABERNETHY-- SOCIAL MEDIA MARKETING
Washington, DC United States
www.TheSalesLounge.com

Pull up a chair and grab your favorite drink and spend some time on the site. Become an 'insider' immediately by subscribing above for your complimentary subscription to my weekly Success * Sales * Social Media award-winning ezine, which will help you right away. Also, check out The Sales Lounge Insider Club™; a five-tiered membership site where I will unlock and lift the velvet rope and welcome you with more in depth materials and support to elevate your business and personal brand. I trust you will find a membership level that is perfect for you and it all starts from an affordable $9.97 per month!

Jennifer Abernethy
The Sales Lounge
Ashburn, VA United States
Contact Phone: 571-223-3887
Click to Contact from Web Site

TOM ANTION -- INTERNET MARKETING EXPERT
Virginia Beach, VA United States
http://www.GreatInternetMarketing.com

Tom Antion, Internet Marketing Expert, will show your audience how to keep from bludgeoning, kicking, cursing, shooting, slapping, spitting on and generally wanting to dismember the people who are supposed to be helping them with their websites. Tom is an internationally acclaimed expert in Internet Marketing for small business who actually makes large sums of money on the Internet. He's not giving book reports, theories or untested ideas like most of the other media hounds who never made a nickel selling anything on the Internet.

Tom Antion
Antion and Associates
Virginia Beach, VA United States
Contact Phone: 757-431-1366
Click to Contact from Web Site

MOHAMMAD BAHARETH
Jeddah, Saudi Arabia
www.bahareth.info

Subliminal Marketing Expert - Author - Business Person - Think Tank - Activist - Social Media Celebrity

Mohammad Bahareth
CEO
Bahareth Enterprises
Jeddah, Saudi Arabia
Contact Phone: +966550559876
Cell: +966550559876
Click to Contact from Web Site

Tom Antion

Internet Money-Making Expert

Tom Antion will show your audience members how to keep from bludgeoning, kicking, cursing, shooting, slapping, spitting on and generally wanting to dismember the people who are supposed to be helping them with their Web sites.

Tom is an internationally acclaimed expert in Internet marketing for small business who actually makes large sums of money on the Internet. He's not giving book reports, theories or untested ideas like most of the other media hounds who never made a nickel selling anything on the Internet.

Big business owners and CEOs aren't too thrilled with Tom when he tells them what morons they are for spending millions of dollars on things that can be done for a few hundred. They really hate it when they find out that Tom got "Best-of-the-Web" in INC. magazine on a site that cost only $650 to create. This site beat out three others that cost more than one million dollars each to create.

Tom has been featured on major news media worldwide, including the Canadian Broadcast Network, the Australian Broadcast Network, Associated Press, the Tokyo Today Show and hundreds of radio, television and print outlets across the United States, including four feature articles in the Washington Post.

Whether in a print or broadcast medium Tom is totally focused on your audience and he knows his job is to give them great tips that will help them succeed, while making you look great for interviewing him. He was media trained by Joel Roberts.

Tom was also the chief spokesperson for CBS-owned Switchboard.com in their "Main Streets Online" outreach program for small business. Switchboard is one of the largest and most heavily visited Web sites on the Internet. Tom beat out thousands of book-learned Ph.D.'s and other pseudo experts for the job.

Tom consistently makes large sums of money while sitting in front of his computer which gave him the idea for his infamous "Butt Camp" Seminars where you learn to make more money sitting on your rear end than going out and working for a living.

ANTION & ASSOCIATES
Box 9558
Virginia Beach, Va. 23450
(757) 431-1366   (800) 448-6280
(Continental USA Only)

Fax: (757) 431-2050   orders@antion.com

INTERNET MARKETING TRAINING CENTER OF VIRGINIA
Virginia Beach, VA United States
http://www.IMTCVA.org

JENNIFER BEEVER -- ONLINE MARKETING - SOCIAL MEDIA EXPERT
Los Angeles, CA United States
http://www.NewIncite.com

The founder of New Incite, Jennifer Beever is the "CMO for Hire" for B2B companies cross-industry with particular focus on technology, green and manufacturing businesses. Jennifer analyzes clients' current marketing situations, plans new marketing programs, and executes the marketing to drive lead and revenue generation. She then sets up results-tracking systems to measure marketing return on investment. Jennifer is an Inbound Marketing Certified Professional, a Certified Management Consultant (CMC) with the Institute of Management Consultants USA, and the author of the B2B Marketing Traction blog.

Jennifer Beever, CMC
CMO for Hire
New Incite
Woodland Hills, CA United States
Contact Phone: 818-347-4248
Cell: 818-347-4248
Click to Contact from Web Site

The Internet Marketing Training Center of Virginia was founded by Small Business Internet Marketing Expert Tom Antion to provide credible training to 1. High school graduates who do not want to attend a traditional college program, 2. People who have been displaced from their job and need a new and highly salable career skill quickly and 3. Small to medium size business owners who want to increase their web presence at a much lower cost by bringing many of the everyday Internet tasks needed in house.

Tom Antion
Internet Marketing Training Center of Virginia
Virginia Beach, VA United States
Contact Phone: 757-431-1366
Cell: 301-346-7403
Click to Contact from Web Site

JEFF KORHAN -- SOCIAL MEDIA FOR SMALL BUSINESS
Chicago, IL United States
www.jeffkorhan.com

Jeff Korhan is a new media marketer and a top-ranked blogger who helps small businesses maximize their Web visibility, reputation, and referrals with social media and Internet marketing. As a social media speaker, consultant, and coach, Jeff applies three decades of marketing experience and an MBA with a special skill for simplifying technology and complex ideas to make them practical and useful for small businesses. Jeff is a former Small Business of the Year owner and a recognized social media expert whose New Media and Small Business Marketing blog is ranked a Top 100 Small Business blog by Technorati.

Jeff Korhan
CEO
JeffKorhan
Naperville, IL United States
Contact Phone: 630-774-8350
Cell: 630-774-8350
Click to Contact from Web Site

TOM NARDONE -- ONLINE PRIVACY EXPERT
Detroit, MI United States
http://www.PriveCo.com

Tom Nardone invented a unique business that allows people to shop in private for embarrassing products. His company now operates 12 retail websites that sell interesting personal items. Over 700,000 customers in more than 70 countries trust him with their deepest secrets. Some customers shop in private to cure hemorrhoids, bad breath, acne, incontinence, and even sexual dysfunction. Others want to keep information about their personal and sex lives private. PriveCo holds everyone's information in the strictest of confidence.

Tom Nardone
President
PriveCo.com
PriveCo Inc.
Troy, MI United States
Contact Phone: 248-457-6874
Contact Main Phone: 248-457-6874
Click to Contact from Web Site

CHAD NELSON -- CHAMPION ONLINE MARKETING
Sacramento, CA United States
www.ChampionOnlineMarketing.com

Champion Online Marketing is a premier internet and digital marketing company. The founder, Chad Nelson, is an expert in internet marketing, has a degree in Managerial Economics from U.C. Davis and has been a successful entrepreneur for over 14 years. Chad's expertise lies in helping local businesses get more customers through the internet and other digital marketing strategies such as mobile text marketing, social media and mobile websites. Chad's expertise, real world experience, education and ability to explain complex marketing strategies so the average, non-expert person can understand them make him an ideal person to speak to on the topic.

Chad Nelson
President
Champion Online Marketing
Folsom, CA United States
Contact Phone: 916-467-9482
Cell: 619-253-8884
Click to Contact from Web Site

ONLINE MARKETING IN A BOX - OFFLINE - ONLINE MARKETING STRATEGIES
Las Vegas, NV United States
OnLineMarketingInABox.com

'Online Marketing In A Box' provides online and online marketing strategies & solutions for businesses. As small business owners themselves since 1994, they know how to measure marketing key metrics and campaigns to get the best results. They combine that experience with best practices and lessons learned from over 20 years of consulting from small companies to Fortune 100 companies to ensure success. Services include mobile technology, social media, websites, search engine optimization (SEO) and fostering communities of loyal customers. Call today to get started.

Kim Snyder & Rob Snyder
Founders
Online Marketing in a Box
Las Vegas, NV United States
Contact Phone: 702-430-1689
Cell: 702-308-4466
Click to Contact from Web Site

THE ONLINE PRIVACY FOUNDATION (OPF)
London, United Kingdom
OnlinePrivacyFoundation.org

The Online Privacy Foundation (OPF) are a small group of expert volunteers who want to raise awareness of online privacy issues through topical research and awareness raising activities. The OPF want to empower people so they can make informed choices about how they use the internet. The foundation, originating out of Basingstoke (near London) in the United Kingdom formed in 2009 after one of the co-founders, Chris Sumner, a computer security professional, had been asked to talk about Computer Security in his local community and identified a clear gap. The foundations mission is to promote safer and more streetwise internet use within the community and push for easier to understand privacy and safety controls.

Chris Sumner
The Online Privacy Foundation (OPF)
Basingstoke, Other United Kingdom
Contact Phone: Prefers Email
Click to Contact from Web Site

DEBBIE WEIL -- CORPORATE BLOGGING EXPERT
Washington, DC United States
http://www.BlogWriteForCEOs.com

Wondering what in heck the blogging buzz is about? Ask Debbie Weil. She is a corporate social media and blogging consultant to clients, such as GlaxoSmithKline, the American College of Radiology and DeVries PR. She is the author of one of the first and most widely praised books about business blogging: 'The Corporate Blogging Book' (Portfolio 2006). She blogs at www.debbieweil.com/blog.

Debbie Weil
WordBiz.com, Inc.
Washington, DC United States
Contact Phone: 202-333-2022
Cell: 202-255-1467
Click to Contact from Web Site

DAVID M. RICH -- EXPERIENCE MARKETING
Boston, MA United States
www.gpj.com/

We create Experience Marketing. We break down walls. And build relationships. After all, audiences today don't see channels, time zones, impressions or conversions. They see (and seek) products and services that fit their needs. Functionally, financially, culturally and socially. A relationship. Person to person, company to customer, brand to buyer, we've been breaking down the walls between clients and their audiences around the world since 1914.

David M. Rich
George P. Johnson Experience Marketing
Boston, MA United States
Contact Phone: 617-535-9822
Click to Contact from Web Site

FREE TECH SUPPORT

BOB RANKIN -- TECH SUPPORT EXPERT
New York, NY United States
http://askbobrankin.com/

Bob Rankin is a technology writer and computer programmer who enjoys exploring the Internet and sharing the fruit of his experience with others. His work has appeared in ComputerWorld, NY Newsday, and other publications. Bob is publisher of Internet TOURBUS, author of several computer books, operator of Flowers Fast! and creator of the Lowfat Linux tutorial.

Bob Rankin
Publisher
Doctor Bob Publications
Airmont, NY United States
Contact Phone: 914-474-5876
Click to Contact from Web Site

TECHNOLYTICS -- STRATEGIC ISSUES
Pittsburgh, PA United States
www.Technolytics.com

The Technolytics Institute (Technolytics) was established in 2000 as an independent executive think-tank. Our primary purpose is to undertake original research and develop substantive points of view on strategic issues facing executives in businesses, government and industry around the world. Our strategic goals focus on improving business performance, creating sustainable competitive advantage, delivering innovation and technology, and managing security. We operate three centers: [Business & Commerce] - [Security & Intelligence] and [Science & Technology].

Public Relations
PR/Marketing
Technolytics
McMurray, PA United States
Contact Phone: 412-760-2773
Contact Main Phone: 888-650-0800
Click to Contact from Web Site

JEFF ALLAN -- MOBILE TECH BUSINESS EXPERT
Tokyo, Japan
www.caferefugee.com/the-people/

Jeff Allan is a global business developer and mobile technology authority. He frequently appears online, in print and on television for outlets that include AOL, Nikkei and CNBC. Jeff's expertise is in the area of emerging technologies and applications that harness the latest in mobile computing devices. He is an authority across most major smart phone and tablet platforms.

Jeff Allan
Cafe Refugee, Inc.
Tokyo, Japan
Contact Phone: 6034997415
Click to Contact from Web Site

CCRadio-2 — AM · FM · WEATHER with
The radio designed for long-range AM Reception

C.CRANE --- RADIO ANTENNA EXPERTS
San Francisco, CA United States
www.CCrane.com

For nearly 30 years, C. Crane has been a hometown company with a hometown way of doing business. That means we take the time to listen to our customers, and enjoy hearing your feedback on our radios, flashlights, garden tools or anything else. We cherish your trust and confidence in our staff and in our products, and we look forward to sharing with you some of the best things we've found — and even designed — to enhance your lives. We hope you enjoy browsing our newly updated website. We're looking forward to serving you.

Jessica Gillette
C.Crane
Fortuna, CA United States
Contact Phone: 707-725-0568
Click to Contact from Web Site

Hilco Industrial, LLC
Auctioneers · Liquidators · Appraisers

HILCO INDUSTRIAL. LLC -- EXPERTS IN INDUSTRIAL MACHINERY AUCTIONS
Detroit, MI United States
www.HilcoInd.com

Hilco Industrial, LLC is a member of the Hilco Trading Co. family of companies and the industry leader in helping companies around the world unlock the hidden value in their underutilized assets. Hilco Industrial, which participates in auctions, liquidations and acquisitions, includes Hilco Industrial Online, Hilco Industrial Europe, Hilco-Bid and Hilco Acetec Mexico. Our auctions and liquidations include machinery and equipment from various industries, including automotive, metalworking, plastics, power generation, high tech, construction, food and beverage processing, and countless more. Our expertise allows to find the most qualified buyers for assets in any field.

Marsha Fales-Wright
Vice President of Marketing
Hilco Industrial, LLC
Farmington Hills, IL United States
Contact Phone: 248-254-9999
Click to Contact from Web Site

IPHONE APP MARKETING, APP REVIEW, IPHONE APP PUBLICITY
Plymouth, MI United States
www.iphoneapppublicity.com

With hundreds of thousands of iPhone and Droid apps available for sale how can any Smartphone App developer get traction with their app? It's simple: Publicity. As a publicist, Scott Lorenz has promoted dozens of Apps and hundreds of products and services using publicity. Apps are becoming so important to our society that the media MUST report on ones that are of interest to their audience. To get the media's attention you need someone who deals with the news media on a daily basis. Learn more about Westwind iPhone App Publicity at http://www.iPhoneAppPublicity. com or contact Lorenz at scottlorenz@iPhoneAppPublicity.com

Scott Lorenz
Publicist
iPhone App Publicity
Plymouth, MI United States
Contact Phone: 734-667-2090
Contact Main Phone: 734-667-2090
Cell: 734-667-2090
Click to Contact from Web Site

STEPHANIE DIAMOND -- MARKETING MESSAGE EXPERT
New York, NY United States
www.marketingmessageblog.com

Stephanie Diamond founder of Digital Media Works, Inc. is a seasoned 25+ year management/marketing professional with experience building profits in a broad range of product and services businesses. She has demonstrated experience in marketing, product development, e-commerce, project management and operations. She worked for eight years as Marketing Director at AOL. When she joined AOL there were less than 1 million subscribers. When she left in 2002 there were 36 million. As she likes to say, 'a lot happened to the Internet in between.' She created a highly successful line of multimedia software products that sold millions of copies for America Online and has developed unique business strategies and products for a variety of companies. She has worked for such media companies as AOL Time Warner, Redgate New Media and Newsweek, Inc.

Stephanie Diamond
New York, NY United States
Contact Phone: 914-765-0720
Click to Contact from Web Site

TIM FERRISS - PRODUCTIVITY,DIGITAL LIFESTYLES AND ENTREPRENEURSHIP
San Francisco, CA United States
http://www.fourhourworkweek.com/blog

Serial entrepreneur and ultravagabond TIM FERRISS has been featured by dozens of media, including The New York Times, National Geographic Traveler, NBC, and MAXIM. He speaks six languages, runs a multinational firm from wireless locations worldwide, and has been a popular guest lecturer at Princeton University since 2003, where he presents entrepreneurial thinking (even as an employee) as a tool for ideal lifestyle design and world change. The 4-Hour Workweek(www.fourhourworkweek.com) is his first book and magnum opus. He is 29 years old.

Tim Ferriss
Author, Princeton University Guest Lecturer
Random House/Crown Publishing
San Francisco, CA United States
Contact Phone:
Click to Contact from Web Site

GARY ROSENZWEIG -- GAME DEVELOPER - APPLE EXPERT
Denver, CO United States
http://clevermedia.com

Gary Rosenzweig is an expert in web-based game development and Apple products. He has written 15 technology books including ActionScript 3.0 Game Programming University, the MacMost. com Guide to Switching to the Mac and My iPad. His company, CleverMedia, Inc., develops and publishes game web sites. Some of its largest sites are GameScene.com, JustSolitaire.com and JustJigsawPuzzles.com. In addition, CleverMedia also produces and publishes the MacMost Now video podcast and MacMost.com site. This is a web site for Apple enthusiasts with tutorials, tips and news. CleverMedia also produces iPhone game apps.

Gary Rosenzweig
CEO
CleverMedia, Inc.
Denver, CO United States
Contact Phone: 720-381-3040
Click to Contact from Web Site

INSTITUTE FOR SOCIAL INTERNET PUBLIC POLICY
Boulder, CO United States
http://www.ISIPP.com/

Our SuretyMail Email Accreditation Program is helping hundreds of companies deliver nearly 2 billion emails a month, and we can help you, too!

SuretyMail
Boulder, CO United States
Contact Phone: 800-759-3818
Contact Main Phone: 800-759-3818
Click to Contact from Web Site

KEVIN SAVETZ -- FREE PRINTABLES
Portland, OR United States
www.SavetzPublishing.com

FORD SAEKS - BUSINESS GROWTH - INTERNET MARKETING - MARKETING
Wichita, KS United States
http://www.ProfitRichResults.com

As one of the worlds' 'Top Business Growth Experts', Ford Saeks specializes in helping organizations find, attract and keep customers through innovative Internet Marketing & Social Media Marketing campaigns. He is the 'go-to' guy when you want to increase targeted lead generation that converts into sales and profits. He has helped thousands of people monetize their websites and social media networking efforts implementing strategies that produce measurable results. Audiences love Ford's interactive approach, fun style and action-oriented focus that allows participants to leave with ideas and action steps that they can implement to produce immediate results.

Ford Saeks
Business Growth Expert
Prime Concepts Group, Inc.
Media Relations and Booking
Wichita, KS United States
Contact Phone: 316-942-1111
Contact Main Phone: 800-946-7804
Cell: 316-207-6718
Click to Contact from Web Site

Kevin Savetz is owner of Savetz Publishing, a company that creates high-quality, content-driven web sites. His more than 90 sites include FreePrintable. net, which offers free business cards, certificates, and other printable documents; and FaxZero.com, a service that lets users send free faxes throughout the U.S. and Canada.

Kevin Savetz
Portland, OR United States
Contact Phone:
Cell: (707) 400-6360
Click to Contact from Web Site

LOREN STOCKER -- 800 NUMBER EXPERT
Los Angeles, CA United States
www.800.Net

Vanity International is the world's premier vanity design firm. We specialize in an emerging area of strategic marketing that can directly increase sales: flawless recall of advertised toll-free numbers and Internet domains. We create Magnetic Brands! We work directly with you and your agency to create and implement an enduring contact strategy. In the process, we provide the highly specialized creative, in-depth research and, ultimately, acquisition of desired vanity numbers and Internet domains-- all without disclosing the actual use or identity of the buyers. We've worked with many Fortune 500 companies and have created and acquired the numbers used for the official catalogs of the NBA, NHL, and other well known promotions including 1-800-Blue-Martini, 1-800-Go-eToys, 1-800-Privacy, 1-800-Jenny-2000, 1-800-No-Load-1 and many, many others. Vanity International maintains direct, real-time access to the North American toll-free registry (SMS/800) and to the Internet Domain Registry.

Loren C. Stocker
Vanity International
Del Mar, CA United States
Contact Phone: 858-792-5000
Click to Contact from Web Site

IRV SCHWARY -- ZENTIREMENT
New Orleans, LA United States
www.zentireman.com

Zentirement ® The Book - coming in 2013. Remember the passion you had when you were a child; renew that passion for success, happiness and meaning. Live the fullest life before and after retirement. Retirement is more than just leaving your job or profession and sitting on a rocker. Follow Zentire Man on Social Media. Work Hard Play Hard Livelife ®

Irv Schwary
Zentire Man
Metairie, LA United States
Contact Phone: 504-837-4025
Click to Contact from Web Site

DOLLARSMARTKIDS ENTERPRISES INC.- FINANCIAL PRODUCTS FOR FAMILIES
Kelowna, British Columbia Canada
www.zelawelakids.com

Nancy Phillips is the author and creator of the Zela Wela Kids financial story books and products. As the founder of DollarSmartKids Enterprises Inc., Nancy's mission is to help create a financially literate society by providing families with resources that help parents teach their children essential personal financial and life success skills. Nancy has an Honors Bachelor of Science degree in Kinesiology and an Executive Master of Business Administration degree. While working in the corporate world for almost twenty years, she held positions in product development, portfolio management and international business.

Ms. Nancy Phillips, HBSc., EMBA
Founder and President
DollarSmartKids Enterprises Inc.
Kelowna, BC Canada
Contact Phone: 250-864-9419
Click to Contact from Web Site

MARVIN H. DONIGER -- FINANCIAL SECURITY EXPERT
Los Angeles, CA United States
booksbydoniger.com/

Marvin H. Doniger, has been an avid investor since his early teens. His perspectives have been developed from his lifelong study of investing, his actual experiences as a registered representative, an individual investor, and as a management consultant to Fortune 500 companies. He is the author of A Common Sense Road Map to Uncommon Wealth, which is a treatise on managing careers and finances, A Common Sense Approach to Successful Investing, in which he first introduced stratamentical analysis, a unique approach for identifying long-term investment opportunities, and Common Sense Prescriptions for Financial Health which presents quaestrology, a unique perspective on managing one's finances. Mr. Doniger received his MBA from Columbia University Graduate School of Business and his BSME from Tufts University. He has taught undergraduate and graduate level courses in production control, inventory management, information technology and finance at Fitchburg State College and Webster University.

Marvin H. Doniger
Doniger & Associates
Laguna Niguel, CA United States
Contact Phone: 949-661-5456
Click to Contact from Web Site

INSTITUTE OF CONSUMER FINANCIAL EDUCATION
San Diego, CA United States
http://www.financial-education-icfe.org

The ICFE, established in 1982, is the nation's only nonprofit organization training and certifying professionals with CE courses in Identity Theft Risk Management, Credit Report Reviewing, Personal Finance Instruction, Make Your Move (a home buying course) and Reverse Mortgage Specialists world-wide. The ICFE's Certificants in turn educate and motivate consumers of all ages on how to improve their spending practices, increase their savings accumulation and use credit safely more wisely. The ICFE is an Official Partner with the Department of Defense in the Financial Readiness Campaign since 2004. In 2011, the ICFE introduced Anti-RFID credit/debit card sleeves to prevent electronic

Paul Richard
President
Institute of Consumer Financial Education
San Diego, CA United States
Contact Phone: 619.239.1401
Click to Contact from Web Site

WILLIAM E. DONOGHUE -- THE FATHER OF SAFE MONEY INVESTING
Boston, MA United States
http://www.donoghue.com

National (registered in all 50 states) SEC Registered Investment Advisors, proactive separate account asset managers, and retirement savings, IRAs, Roth IRAs, tax-managed accounts, mutual fund separate accounts, variable annuities and variable insurance sub-accounts, managed separate accounts of Exchanged-traded fund (ETFs), high-return low-risk five-star- rated separate accounts, Power Income Portfolio, Power Sector Portfolio, independent broker-dealers and financial advisors, proactive asset managers managing portfolios of ETFs and mutual funds.

William E. Donoghue
Chairman
W. E. Donoghue Co., Inc.
Healdsburg, CA United States
Contact Phone: 707-395-0147
Contact Main Phone: 800-642-4276
Cell: 206-954-4762
Click to Contact from Web Site

MATT HARRISON -- THE PROMETHEUS INSTITUTE -- A PUBLIC POLICY ORGANIZATION
Los Angeles, CA United States
www.ThePrometheusInstitute.org

The Prometheus Institute is a public policy organization dedicated to discovering independent policy solutions to pressing national issues, and creatively marketing these ideas to the people of the United States, especially the younger generations. Existing policy organizations generally seek to forward their ideas through elite scholarship and occasional congressional testimony, but rarely through popular means. The Prometheus Institute is the first public policy organization dedicated to utilizing the power of marketing to empower the citizenry with the tools and knowledge to advocate for policy change. Through issue-oriented initiatives and other innovative programs, the Institute is constantly pursuing public policy advocacy.

Scott Lorenz
Publicist
Westwind Communications Public Relations
Plymouth, MI United States
Contact Phone: 734-667-2090
Cell: 248-705-2214
Click to Contact from Web Site

William E. Donoghue

"Proactive Fund Investing Guru"

Proactive Fund Investing Advocate Manager

Today's volatile markets demonstrate that traditional "Buy and Hold" strategies alone are unlikely to be effective. Donoghue's proactive investing strategies seek to earn high-return, low-risk returns by avoiding known risks and diversifying to reduce unknown risks.

A mutual fund expert for 43 years, an asset manager for 20 years and a proactive sector fund and ETF portfolio manager for 10 years, Donoghue offers innovative portfolios, using Sector Rotation, Long/Short Investing, Power Income and Tactical Growth strategies in taxable, potentially tax-free and tax-deferred accounts.

William E. Donoghue
Chairman, W. E. Donoghue & Co., Inc.
Registered Investment Advisors
260 N. Main Street
Natick, Massachusetts 01760
800-642-4276

Chairman's Office: 206-281-8188
(Seattle)
or 206-954-4762 (Cell)

www.donoghue.com
guru@donoghue.com

SHARON B. JONES -- PERSONAL FINANCE EXPERT
Upper Marlboro, MD United States
http://www.SharonBJones.com

Sharon B Jones is a personal finance expert, educator and motivational speaker. She is known as the 'financial life coach' with an inspiring message on how to get financially fit and live joyfully ever after. Jones led customer-focused coaches' clinics for financial business leaders. She is recognized by the President's Advisory Council on Financial Literacy for co-facilitating the first White House Roundtable on Financial Literacy and national initiatives to advance financial literacy in America.

Sharon B. Jones
Personal Finance Expert
Capitol Heights, MD United States
Contact Phone: 301-943-9169
Click to Contact from Web Site

BELINDA ROSENBLUM -- OWN YOUR MONEY LLC
Boston, MA United States
http://www.ownyourmoney.com/

Belinda Rosenblum, CPA is helping thousands of people discover how 'owning your money' creates certainty, security, and the life of financial independence they deserve. Belinda is the President of OwnYourMoney.com, a financial coaching and education company teaching individuals, couples and business owners how to make personal finance and small business success rewarding, manageable, and profitable. Belinda's ability to inspire action in others is fueled by her passion for helping people appreciate their self-worth and realize their financial goals.

Amanda Troisi
Executive Assistant
Own Your Money LLC
Littleton, MA United States
Contact Phone: 855-866-6398
Click to Contact from Web Site

JEFF HARRIS -- INDEPENDENT PENSION CONSULTANT
York, SC United States
www.jeffharrisria.com/

Jeff Harris an Independent Pension Consultant in York, SC. Says: 'For millions of Americans retirement dreams have turned into a hopeless nightmare.' He's part of an elite group of professionals who've earned the Accredited Investment Fiduciary Analyst® (AIFA) professional designation through The Wharton Business School in San Francisco, CA. In his new book, 'Rays of Hope for Shattered Dreams: A Simple Fix for 401(k)s', he outlines a step-by-step process designed to help Americans get their retirement plans back on track. Mr. Harris has been featured in Readers Digest (Dec 07), The Wall St. Journal (July 09).

Jeffrey B. Harris
Senior Partner
Jeff Harris & Associates, Inc
York, SC United States
Contact Phone: 803-684-1075
Cell: 803-487-7103
Click to Contact from Web Site

C. LEO SCHIKHOF - FATCA, IMPACTS AND IMPLEMENTATION

Zurich, Switzerland
www.linkedin.com/profile/view?id=
39622842&trk=tab_pro

Leo Schikhof is an expert in the increasingly important Legal & Compliance area in the Financial Industry. Currently focusing on Fatca, he assists financial institutions in assessing its impact and compiling the strategic and operational considerations as regards this American legislation. He has over 25 years of experience in Financial Services, is qualified in English law and resides in Europe.

C. Leo Schikhof
none
Uster, Switzerland
Contact Phone: +41798487183
Cell: +41 79 8487183
Click to Contact from Web Site

GREG WOMACK -- CERTIFIED FINANCIAL PLANNER

Oklahoma City, OK United States
http://www.womackadvisers.com

For 25 years, Greg Womack has been an active professional in the financial services industry. His business experience teamed with his simple, yet dynamic, delivery of financial core concepts makes him a great guest speaker for any organization. Greg is a certified financial planner (CFP) and serves as President and Principal of Womack Investment Advisers, Inc. (WIA), an independent registered investment advisory firm registered with the Securities Exchange Commission. His practice focuses on providing clients with a wide range of planning services, with an emphasis on investment management and fee-based planning.

Greg Womack, CFP
President
Womack Investment Advisers
Edmond, OK United States
Contact Phone: 405-340-1717
Click to Contact from Web Site

JK HARRIS AND COMPANY, LLC -- TAX PROBLEMS AND SOLUTIONS

Charleston, SC United States
www.jkharris.com

JK Harris & Company, based in Goose Creek, S.C., is the nation's largest tax representation company and can meet with customers, by appointment only, in over 325 locations nationwide. JK Harris also provides services for tax return preparation, and audit representation.

Gina Anton
Director of Corporate Communications
JK Harris and Company, LLC
Goose Creek, SC United States
Contact Phone: 843-576-2255
Contact Main Phone: 843-576-2255
Cell: 843-729-6630
Click to Contact from Web Site

JOHNSON JACOBSON WILCOX CPAS
Las Vegas, NV United States
jjwcpa.com

Founded in 1995, Johnson Jacobson Wilcox is a firm that thinks way outside all those little boxes on a spreadsheet. It's their job to not only know their business and the ins and outs of clients' businesses, but to also maintain an objective perspective so they can help them make strategic business decisions. To learn more go to www.jjwcpa.com.

ImageWords
Las Vegas, NV United States
Contact Phone: 702-255-8288
Click to Contact from Web Site

STANLEY M. BURNSTEIN -- TAX PLANNING EXPERT
Kansas City, MO United States

Career Overview: From 1962 to 1966, Stanley Burnstein was a member of the tax department of Arthur Andersen & Co. providing tax planning for business owners, high net worth inpiduals, trusts, and estates. Stanley lectures extensively throughout the country to business and professional organizations, and counsels family-owned businesses and investors. Stanley has a talent for explaining very technical subjects in an understandable manner.

Brad Butler
Hollywood, CA United States
Contact Phone: 323-461-3921
Click to Contact from Web Site

THE BABY BOOMERS RETIREMENT NETWORK (BBRN) -- RICHARD ROLL
Stamford, CT United States
www.mybbrc.com

BBRN Chairman Richard J. Roll is a nationally known consumer finances expert, Harvard MBA, and best-selling author (with Hugh Downs) in the field of retirement planning. As an energetic guest and an acknowledged expert/thought leader on Baby Boomer retirement issues, he has been interviewed by hundreds of the nation's leading media such as CNBC, MSNBC, Money Magazine and Forbes. Richard is available for interviews and quotes pertaining to all areas Baby Boomers are facing today from fitness to finance and everything in between. In his new book, The 7 Rules of Retirement.

Richard Roll
Chairman
Stamford, CT United States
Contact Phone: 203-253-7077
Contact Main Phone: 203-253-7077
Cell: 203-253-7077
Click to Contact from Web Site

Greg Womack, CFP
Financial Expert

Greg Womack, a 20-year veteran in the financial services industry is a certified financial planner™ (CFP®) and president of Womack Investment Advisers, Inc., an independent, registered investment advisory firm. He is an active member of his community and a 19-year member of the Rotary Club of Edmond/Central.

He is the author of "Wisdom & Wealth: A Christian's Guide to Managing Your Life and Finances," and has been quoted in USA Today, Barron's, The Wall Street Journal, U.S.News & World Report, TheStreet.com and appearances on CNBC. Womack is also a member of the Ed Slott Elite Advisor's Network. (For more info, visit www.irahelp.com.)

About the firm:

Womack Investment Advisers, Inc., is an independent investment advisory firm, registered with the U.S. Securities and Exchange Commission (SEC). It provides fee-based investment management and financial planning services. It also provides comprehensive wealth management to help unite clients with their life goals.

Visit www.womackadvisers.com for more information. Greg Womack is a registered principal and representative with Cambridge Investment Research, Inc. (CIR), member SIPC/FINRA. Womack and CIR are non-affiliated companies.

Create   Preserve   Continue

Greg Womack, CFP
Womack Investment Advisers
1366 East 15th Street
Edmond, Oklahoma
73013

WOMACK
INVESTMENT ADVISERS
PLAN FOR LIFE. PLAN FOR WEALTH.

www.WomackAdvisers.com

greg@womackadvisers.com

Media contact,
Amber Johnson:

Phone: 405-340-1717
Fax: 405-340-6091

amber@womackadvisers.com

CHRIS COOPER, CFP, EA -- FEE-ONLY FINANCIAL PLANNER
San Diego, CA United States
www.chriscooper.com

Chris Cooper, a California Licensed Professional Fiduciary #615, is the owner and founder of Chris Cooper & Company, Inc., a fee-only financial planning firm working with people who own small businesses, with persons preparing to retire, and very elderly persons. Chris provides counseling and guidance in the areas of investments, taxation, and estate preservation. As a practitioner he invests and manages money, does personal and business tax returns and representation, and comprehensive financial planning consultations. Chris is also the founder and president of ElderCare Advocates, a free standing, long term care consultancy.

Chris Cooper, CFP, EA
Chris Cooper & Company
San Diego, CA United States
Contact Phone: 800-352-7674
Click to Contact from Web Site

KATHLEEN BURNS KINGSBURY, WEALTH PSYCHOLOGY EXPERT
Boston, MA United States
http://www.kbkwealthconnection.com

Wealth Psychology Expert, Internationally Published Author, Columnist, Graduate Business School Professor and Founder, KBK Wealth Connection. She has a Master's Degree in psychology, a Bachelor's Degree in Finance and is an expert on facilitating intergenerational wealth conversations, raising financially literate children, advising couples and women and wealth. She is a licensed counselor and accredited coach. Her third book, How To Give Financial Advice to Women: Attracting and Retaining High-Net-Worth Female Clients (McGraw-Hill, 2012) is based on her 20 years of experience inspiring professionals and clients to make positive behavioral changes to improve their health and their wealth. Contact 617-803-6046.

Kathleen Burns Kingsbury
Wealth Psychology Expert
KBK Wealth Connection
Easton, MA United States
Contact Phone: 617-803-6046
Cell: 617-803-6046
Click to Contact from Web Site

SUSAN MANGIERO, PH.D., CFA, FRM AIFA -- BUSINESS CONSULTANT
New York, NY United States
www.GoodRiskGovernancePays.com

Dr. Susan Mangiero, CFA, FRM, AIFA has over 20 years of experience in the areas of investment best practices, risk management and valuation. She has served as an expert witness, testified before the ERISA Advisory Council, OECD and the International Organization of Pension Supervisors on the topics of hedge fund and derivatives-related risk management and valuation. She served as the risk management expert on the World Bank team on behalf of the Chilean pension regulator. She authored Risk Management for Pensions, Endowments and Foundations and is the creator of www.PensionRiskMatters.com and www.GoodRiskGovernancePays.com.

Susan Mangiero
FTI Consulting
New York, NY United States
Contact Phone: 646-453-1241
Cell: 203-400-8176
Click to Contact from Web Site

JONATHAN M. BERGMAN, CFP, EA - FINANCIAL ADVISOR

Scarsdale, NY United States
PalisadesHudson.com

As chief investment officer and chairman of the firm's investment committee, Jonathan M. Bergman, CFP®, EA, directs a team of portfolio managers and associates focused on finding the most efficient and cost-effective ways to implement client portfolio strategies. He oversees more than $1 billion in client assets, including all aspects of investment strategy, portfolio management, due diligence, and manager selection. He is also expert in estate planning and income and estate tax.

Henry Stimpson
Stimpson Communications
Wayland, MA United States
Contact Phone: 508 647 0705
Click to Contact from Web Site

MIKE BONACORSI, CFP® -- CERTIFIED FINANCIAL PLANNER ™

Boston, MA United States
http://MikeBonacorsi.com

Mike Bonacorsi is president of Mike Bonacorsi, LLC, a financial planning and wealth management firm. He is a Professional Speaker addressing the Baby Boomer generation, author of the book 'Retirement Readiness-Creating Your Vision, Knowing Your Position , and Preparing for Your Futureand a contributing author to the book "65 Things To Do When You Retire." Mike hosts a local radio show "The Mike Bonacorsi Show" on WSMN Radio, and his Retirement Readiness Minute can be heard nationally each night on America Tonight Radio.

Mike Bonacorsi, CFP®
Amherst, NH United States
Contact Phone: 603-769-3111
Click to Contact from Web Site

MOSAIC FINANCIAL PARTNERS, LLC

San Francisco, CA United States
www.mosaicfp.com

At Mosaic Financial Partners, Inc. our mission is to improve your life by providing caring knowledgeable financial advice and individualized solutions that enable you to attain your lifetime goals and aspirations. There are many pieces to your financial life. To achieve your goals, these pieces must come together, like a mosaic, to form an integrated picture that will give you the clarity and confidence for financial peace of mind. Financial planning is a life-time process that addresses your ever-changing circumstances and is the foundation for our advice and service to you.

Frances Larose
The Larose Group, LLC
San Francisco, CA United States
Contact Phone: 650-548-6700
Click to Contact from Web Site

SCHAMMOND ADVISORS
Boston, MA United States
www.schammond.com

Susan C. Hammond, CPA, MST of scHammond Advisors consults with CEOs of small to mid-size companies and nonprofit organizations on the formation of advisory boards, improving governance, and effective financial management. A recognized expert on advisory boards, she is the author of the Advisory Board Kit: A Comprehensive Guide to Establishing an Advisory Board. Susan has served as a contract CFO/COO for technology companies, professional service firms, and nonprofit organizations. Susan is a co-founder of the Center for Women & Enterprise and the South Shore Women's Network.

Susan C Hammond, CPA, MST
Principal
scHammond Advisors
Duxbury, MA United States
Contact Phone: 781-837-1999
Contact Main Phone: 781-837-1999
Cell: 617-842-2158
Click to Contact from Web Site

EATLASAMERICAINSURANCE.COM --- ATLAS AMERICA TRAVEL INSURANCE
Glen Allen, VA United States
www.eatlasamericainsurance.com

Atlas America Insurance provides a comprehensive coverage for non-U.S. citizens in the US. Atlas America Insurance offers medical coverage from 5 days to 12 months for Non US citizens visiting US for pleasure, bussiness or study. There is coverage for both inpatient/ outpatient medical expenses, emergency medical evacuation, acute onset of pre-existing condition, coverage for lost luggage that has been checked and much more.

Chiranth Nataraj
President & CEO
Glen Allen, VA United States
Contact Phone: 877-593-5403
Click to Contact from Web Site

NATIONAL ASSOCIATION OF MUTUAL INSURANCE COMPANIES
Indianapolis, IN United States
http://www.NAMIC.org

We are 1,400 property/casualty insurance companies serving more than 135 million auto, home and business policyholders, with more than $196 billion in premiums accounting for 50 percent of the automobile/homeowners market and 31 percent of the business insurance market. We are the largest and most diverse property/casualty trade association in the country, with regional and local mutual insurance companies on main streets across America joining many of the country's largest national insurers who also call NAMIC their home. More than 200,000 people are employed by NAMIC members.

Brent Bahler
National Association of Mutual Insurance Companies
Indianapolis, IN United States
Contact Phone: (317) 575-5250
Click to Contact from Web Site

DAN WEEDIN -- CRISIS LEADERSHIP AND INSURANCE CONSULTANT
Seattle, WA United States
http://www.DanWeedin.com

Dan Weedin turns risk into reward! He is a crisis leadership, insurance and risk management consultant helping business owners and organizations accelerate the risk management decision-making process and improving the quality of those decisions. The bottom line results are reduced costs, improved protection, and enhanced peace of mind. In addition, he helps clients develop strategy to effectively respond to crisis to maximize growth and enhance reputation.

Dan Weedin
Toro Consulting, Inc.
Poulsbo, WA United States
Contact Phone: 360-271-1592
Click to Contact from Web Site

JACKIE LAPIN -- THE ART OF CONSCIOUS CREATION
Agoura Hills, CA United States
www.TheArtofConsciousCreation.com

Jackie Lapin is the author of 'The Art of Conscious Creation, How You Can Transform the World,' a number-one best seller on Amazon.com and the upcoming 'Practical Conscious Creation: Daily Techniques to Manifest Your Desires.' (Findhorn Press, Fall 2011). As an author, speaker and 'Conscious Creation' and 'Law of Attraction' coach, Lapin travels the world, teaching people how they can shape their personal future and the future of the planet. Her practical step-by-step process motivates persons to take charge of their lives and prosper in business and thrive in their personal lives.

Jackie Lapin
The Art of Conscious Creation
Agoura Hills, CA United States
Contact Phone: (888) 9-MANIFEST
Click to Contact from Web Site

OVERCOMING JOB BURNOUT
Berkeley, CA United States
docpotter.com

When work goes bad, life is hell. Burnout is a kind of job depression caused by feeling powerless, not stress. Reducing stress is essential to preserve health, but doing so does not stop burnout, which is a motivational problem. Docpotter offers 8 proven strategies for renewing enthusiasm for work and overcoming burnout: Pace Yourself, Manage Stress, Build skills, Cultivate social support, Tailor the job, Change jobs, Think powerfully, and Develop detached concern. Packed with practical steps to implement today. Includes quizzes: 'Am I Burning Out?,' 'Burnout Potential of My Job', 'Is My Staff Burning Out?.'

Dr. Beverly Potter
Author
Overcoming Job Burnout
Oakland, CA United States
Contact Phone: 510-420-3669
Click to Contact from Web Site

PERSONAL BEST CONSULTING -- DR. LEIF H. SMITH
Hilliard, OH United States
http://www.PersonalBestConsulting.com

Dr. Leif H. Smith is an expert in improving on-the-job leadership and performance. He is the publisher of 'Personal Bests,' a monthly newsletter designed to offer tips and techniques to immediately improve personal productiveness. Dr. Smith has been quoted in The New York Times, Entrepreneur Magazine, and other publications. His clients have included America Online, The American Lung Association, The Ohio State University Department of Athletics, and The University of Iowa, among others.

Dr. Leif H. Smith
President
Personal Best Consulting
Hilliard, OH United States
Contact Phone: 614-870-8742
Click to Contact from Web Site

VICKI RACKNER MD --- SELLING TO DOCTORS

Seattle, WA United States
www.TargetingDoctors.com

Would you like to increase your power of persuasion with physicians? Master B2D Communication? -- Author, speaker and consultant Dr. Vicki Rackner helps you understand how doctors think, quickly build rapport and persuade doctors to buy your ideas, products and services. Whether you work with doctors all day long or you're just breaking onto the physician niche, you can: Dramatically improve your ability to reach physicians, Graciously ask for referrals, Talk so doctors will listen, Craft offers doctors love, Avoid the land mines that blow up sales, Secure your role as a trusted advisor - Make more sales. Accelerate your business growth by working more effectively with physicians.

Vicki Rackner MD
Targeting Doctors
Mercer Island, WA United States
Contact Phone: (425) 451-3777
Click to Contact from Web Site

SHARON SPANO, CSP -- CORPORATE BURNOUT EXPERT

Heathrow, FL United States
http://www.sharonspano.com/

Sharon Spano, CSP is President of Spano & Company, Inc., one of the most in-demand human and organizational development firms in the country. Sharon is a workforce expert with expertise in transforming corporate cultures, revitalizing people, Principled Leadership™, corporate resiliency in a down market, integrity in the workplace, corporate wellness, overcoming burnout, and strategies for life and work balance. As a Corporate-Health Strategist™, Sharon is dedicated to maximizing human potential in corporate America. Her passion for the revitalization of integrity in the workplace, together with her proven processes, is guaranteed to catapult you and your team to unexpected levels of performance and increased bottom-line results. A Certified Speaking Professional, Sharon has delivered keynote addresses around the country. Her most recent book, 'Isabel's God' is a must read for anyone in health care. Watch for her upcoming release, The Best Stressed Woman: Walking with God through Adversity.

Sharon Spano
President
Spano & Company, Inc.
Heathrow, FL United States
Contact Phone:
Contact Main Phone: 407-333-0224
Cell: 407.247.1419
Click to Contact from Web Site

MARGO BERMAN - CREATIVE MARKETING EXPERT

Miami, FL United States
http://www.unlocktheblock.com/

Margo Berman -- Author, Marketer, Professor, Inventor, Speaker -- Margo, a creativity and marketing expert, is an award-winning creative director and advertising professor. She founded her own ad agency, Global Impact, handling clients like American Express. Margo hosted an interview talk show in Miami. Her book, Street-Smart Advertising: How to Win the Battle of the Buzz, was the featured Business Book in Delta Sky Magazine, June 2008. She created two national award-winning 6-CD webinar sets on Street-Smart Advertising. Her second advertising book, The Brains Behind Great Ad Campaigns, was released in 2009. Margo invented tactikPAK®, a patented system of learning. Margo has co-authored three books on spirituality. A keynote speaker and NSA member, Margo delivers dynamic programs like Creativity to Shatter The Gray Matter® and Mental Peanut Butter®. She has received numerous scholarly awards, including Woman of the Year in Communications Education, national Clarion Awards, and Kauffman Faculty Scholar.

Margo Berman
Creative Catalyst Unlock The Block
North Miami Beach, FL United States
Contact Phone: 305-949-7711
Click to Contact from Web Site

Corporate-Health Strategist™

SHARON SPANO, CSP

Healthy Culture. Healthy Profits.

Leading Workforce Expert Specializing in:

Transforming Corporate Cultures

Revitalizing People

Principled Leadership™

Corporate Resiliency in a Down Market

Integrity in the Workplace

Corporate Wellness

Overcoming Burnout

Strategies for Life and Work Balance

Sharon Spano is the President of Spano & Company, one of the most in-demand human and organizational development firms in the country. As a Corporate Health Strategist, she is dedicated to maximizing human potential in corporate America. Her passion for the revitalization of integrity in the workplace, together with her proven processes, is guaranteed to catapult you and your team to unexpected levels of performance and increased bottom-line results. It's about …

Purpose. People. Profit.

Phone: 407-333-0224 • 407-247-1419

Sharon@ SharonSpano.com or Charles@SharonSpano.com

www.SharonSpano.com

1349 South International Parkway • Suite 2401• Heathrow, Florida • 32746

DENNIS CHARLES -- CAREER EXPERT
Boston, MA United States
www.CharlesCareers.com

I was born in the East End of London. I am a former professional soccer player, coach and referee, musician and DJ. In between all this I had spells as a high school teacher and I left school at 16 and worked in a plastics factory for four mind-numbing years. One day I decided I'd had enough and put on my running shoes and ran to the local college. Using what I'd learned on the street, I convinced them to accept me on a Phys. Ed. degree, without any formal qualifications.

Dennis Charles
Framingham, MA United States
Contact Phone: 508-505-6327
Click to Contact from Web Site

JOHN P. DENTICO LEADERSHIP AND SIMULATION EXPERT
Annapolis, MD United States
www.leadsimm.com

Dr. John Dentico is a leadership development and simulation-learning expert who speaks, writes, consults and trains 21st Century leaders. He is the founder of LeadSimm LLC a one-of-a-kind 21st Century leadership development and simulation learning company. With more than 30 years of experience in leadership, learning and simulation design and development, he is convinced that there is no problem too hard, no challenge too great, and no issue too complex that it cannot be solved by the collaborative actions of a focused group of committed people. He understands that the best way to learn leadership is to practice leadership in as close to the real world decision making environment as possible because then and only then will a potential leader learn how to create leadership dynamics, the real power of 21st Century organizations.

Dr. John P. Dentico
President/Principal
LeadSimm LLC
Annapolis, MD United States
Contact Phone: 443-994-1151
Click to Contact from Web Site

JAMES D. FELDMAN -- THE INNOVATOR
Chicago, IL United States
www.ShiftHappens.com

Jim Feldman is the creator of Shift Happens!® and a professional Change Management speaker. As the owner of several businesses and consultant to Fortune 500 companies, Jim has been on the receiving end of changes in business. He has both failed and succeeded, using both experiences to create a roadmap to change. He shares funny stories, valuable techniques and creative problem solving in a hilarious and content-rich presentation, article or interview. Jim customizes each speech or interview to meet your needs. He researches your company or organization and creates a plan for change using real world examples. He has been known to leave the audience with several solutions to these changes which they can implement immediately. He is consistently named the top speaker at conferences and was also named one of the Top 100 Motivators of the Last 100 Years by Incentive Magazine. Call us at 312-527-9111 to make Shift Happen!

James Feldman
Professional Speaker
Shift Happens
Chicago, IL United States
Contact Phone: 312-527-9111
Cell: 312-909-9700
Click to Contact from Web Site

Margo Berman
Creative Marketing Expert

Hire the Right Brain
for sponBRAINeous combustion®

When your Creative Juices Need Recharging,
This Creative Catalyst Will Show You HOW TO:

- Ignite your creativity ... instantly
- Think conceptually
- Discover Mental Peanut Butter® branding
- Master exciting problem-solving methods
- Brainstorm with Shatter the Gray Matter®

Strap on your seat belt
for one fast-paced session!

Margo Berman -- author, inventor, trainer, keynote speaker -- is a creativity, branding and marketing expert with more than 20 years as an award-winning creative director and advertising professor.

She is the inventor of "tactikPAK®," a patented system of learning in nine business disciplines.
In addition, she is the creator of
Mental Peanut Butter®
Training ... For Industrial
Strength Branding
That Sticks to the
Roof of Your Brain™.
Margo's first book
was "Street-Smart
Advertising: How to Win
the Battle of the Buzz."

In 2009, she released
her second book:
"The Brains Behind
Great Ad Campaigns."

Margo Berman
Creative Catalyst:Unlock The Block

3733 NE 163 Street, N. Miami Beach, Florida 33160

305-949-7711   Fax: 305-947-3334

E-mail: unblockit@aol.com

www.UnlockTheBlock.com

VOSS W. GRAHAM -- INNERACTIVE CONSULTING
Memphis, TN United States
http://www.inneractiveconsulting.com

Expertise getting people to the next level of performance. Expertise in executive, manager and fast-tracker coaching. Provide insight for effective communication for individuals and teams. Experienced in Major Account Selling - moving sales teams and management from transactional to key account selling. Guide selection process using assessments and the interpretation of assessments to get the right people for the right jobs. Aligning performance with strategic objectives for accelerating growth. Author - Three Games of Selling.

Voss W. Graham
CEO / Sr. Business Advisor
InnerActive Consulting Group, Inc.
Cordova, TN United States
Contact Phone: 901-757-4434
Cell: 901-230-4036
Click to Contact from Web Site

TOM HINTON -- 10,000 DAYS FOUNDATION
San Diego, CA United States
www.TomHinton.com

Tom Hinton is recognized as America's Personal Growth Expert and is frequently interviewed on such topics as Work-Life Balance, Personal Growth, and Creating a Lasting Legacy. Tom helps his clients achieve the life of their dreams through his popular personal growth seminars and consulting strategies. Tom is also a popular speaker because of his inspirational messages, content-rich programs and entertaining style on topics such as: Achieving a Work-Life Balance that Works for You! and Living the Life of Your Dreams. Tom's new book, 10,000 Days: The Rest of Your Life, the Best of Your Life, is available on Amazon.com

Tom Hinton
President & CEO
10,000 Days Foundation
San Diego, CA United States
Contact Phone: 800-544-0414
Contact Main Phone: 760-787-0414
Cell: 858-449-9055
Click to Contact from Web Site

SHEL HOROWITZ, MARKETING CONSULTANT - GREEN AND PROFITABLE
Springfield, MA United States
GreenAndProfitable.com
MA

Need to establish your brand's green credentials or interview an expert? Green marketing consultant and copywriter Shel Horowitz of GreenAndProfitable.com can help: licensing content, providing informational programs, and materials, even walking you through specific steps to go more green affordably and ethically. Resources to reach the green consumers AND green practitioners. Shel is the award-winning primary author of Guerrilla Marketing Goes Green, and has written seven other books including Grassroots Marketing: Getting Noticed in a Noisy World. He speaks internationally about green marketing and green business, and writes the monthly Green And Profitable, at http://greenandprofitable.com

Shel Horowitz
Marketing Consultant/Copywriter/Author
GreenAndProfitable.com
Hadley, MA United States
Contact Phone: 413-586-2388
Contact Main Phone: 413-586-2388
Cell: 413-586-2388
Click to Contact from Web Site

Dr. John P. Dentico
The Simulation Doctor

Don't be a Victim of the Future-*Change it!*
Anticipate Tomorrow's Difficult Decisions Today!

Dr. John P. Dentico works with organizations that want to preclude and mitigate future catastrophes. To achieve this, he creates and facilitates realistic, custom designed simulations where people experience strategies that prevent or avoid tragic events before they become reality. *You Can't Afford To Play Games With The Future!* Simulate the crisis facing you and your organization and build leadership capacity to develop and implement comprehensive solutions that work.

Think and Act Strategically--Streamline Your Approach
Gain Greater Levels of Efficiency and Effectiveness

Sample Simulations:
- Counter Terrorism
- Disaster Preparedness
- Organizational Change
- Leadership Development
- Insurance Risk Mitigation
- Mass Transit Safety and Security
- Mergers and Acquisitions
- Threat and Vulnerability Analysis
- School Safety
- New Product/Service Introduction

John P. Dentico, Ed. D. is President of LeadSimm a simulation and leadership development practice. Dr. Dentico has over 29 years of simulation experience and is a nationally recognized authority in the development and use of simulations to accelerate comprehensive learning and develop leadership capacity. His LeadSimm© Leadership development simulation program was specifically cited by the United States Department of Justice as one of America's Best Leadership development programs.

Dr. John P. Dentico--The Simulation Doctor
Ph: 443-994-1151, DrJohn@thesimulationdoctor.com
www.thesimulationdoctor.com

ROGER D. ISAACS
Chicago, IL United States
www.talkingwithgod.net

Roger D. Isaacs is an independent scholar who began researching the Hebrew Bible in the 1950s alongside his father, noted hematologist and biblical scholar, Dr. Raphael Isaacs. After his father's death in 1965, Isaacs launched into independent research which has resulted in the book 'Talking With God' and other forthcoming volumes.

Julie Shallow
Assistant
Philip Reese
Richmond, VA United States
Contact Phone: 888-445-6111
Click to Contact from Web Site

AL LAUTENSLAGER -- CERTIFIED GUERRILLA MARKETING COACH
Chicago, IL United States
www.market-for-profits.com/

Al Lautenslager is a marketing/PR consultant, speaker, author, entrepreneur and business owner. He is the best-selling, co-author of Guerrilla Marketing in 30 Days and a featured business coach on Entrepreneur.com. He is the principal of Market for Profits, a Chicago-based marketing consulting firm and president of a commercial printing and mailing company in Wheaton, IL. Recently Al joined forces with Donald Trump and former Apprentice Television show contestants in the Apprentice Legend Millionaire Forum.

Al Lautenslager
Author, Speaker, Entrepreneur, Business Owner,
Certified Guerrilla Marketing Coach
Wheaton, IL United States
Contact Phone: (630) 740-1397
Click to Contact from Web Site

RODNEY M. LOESCH JD, CFP, CDFA
Moberly, MO United States
www.tricycleleadership.com

Rodney is an expert in creating collaborative, accountable, innovative leadership teams for trade assoctions and Fortune 1000 firms. He has 30 years consulting and speaking experience with execuitves & high-achieving professionals in organizations such as, AIG, Torchmark and Hummana. A former sales manager and trainer for the Multi-National Eutectic Corporation, overseeing 300+ sales professionals and personally managing key multi-million dollar industrial sales accounts. A media resource, Rodney has been quoted and published in Kiplinger's, Christian Science Monitor and the KC Star. Spoken to over 50,000 people coast to coast. Avocation as a USGA/ NCAA golf rules official.

Rodney M. Loesch JD, CFP,CDFA
President
Tricycle Leadership Inc.
Moberly, MO United States
Contact Phone: 1-877-505-5101
Click to Contact from Web Site

LETHIA OWENS - PERSONAL BRANDING AND SOCIAL MEDIA STRATEGIST
St. Peters, MO United States
www.LethiaOwens.com

Lethia Owens is the president and CEO of Lethia Owens International, Inc. and she is internationally recognized as a personal branding expert, speaker, author and coach. She uses high value content, dynamic keynote presentations and engaging training programs to show others they too can achieve extraordinary results - if they have the right skills and attitude. Through the use of real-life stories and common sense strategies, she awakens the potential in audiences to think, work and live powerfully. She has had the opportunity to travel and speak in 49 of the 50 United States plus Dubai - UAE.

Lethia Owens
Personal Branding Strategist
Lethia Owens International, Inc.
St. Peters, MO United States
Contact Phone: 636-244-5041
Contact Main Phone: 636-244-5041
Pager: 314-517-6201
Cell: 314-517-6201
Click to Contact from Web Site

JOELLYN (JOEY) SARGENT - STRATEGIC MARKETING CONSULTANT
Atlanta, GA United States
www.brandsproutmarketing.com

Joellyn Joey Sargent is Principal of BrandSprout LLC, a strategic marketing and management consulting firm dedicated to helping growing companies turn daunting business challenges into compelling success stories. Joey provides fresh business perspectives and keen strategic insights for business owners and entrepreneurs. She accelerates business growth with programs that create visibility, engage customers and increase sales. Joey is a warm and engaging speaker, drawing on over 20 years of experience as a corporate marketing executive in the B2B and technology space. She holds an MBA from Embry Riddle Aeronautical University and is working on her first book.

Joellyn Sargent
Principal
BrandSprout LLC
Milton, GA United States
Contact Phone: 678-823-8228
Click to Contact from Web Site

EDWARD SEGAL -- GETTING YOUR 15 MINUTES OF FAME
San Francisco, CA United States
www.EdwardSegal.com/

PR guru Edward Segal is an expert on the good, bad and ugly ways individuals and organizations behave and react in the public spotlight. Segal's advice is based on his experience as a journalist, public relations consultant and congressional press secretary. He is a former PR consultant to more than 500 corporations and organizations including Marriott, Ford, E-Myth Worldwide and the Consumer Electronics Association. He was senior media relations consultant for Ogilvy Public Relations Worldwide and was the marketing strategies columnist for The Wall Street Journal's StartUpJournal.com. Segal is the author the PR handbook, Getting Your 15 Minutes of Fame.

Edward Segal
Sebastapol, CA United States
Contact Phone: 415-218-8600
Click to Contact from Web Site

PROFESSOR BOB BOYD -- HOME-BASED BUSINESS

Los Angeles, CA United States
smsprovensystem.com/

Doctors of Business Administration 'Studies' (all but dissertation). Best Selling Author, Entrepreneur, Problem Solver, and the Founder and CEO of Successful Marketing Solutions, LLC. Emeritus Professor of Business and Management and has a lifetime community college instructors credential. Commission as a captain in the Naval Volunteers Reserve of the United States Volunteer-Joint Services Command, to lead a group of outstanding individuals that will develop guidelines to establish that organization's first Board of Directors.

Professor Bob Boyd
Founder, CEO and Problem Solver
Successful Marketing Solution LLC
Inglewood, CA United States
Contact Phone: 310-491-5235
Click to Contact from Web Site

CONTENTED COW PARTNERS, LLC -- WORKPLACE EXPERTS

Jacksonville, FL United States
www.ContentedCows.com

No organization can compete in today's tough economy without the willing, enthusiastic engagement of everyone on the payroll. When it comes to the topic of people and profit, we wrote the book... literally. Based on years of research on the leadership and employee relations practices of some of America's best managed companies, plus 30 years' combined management experience, we address and can comment knowledgeably on: workplace issues, turnover, morale, leadership, retention, recruitment, and HR best practices.

Richard Hadden, CSP
Managing Partner
Contented Cow Partners, LLC
Jacksonville, FL United States
Contact Phone: 904-720-0870
Cell: 904-813-4322
Click to Contact from Web Site

RANDALL CRAIG -- SOCIAL MEDIA AND WEB STRATEGY EXPERT

Toronto, Ontario Canada
http://www.RandallCraig.com

Author of six books, including Social Media for Business, the Online PR and Social Media series, and best-seller Personal Balance Sheet, Randall founded several successful start-ups, held a long-time position at a 'big-four' consulting firm, and was a public company executive. Currently president of consulting firm Pinetree Advisors, he is also an MBA School lecturer and weekly columnist on Monster. With a national media profile, SINCE 1994 he is been an expert on Web/Social Media Strategy, Social Media Risks, Networking, and Social Media Career planning/Job Search. Web site has hundreds of articles and story ideas.

Randall Craig, CFA, MBA, CMC
President
Pinetree Advisors Inc.
Toronto, ON Canada
Contact Phone: 416-256-7773
Cell: 416-256-7773 x101
Click to Contact from Web Site

DAVID W. DELONG -- FUTURE WORKFORCE SKILLS
Boston, MA United States
www.SmartWorkForceStrategies.com

Dr. David DeLong, researcher, consultant and speaker, solves talent management problems created by leadership shortages, skills gaps, poor succession planning and inadequate knowledge transfer. He also helps aging baby boomers and new college graduates get employed faster in today's job market. David, a research fellow at the MIT AgeLab, has also been an adjunct professor at Babson College. He is co-author of The Executive Guide to High-Impact Talent Management (McGraw-Hill). Also author of Lost Knowledge: Confronting the Threat of an Aging Workforce. And author of forthcoming Graduate to a Great Job! How to Make Your College Degree Pay Off.

Dr. David W. DeLong
President
David DeLong and Associates, Inc.
Concord, MA United States
Contact Phone: 978-369-5083
Cell: 978-369-5083
Click to Contact from Web Site

MIKE PALUMBO -- EXECUTIVE RECRUITER -- CAREER INSIDER
Fairhope, AL United States
www.askmikepalumbo.com

Hi, my name is Mike Palumbo and I am the founder of The Palumbo Company, an executive search and professional recruiting firm that has filled hundreds of executive and managerial positions worldwide. I'm dealing with career issues everyday! I know the games! I can teach you how to 'get-in' and get that dream career you've always wanted. As a business owner, author, broadcaster, blogger and motivational speaker, I can cut through all the noise and give you the truth as only a 'career insider' can! My goal is to help people reach their full potential and stop wasting their talents!

Mike Palumbo
Fairhope, AL United States
Contact Phone: 251-990-3385
Contact Main Phone: 251-990-3385
Cell: 251-459-3133
Click to Contact from Web Site

AVIV SHAHAR --LEADERSHIP DEVELOPMENT EXPERT
Seattle, WA United States
www.AvivConsulting.com

Aviv Shahar is president of Aviv Consulting, LLC., world leader in the delivery of transformational learning and development solutions. Aviv helps CEOs, executives and top teams to create breakthrough results and realize greatness. Aviv has worked with executives fortune 100 companies in over 20 countries including Canada, Germany, Brazil, Taiwan, UK, Mexico, Holland, Czech Republic, Israel, and the US. Clients' return to work with Aviv becuase his collaborations create profound results: enhanced effectiveness, winning strategies, increased revenue, impactful leadership and happier & healthier Teams.

Aviv Shahar
President
Aviv Consulting
Woodinville, WA United States
Contact Phone: 425-415-6155
Click to Contact from Web Site

DR. MAYNARD BRUSMAN - WORKPLACE EXPERT AND EXECUTIVE COACH
San Francisco, CA United States
http://www.workingresources.com

Dr. Maynard Brusman is a workplace psychologist and the president of Working Resources. We help companies assess, select, coach, and retain top talent. Maynard is a recognized expert in executive coaching, leadership development, career coaching, coaching attorneys, succession planning, executive selection, pre-employment selection and assessment of emotionally intelligent people. He facilitates leadership retreats nationally and in Costa Rica. He has appeared in a variety of media including the Wall Street Journal, USA Today, San Francisco Chronicle, NBC, and Fast Company. The Society for Advancement of Consulting has awarded Dr. Maynard Brusman two rare 'Board Approvals' in leadership development and executive coaching.

Dr. Maynard Brusman
Consulting Psychologist and Executive Coach
Working Resources
San Francisco, CA United States
Contact Phone: 415-546-1252
Click to Contact from Web Site

SANDRA A. SHELTON
Dallas, TX United States
www.sandrashelton.com

Sandra Shelton, BA,MEd.,CTACC Sandra A. Shelton, B.A., MEd., CTACC delights audiences and tells it like it is with passion, humor, and her personable attraction factor that draws in even the most resistant participant. As a thought leader in workforce engagement, communication, leadership development, and community development her decidedly unique perspective comes from hands-on experience, academic and corporate leadership, nonprofit executive, and business entrepreneur. She has given over 2,600 presentations in 15 countries for more than two decades consistently moving listeners to a higher business perspective for solid relationships that move the organization's goal forward and each individual's potential higher.

Sandra A. Shelton
Sandra A. Shelton
Fort Worth, Texas, TX United States
Contact Phone: 827 230 4523
Cell: 817 714 7377
Click to Contact from Web Site

KAREN SUSMAN -- KAREN SUSMAN AND ASSOCIATES
Denver, CO United States
www.karensusman.com

Karen's an expert on Humor, Life Balance, Stress, Presentation Skills, Networking and Building Community/Association Involvement. Trial attorneys hire Karen to prepare their clients for deposition and cross-examination. Since 1983, she's spoken internationally to organizations like INC Magazine, NBC, Marriott, American Society of Association Executives and National League of Cities. Her guidebooks on Networking, Time Management, Community Involvement and Humor at Work are crammed with doable ideas. She's the author of the forthcoming book on presentation skills: Connect or DieTM. If you're looking for content plus mirth for interviews, articles and presentations, contact Karen. You'll like what you hear.

Karen Susman
Speaker/Author/Consultant
Karen Susman and Associates
Denver, CO United States
Contact Phone: 303-756-6939
Contact Main Phone: 888-678-8818
Cell: 720-545-7110
Click to Contact from Web Site

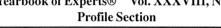

DALE IRVIN -- VERY FUNNY SPEAKER
Chicago, IL United States
http://www.youtube.com/user/ProSummarizer

AMERICAN PAYROLL ASSOCIATION
San Antonio, TX United States
http://www.AmericanPayroll.org

**SYLVIA HENDERSON -
INTERPERSONAL SKILLS EXPERT**
Washington, DC United States
www.springboardtraining.com

'Very Funny Speaker': Dale Irvin is the world's only 'Professional Summarizer.' He attends your meeting, paying attention to every word spoken by every speaker and noticing every detail of the event. Then, throughout the day, he will 'summarize' the event with a comedy monologue, written on the spot. One of his clients best described his performance, when she said: 'What Billy Crystal brings to the Academy Awards, you brought to our meeting.'

The American Payroll Association (APA) is the nation's leader in payroll education, publications and training. The nonprofit association conducts more than 300 payroll training conferences and seminars each year and publishes a library of resource texts and newsletters. National Payroll Week, APA's celebration of synergy between America's workers and payroll professionals, aims at educating the public about the payroll function. APA's Executive Director, Dan Maddux, has made numerous television and radio appearances. APA is the industry's collective voice in Washington, D.C.

Sylvia Henderson helps people SHOW they are as great as they say they are, effecting change from the outside, in. She is your expert on interpersonal 'people skills' for workplace, business, and life success. When sales relationships, customer service, professionalism, attitudes, or workplace interaction and communications are issues, Sylvia can help you and your organization. Henderson can teach you to be on time, all the time! Sylvia holds education and business degrees and has 30+ years of service, training, leadership, and management experience that shapes her expertise. She served on and led nonprofit boards and speaks and trains in her volunteer roles. She rides motorcycles and integrates biker analogies and metaphors into her business programs. Her two Welsh Corgis allow her to live in the Washington DC area.

Dale Irvin
Downers Grove, IL United States
Contact Phone: 630-852-7695
Click to Contact from Web Site

Mark Coindreau
Public Relations Manager
American Payroll Association
San Antonio, TX United States
Contact Phone: 210-226-4600
Click to Contact from Web Site

Sylvia Henderson
Chief Everything Officer (CEO)
Springboard Training
Olney, MD United States
Contact Phone: 301-260-1538
Contact Main Phone: 301-260-1538
Click to Contact from Web Site

Interpersonal Skills Expert
Sylvia Henderson

Sylvia Henderson helps organizations thrive by working with their people to show they are as great as they say they are. Henderson does this through her business – Springboard Training – by partnering with clients to learn what they need and how she can provide solutions that meet those needs. She works with staff and administrative-level employees, supervisors, managers and decision-makers in businesses, associations, non-profits, government agencies and educational institutions.

Henderson is your expert on interpersonal "people skills" and professional behaviors that lead to success. She has more than 30 years of experience consulting, training, speaking, writing, and leading teams, departments, and boards of directors, implementing the skills and behaviors that support her expertise. Her programs integrate her motorcycle avocation with solid business and life success principles.

Benefits of using Henderson's talents:
- Mitigate conflict situations.
- Minimize communications breakdowns.
- Improve performance – individual, team, organizational.
- Contribute to positive morale.
- Build positive relationships.
- Improve customer service and sales results.
- Present a positive corporate image and brand.
- Create a better management and leadership culture.

Henderson writes, co-writes and is a published author on communication, leadership, professionalism, success – and motorcycle-related topics. Books, learning aids and job-reference materials, articles, blogs, and online media are components of her catalog. She is featured in a variety of media and interviews as the main guest on radio programs.

Media credits include host of her own television program "Think About It!" on MMC-TV16, a weekly talk program on personal, professional and business development topics.

Henderson is a volunteer trainer for and life member of the Girl Scouts of the USA. She participates in breast cancer walks in Washington D.C. She is past national president of Women On Wheels® Motorcycle Association and has received the American Motorcyclist Association's MVP recognition. She is past president of the D.C. chapter of the National Speakers Association and is a DTM-level Toastmaster. She is owned by two Welsh Corgis and rides a Honda Shadow 1100 motorcycle.

Interpersonal Skills Include, Yet Are Not Limited to:

- Respecting time and managing priorities.
- Creating positive impressions and perceptions.
- The value of speaking well.
- Setting and achieving goals.
- Demonstrating positive work ethics.
- Remaining personally authentic while making choices for success.
- Communication and public speaking skills.
- "Small talk" and conversational skills.
- Workplace behaviors and professionalism.
- Presenting professionally in person, on the phone and in video.
- Motivation, self-esteem and positive attitudes.

Sylvia Henderson
P.O. Box 588, Olney, Maryland
(Washington, D.C.)
301-260-1538
Sylvia@SpringboardTraining.com

RUTH SIRMAN, CANMEDIATE INTERNATIONAL - WORKPLACE CONFLICT EXPERT
Ottawa, Ontario Canada
wwwcanmediate.com

Ruth Sirman, Workplace Conflict Expert is a veteran in the world of Alternative Dispute Resolution, Organizational Conflict and Restorative Justice. Specializing in complex, multi-stakeholder interventions in workplaces, organizations, communities and churches, Ruth's knowledge of human behavior, her quick wit and humor based "down home" practicality have made her a much sought after speaker, trainer, mediator and writer nationally and internationally. Ruth teaches the techniques and strategies she has used to support more than 50 organizations and 5,000 people to resolve tough complex conflicts, manage difficult relationships and create sustainable change in their lives. For more information check out www.canmediate.com

Ruth Sirman
President and Senior Mediator, Speaker and Trainer
CanMediate International
Almonte, ON Canada
Contact Phone: 613-256-3852
Click to Contact from Web Site

BILL WAGNER -- ACCORD MANAGEMENT SYSTEMS
Los Angeles, CA United States
www.accordsyst.com

Accord Management Systems provides clients with the necessary tools to assess, engage, and retain the most valuable asset in any organization, its people. Our clients utilize a series of surveys & assessments that scope job requirements, evaluate how potential employees fit into those jobs, and identify changes that will keep employees engaged, which are all keys to improving productivity in today's business environment.

Bill Wagner
Accord Management Systems
Thousand Oaks, CA United States
Contact Phone: 805-230-2100
Click to Contact from Web Site

ROBIN L. GRAHAM -- INNERACTIVE CONSULTING GROUP INC.
Memphis, TN United States
www.inneractiveconsulting.com

Specialist in bridging the knowing-doing gap. Rather than spending additional time, effort and dollars on standard Sales, Leadership, Teamwork, Wellness and other initiatives - redirect the focus to where success ultimately resides. The inner mind-set, thoughts and beliefs of the individuals involved. Knowing what to do, how to do it and why it is important is not enough. Achieve sustainable success by accessing and aligning subconscious thoughts, decisions, and actions with external goals.

Robin L. Graham
President
InnerActive Consulting Group Inc.
Cordova, TN United States
Contact Phone: 901-757-4434
Click to Contact from Web Site

MOMPRENEURS
Scarsdale, NY United States
www.mompreneursonline.com

Ellen H. Parlapiano and Patricia Cobe are authors of Mompreneurs®: A Mother's Practical Step-by-Step Guide to Work-at-Home Success. Moms themselves, they are authorities on balancing home business and family needs. The Mompreneurs® have shared their work-from-home expertise on TV and radio, in newspapers and magazines, and as regular contributors to iVillage.com. Their new book on Internet businesses will be out in 2001. Additional Contact: Patricia Cobe: (914) 472-8060 - FAX (914) 723-5171 E-mail: Momprenp@aol.com

Ellen H. Parlapiano
Mompreneurs
Scarsdale, NY United States
Contact Phone: 914-472-7322
Click to Contact from Web Site

*Call ASAP

KATE ZABRISKIE - TRAINING SEMINARS, WORKSHOPS AND KEYNOTES
Washington, DC United States
www.businesstrainingworks.com

Business Training Works - Onsite training provider answers your questions about soft-skills: customer service, communication skills, business etiquette, business writing, time management, presentation skills, train the trainer, creativity and critical thinking, negotiation, supervision skills, and the other basics that people need to be successful at work. Founder, Kate Zabriskie and her team of trainers work with the Fortune 500, government, and small businesses to improve business results. Are you wondering which fork to use? We can help. Do you need to know how to write clear sentences that get results? We can help. Are you trying to improve customer service? We can help. THE BOTTOM LINE: WE CAN ANSWER HARD QUESTIONS ABOUT SOFT SKILLS Our clients include: Earthlink, Microsoft, Boeing, United States Government, Toyota, The University of Maryland, Georgetown University, and hundreds of other organizations. From communication skills to getting organized and staying that way, we're happy to tell you what we know. You ask the question. We'll answer it or recommend someone who can.

Kate Zabriskie
Owner
Business Training Works, Inc.
Port Tobacco, MD United States
Contact Phone: 301.934.3250
Contact Main Phone: 800.934.4825
Cell: 240.412.3955
Click to Contact from Web Site

NATIONAL BORDER PATROL COUNCIL
Campo, CA United States
http://www.nbpc.net

The National Border Patrol Council is the labor organization that represents the more than 17,000 front-line Border Patrol employees responsible for enforcing U.S. immigration laws. It strongly advocates for secure borders and fair treatment of the dedicated men and women who patrol them. In order to achieve these goals, the Council lobbies Congress, negotiates with DHS, represents employees in various proceedings, and provides the news media with reliable and candid information from a front-line perspective.

T.J. Bonner
President
National Border Patrol Council
Campo, CA United States
Contact Phone: 619-478-5145
Click to Contact from Web Site

GEOFF DRUCKER--DISPUTE RESOLUTION

Arlington, VA United States
http://www.mccammongroup.com/
professionals-training/drucker.asp
VA

A winning combination of real world experience and academic credentials. Geoff is a seasoned trial lawyer, deal negotiator, and dispute system designer. He teaches Conflict in Organizations, Negotiation, Alternative Dispute Resolution, and Mediation in prestigious graduate and professional programs. His forthcoming book (November, 2011), Resolving 21st Century Disputes: Best Practices for a Fast-Paced World, explains how to prevent and respond to common forms of "irrational" and dysfunctional behavior at work and at home.

Geoff Drucker
Arlington, VA United States
Contact Phone: 703-582-9971
Click to Contact from Web Site

ROGER H. MADON -- LABOR ARBITRATOR - LABOR ATTORNEY

New York, NY United States
www.arb-med.net

Roger H. Madon, Labor and employment law Arbitrator/Mediator: Born Brooklyn, New York, December 13, 1936; admitted to bar, 1973, New York; 1989, District of Columbia; 2003, Commonwealth of Massachusetts. Education: University of Vermont (B.A., 1958); St. John's University (J.D., 1972); New York University (LL.M., Labor Law, 1978); Pace University (LL.M., Environmental Law, 1989). Lecturer: labor and employment law, environmental law and international transactions. Represented both labor and management for 38 years. Have been an advocate in over 2000 arbitrations and negotiated over 1500 collective bargaining agreements. Affiliated with Talk Radio News Network, and talk radio host on Paltalk News Network.

Roger H. Madon
Abitrator/Mediator/Attorney
Madon Malin, P.C.
New York, NY United States
Contact Phone: 212-759-9740
Cell: 917-270-6829
Click to Contact from Web Site

DOUGLAS M. MCCABE, PH.D. -- EMPLOYEE RELATIONS EXPERT

Washington, DC United States

Dr. Douglas M. McCabe is Professor of Labor Relations, Human Resource Management, and Organizational Behavior at Georgetown University's School of Business in Washington, DC. He is the author of more than 200 articles, papers, monographs and speeches presented at professional and scholarly meetings in the field of employee relations. He is also an active domestic and international management consultant. Dr. McCabe has appeared more than 200 times on television and radio.

Douglas M. McCabe, Ph.D.
Professor of Management
Georgetown University
Washington, DC United States
Contact Phone: 202-687-3778
Click to Contact from Web Site

Get the answers to the hard questions about soft skills.

Onsite training provider can answer your questions about soft skills: customer service, communication, business etiquette, business writing, time management, presentation skills, train the trainer, change management, military writing, creativity and critical thinking, cross-cultural management, negotiation, supervision skills, and the other basics that people need to be successful at work.

Are you wondering which fork to use?
We can help.

Do you need to know how to write clear sentences that get results?
We can help.

Are you trying to improve customer service?
We can help.

*Call ASAP

From communication skills to getting organized and staying that way, we're happy to tell you what we know. You ask the questions. We'll answer them or recommend someone who can.

Our clients include: Earthlink, Microsoft, Boeing, United States Government, Toyota, The University of Maryland, Georgetown University, Northrop Grumman, and hundreds of other organizations.

ALL CALLS ANSWERED
(301) 934.3250 | info@businesstrainingworks.com

NATIONAL ASSOCIATION OF LETTER CARRIERS, AFL-CIO
Washington, DC United States
http://www.nalc.org

The 300,000-member National Association of Letter Carriers (AFL-CIO) union represents active and retired city delivery letter carriers of the U.S. Postal Service in all 50 states and U.S. jurisdictions. NALC President Fredric V. Rolando is available to provide insight and information regarding: Postal Issues, Organized Labor, Politics, Legislation, Grievance and Arbitration Procedures, and efforts to Stamp Out Hunger.

Philip Dine
Director of Public Relations
National Association of Letter Carriers(AFL-CIO)
Washington, DC United States
Contact Phone: 202-662-2489
Contact Main Phone: 202-393-4695
Click to Contact from Web Site

LISA ANDERSON M.B.A. - - BUSINESS AND MANAGEMENT EXPERT
Claremont, CA United States
http://lma-consultinggroup.com

Lisa Anderson is a senior supply chain and operations executive and founder and President of LMA Consulting Group,Inc. She works with executive leaders and management teams to transform people + process = profit. Lisa's primary focus is on delivering results - improving the client's condition. As a business consultant, executive coach, speaker and author, she has helped companies improve their business performance, resulting in increased profitability, cash flow, and customer service levels.

Lisa Anderson
LMA Consulting Group, Inc.
Claremont, CA United States
Contact Phone: 909-630-3943
Click to Contact from Web Site

TIM HALLORAN -- THE BRAND GUY
Atlanta, GA United States
www.timhalloran.com

Does your brand need therapy? Tim Halloran, the brand guy, is a renowned consultant, speaker, and educator who understands the relationships between brands and consumers. He has appeared on major TV, radio, and print publications. His unique perspective emerges from over 19 years of consumer branding and new product development at such international firms as Coca-Cola. Tim provides brand 'illumination' for such products as consumer goods/services, professional athletes, and individuals. In addition, Tim is a highly rated marketing faculty member at Emory University's top rated Goizueta Business School. Tim is available for interviews and speaking engagements.

Tim Halloran
The Brand Guy
Brand Illumination
Atlanta, GA United States
Contact Phone: 404-218-4117
Contact Main Phone: 404-218-4117
Cell: 404-218-4117
Click to Contact from Web Site

Employee Relations Expert

DOUGLAS M. MCCABE, PH.D.

McDonough School of Business
Georgetown University
Washington, D.C.
202-687-3778

McCabeD@Georgetown.edu

Dr. Douglas M. McCabe is Professor of Labor Relations, Human Resource Management, and Organizational Behavior at Georgetown University's School of Business, Washington, D.C. He is the author of more than 200 articles, papers, monographs and speeches presented at professional and scholarly meetings in the field of employee relations. He is also an active domestic and international management consultant.

Considered by the media to be an expert in his field, Dr. McCabe has appeared more than 200 times on international, national, and local television and radio as the networks have sought his views on critical issues in employee relations.

His television credits include being interviewed on "ABC World News Tonight," "NBC Nightly News," "CBS Evening News," and "PBS NewsHour" as well as CNN's "Crossfire" and "Inside Politics."

His print media credits include being quoted in *Business Week, U.S. News & World Report, USA Today, The Washington Post, The Los Angeles Times, The New York Times, The Chicago Sun-Times, The Chicago Tribune, The Milwaukee Journal* and *The Detroit News.*

Furthermore, Dr. McCabe is a premier executive education professor. He has conducted more than 300 management development programs in the area of employee relations. Also, he is a member of the Society for Human Resource Management. He holds a Ph.D. from Cornell University and is a member of Phi Beta Kappa.

Analysis provided on the following topics:

■ **Labor-Management Relations**

■ **Human Resource Management**

■ **Organizational Behavior**

■ **Employee Relations**

■ **International Industrial Relations**

■ **Management Consulting Practices**

■ **Global Employment Trends**

■ **Ethical Issues in Management**

■ **Negotiation**

■ **Mediation**

■ **Arbitration**

■ **International Business Negotiation**

MARK HOLMES -- SALESONOMICS
Springfield, MO United States
www.salesonomics.com

Mark Holmes is one of America's most sought after B2B sales consultants and speakers on increasing sales in tough business sectors. He is the author of Salesonomics (2011) and the best-seller Wooing Customers Back (1994, 1995, 2005). His clients include TETRA Technologies, SWIRE Oilfield Services, Bass Pro Shops, ServiceMASTER, Cisco Systems, Silver Dollar City, Mueller BioPharm and a host of small businesses in over twenty industries. Mark is an entrepreneur and has owned several companies including a marketing firm, fitness center, as well as a failing AM radio station which he tripled sales in six months then sold the station for a nice profit. He is an engaging interview and his ideas are in-demand by the Wall Street Journal, FOX Business Network, BNET, Sales & Marketing Management, the Chicago Tribune and Drake Business Review. Discover why Mark's ideas are in demand by thousands of sales and management professionals.

Mark Holmes
President
Consultant Board Inc.
Salesonomics®
Springfield, MO United States
Contact Phone: (417) 883-7434
Cell: (417) 848-6560
Click to Contact from Web Site

OPTIMIZE INTERNATIONAL-OPTIMIZING THE RESULTS OF EXECUTIVE TEAMS
Boston, MA United States
www.OptimizeIntl.com

Steve Lishansky is The Executive Optimizer, known for working with leaders and executive teams in creating clarity, focus, and impact that drives superior results, and developing the skills to sustain them. Steve is recognized as a thought leader and innovator in enhancing executive's skillfulness in leading organizational change, and building highly effective, value-based relationships - both between leaders and their people, as well as between senior technical and professional experts and their internal and external clients. Founder of the first Executive Coaching Institute in the world, Steve delivers exceptional results through coaching, facilitation of executive teams, riveting speaking and training.

Steve Lishansky
CEO
OPTIMIZEInternational
Hollis, NH United States
Contact Phone: 978-369-4525
Contact Main Phone: 978-369-4525
Cell: 978-828-3000
Click to Contact from Web Site

ANTHONY SIGNORELLI -- CONSULTANT IN SALES FORCE EFFECTIVENESS
St. Paul, MN United States
www.signorelli.biz

Anthony Signorelli is President and Principal Consultant of Signorelli & Associates, Inc. As a consultant, Signorelli provides consulting services in sales force effectivenes to clients, such as ThomsonReuters, Medtronic, BioShpere Medical, Fairview Health System, Rosemount and many others. As a speaker, Signorelli addresses issues of sales leadership and sales rep productivity, effective training, and other dynamic programs that keep people engaged. Audiences walk away with new ideas to improve their performance. Signorelli is a member of American Society for Training and Development, Association of Business Process Management Professionals, Sales Management Association, American Management Association, and the National Association of Sales

Anthony Signorelli
Principal Consultant
Sitllwater, MN United States
Contact Phone: 888-828-3666
Click to Contact from Web Site

0

Mark Holmes

Expert in Influencing Employee Performance

"Companies today only have three things left to compete with: the ability to adapt, the ability to increase sales, the ability to create and sustain customer loyalty. All three require engaged, willing employees."

Mark Holmes knows what employees and customers really want.

For 24 years, he interviewed thousands of employees and managers in more than 20 industries, and many of the insights landed in his book, "The People Keeper." Holmes's customer service firm surveyed and evaluated more than 10,000 customer experiences, and the rich insights led to his top-selling allegorical book, "Wooing Customers Back."

Holmes has a unique ability to craft exactly what an audience, a sales team or an executive will respond to. He takes mystifying workplace challenges and simplifies them with useful, effective tools.

www.ManageMyEmployees.com

417-883-7434   mark@managemyemployees.com

www.ThePeopleKeeper.com

CHANGE MASTERS INCORPORATED
Minneapolis, MN United States
www.ChangeMasters.com

Change Masters® Incorporated has coached over 2,000 individual executives and technology leaders to master effective communications in their rapidly changing organizations since 1986. Customers include over 25 Fortune 100 companies and over 150 companies in total. Tom is co-author of 'Seeing Yourself as Others Do - Authentic Executive Presence at Any Stage of Your Career.' He has been featured in major newspapers, conducted radio interviews and is a professional member of the National Speakers Association.

Thomas Mungavan, MBA, CSP
President
Change Masters® Incorporated
Minneapolis, MN United States
Contact Phone: 763-231-6410
Contact Main Phone: 1-800-CHANGE-1
Cell: 763-476-4200
Click to Contact from Web Site

PHYLLIS EZOP --- GROWTH STRATEGY EXPERT
LaGrange Park, IL United States
www.ezopandassociates.com/

Phyllis Ezop is a growth strategy expert who examines and analyzes the causes of business growth. She has been quoted in the New York Times and other publications.

Phyllis Ezop
Ezop and Associates
LaGrange Park, IL United States
Contact Phone: 708-579-1711
Click to Contact from Web Site

Home of The Standing O'

OVATIONS INTERNATIONAL INC. -- MATTHEW COSSOLOTTO
New York, NY United States
www.Ovations.com

A former aide to House Speaker Jim Wright and Representative Leon Panetta, Matthew served as CEO-level speechwriter at MCI, GTE, and Pepsi-Cola International. Launched Ovations International in 1996. Author of All The World's A Podium and The Real F Word - The 7 FAILURE Traps of Highly Disempowered People (and what to do about them). Visit www.ovations.com and www. TheRealFWord.com. Matthew spent his junior year studying in Lund, Sweden. He's now forming a nonprofit called Study Abroad Alumni International -- building a community of global citizens. Visit www.StudyAbroadAlumniInternational. org and www.StudyAbroadAlumni.ning.com.

Matthew Cossolotto
President/Author/Speaker
Ovations International, Inc.
'Home of the Standing O'
Yorktown Heights, NY United States
Contact Phone: 914-245-9721
Click to Contact from Web Site

MATTEO PEDERZOLI - ADVOCACY, PARTNERSHIP BUILDING REVERSE INNOVATION
Brussels, Belgium
http://be.linkedin.com/in/matteopederzoli

Track record presenting to financial services audiences of hundreds spanning 20 countries. Topics include professionalism, ethical selling, client advocacy (client-centric tools), NLP and behavioral finance. Quoted in international media. Facilitates performance improvements and organizational growth through change / activity management within the non- and for-profit sectors. Accomplished Association Business Executive: demonstrated in-depth analytical and strategic ability to facilitate operational and procedural planning throughout experience in international organization management - creating value via reverse innovation.

Matteo Pederzoli
Brussels, Belgium
Contact Phone: +32495616939
Click to Contact from Web Site

DR. HOWARD RASHEED -- IDEA ACCELERATOR TECHNOLOGIES
Wilmington, NC United States
http://www.idea-act.com/

Dr. Howard Rasheed is founder of The Institute for Innovation and CEO of Idea Accelerator Technologies. Idea Accelerator Technologies specializies in innovation, group collaboration and brainstorming, providing a methodology that stimulates creativity, a web-based application that alleviates the traditional barriers to effective planning and facilitation services for clients who want a turn-key project. His upcoming book, The Six Steps to Collective Genius is based on his proprietary Idea Accelerator Methodology. Dr. Rasheed is Associate Professor of Strategy and Entrepreneurship at the University of North Carolina Wilmington and holds a Ph.D. from The Florida State University.

Dr. Howard Rasheed
Institute for Innovation, Inc.
Wilmington, NC United States
Contact Phone: 877-789-8899
Contact Main Phone: 877-789-8899
Cell: (910) 431-1233
Click to Contact from Web Site

MICHAEL J. HERMAN - INSPIRATION MOTIVATION ATTITUDE SALES SPEAKER
Burbank, CA United States
www.michaeljherman.com/

Michael J. Herman is a recognized authority by most in the media on the topics of success, entrepreneurialism, and sales. *4,300 published articles in more than 300 publications since 1997 *'Mr. Motivation is uniquely qualified to speak and write on the topics of motivation, attitude, and sales.' *He's delivered more than 2,200 presentations since 1986, Michael J. Herman is recognized as one of America's leading authorities on Attitude, Sales, and Motivation. Having done it all. Not only success, but proven techniques for transmuting failure.

Michael J. Herman
President, CEO
The Motivational Minute Publishing Company
Burbank, CA United States
Contact Phone: 818-843-7783
Contact Main Phone: 818-843-7783
Cell: 818-441-9288
Click to Contact from Web Site

RICHARD MARTIN -- CANADIAN LEADERSHIP AND STRATEGY CONSULTANT
Montreal, Quebec Canada
http://www.alcera.ca

Richard Martin is founder and president of Alcera Consulting Inc. He brings his business and military leadership experience to bear for organizations and executives seeking to exploit change, maximize opportunity, and minimize risk. He has helped executives and organizations in both the private and public sectors to develop and implement corporate strategy, assess and mitigate risks and threats of all kinds, adapt structures and processes for the achievement of corporate strategic objectives, and create lasting improvements in individual and organizational performance.

Richard Martin
President
Alcera Consulting Inc.
N.D. Ile-Perrot, QC Canada
Contact Phone: 514-453-3993
Click to Contact from Web Site

GREG MACIOLEK - SPEAKER, AUTHOR, BUSINESS CONSULTANT
Knoxville, TN United States
www.imrtn.com/speaker.php

Speaker, author, consultant and session facilitator, Greg Maciolek focuses on the loss of productivity of workers through their mismanagement by owners and managers. He promotes the use of assessments for hiring and developing all employees. His insights into leadership, management, communications, performance feedback and hiring the right person for the job all combine into making Greg a top consultant to businesses. He is published in nine books. He is a former Air Force fighter pilot and commander.

Gregory Maciolek
President
Integrated Management Resources, Inc.
Knoxville, TN United States
Contact Phone: 800-262-6403
Contact Main Phone: 865-675-5901
Click to Contact from Web Site

CHOICE MAGAZINE -- PROFESSIONAL COACHES TRADE MAGAZINE
Toronto, Ontario Canada
http://choice-online.com

choice, the magazine of professional coaching, celebrating over 7 years as the quarterly professional magazine committed to being the unbiased source of information about professional coaching. Filled with articles, news, information & advertising related to professional coaching. It serves anyone who uses coaching, as well as those who are seeking information about professional development, human resources, management, personal & business dynamics & growth. choice is delivered anywhere in the world in print and/or electronic versions. A must read for anyone using coaching in their lives and careers. www.choice-online.com

Garry T. Schleifer, PCC
Choice Magazine
Toronto, ON Canada
Contact Phone: 416-925-6643
Click to Contact from Web Site

TOM CLARK -- EXECUTIVE COACHING
Lexington, KY United States
www.art-of-growth.com

I provide Mindfulness Based Executive Coaching, Change Leadership, Counseling & Teaching Mindfulness Meditation and Mindfulness Based Stress Reduction. I bring a contagious passion for life and a unique combination of experience professionally, academically, and in life. I was an international CEO and senior executive for 13 years. I was a senior level consultant in operations strategy and lean manufacturing. I have been running my business, the Bradford Clark Group since 1996 which focuses on Leadership & Organization Profiling and Assessment, Mindfulness Based Leadership Development & Executive Coaching, Change Management and teaching Mindfulness Meditation and Mindfulness Based Stress Reduction.

Tom Clark
the Bradford Clark Group
Lexington, KY United States
Contact Phone: 859-550-1655
Cell: 859-550-1655
Click to Contact from Web Site

FRANCIE DALTON -- CERTIFIED MANAGMENT CONSULTANT
Washington, DC United States
www.DaltonAlliances.com

Our mission at Dalton Alliances, Inc. is to provide organizations with a broad range of consulting services in the communication, management and behavioral sciences. We measurably enhance the success of our client companies by providing: 360 Degree Leadership Assessments and Customized Surveys, including, employee and member surveys, and constituent, augmented by follow up services and next steps. Professional Development Workshops, including Motivating the Unmotivated, Professional Presenting, Accelerated Problem Solving, Developmental Delegation, Conflict Management, and many others.

Rachel Dittman
Marketing Associate
Dalton Alliances
Columbia, MD United States
Contact Phone: 410.715.0484
Cell: 410.978.4868
Click to Contact from Web Site

TONY DOVALE - LIFE MASTERS
Johannesburg, South Africa
www.tonydovale.com

Tony Dovale is available for Professional Beyond Motivatioal Speaking Gigs, Business Keynotes, Leadership development sessions, REAL Appreciative Team Building process, Executive Coaching and professional presentations on New World of Happiness at work, Tribal Leadership. Tony is also the Author of The Action Advantage talks, workshops, sessions and Tribe Buildings Workshops.

Tony Dovale
Life Masters
Johannesburg, South Africa
Contact Phone: ++27834476300
Click to Contact from Web Site

MARSHA EGAN -- WORKPLACE PRODUCTIVITY COACH AND E-MAIL EXPERT
Nantucket, MA United States
www.inboxdetox.com

Marsha Egan, CPCU, PCC,is an ICF certified workplace productivity coach. Celebrated speaker, facilitator, executive coach, author, and internationally recognized e-mail productivity expert, she has coached leaders from some of the country's top companies and built a thriving coaching practice. Named one of PA's 50 Best Women in Business, she brings over twenty-five years of outstanding corporate and volunteer experience to her workplace productivity and executive coaching firm, The Egan Group, Inc. Having been featured in countless media outlets, includint ABC Nightly News, CNN, and USA Today, she is an internationally sought expert in goal, life and inbox management.

Marsha Egan, CPCU, PCC
CEO
InboxDetox.com, a division of The Egan Group, Inc.
Nantucket, MA United States
Contact Phone: 610-777-3795
Contact Main Phone: 877-749-4036
Cell: 610-780-1640
Click to Contact from Web Site

DAVID RIKLAN -- SELFGROWTH.COM
Morganville, NJ United States
http://www.selfgrowth.com

David Riklan is the president and founder of Self Improvement Online, Inc., the leading provider of self-improvement and personal growth information on the Internet. David's company was founded in 1998 and now maintains four websites on self-improvement and natural health: SelfGrowth.com SelfImprovementNewsletters.com, SelfGrowthMarketing.com and NaturalHealthWeb.com. SelfGrowth.com attracts over 1.2 million visitors per month, and David's six email newsletters reach over 950,000 weekly subscribers on the topics of self-improvement, natural health, personal growth, relationships, home business, sales skills, and brain improvement. His first book, Self Improvement: The Top 101 Experts Who Help Us Improve Our Lives, has been praised by leading

SelfGrowth.com
Morganville, NJ United States
Contact Phone: 732-617-1030 ext 101
Click to Contact from Web Site

DAVID ROHLANDER - THE CEO'S COACH
Los Angeles, CA United States
http://www.DAvidRohlander.com

When you want an articulate, candid and experienced point of view, call David G. Rohlander. A professional speaker, executive coach and Chairman of The CEO's Forum, David's passion is helping executives and organizations become the best that they can be. His life experience is useful. David's career consists of military, academic, corporate and entrepreneurial successes. Military experience is highlighted by leadership roles and being a USAF combat fighter pilot. David's teaching includes being an adjunct professor at six universities in the southwestern US. At Merrill Lynch David became a Regional Tax Investment Specialist and was appointed to the firm's Management Advisory Council. As an entrepreneur, he started and ran two companies, syndicated and developed real estate and still leads DGR Communications, a division of Rohlander, Inc. David is an Executive Coach and Professional Speaker.

David Rohlander
CEO
DGR Communications
Orange, CA United States
Contact Phone: 714-771-7043
Cell: 714-307-4438
Click to Contact from Web Site

DAVID G. ROHLANDER

DGR

The CEO's Coach

Get Real. Get Successful.

Your current business success is the result of years of hard work, smart choices and maybe a bit of luck. When you want to soar to the next level, it is essential to get an experienced point of view. I've been coaching executives and transforming organizations since 1979.

Working together, I will be a catalyst to help you focus, find purpose, gain perspective and then clarify and achieve your goals. Improved insight and renewed passion will enable you to create a masterpiece both professionally and personally for yourself and the world. *– DGR*

You will receive insight and wisdom from David based on his wide and varied experience as a former USAF combat fighter pilot, member of Merrill Lynch's Management Advisory Council, real estate syndicator and developer, and adjunct university professor. Founder and CEO of two companies, David continues his work of executive coaching and professional speaking while leading DGR Communications. David's MBA in finance is from California State University Fullerton, and his BA degree in literature and history is from Westmont College. Get real impact, relevance and results. Call today.

DAVID ROHLANDER · THE CEO'S COACH

David@DavidRohlander.com

714.771.7043

DGR Communications • PO Box 2558 • Orange, California 92859-0558

JOHN DI FRANCES
Wales, WI United States
www.difrances.com

DR. SARAH LAYTON -- BLUE OCEAN STRATEGY CONSULTANT
Orlando, FL United States
www.corporatestrategy.com/

JOHN COLLARD -- TURNAROUND INTERIM MANAGEMENT EXPERT
Annapolis, MD United States
www.StrategicMgtPartners.com

Our principal has been advisor to Presidents Bush (41&43), Clinton, Yeltsin, World Bank, EBRD, Investors on turnaround management and equity investing techniques. A leading turnaround management firm specializing in interim manager leadership, corporate renewal governance, asset & investment recovery, litigation support, M&A, equity investing in distressed troubled companies. We serve as CEO, Director, advisor to private equity investment funds, start-up and middle market companies representing the private equity, investment, manufacturing, defense, electronics, engineering services, computer, telecommunications, high tech, printing, job shop and marine industries. John is CTP, CITM, and inducted to Turnaround Management, Restructuring, Distressed Investing Industry Hall of Fame.

John M. Collard
Strategic Management Partners, Inc.
Annapolis, MD United States
Contact Phone: 410-263-9100
Click to Contact from Web Site

John DiFrances is a noted senior executive advisor and professional speaker. His nearly thirty years of international business experience include: defense, petroleum, medical, service, construction, manufacturing, export, nonprofit, government and other sectors. His clientele reaches from North America to Europe and Asia. John is a noted keynote conference and retreat speaker specializing in Leadership, Innovation and Synergy issues as they relate to corporate, government, nonprofit and academic organizations. He is also a prolific writer.

Nancy Miskelley
Director of Public Relations
DI FRANCES & ASSOCIATES, LLC
Wales, WI United States
Contact Phone: 262-968-9850
Contact Main Phone: 262-968-9850
Click to Contact from Web Site

Helping her clients make their competition irrelevant through value innovation is what Dr. Sarah Layton is all about. Recognized around the world for her ability to lead clients through activities that result in, not just identifying ways to find new untapped markets for the future, but to identify immediate ways they can become more competitive in their current environment. In just two days with a focused client, she can begin to show how they are similar to their competition and what they need to do to find new markets to serve. Qualified by the Blue Ocean Strategy® Initiative Centre - London in Blue Ocean Strategy® framework, concepts and tools, Dr. Layton, after 18 years of leading traditional strategic planning processes, believes this is the way of the future in strategy development. If a company wants to grow profitably into the future, traditional tools of strategic planning such as the SWOT analysis, brain storming, financial history, and customer surveys won't get you there.

Dr. Sarah Layton
Corporate Strategy Institute
Orlando, FL United States
Contact Phone: 407-876-2785
Click to Contact from Web Site

DEREK MILLS - THE STANDARDS GUY®
Birmingham, United Kingdom
www.derek-mills.com

When you meet Derek Mills, it's hard to imagine him as anything but charismatic, elegantly turned out in a suit with open neck shirt, completely comfortable in his own self. The challenge of being a stutterer since the age of 13 due to the shock of a sudden death in his family, remained with him as he entered the world of Financial Services. Derek is the creator of the '10 Second Philosophy®'. This unique approach guides you to set Standards instead of goals to achieve happiness and success.

Sonja Graham
Shirley, Solihull, West Midlands, West Midlands
United Kingdom
Contact Phone: +44 121 215 0909
Click to Contact from Web Site

AMY BETH O'BRIEN -- SPEAKER - AUTHOR - COACH
Boston, MA United States
www.AmyBethObrien.com

Amy is the four-time, award-winning author of Stuck with Mr. Wrong? Ten Steps to Starring in your own Life Story and Amazon Best-Selling co-author of A Juicy, Joyful Life. She is a certified coach and mind/body yoga instructor. She helps people who feel stuck. Whether they're working in a job they don't like, they long for more creative freedom, or have trouble identifying exactly what it is they want, Amy helps them remove blocks that hold them back and take steps to achieving their goals and dreams.

Amy Beth O'Brien
Wrenton, MA United States
Contact Phone: 978.500.0066
Click to Contact from Web Site

SUCCESSFUL TRANSITION PLANNING INSTITUTE
Cambridge, MA United States
www.SuccessfulTransitionPlanning.com/

Jack Beauregard is a nationally recognized expert and award-winning author whose work helps Baby Boomers create a new paradigm by transforming traditional retirement into the Platinum Years--an exciting, meaningful new stage of life. As CEO and founder of the Successful Transition Planning Institute, Jack helps Baby Boomer business owners, senior executives, and professional advisers learn how to integrate the Head and Heart issues that create successful personal and business transitions and fulfilling new lives.

Jack Beauregard
Founder, CEO
Successful Transtion Planning Institute
Cambridge, MA United States
Contact Phone: 617.576.5728
Cell: 617.267.9727
Click to Contact from Web Site

CHRIS DEVANY -- PINNACLE PERFORMANCE IMPROVEMENT WORLDWIDE

Wayland, MA United States
www.ppiw.com

Chris DeVany is the founder and president of Pinnacle Performance Improvement Worldwide, a firm which focuses on management and organization development. Pinnacle's clients include such organizations as Visa International, the Society for Human Resource Management (SHRM), U.S. Department of Housing and Urban Development, Sprint, American Counseling Association, Aviva Insurance, Microsoft, U.S. Patent and Trademark Office, Big Brothers and Big Sisters, Hospital Corporation of America, Schlumberger, Morgan Stanley, Boston Scientific, US HealthCare and over 500 other organizations in 22 countries. He has published numerous articles in the fields of project management, management, sales, team-building, leadership, ethics, customer service, diversity and work-life

Chris DeVany
President
Pinnacle Performance Improvement Worldwide
Wayland, MA United States
Contact Phone: 877-832-6790
Contact Main Phone: 508-358-8070
Pager: 617-308-8070
Cell: 617-308-8070
Click to Contact from Web Site

PATRINA M. CLARK, HCS, SPHR - PIVOTAL PRACTICES CONSULTING LLC

Washington, DC United States
pivotalpractices.com

Patrina has more than 25 years of experience in effective change management, performance improvement, strategy development, and organizational development. She has held leadership positions at the U.S. Government Accountability Office (GAO), Federal Election Commission (FEC), Department of Navy, and Internal Revenue Service (IRS). Her consulting firm, Pivotal Practices Consulting LLC, specializes in people-centered performance optimization. Patrina is certified as a Human Capital Strategist (HCS) and a Senior Professional in Human Resources (SPHR). She holds a Master of Science in Management (MSM) with a concentration in Human Resource Management from the University of Maryland. Patrina has also completed numerous graduate certificates in leadership, human resources, and project management from world-renowned institutions including Harvard Business School, Georgetown University, Cornell University, and George Washington University that combined with her extensive professional experience provide a global, well-rounded perspective for effectively and credibly addressing individual, team, and organizational challenges.

Patrina Clark
Pivotal Practices Consulting LLC
Hyattsville, MD United States
Contact Phone: 301-927-2389
Cell: 443-481-8511
Click to Contact from Web Site

ALAN SKRAINKA -- INVESTMENT MANAGER

St. Louis, MO United States
http://www.linkedin.com/pub/alan-skrainka-cfa/26/511/4a1

Alan Skrainka is a seasoned money manager and investment professional with 30 years of experience. Quoted in financial publications and interviewed by reporters across the country, Alan provides investment insight and analysis to investors, fellow advisors and financial journalists on the economy and markets. As Chief Investment Officer at Cornerstone Wealth Management, Alan Skrainka is responsible for managing the Cornerstone Model Wealth Program and serves as Chairman of the Investment Policy Committee. Securities offered through LPL Financial. -- Helping others understand the economy and the complex world of investing is Alan's passion. He's available for media interviews and seminars.

Alan Skrainka
Cornerstone Wealth Management
Des Peres, MO United States
Contact Phone: 314-394-1670
Contact Main Phone: 314-394-1670
Cell: 314-497-4191
Click to Contact from Web Site

SOCIETY FOR ADVANCEMENT OF CONSULTING, LLC
Boston, MA United States
http://www.consultingsociety.com

Society for Advancement of ConsultingSM LLC is dedicated to the advancement of independent consultants and solo practitioners. Our mission is to build the business, competencies, and 'voice' of consultants in the business community and within the organizational world.

Alan Weiss
Society for Advancement of Consulting
East Greenwich, RI United States
Contact Phone: 401-886-4097
Click to Contact from Web Site

GLEN BOYLS -- RISK MANAGEMENT - BUSINESS CONTINUITY EXPERT
Washington, DC United States
www.amxi.com

Mr. Boyls has been actively involved in Risk Management and Business Continuity Planning for the last twelve years of his twenty-five management consulting career. He is a Certified Business Continuity Professional, and a member of the Disaster Recovery Institute International, Association of Contingency Planners, Professional Risk Manager's International Association and the National Economist Club. Mr. Boyls has helped clients achieve over $1 billion in stakeholder value through risk mitigation, financial and operational improvements, program management and IT project turnarounds. Mr. Boyls founded AMX in 1991, is an alumnus of Ernst & Young, and has a graduate degree in Economics.

Glen Boyls
President
AMX International, Incorporated
Fairfax Station, VA United States
Contact Phone: 703-864-7046
Cell: 703-864-7046
Click to Contact from Web Site

MARK FAUST -- MANAGEMENT CONSULTANT
Cincinnati, OH United States
www.EchelonManagement.com

Since founding Echelon Management International in 1990, Faust has been a growth and turnaround consultant, syndicated writer, professional speaker, and executive coach to owners and CEOs. He has worked directly with and interviewed a dozen Fortune 500 CEOs as well as dozens of turnaround CEOs. His client companies have included companies such as P&G, IBM, Monsanto, Apple, Syngenta, Bayer, and John Deere, as well as smaller, closely held organizations, government agencies, and even nonprofits. He has been an adjunct COO, a VP of sales, a board member/advisor, and an adjunct professor at the University of Cincinnati and Ohio University.

Mark Faust
Echelon Management International
Cincinnati, OH United States
Contact Phone: 513-621-8000 ext 1
Cell: 513-623-8000
Click to Contact from Web Site

Patrina M. Clark, HCS, SPHR

Talent Strategist – People Person

- ● **Speaking engagements**
- ● **Meeting facilitation**
- ● **Customized workshops and seminars**
- ● **Strategic human resources consulting**
- ● **Executive coaching & leadership development**
- ● **Team building**
- ● **Public management consulting**

Patrina is President and Founder of Pivotal Practices Consulting LLC, a metro Washington, D.C.-based global management and strategic human resources consulting firm, specializing in people-centered performance optimization.

Patrina has more than 25 years of experience in leadership, effective change management, performance improvement, strategy development, and organizational development. She has held leadership positions at the U.S. Government Accountability Office (GAO), Federal Election Commission (FEC), Department of Navy and the Internal Revenue Service (IRS). She is passionate about employee engagement and commitment and has a special affinity for public servants.

PHONE:
301.927.2389 (phone)
1.855.85.PIVOT
(toll-free/fax)

EMAIL:
info@pivotalpractices.com
WEB:
http://pivotalpractices.com

INSTITUTE OF MANAGEMENT CONSULTANTS USA. INC.
Washington, DC United States
http://www.imcusa.org

Setting the standard for excellence and ethics in consulting since 1968, IMC USA is the premier professional association and sole certifying body for management consultants in the United States. Get a fresh perspective on consulting to management, business, government and non-profit organizations from IMC USA's member experts, who bring independence and objectivity to topics and trends in these sectors, and must adhere to a robust, adjudicable Code of Ethics. Our Certified Management Consultants® must meet or exceed global professional standards in ethics, consulting competencies, managing client relationships, project management, and personal conduct. Our organization is a charter member of the International Council of Management Consulting Institutes (IC-MCI), a 46-nation body that sets global standards for technical competence and professional conduct for management consultants. To find an expert member or Certified Management Consultant (CMC®), please contact Jane Blume at 505-294-1976, jblume@desertskycommunications.com.

Jane Blume CMC
Media Contact
Desert Sky Communications
Albuquerque, NM United States
Contact Phone: 505-294-1976
Contact Main Phone: 505-294-1976
Cell: 505-980-1874
Click to Contact from Web Site

CEO TONY JIMENEZ - FASTEST GROWING HISPANIC OWNED BUSINESS IN US
Vienna, VA United States
www.microtech.net

Tony Jimenez is the Founder and President & CEO of MicroTech - America's No. 1 Fastest-Growing Hispanic-Owned Business. Employing 400 highly skilled professionals, Tony has grown MicroTech into a multi-million dollar technology business. A military veteran and advocate for the Veteran and Hispanic communities, his public speaking topics include Entrepreneurship, Government Contracting, and Diversity Business. Among his business awards: Business Legend; Federal 100; Top CEO Philanthropist; Veteran Champion; Minority Business Leader. Tony has been profiled in INC., Washington Post, CNN, Business Week, American Legion, Veterans Business Journal, Federal Computer Week, Washington Business Journal, Hispanic Business, Executive Biz, SmartCEO

Michael Jordan
Sr. Marketing Manager
MicroTech
Vienna, VA United States
Contact Phone: 703-891-1073
Click to Contact from Web Site

ROBERT JORDAN -- AUTHOR - HOW THEY DID IT - PRESIDENT - INTERIMCEO
Chicago, IL United States
www.interimceo.com

Robert Jordan is an Inc. 500 CEO who founded and published Online Access, the first Internet-coverage magazine in the world. After the sale of Online Access, Jordan launched two companies: RedFlash, an interim management team; and interimCEO/interimCFO, the worldwide network for interim, contract, and project executives. Jordan is author of 'How They Did It: Billion Dollar Insights from the Heart of America', which will launch November 16, 2010. ordan received his bachelor's degree from the Honors College at the University of Michigan and his MBA from the Kellogg School of Management at Northwestern University.

Robert Jordan
CEO
InterimCEO, Inc.
Northbrook, IL United States
Contact Phone: 847-849-2800
Click to Contact from Web Site

Institute of Management Consultants USA

Get a fresh perspective on management and business.

When you need a reliable, independent and objective interview source on topics and trends in business and management, tap into one of the nation's largest corps of knowledge and thought leadership -- members of the Institute of Management Consultants USA (IMC USA).

Look for IMC USA Certified Management Consultants (CMC®) and Professional Members, who are authorities in:

> Ethics, leadership, change management, human resources, engineering, technology, risk management, operations, reengineering, supply chain, manufacturing, retail, biotech, government, military, finance, outsourcing, teambuilding, international business and trade, information security, small business, family business, intellectual property, marketing, profit marketing, governance, strategy, and more.

Search thousands of experts by key word, area of expertise or industry at www.imcusa.org.

The CMC (Certified Management Consultant) is an internationally recognized certification mark awarded by the Institute of Management Consultants USA as evidence of meeting the highest standards of consulting and adherence to the ethical canons of the profession. Less than 1% of all consultants have achieved this certification. IMC USA is the premier professional association and sole certifying body for management consultants in the U.S. and a member of the 43-nation International Council of Management Consulting Institutes.

Contact: experts@imcusa.org or Megan Renner, 800-221-2557

JOHN MARTINKA -- PARTNER ON-CALL NETWORK
Seattle, WA United States
http://www.partneroncall.com/johnmartinka/

Business owners, 'Without an Exit Strategy you Have No Strategy.' Planning and preparation can help dramatically in this area. There will be glut of businesses for sale in the 2010 decade. Stand out from the crowd by taking the time to have an exit/succession plan and prepare your company (and yourself) for the next stage be it a transfer or sale. Do you want to buy the right business the right way? Up to 80% of profitable businesses for sale are on the hidden market and we know to find them. These sellers don't advertise or employ a broker.

John Martinka
Partner On-Call Network
Kirkland, WA United States
Contact Phone: 425-576-1814
Click to Contact from Web Site

DONALD MCLACHLAN -- STRATEGIC PLANNING EXPERT
Austin, TX United States
www.silverquest.com

Donald McLachlan is a strategic planning expert, organizational designer, executive coach, and keynote speaker. He specializes in making problems go away and making dreams come true--sort of a combination of John Wayne and Walt Disney. Donald's client list includes Fortune 500 companies, healthcare systems, financial service firms, and major universities and colleges. His competencies include: Strategy, Growth, Innovation, Operations, Risk Management, Transformation, Leader Development, and Conflict Resolution. He partners with his clients to discover new insights and deliver customized solutions. Donald enjoys helping executives consistently make intelligent decisions that maximize opportunities, build capabilities, and increase long term competitive advantage.

Donald McLachlan
President and CEO
Silverquest Consulting Group
SilverQuest
Georgetown, TX United States
Contact Phone: 800-798-6540
Cell: 512-751-0102
Click to Contact from Web Site

D. ANTHONY MILES, PH.D., MCP, RBA, CMA, MBC
San Antonio, TX United States
www.mdicorpventures.com

Dr. D. Anthony Miles, is CEO and founder of Miles Development Industries Corporation®, a venture consulting practice and venture capital acquisition firm. Miles is a leading expert in the areas of entrepreneurial risk, entrepreneurship, and business model development. He has over 20 years experience in the private sector. He has held positions with fortune 500 companies. He consulted and developed a business plan and strategic plan for Brooks City-Base, a former military base that was under Base Realignment Closure (BRAC) in San Antonio, Texas. His background is in entrepreneurship/small business, venture capital, marketing, management, economic development, banking and industry research.

D. Anthony Miles, Ph.D.
CEO/Founder and Consultant
Miles Development Industries Corporation
San Antonio, TX United States
Contact Phone: 210-362-0460
Contact Main Phone: 210-362-0460
Cell: 210-362-0460
Click to Contact from Web Site

EUGENE A. RAZZETTI -- CERTIFIED MANAGEMENT CONSULTANT
Alexandria, VA United States
www.corprespmgmt.com

Do YOU want to have a Corporate Responsibility Management System that will: - Implement, maintain, and improve a high standard of ethical character in your organization, protecting both you and your personnel - Consolidate and comply with already-established Corporate Responsibility policies and regulations - Be certified by an external registrar recognized worldwide - Ensure adherence to your fiduciary as well as moral responsibilities as a corporation - Be confirmed by periodic self audits that the management system is maintained in accordance with an established Standard? AND Do YOU want the longevity and profitability that comes from building an effective, self-sustaining organization?

Eugene A. Razzetti
Eugene A. Razzetti, Management Consultant
Alexandria, VA United States
Contact Phone: 703 823 5238
Cell: (703) 309-2533
Click to Contact from Web Site

J. LANCE REESE --- SILVER PEAK CONSULTING
Idaho Falls, ID United States
http://www.silverpeakconsulting.com

J. Lance Reese is president and CEO of Silver Peak Consulting, Inc., a global consulting business based in Idaho Falls, Idaho. Lance is an accomplished consultant and coach, and is a sought after speaker. Prior to founding Silver Peak Consulting, Lance served as COO and CIO of global corporations ranging from $10M to $1B in revenues for over 17 years. Lance is The Technology Strategist. His expertise lies in leveraging technology to drive revenue and increase profitability. He teaches business leaders and managers the principles and methodologies needed to grow their businesses by maximizing the return from their technology investment. He expects and obtains world-class results from every team that he works with.

J. Lance Reese
Silver Peak Consulting
Idaho Falls, ID United States
Contact Phone: (208) 522-1693
Click to Contact from Web Site

REBECCA RYAN --- CAREER MANAGEMENT FOR THE ENTERPRISING WOMAN
Sydney, NSW, Australia
http://www.mindality.com.au/#!mindality-home

Mindality provides consulting and coaching in personal and professional development. We specialise in Cognitive Behavioural Coaching (CBC) and interpersonal communication to support you in your life, relationships and career. In particular, our focus is on women in business and the unique challenges women face not only in business and in their careers, but also the effects traditional family pressures (including raising children) can have on them. CBC can be used to improve all aspects of your life and although our focus is on your career and the workplace, you will find that the self awareness, skills and techniques you learn will help you in numerous area's of your life.

Rebecca Ryan
The Mind Collaborative
Drummoyne, New South Wales Australia
Contact Phone: 8003 6707/+61 404 12
Click to Contact from Web Site

SUMMIT CONSULTING GROUP, INC. -- ALAN WEISS, PH.D.
East Greenwich, RI United States
http://www.summitconsulting.com

Alan Weiss, Ph.D., is one of the most highly regarded independent consultants in the country, according to the New York Post. He is the author of the best-selling Million Dollar Consulting (McGraw-Hill), as well as 45 other books appearing in 9 languages. He is the only non-journalist ever awarded the Lifetime Achievement Award by the American Press Institute, and is one of only two people in history named as a Fellow of the Institute of Management Consulting and as a member of the Professional Speakers Hall of Fame.

Crysta Ames
Office Manager
Summit Consulting Group, Inc.
East Greenwich, RI United States
Contact Phone: 401-884-2778
Click to Contact from Web Site

THOUGHT LEADING WOMEN
San Francisco, CA United States

Imagine a world where your concept of someone with profound ideas is a woman. Because when you think about it, most people who change the way we think - experts on TV, scientists, economists, business gurus, and the like, are men. I develop talented, driven women (and a man or two, of course) in a variety of fields, who have big ideas no-one else has thought of, to be acknowledged as the undisputed go-to, leading authority in their area of expertise. Using my 3D Influencer™ process, we define their idea, develop it (usually in book form), and spread the word through branding, packaging and promotion, to make their big idea accessible to a wide audience. Catch a snippet of my thinking about this in my response to a Business Week article on personal branding, which they published:

Roberta Guise
San Francisco, CA United States
Contact Phone: 415-979-0611
Click to Contact from Web Site

DRAY WHARTON -- MANAGEMENT CONSULTANT
Denver, CO United States
www.whartonandcompany.com

Wharton & Co. is a management consultancy based in the Denver metro area. We work with a number of other management and technology professionals to help businesses improve productivity, increase profits, implement change, and address challenges. Our goal is to bring value and expertise to our clients and build long-term relationships. Our work focuses on productivity frameworks and we work with individuals, teams, groups and entire companies to introduce and lead change.

Dray Wharton
Principal
Wharton & Co. LLC
Aurora, CO United States
Contact Phone: 303-317-6519
Click to Contact from Web Site

JIM CAMP - NEGOTIATION EXPERT
Dublin, OH United States
www.startwithno.com

From 'Start With No' by Jim Camp: Win-Win Will Get You Killed. How often over the past couple of decades have we read or heard the phrase 'win-win'? Thousands, I guess. Enough, I know. The term has become a clich [e92069]n our culture, the only acceptable paradigm for personal interaction of any sort. It all sounds so good, what stick-in-the-mud could possibly disagree that win-win is the model to use in negotiation? Well, I disagree. Based on my nearly 20 years of experience as a negotiation coach, I believe win-win is misguided, and I 'Start With No.'

Jim Camp
Founder/CEO
Camp Negotiation Systems
Vero Beach, FL United States
Contact Phone: 614-764-0213
Cell: 614 296 4901
Click to Contact from Web Site

SHAWN CASEMORE - OPERATIONAL PERFORMANCE AND LEADERSHIP DEVELOPMENT
Toronto, Ontario Canada
www.CasemoreAndCo.com

Shawn Casemore has spent nearly two decades managing teams and advising business leaders on improving their operational performance. He has worked with dynamic companies including Magna International, Arvin Meritor, Bellwyck Packaging Solutions and Bruce Power. A recognized speaker and writer, Shawn's provocative views have been published in print and online in several industry publications including the Globe and Mail, purchasing b2b, CFO.com and Enterprise Apps Today. He frequently speaks to business owners and executives at national and regional conferences on the topics of operational efficiency and leadership.

Shawn Casemore
President
Casemore and Co
Owen Sound, ON Canada
Contact Phone: (519) 470-7697
Contact Main Phone: (519) 470-7697
Click to Contact from Web Site

GLOBAL STRATEGIC MANAGEMENT SOLUTIONS
Palm Beach Gardens, FL United States
www.globalstrategicmgmt.com

Doreen is an engaging guest speaker who can offer plenty of hands-on experience and practical tips for audiences on leadership. Both organizations and individuals have come to rely upon Dr. McGunagle year after year for her strategic insights and results-focused action plans. Doreen's ability to get to the root causes in performance breakdowns has guided organizations to achieve performance breakthroughs that show up readily in the balance sheet and beyond. She discovered her passion for creating effective leaders early in her career. Her mentors reinforced that effective leaders transform people, teams, and organizations to achieve extraordinary results. Check Dr. McGunagle' availability for your next function!

Doreen M. McGunagle, Ph.D.
CEO
Global Strategic Management Solutions, Inc.
Palm Beach Gardens, FL United States
Contact Phone: 561.208.1071
Cell: 561.310.7537
Click to Contact from Web Site

CHAS KLIVANS -- THE CEO'S NAVIGATOR
Orange County, CA United States
www.InnovationTwo.Us

Chas Klivans' personal journey helped him develop a real life survival prototype during seven years existing in hostile territory, which he then applied to get out alive from an Afghanistan prison and afterward to escape capture from the Maoist Terrorists in the Amazon jungle. The prototype later evolved into a business survival tool kit called Innovation [b2] which has been field-tested in real companies for the past 28 years with Chas, as CEO or Co-Founder, leading teams through adversity to achieve ambitious results.

Chas Klivans
The CEO's Navigator
Tustin, CA United States
Contact Phone: 714-508-5972
Click to Contact from Web Site

LARRY LAROSE -- PERFORMANCE COACH
Washington, DC United States
www.larrylarose.com

The Business Troubleshooter: Power Presentation and Performance Coach. I Make You Positively Memorable! Combining the Art of Business and Theater to Discover the Award Winning 'Performer' in YOU! Larry LaRose is an award winning actor and veteran of over 60 stage production and he is also the recipient of over 35 business management and development awards. By combining this unique set of skills Larry can help you, your staff and your employees give an award winning performance every day in your business and your life. Because when you ACT like a winner, you PERFORM like a winner!

Larry LaRose
Innovative Creative Solutions, LLC
Bowie, MD United States
Contact Phone: 301-809-6437
Click to Contact from Web Site

SUZANNE O'CONNOR -- QUALITY IMPROVEMENT EXPERT
Boston, MA United States
www.SuzanneOConnor.com

For more than 30 years Suzanne has been involved in direct patient contact in a wide variety of health care settings. This has given her an in-depth understanding of what patients need and how to increase trust, satisfaction, and their motivation to take care of their health. She has been a healthcare organizational consultant for almost 20 years, guiding major changes in many hospital, home care, hospice, and rehabilitation organizations. She consults with out-patient and in-patient health care leaders and staff to create productive teams and system improvements and create loyal customers and staff.

Suzanne O'Connor
Andover, MA United States
Contact Phone: 978-475-4862
Click to Contact from Web Site

GARY W. PATTERSON -- ENTERPRISE RISK MANAGEMENT EXPERT
Atlanta, GA United States
http://www.FiscalDoctor.com

Gary works with leaders to uncover blind spots so they can make better business decisions. This helps leaders avoid costly problems and increase profits. He also carrys out rigorous due diligence and enterprise risk management (ERM) reviews, and partnering with those leaders on critical fiscal and financial projects. Dramatically accelerate correct fiscal leadership decisions! Risks are what really go wrong when you are not looking: stupid things like bounced checks, losing your best customers or best people when you are blindsided. Gary helps you create peripheral vision in your business so you are not blindsided. You need a perspective of business under the microscope and to have lived to tell the tale. Author of Stick Out Your Balance Sheet and Cough: Best Practices for Long-Term Business Health, The Fiscal Fitness System: Understanding Balance Sheets, Income Statements, and Cash Flow and Million Dollar Blind Spot: 20/20 Vision into Financial Growth.

Gary W. Patterson
Trusted Advisor
FiscalDoctor Inc.
Alpharetta, GA United States
Contact Phone: 781-237-3637
Contact Main Phone: 678-319-4739
Cell: 781-237-3637
Click to Contact from Web Site

PHIL SYMCHYCH -- STRATEGIC ADVICE CONSULTANT
Regina, Saskatoon Canada
www.businesssuccessforlife.com

Phil Symchych is an expert in accelerating profitable growth. With over 20 years of experience, Phil provides strategic and financial advice to help small business and mid-market companies to dramatically increase profits, enhance business valuation, and create transition and exit plans for entrepreneurs. As an MBA and Chartered Accountant, Phil has the holistic perspective and detailed approach that provides pragmatic advice and fast results to help business owners maximize their results and profits. He has raised millions in financing and turned busy entrepreneurs into multimillionaires.

Phil Symchych
Symco & Co.
Regina, SK Canada
Contact Phone: 306-569-9111
Click to Contact from Web Site

JOHN J. TRACY, JR. CMC -- LOGISTICS EXPERT
South Orange, NJ United States
http://www.tracy-hayden.com/

Experienced Logistics (Supply Chain, Inventory Management and Materials Management, Physical Distribution, Warehousing, Materials Handling, Information Systems and Organization) Consultants, Tracy-Hayden Associates works closely with its clients to achieve client objectives and goals.

John J. Tracy, Jr. CMC
Tracy-Hayden Associates
South Orange, NJ United States
Contact Phone: 973-736-6111
Click to Contact from Web Site

CARL VAN -- EMPLOYEE AND MANAGEMENT PERFORMANCE
New Orleans, LA United States
www.insuranceinstitute.com

Carl Van, Claims Expert, is one of the most highly sought-after keynote speakers and presenters at conferences in the U.S. and Canada. With over 70 published articles and two books on the characteristics of truly exceptional performers, Carl Van is called upon over 120 times per year to present on his expertise in claims and employee performance. He is President of International Insurance Institute, publisher of Claims Education Magazine, creator of Claims Education On Line, Board President of Claims Education Conference and Claims Executive Academy, and owner of ClaimsProfessionalBooks.com. His new book is entitled 'Gaining Cooperation.'

Carl Van
International Insurance Institue
Gretna, LA United States
Contact Phone: 888-414-8811
Cell: 615-479-2633
Click to Contact from Web Site

JOHN DOEHRING -- MANAGEMENT CONSULTING
Boston, MA United States
http://www.jdoehring.com/

J. Doehring & Co. provides management consulting, executive education, and professional speaking services primarily focused on the markets of professional services firms and their leaders. We advise senior management on issues of significance, and collaborate with client organizations to achieve extraordinary business performance improvement and success. Areas of special focus include business strategy design and implementation; marketing and business development results; leadership development, succession planning, and transition; and operations turnaround, transformation, and sustainable excellence. John Doehring is a recognized and highly regarded strategist, engaging and thought provoking educator, and passionate and high energy keynote speaker. John has worked in and led organizations both large and small, and he is a successful entrepreneur now twice-over. John speaks regularly to audiences in both public conference and seminar settings and in private client venues - he's spoken to and helped hundreds of organizations and their leaders across the spectrum of business.

John Doehring
J. Doehring & Co., LLC
Pepperell, MA United States
Contact Phone: 978.433.6848
Cell: 978.877.9148
Click to Contact from Web Site

LINDA POPKY - LEVERAGE2MARKET ASSOCIATES, INC.
San Francisco, CA United States
www.leverage2market.com

Linda Popky, President of Leverage2Market Associates, Inc. is a senior marketing professional, author, speaker, and educator who helps transform organizations through powerful marketing results. Leverage2Market works with a wide range of organizations from startups and small businesses to Fortune 100 companies to get the best possible return on each marketing investment.

Linda Popky
President
Leverage2Market Associates
Redwood City, CA United States
Contact Phone: 650 281-4854
Click to Contact from Web Site

Gary Patterson

FiscalDoctor™
Enhancing Growth & Profitability

Gary Patterson has more than 30 years of senior management experience with high-growth technology, manufacturing and service companies. He has worked with more than 200 companies — from start-ups to Inc 500 to Fortune 500 — providing high-level strategic guidance and expertise, helping them successfully navigate that often murky pathway to exceptional growth and profitability.

As a trusted advisor, Patterson's FiscalDoctor™ helps CEOs, board members, executive teams, private equity investors and owners achieve fiscal health. From a quick financial assessment to a comprehensive financial management review, Fiscal Doctor™ will heal what ails you.

Patterson's extraordinary track record includes building two start-ups (each achieving $10 million revenue their first year), diagnosing company oversights to save $150K to $3 million annually; guiding a young company through a liquidity search, resulting in $25 million in financing, and; helping a company broaden its client base 525 percent, increasing revenue from $16 million to $100 million.

His international experience includes serving as European coordinator for the global enterprise-wide application software pilot program for a Fortune 500 company.

Patterson holds an MBA in Finance and Operations from Stanford University, a BA in Accounting from the University of Mississippi and a CPA.

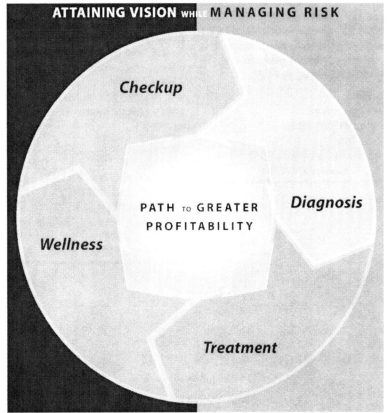

ATTAINING VISION WHILE MANAGING RISK

Checkup

Diagnosis

PATH TO GREATER PROFITABILITY

Wellness

Treatment

Gary W. Patterson
21 Westerly Street, Suite 7, Wellesley, Massachusetts 02482
781.237.3637
gary@FiscalDoctor.com ■ www.FiscalDoctor.com

RICK MAURER -- CHANGE MANAGEMENT EXPERT

Arlington, VA United States
www.BeyondResistance.com

Leading change. Two-thirds of major changes in organizations fail. That's a lot of wasted money, time and opportunities. Resistance is the primary reason these initiatives fail - and Rick Maurer wrote the book on resistance. (Beyond the Wall of Resistance) He advises leaders of organizations on change. His opinion is sought by major media. Learn why his Change without Migraines approach is so popular - and practical. He can address why mergers and other new projects fail - and offer proven strategies to avoid the pitfalls.

Rick Maurer
Maurer & Associates
Arlington, VA United States
Contact Phone:
Contact Main Phone: 703-525-7074
Click to Contact from Web Site

DAVID MOREY -- THE UNDERDOG ADVANTAGE

Washington, DC United States
www.playoffense.com

It's the toughest environment in business history. Today, 95% of start-up businesses fail by their 10th year—as do 80% of corporate products. Consumer research shows unprecedented distrust, cynicism and even anger. For all companies, these are remarkably topsy-turvy times. It's the toughest time in history for the incumbent. David Morey is one of America's most sought after speakers. He brings alive the insurgent strategies that helped him win presidential campaigns on four continents— and add market value and profit to some of the world's greatest companies. He shows audiences how to win.

David Morey
Vice Chairman
Core Strategy Group
Washington, DC United States
Contact Phone: 888-626-9776
Contact Main Phone: 202-223-7945
Cell: 404-682-5460
Click to Contact from Web Site

MELVIN J. GRAVELY II PH.D. - INSTITUTE FOR ENTREPRENEURIAL THINKING, LTD.

Cincinnati, OH United States
http://www.entrethinking.com

If you own a business, you will want to know this guy! He is the Entrepreneurial Coach Mel Gravely is a recognized expert, author and national speaker on the subjects of entrepreneurship and small business development. As the founder of the Institute For Entrepreneurial Thinking, Mel has helped thousands of entrepreneurs get the results they expect. Entrepreneurs: He is one, he's coached them & no one knows them better. Entrepreneurs: He is one, he's coached them & no one knows them better. What are the four principles every entrepreneur better know? What are the three moves guaranteed to improve your business? Why marketing never works & how you can get customers anyway. What are the two things you must know about getting capital? How has the 'new economy' ruined entrepreneurship? How can you grow a 'solo business' and still keep it solo? What is the one, overwhelming reason businesses fail and how you can avoid it?

Robin Bischoff
Program Manager
Institute For Entrepreneurial Thinking, LTD.
Cincinnati, OH United States
Contact Phone: 513-469-6772
Click to Contact from Web Site

Melvin J. Gravely II, Ph.D.

Author of

When Black & White Make Green

Expert on Minority Business Development

Dr. Melvin Gravely is professionally dedicated to developing capacity and opportunity for minority entrepreneurs. Dr. Gravely is a sought-after keynote speaker and respected advisor to major corporations, chambers of commerce executives, urban city leaders and NMSDC affiliates.

Dr. Gravely is a frequent guest on radio stations and has been featured in many national publications. After ten successful years working for a large corporation, he co-founded a civil engineering firm and grew it to a multimillion-dollar company. He is the author of five other books, including "The Lost Art of Entrepreneurship."

Leading the Next Evolution of Business & Race

As founder of the Institute for Entrepreneurial Thinking, Dr. Gravely's mission is to help clients improve the outcomes of minority business development initiatives.

He is the leading authority on issues related to minority business development.

Clients look to Dr. Gravely to assist them in overcoming the legacy of missed expectations and in creating strategies that produce tangible outcomes.

Core Principles That Highlight His Approach

- Professional Interactions
- Balanced Perspective
- Practical Approach
- Market Driven Solutions

Frequently Requested Topics

- Economic Inclusion
- Partnering to Prosper
- Minority Business Development
- Supplier Diversity
- The Power of Entrepreneurial Thinking
- The Lost Art of Entrepreneurship

"Mel Gravely has spoken several times to the members of the American Chamber of Commerce Executives (ACCE) and has consulted for several chambers. He brings lively, important and original perspective to the key topic of minority and small business development. Chamber executives appreciate his practical approach."

-- *Mick Fleming, President and CEO*
American Chamber of Commerce Executives

The Institute for Entrepreneurial Thinking, Ltd.

P.O. Box 621170
Cincinnati, Ohio 45262-1170
Telephone: 513-469-6772
Fax: 513-793-6776

Melvin Gravely II, Ph.D.
Managing Director
513-469-6772, ext. 12
Email: Mel@entrethinking.com

ED RIGSBEE -- STRATEGIC ALLIANCE AND BUSINESS RELATIONSHIP EXPERT

Los Angeles, CA United States
www.edrigsbee.com

Author of 'Developing Strategic Alliances.' One of America's most prolific authors on the subject of Business Growth from Smart Strategic Alliances, Ed Rigsbee is a consultant and advisor to world class clients such as Toyota, 3M, Dun & Bradstreet, BE Aerospace, George Fischer Signet, Mead, Siemens, Roland, Best Buy and others. He travels internationally to assist organizations in building strategic alliance relationships and to improve their total effectiveness and profitability. As a strategic alliance consultant, Rigsbee will help you develop and implement smart strategic alliances for continued business growth. His other books include: 'PartnerShift--How to Profit from the Partnering Trend,' 'The Art of Partnering.' 'Kids, Parents & Soccer.' To access all of Ed Rigsbee's content-specific Web sites and blogs, visit www.EdRigsbee.com.

Ed Rigsbee, CSP
President
Developing Strategic Alliances
Thousand Oaks, CA United States
Contact Phone: 805-444-0957
Cell: 805-444-0957
Click to Contact from Web Site

DR. JULIA SLOAN -- GLOBAL STRATEGIC THINKING EXPERT

New York, NY United States
www.sloaninternationalconsulting.com

Dr. Julia Sloan is a leading international authority on learning strategic thinking. The author of the definitive book, Learning to Think Strategically, she is widely recognized for her pioneering work in the application of complex cognitive theory to everyday global strategic thinking practice. Julia draws on 20+ years global business experience in emerging economies and is available for: interviews, speaking, consulting & seminars. Julia earned a doctorate from Columbia University; master's studies at Yale University and University of Alaska; and undergraduate studies at Kent State University.

Dr. Julia Sloan
Principal
Sloan International Consulting
New York, NY United States
Contact Phone: 212-362-9455
Click to Contact from Web Site

MAURICE EVANS -- VIRAL MARKETING EXPERT -- ABUNDANT LIFE COACH

Tampa, FL United States
www.igrowyourbiz.com

Maurice W. Evans, aka 'Mr. iGROWyourBiz' is a Business and Abundant Life Coach. He is a Licensed Pastor, Certified Guerrilla Marketing Trainer and Certified John Maxwell Coach, Speaker and Trainer. He's the original creator of the social network NetworkingCity.com. Maurice is an author, dynamic conference speaker and viral marketing Expert. His firm offers a money back guarantee and focuses on helping businesses grow their brand using proven methods and technologies. His ministry focuses on helping people discover their purpose, live life abundantly and experience their destiny. To book coaching or speaking engagements with Maurice call Toll Free 1-800-691-2WIN or http://www.iGROWyourBiz.com

Maurice Evans
CEO
iGROWyourBiz
Viral Marketing Expert
Tampa, FL United States
Contact Phone: 800-691-2WIN
Contact Main Phone: 800-691-2WIN
Cell: 530-763-2867
Click to Contact from Web Site

JUDI MOREO -- A SPEAKER WITH SUBSTANCE AND STYLE
Las Vegas, NV United States
http://www.judimoreo.com/home.htm

Judi doesn't just talk about success. . .She Lives It! In 2003, the US Business Advisory Council named her "Nevada Business Person of the Year" and the Las Vegas Chamber of Commerce awarded her company, Turning Point International, with a "Circle of Excellence" Award. In 1986, the Chamber also honored her as "Woman of Achievement - Entrepreneur." Today, she lives in Las Vegas, Nevada and serves as President of Turning Point International, a performance improvement company with offices in Las Vegas and Johannesburg. Her client list reads like a Who's Who of the World's Most Prestigious Companies and Organizations.

Judi Moreo
President
Turning Point International
Las Vegas, NV United States
Contact Phone: 702-896-2228
Cell: 702-283-4567
Click to Contact from Web Site

ASSOCIATION FOR STRATEGIC PLANNING
Los Angeles, CA United States
http://www.StrategyPlus.org/

The Association for Strategic Planning (ASP) is the preeminent professional association for those engaged in strategic thinking, planning, and action. ASP has members in 40 states and several foreign countries, as well as active chapters operating in 14 metropolitan areas. Several others are in formation. The chapters serve the local area with networking and educational programs geared to the subject of strategic planning. ASP offers a strategic planning certification program based on a rigorous Body of Knowledge.

Jennifer Beever
P.R. Contact
Association for Strategic Planning
Los Angeles, CA United States
Contact Phone: 818-347-4248
Cell: 818-347-4248
Click to Contact from Web Site

D. KEVIN BERCHELMANN - SPEAKER -- STRATEGIST -- EXECUTIVE FACILIT
Houston, TX United States
http://www.triangleperformance.com

Kevin Berchelmann is an expert in management, leadership, and strategy, specializing in organizational development and value-added human capital strategies. With 20+ years of senior executive experience before starting his successful consulting firm, Triangle Performance, LLC, Kevin is an engaging and sought-after speaker, and his firm was recently awarded #9 on Houston's 'Fast 100,' fastest-growing privately held companies. Client list includes Fortune 100 (Archer-Daniels Midland, Sprint) through small, family-owned businesses located across the country.

D. Kevin Berchelmann
President & Founder
Triangle Performance, LLC
Spring, TX United States
Contact Phone: 281-257-4442
Click to Contact from Web Site

LOREEN SHERMAN, MBA - BUSINESS CONSULTANT & LEADERSHIP SPEAKER
Calgary, Alberta Canada
www.loreensherman.com

A specialist on organizational leadership development, Loreen Sherman appears at business conferences to translate strategic vision into clear SMART (specific, measurable, attainable, realistic and timeline) goals for executive leadership and mentor them to success. Loreen knows how to assess and evaluate high performance teams. You want growth, don't you? 81% of companies with ongoing management programs had strong business results. Connect with Loreen, a seasoned master in leadership and a business expert. Let her diagnostic insights outline solutions. Invite Loreen to speak and find out how your firm or organization can be more productive and innovative. Hurry, call 1.877.896.7292 today!

Loreen Sherman, MBA
Business Consultant & Leadership Speaker
Star-Ting Incorporated
Calgary, AB Canada
Contact Phone: 403.289.2292
Click to Contact from Web Site

ANGELA DINGLE -- EX NIHILO MANAGEMENT, LLC
Washington, DC United States
www.thefemaleentrepreneur.blogspot.com/

Angela Dingle, President of Ex Nihilo Management, LLC, is a Certified Management Consultant (CMC) with over 20 years of experience in business, leadership, IT governance, risk management, compliance, systems engineering and quality assurance. She holds a MS in Management Information Systems from Bowie State University, a BS in Computer Science from DeVry Institute and is Certified in the Governance of Information Technology (CGEIT). She is a National Partner and Diversity Co-Chair for the Executive Advisory Board of Women Impacting Public Policy (WIPP), and VP of Professional Development for the Institute of Management Consultants National Capital Region (NCR).

Angela Dingle
President
Ex Nihilo Management, LLC
Washington, DC United States
Contact Phone: 202-379-4884
Click to Contact from Web Site

BETH CAMPBELL DUKE -- PERSONAL BRANDING
Victoria, British Columbia Canada
http://CampbellDuke.com

Beth Campbell Duke is a former high school teacher who now runs CampbellDuke Personal Branding helping people find or create work they LOVE. Personal Branding helps people discover and build on their strengths, create an effective online 'brand' and understand and work their personal networks. Beth's new youth program, Werd OUT, helps engage high school students in their own education and sets them on the road to personal and work-life success. Find out more at CampbellDuke.com and WerdOUT.ca.

Beth Campbell Duke
Principal
CampbellDuke Personal Branding
Fanny Bay, BC Canada
Contact Phone: 250-335-1752
Contact Main Phone: 250-335-1752
Cell: 250-650-1527
Click to Contact from Web Site

D. Kevin Berchelmann

Thought-leader, Expert Consultant,
Strategist, Executive Facilitator

IMPROVING MANAGER AND ORGANIZATION PERFORMANCE

D. Kevin Berchelmann, president, CEO and principal consultant, is a highly acclaimed strategist and thought leader in executive, management and organization performance.

Bottom line: Leadership is a learned skill, and management performance can change the course of any -- ANY -- organization. The key is in the "learning," and contrary to the plethora of trainers in this business, few can actually "develop" leaders successfully.

From executive teambuilding, strategy development and compensation, to individualized coaching, performance improvement and retention, Berchelmann has been incredibly successful in delivering results and measurable value in this critical environment.

These results most recently include:

- Management and leadership development for multiple levels of a Fortune 50 manufacturer;

- Executive and incentive compensation for a publicly traded construction company;

- Executive development and succession planning for a $750M services firm;

- Strategy and HR advisor to several firms of various sizes, industries and markets.

Triangle Performance was recently named #9 on Houston's Fast 100 fastest growing, privately held companies.

A decorated 13-year Armed Forces veteran, Berchelmann has a corporate background which includes senior executive roles in human resources, operations and general management for multiple Fortune 1000 and privately held firms. Company profiles and industries include technology, manufacturing, professional services, construction, not for profit and biopharmaceutical. Additionally, he has extensive experience with investor-led, vendor-backed start-up and ongoing firms.

Berchelmann is a sought-after speaker, invited to present, "Contingency Retention: Keeping the Key Employee," at the Winning the War for Talent: Recruiting and Retaining Employees conference held in San Francisco, and "Motivation & Performance Incentives: Creating Star Performers," at the Customer Care Summit in Las Vegas. His presentation for the International Zinc Association, "Human Resources -- a Global Focus," was lauded as the best presentation during the five-day international executive event, Zinc College in Golden, Colo.

D. Kevin Berchelmann

Founder and President
Triangle Performance, LLC
6046 FM 2920 #320
Spring, Texas 77379
281.257.4442
866.831.7645 Fax
kevinb@triangleperformance.com
www.triangleperformance.com

"Kevin Berchelmann is... a human capital expert."
The Harvard Business Press

"Kevin... is a prominent strategist and thought-leader in effective human capital strategy."
ASQ's Journal for Quality and Participation

TRIANGLE
PERFORMANCE, LLC

MARKETING AND BRANDING ADVICE FOR THE REST OF US

Roberta Guise has answers about branding, promotions, getting known, being acknowledged as a leading authority, and using social media effectively.

KEY TOPICS

- How to find out what customers really want and value
- What to do to be sure one's marketing efforts pay off
- Effective marketing strategies in a Web 2.0 world
- Marketing pitfalls—what to do to avoid them and save a ton of money
- How to compete, get known and be extra in a most competitive marketplace
- 5 key steps to becoming an innovative marketer
- Ways to cater for customers to the point of obsession
- The 5 essential steps for successful women to become thought leaders

Roberta Guise
Small Business Marketing Expert

**Incisive.
Timely.
Thoughtful.**

Let Roberta's ideas capture your readers' imagination.

ROBERTA GUISE, MBA -- SMALL BUSINESS MARKETING EXPERT

San Francisco, CA United States
www.GuiseMarketing.com

Marketing and PR consultant Roberta Guise advises small business owners, independent professionals and non-profits on how to build a profitable stable of customers, save money on ineffective promotions, and get known through branding, precision marketing and public relations. Roberta also enables successful women to become thought leaders. She coaches clients one-one-one, and writes and speaks on how to get a distinctive marketing edge and be extraordinarily visible. For a lively mix of her ideas and opinions, read her articles at www.guisemarketing.com/bevisible-blog, and podcast profiles of influential women at www.guisemarketing.com/straighttalk

Roberta Guise, MBA
Guise Marketing and PR
San Francisco, CA United States
Contact Phone: 415-979-0611
Click to Contact from Web Site

DEBBIE LACHUSA: MONEY SUCCESS HAPPINESS AUTHOR & SPEAKER

San Diego, CA United States
www.debbielachusa.com

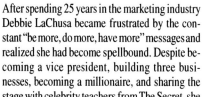

After spending 25 years in the marketing industry Debbie LaChusa became frustrated by the constant "be more, do more, have more" messages and realized she had become spellbound. Despite becoming a vice president, building three businesses, becoming a millionaire, and sharing the stage with celebrity teachers from The Secret, she realized she still didn't feel successful, happy, or rich, and was still chasing more. She discovered she wasn't alone and set out to break the spell, transform herself, and inspire others to stop chasing money, success, and happiness and discover how to a live a happy, healthy, and wealthy life.

Debbie LaChusa
Founder and President
DLC Marketing, Inc.
Santee, CA United States
Contact Phone: 619-334-8590
Cell: 619-840-8619
Click to Contact from Web Site

NATHAN R MITCHELL--SMALL BUSINESS EXPERT

Tulsa, OK United States
www.clutchconsulting.net

Nathan R Mitchell, Founder of Clutch Consulting, is a Small-Business Coach, Author, & Speaker. Nathan is dedicated to helping small-business owners and aspiring entrepreneurs reach new levels of success in their business and personal life through services that are empowering and insightful. Nathan's passion for business and entrepreneurship, and for the winners who pursue it, started in young adulthood, and has stayed with him to this day. He has earned a Bachelor of Science Degree in Entrepreneurial Management, and an MBA from Missouri State University. He is currently authoring his fist book on entrepreneurship, 'Give Me The Ball!'

Nathan R Mitchell
Small Business Coach
Clutch Consulting LLC
Tulsa, OK United States
Contact Phone: 918-894-6953
Cell: 918-851-7246
Click to Contact from Web Site

MARKETING AND BRANDING ADVICE FOR THE REST OF US

Roberta Guise has answers about branding, promotions, getting known, being acknowledged as a leading authority, and using social media effectively.

KEY TOPICS

- How to find out what customers really want and value
- What to do to be sure one's marketing efforts pay off
- Effective marketing strategies in a Web 2.0 world
- Marketing pitfalls—what to do to avoid them and save a ton of money
- How to compete, get known and be visible in a noisy, competitive marketplace
- 3 key steps to becoming an innovative marketer
- Ways to care for customers to the point of obsession
- The 5 essential steps for successful women to become thought leaders

Roberta Guise
Small Business Marketing Expert

Incisive. Timely. Thoughtful.

Let Roberta's ideas capture your readers' imagination.

Marketing and PR expert *Roberta Guise* advises small business owners, independent professionals and non-profits on how to build a profitable stable of customers, save money on ineffective promotions, and get known through branding, precision marketing and public relations.

An award-winning marketer, Roberta also enables successful women to become thought leaders. For a lively mix of her ideas and opinions, read her articles at www.guisemarketing.com/bevisibleblog, and podcast profiles of influential women at www.guisemarketing.com/straighttalk

Be Visible!

Roberta Guise, MBA | Roberta@guisemarketing.com
Guise Marketing & PR: **415.979.0611**
www.guisemarketing.com

PAUL M. RAND - WORD OF MOUTH & SOCIAL MEDIA MARKETING
Chicago, IL United States
www.zocalogroup.com

Paul is widely regarded as an industry leader and innovator in marketing, social and digital media, mobile media, word of mouth and public relations, helping brands become the most talked about and recommended in their categories. As the current President and CEO of Z [f363616c]o Group, he also serves on the Board of the Better Business Bureau (BBB), is the immediate past president and current board member of the Word of Mouth Marketing Association (WOMMA), and is a leader of the Dean's Advisory Board for DePaul University's Graduate School of Business. Paul also served as a Partner, Executive Committee member and the Global Chief Development and Innovation Officer for Ketchum, one of the world's leading public relations firms, and was the Director of Ketchum's Global Technology Practice and Managing Director for its Midwest operations. He also founded and served as CEO of the Midwest's largest independent corporate and technology communications firm.

Paul M. Rand
President/CEO
Zocalo Group
Chicago, IL United States
Contact Phone: 312-596-6300
Click to Contact from Web Site

MARK LEBLANC -- SMALL BUSINESS SUCCESS
Minneapolis, MN United States
www.SmallBusinessSuccess.com/

Mark LeBlanc started Small Business Success in 1992, and has been working with and speaking for groups of business owners, and professionals who want to grow and sell more products and services. No one has created a more comprehensive business development philosophy than Mark. His flagship presentation, Growing Your Business! contains the wisdom, insights, strategies, and ideas for taking a business or professional practice to a new level of success. He can serve your organization in a variety of ways, but ultimately, to meet the best of what you need and want. His strategies are streetsmart, practical, and can be easily understood and accessed. His content is driven by 16 core principles and formulas, of which, any one can have immediate impact. When principles and formulas are integrated, an owner can create a wave of momentum that is unstoppable.

Mark LeBlanc
Minneapolis, MN United States
Contact Phone: 858-456-4010
Click to Contact from Web Site

ONECOACH, INC -- SMALL BUSINESS GROWTH EXPERTS
San Diego, CA United States
http://onecoach.com/

Founded in 2005 by small business experts, John Assaraf and Murray Smith, OneCoach is the world's leading franchisor for small-business growth services. OneCoach helps entrepreneurs grow their businesses faster by mastering the mindset for success, and then helping them attract more clients. OneCoach franchisees provide entrepreneurs with customized solutions to grow their small businesses. The OneCoach small business coaching services include interactive coaching, expert resources and networking. The OneCoach Business Growth Network™ combines the latest scientific research with proven strategies to give every small-business owner the best chance for achieving success.

John Assaraf
OneCoach, Inc.
Solana Beach, CA United States
Contact Phone: 419-878-3023
Cell: 419.304.6871
Click to Contact from Web Site

Business Development

Mark LeBlanc is your go-to resource on the core issues business owners face on a daily basis.

- *Doing Business In Times of Change*

- *Staying Focused In a Down Market*

- *Strategies for Navigating Growth*

- *Putting More Money In Your Pocket*

Mark LeBlanc of Small Business Success has special expertise on the core issues that business owners and professionals face on a daily basis. His flagship presentation and book, "Growing Your Business!" are ideal on addressing how to sell more products and services. Attendees walk away feeling more focused, able to attract more prospects, stimulate more referrals, and ultimately, craft a plan for generating more business.

LeBlanc has been on his own virtually his entire adult life, owned several businesses and now speaks and writes on the street-smart strategies for achieving in times of challenge and change. He can deliver an inspirational can-do keynote, a content-rich general session, hands-on workshop and/or a multi-day program.

His comprehensive, one-of-a kind, business development philosophy, that has the right blend of wisdom, strategies, insights, and ideas that can be implemented immediately. His new book, "Growing Your Business When YOU Are The Business," will be in bookstores later this year.

LeBlanc is a seasoned veteran with the National Speakers Association and its immediate past president. His style is magnetic, approachable and laced with a unique sense of humor.

Small Business Success
63 South 1st Street, Suite B4
Minneapolis, Minnesota 55401

800-690-0810
Mark@SmallBusinessSuccess.com
Cell: 858-945-4769

www.MarkLeBlanc.com

BDN -- BRAND DEVELOPMENT NETWORK
Kenilworth, IL United States
http://www.bdn-intl.com

Richard Czerniawski and Mike Maloney, international experts in the fields of brand positioning, brand marketing, advertising and creating "brand" loyalty, have managed leading brands for some of the world's most admired companies. Additionally, they have authored hundreds of articles on marketing management, taught marketing for large multi-national corporations and have served as guest lecturers for business and management schools. Richard and Mike are principals with Brand Development Network International, a marketing resource firm that provides consulting, through Brand Development Network Implementation, and training services, through Brand Development Network Institute, to assist companies across a wide range of industries, and their brand marketing teams, develop strategies and initiatives that create brand loyalty in the marketplace. Mr. Czerniawski and Mr. Maloney are the authors of Creating Brand Loyalty: The Management of Power Positioning and Really Great Advertising.

Lori Vandervoort
Director of Operations
BDN -- Brand Developement Network
Central Division Offices
Chanute, KS United States
Contact Phone: 800-255-9831
Contact Main Phone: 620-431-0780
Click to Contact from Web Site

THOMAS J. WINNINGER -- PRICING STRATEGY EXPERT
Minneapolis, MN United States
www.Winninger.com

Thomas Winninger is the founder of WINNINGER Resource Companies, Inc. a Minneapolis based group that provides products, services and technologies that drive market leadership based on differentiation. Thom believes that the only true differentiator is smart thinking. As a successful businessman who speaks, Thom has applied his strategies to his own companies as well as others to capture and sustain market leadership in challenging economies. His companies include IntroSpect Research, TeamTrac, and Winninger Works Productions and Visionscope. He also sits on the board of number of profit and non-profit organizations.

Thomas J. Winninger
Edina, MN United States
Contact Phone: 952-896-1900
Click to Contact from Web Site

AMANDA SETILI --- STRATEGY CONSULTANT
Atlanta, GA United States
www.setili.com

Setili & Associates provides Coca-Cola, Delta Air Lines, The Home Depot, Wal-Mart and other organizations with unbiased advice about strategic direction. Managing partner Amanda Setili has advised organizations in the consumer and industrial products, financial services, technology, and retail industries. Before starting Setili & Associates, Setili served as director of marketing for Global Food Exchange, consulted for McKinsey & Company, served as chief operating officer of Malaysia's leading Internet services company, and was an engineer with Kimberly-Clark. Setili served as an adjunct professor at Emory University. She earned her degree chemical engineering at Vanderbilt and her MBA at Harvard.

Amanda Setili
Setili & Associates, LLC
Atlanta, GA United States
Contact Phone: 404-378-0400
Click to Contact from Web Site

MICHAEL CANNON -- SALES CONSULTANT
San Francisco, CA United States
http://www.silverbulletgroup.com

Michael Cannon is an internationally renowned sales and marketing effectiveness expert and best-selling author, recently coauthoring with Jay Conrad Levinson ('Guerrilla Marketing'), et al., 'Marketing Strategies That Really Work! Promote Your Way to Millions.' Founder and CEO of the Silver Bullet Group, he has over 20 years of sales, marketing, management, and founder's experience in the enterprise software, telecommunications, wireless, and professional services industries. Michael has addressed audiences around the world, including the American Marketing Association.

Michael Cannon
CEO
Silver Bullet Group, Inc.
Walnut Creek, CA United States
Contact Phone: 925.930.9436
Click to Contact from Web Site

CRAIG ELIAS -- TRIGGER EVENT SELLING EXPERT
Calgary, Alberta Canada
www.ShiftSelling.com/About

Craig Elias is the creator of Trigger Event Selling™, and the Chief Catalyst of SHiFT Selling, Inc. For almost 20 years, Elias has used Trigger Event strategies to become a top sales performer at every company that has hired him - including WorldCom where he was named the number one salesperson within six months of joining the company. Trigger Event strategies have earned Elias coverage on NBC news, in The New York Times, The Wall Street Journal, The Globe and Mail, The National Post, Nikkei Marketing Journal, Business 2.0, Sales and Marketing magazine, Venture Magazine, Calgary Inc.

Craig Elias
Shift Selling, Inc.
Calgary, AB Canada
Contact Phone: +1.403.874.2998
Click to Contact from Web Site

LENANN MCGOOKEY GARDNER -- YOUCANSELL.COM
Albuquerque, NM United States
http://www.youcansell.com/

Lenann Gardner is an expert in state-of-the-art selling. She teaches the most recent research about how people successfully sell today, making those skills easy-to-understand and use. A past #1 sales rep at Xerox Corporation, Lenann has helped hundreds of professionals bring in millions of dollars in revenue. She authored Got Sales? The Complete Guide to Today's Proven Methods for Selling Services, nominated for the Axiom Book Award as the year's best sales book.

Gail Rubin
P.R. Director
G/R/P/R
Albuquerque, NM United States
Contact Phone: 505-265-7215
Click to Contact from Web Site

DENNY HATCH -- DIRECT MAIL EXPERT

Philadelphia, PA United States
www.DennyHatch.com

Denny Hatch, author, journalist and founder and editor of the e-newsletter, BusinessCommon-Sense.com. He is a freelance writer, designer and consultant on direct mail/direct marketing and the author of six books on marketing and business as well as three novels. His most recent book: CAREER-CHANGING TAKEAWAYS!—Quotations, Rules, Aphorisms, Pithy Tips, Quips, Sage Advice, Secrets, Dictums and Truisms In 99 Categories of Marketing, Business and Life.

Denny Hatch
Denny Hatch Associates, Inc.
Philadelphia, PA United States
Contact Phone: 215-627-9103
Click to Contact from Web Site

MARKETING SOLUTIONS -- PROFESSIONAL BUSINESS OF BEAUTY

Fairfax, VA United States
www.mktgsols.com

Specialists in the professional business of beauty! The leading marketing, advertising, public relations and consulting services agency in the salon and beautycare industries. Nationally recognized experts and spokespersons on: professional haircare, beautycare, nailcare & skincare, total hair & beauty makeovers, hair fashion trends, salon & day salons, salon & spa services, medical spas & plastic surgery, salon & medical retail products, and anti-aging. They have salons, dayspas, medical services, national and international haircare and beautycare companies as clients.

Larry H. Oskin
President
Marketing Solutions
Fairfax, VA United States
Contact Phone: 703-359-6000
Click to Contact from Web Site

DANIEL MILSTEIN -- ABC OF SALES

Detroit, MI United States
http://www.ABCofSales.com

A motivated, driven, determined, successful, and savvy businessman, the CEO of Ann Arbor based Gold Star Mortgage Financial Group is passing the secrets of his success on to others in the sales business. A super success in mortgage sales, he has recently published The ABC of Sales as a guide for professionals who want to soar in sales, revive their sales careers, or position their companies among the elite. Gold Star is one of Inc. Magazine's 500 fastest growing companies in America for two consecutive years, 2009 & 2010

Scott Lorenz
Westwind Communications
Plymouth, MI United States
Contact Phone: 734-667-2090
Click to Contact from Web Site

ERIC BLOOM -- MARKET RESEARCH
Boston, MA United States
http://www.ManagerMechanics.com

We combine the strength of our IT background with proprietary technology and blended learning to provide superior training in a choice of formats, as well as automated training needs assessments and online testing using our Survey Plus Platform, and one-on-one manager mentoring.

Eric Bloom
Manager Mechanics
Ashland, MA United States
Contact Phone: 855-286-1110
Click to Contact from Web Site

EMPLOYEE INVOLVEMENT ASSOCIATION
Detroit, MI United States
www.eianet.org

An internationally recognized organization serving professional managers and administrators of employee involvement and suggestion programs for over 64 years by providing quality educational programs, publications, benchmarking and networking opportunities. Our members are leaders in ideas and suggestions systems. Employee Involvement is the keystone of organizational development, nurturing the empowerment of people. EIA is committed to increasing organizational effectiveness through the imagination of employees. Our members work in a broad range of industries who understand that their employees have the ideas to help make their companies more productive and profitable.

Paula Davis
Employee Involvement Association
Auburn Hills, MI United States
Contact Phone: 248.253.9252
Click to Contact from Web Site

EPM COMMUNICATIONS -- RESEARCH ON CONSUMER BEHAVIOR & LICENSING
New York, NY United States
http://www.epmcom.com

EPM publishes newsletters and research studies about the licensing of consumer products, content licensing, and consumer behavior. The Licensing Letter provides proprietary estimates of retail sales of licensed merchandise worldwide, reports on the latest deals, and provides contact information for key decision-makers among owners of intellectual property, manufacturers of licensed goods, and others. Content Licensing covers the marketing of entertainment and media across platforms. And Research Alert, Youth Markets Alert, and Marketing To Women provide extensive data and reporting on consumer behavior. EPM President Ira Mayer is a frequent speaker on retail, business and consumer trends.

Ira Mayer
President and Publisher
EPM Communications, Inc.
New York, NY United States
Contact Phone: 212-941-1633
Contact Main Phone: 212-941-0099
Click to Contact from Web Site

UNA MEDINA, PH.D. -- BEHAVIORAL AND CHAOS EXPERT
Albuquerque, NM United States
www.innovation.cc/editorial-board/medina.htm

Una E. Medina, Ph.D., Behavioral and Chaos Science: Author of "Happiness in Chaos: 7 Secrets to Living Well when the World is Falling Apart," Dr. Medina publishes in behavioral chaos science. Alumna of New England Complex Systems Institute, MIT and Systems Science at Portland State University, she conducts research for the National Institutes of Health on winning in a chaotic world, edits at the Innovation Journal and considers herself a friendly scientist, who harnesses chaos science to grow happiness for everyday people.

Una Medina, Ph.D.
Behavioral and Chaos Science
Albuquerque, NM United States
Contact Phone: 505-264-3478
Click to Contact from Web Site

  THE RESEARCH DEPARTMENT

Focus Groups and Other Qualitative Market Research

THE RESEARCH DEPARTMENT -- FOCUS GROUPS AND QUALITATIVE MARKET RESEARCH
New York, NY United States
researchdepartment.us.com

Alexa Smith is a leading expert on consumer attitudes and behavior. As a focus group moderator and market research practitioner for over 20 years, Ms. Smith has been quoted in many publications, has written byline articles and is a frequent speaker and lecturer on consumer trends, attitudes and habits.

Alexa Smith
President
The Research Department
New York, NY United States
Contact Phone: 212-717-6087
Click to Contact from Web Site

RON KARR -- CSP -- SALES LEADERSHIP EXPERT
New York, NY United States
www.ronkarr.com

Lead Sell or Get Out of the Way--Sales--Leadership - THE TITAN PRINCIPLE Sales -- Negotiations -- Customer Service -- The Key to Market Domination -- Call today and find out how the TITAN PRINCIPLE will help your audience: Increase Client $ Value -- Differentiate from the Competition -- Gain Customers -- Increase Market Share -- Position Themselves as a Valued Resource Sell on Value -- Partner for Influence -- Increase Profits.

Ronald Karr
President
Karr Associates, Inc.
Westwood, NJ United States
Contact Phone: 201.666.7599
Cell: 201.914.3895
Click to Contact from Web Site

Living Well when the World is Falling Apart
.CX the website

harnessing chaos science to grow happiness in everyday life

"*extremely insightful* with helping me deal with difficult situations *at work and in my daily life... solutions were very easy to implement* and have completely turned our team around... scientific research guided her recommendations... an expert in behavior change."
—Lori Truster, Account Manager, Goodman Interior Structures

"...thinks outside of the box... *creative solutions to problems*."
—Cecily Froemke, M.S., Clinical Systems, Axis Clinical Software

"...*an innovative analyst* and systems modeler... *insightful ideas*... addressing tough problems such as poverty, terrorism, and social behavior change."
—Wayne Wakeland, Ph.D., Systems Science Graduate Program, Portland State University

"...*a global consciousness*. Her voice and perspective are well respected and much needed."
—Amber Lopez-Lasater, Ph.D., Communications Director, SEIU Nevada

"...*a key presentation* to an audience of several hundred [scientists, International Conference on Complex Systems]. It was very well received."
Yaneer Bar-Yam, Ph.D., President, New England Complex Systems Institute

"...*a stellar example of professionalism and expertise*... cheerful and focused... *keen ability to assess and respond quickly and accurately* in every situation."
—Heather Rowley, President, Rowley Enterprises Inc.

"...chang[ed] my marketing strategy... *turning competitors into revenue sources... new accounts will ultimately pursue my business*."
—Francine Olmstead, MD, CEO, NM Travel Health

"... worked with me to *understand the likely mental processes* [web] users were experiencing... suggested the "sales pitch" and where to put it in the program... *donations per user increased 317% [in 79 days]*."
—Reid Hester, Ph.D., Clinical Psychologist Director, Research Division, Behavioral Therapy Associates, LLP

"... *increased enrollment* in PNM weatherization workshops *by 500%*... changed client behavior, recruited new clients... a snowball effect: they referred friends, neighbors, and family who also became clients... [spread] from New Mexico to... Texas." and "...Una led a full day workshop for members of my PNM Resources Speakers Bureau, a large group [300] of corporate communicators... *three years later I am still hearing* from my speakers that this was *one of the most valuable learning days they have spent at this company*."
Sharon Rogers, Senior Community Liason, PNM Resources, Public Service Company of New Mexico

"... the opportunity to *think differently and relate* to those we most want to help *in ways that reach them*... youth *we would not otherwise have reached* the gift of productive and fulfilled lives." "I was truly humbled... to see ourselves and the children we serve in new ways... Dr. Medina has made a huge difference to me and to Scouting." "...*thought provoking*... how cultural barriers can be recognized and overcome... knows how to successfully engage her audience in *finding viable solutions to problems*." "... stimulating persuasion techniques... the one that resonated most with me was *how to persuade people without talking*... the *high point of my weekend... well worthwhile!*"
—International Scouting Executives and Alison K. Schuler, President, Western Region Area 6, Boy Scouts of America

Puzzling problems? Impossible problems?

CX = complexity/chaos science, for solving the impossible.

CX secrets are yours. Claim them. Find out how they work.

Happiness in Chaos
7 Secrets to Living Well when the World is Falling Apart

Una E Medina PhD

3512 Yipee Calle Ct NW • Albuquerque, NM 87120 • 505-264-3478 • UnaMedina@me.com • www.UnaMedina.com • www.una.cx

STEPHEN R. BALZAC, LEADERSHIP DEVELOPMENT EXPERT
Stow, MA United States
www.7stepsahead.com

Stephen R. Balzac, 'The Business Sensei,' helps leaders grow their organizations. He is an author, speaker, consultant, and the president of 7 Steps Ahead, LLC. His articles have appeared in a number of journals, including The Journal of Interactive Drama, The IBM Systems Journal, Mass High Tech, Enterprise Management Quarterly, The CEO Refresher, The Journal of Corporate Recruiting Leadership, Performance & Profits, Corp! Magazine, Analog SF/F and the Worcester Business Journal. Steve is the author of 'The 36-Hour Course in Organizational Development,' published by McGraw-Hill.

Stephen R. Balzac
President
7 Steps Ahead, LLC
Stow, MA United States
Contact Phone: 978-298-5189
Click to Contact from Web Site

DON BENTON -- MARKETING EXPERT
Portland, WA United States
www.donbenton.com

Don Benton is an advertising expert with specific yellow pages, television and newspaper expertise. He has trained sales teams at over 600 television stations in the US, and Canada. He has consulted with thousands of business owners on their advertising and marketing plans. Senator Benton also consults several law firms and advises them on their marketing and advertising strategies. His company, The Benton Group, conducts training and counseling for companies such as Viacom, CBS, Fox Broadcasting and the Walt Disney Company. A sought after public speaker and author of two books, Senator Benton is the nations leading expert on small business advertising.

Don Benton
CEO
The Benton Group
Vancouver, WA United States
Contact Phone: 360-574-7369
Click to Contact from Web Site

STUART CROSS -- MORGAN CROSS CONSULTING
Newark-on-Trent, United Kingdom
www.morgancross.co.uk

Stuart Cross helps some of the world's top companies achieve rapid, sustainable profit growth. Rick Mils, Strategy SVP of Alliance Books says: "I would recommend Stuart to any company looking for creative solutions to challenging strategic issues" and Stephen Ford, Strategy SVP of for Avon, says, "Stuart used his excellent strategic skills to help us drive significantly higher levels of growth for the business."

Stuart Cross
Morgan Cross Consulting
Newark-on-Trent, None United Kingdom
Contact Phone: +44 (0)1636-52611
Click to Contact from Web Site

In today's sales world, there's no room for followers. But there's plenty of room for leaders. Competition is intense, and if you don't take a leadership role in producing results for your clients, someone else will. In "Lead, Sell, or Get Out of the Way," Ron Karr outlines a repeatable process based on the powerful idea that great sellers lead relationships in the same way that great leaders sell ideas.

No matter what you sell, you must communicate persuasively and effectively what it is you can offer clients.

However, sales leaders do even more than that. They raise the bar by finding new opportunities and creating new levels of performance for their customers. They don't just sell products or services; they sell outcomes that transform a customer's world, and they assume personal responsibility for those outcomes.

This customer-focused mindset is the key to Karr's proven leadership selling process. Based on decades of research with companies of all sizes, Karr reveals what great sellers do and shows how anyone can implement the same powerful principles.

"Karr's book illustrates what we believe: that knowing your customers' needs is the single most important factor in building sales. Business starts with the sale. To make profitable sales, you need to understand your customer and create a timely value proposition. This book shows you how to do both."
— Larry Kellner, Chairman and CEO, Continental Airlines

RON KARR
Business Development Expert

LEAD, SELL, OR GET OUT OF THE WAY
THE 7 TRAITS OF GREAT SELLERS
RON KARR

Karr Associates, Inc.
372 Kinderkamack Rd.
Westwood, N.J.   07675
Tel: 201-666-7599
Fax: 201-666-7539
Cell: 201-914-3895
E-mail: ron@ronkarr.com
Web: ronkarr.com
Book Web site:
leadsellorgetoutoftheway.com
Blog: ronkarr.net

BARBARA FAGAN -- SOURCE POINT TRAINING -- MASTER COACH
San Francisco, CA United States
www.SourcePointTraining.com

Barbara Fagan is a pioneer in the professional coaching field and is a strong advocate for the value of leadership development and training. She is a Master Coach with over 7,000 hours spent in individual coaching sessions. She has coached business professionals involved in early-stage development as well as those managing major change initiatives. She co-founded Source Point Training in late 2009 and is a member of the International Coach Federation, International Association of Coaches and American Society for Training and Development. Barbara is a keynote speaker for many professional business organizations.

Ray Wyman Jr
Corp Communications
Source Point Training
Orange, CA United States
Contact Phone:
Contact Main Phone: 7149973808
Cell: 714-330-2232
Click to Contact from Web Site

ANNE GRAHAM -- INSPIRING TOMORROW'S LEGENDARY COMPANIES
Vancouver, British Columbia Canada
www.LegendaryValue.com

Creating organic growth to satisfy investor expectations is becoming increasingly difficult, given the high failure rate of most new products, mergers, and acquisitions. The Create the Value™ phase helps you revitalize your market position and growth opportunities in uncommon ways, strengthen your foundations for value creation, use market insights to prepare for the future, and build your team so that you can profit from next generation customer needs in ways that are virtually impossible for your competitors to duplicate.

Anne Graham
Managing Director
The Legendary Value Institute
Vancouver, BC Canada
Contact Phone: 604-830-3990
Click to Contact from Web Site

SCOTT HUNTER -- LEADERSHIP EXPERT
Irvine, CA United States
www.unshackledleadership.com

Scott Hunter, BEE, JD, CSP, is a nationally recognized expert in the fields of leadership, teambuilding and business success. He has been transforming the culture of organizations for over two decades, through keynote speeches, workshops, retreats and management team coaching. Hunter is the author of 'Unshackled Leadership, Building Businesses Based on Faith, Trust, Possibility and Abundance,' which has received successful reviews and garnered a following among executives, professionals and students. He has been recognized as an expert on more than 50 radio talk shows and appeared on a number of television news programs. He has also authored dozens of articles on creating extraordinary organizations and has a number of audio programs on the same topic.

Scott Hunter, CSP
President
The Hunter Partnership Alliance
Irvine, CA United States
Contact Phone: 714-573-8855
Contact Main Phone: 714-573-8855
Cell: 714-309-1099
Click to Contact from Web Site

SCOTT HUNTER
BUSINESS LEADERSHIP

Scott Hunter has been transforming organizations for over two decades through keynote speeches, workshops, retreats and management team coaching.

Since 1985, Hunter has helped hundreds of businesses, delivered over 1,000 speeches and worked with over 250,000 individuals as a business coach and speaker. He has conducted hundreds of corporate retreats, consistently producing breakthroughs in the participants' personal and professional lives -- and setting the stage for the companies they manage to achieve results that go far beyond their expectations.

After a stalled legal career, Hunter began to research what it takes for people to produce extraordinary results in their personal lives and careers and for companies to break through to new levels of profitability and success. He took classes, read books and signed up for one seminar after another.

Hunter turned his whole life around and now teaches companies how to make the same success journey he made. Using what he learned painfully -- through trial and error -- he realized he could guide others to move to their own success goals, bypassing costly, time-consuming detours.

Today, Scott Hunter works as a successful business coach and speaker -- a recognized expert, featured on radio talk shows and television news programs. He speaks to thousands of people each year and shares advice with CEOs of corporations of all sizes. His first book, "Making Work Work," has received successful reviews and garnered a following among executives, professionals and students.

His latest book, "Unshackled Leadership: Building Businesses Based on Faith, Trust, Possibility and Abundance," reveals a groundbreaking 15-step program that enables business leaders to become unstuck from conventional and disempowering thinking and create positive and dramatic change within their companies.

Scott Hunter changes the way business leaders think. Why?

Because people who are successful think differently than people who are not. Successful leaders make conscious and wise choices, create relationships based on trust and respect, have a clear sense of purpose, take responsibility for their actions and live with grace and ease.

Scott Hunter
The Hunter Partnership Alliance
55 Sconset Lane   Irvine, California 92620
Phone: 714-573-8855
Fax: 714-573-8860
E-Mail: scott@thpalliance.com

For more information about Scott Hunter and the Unshackled Leadership model, please visit **www.UnshackledLeadership.com**.

To schedule an interview with Scott, please contact him at the phone number or e-mail above.

ANDREW MILLER -- OPERATIONAL EFFECTIVENESS AND EFFICIENCY EXPERT

Toronto, Ontario Canada
www.ACMConsulting.ca

For more than a decade, Andrew Miller has been working with organizations to generate dramatic operational and financial improvements and helping companies do things faster and better. Andrew works with companies to improve their performance and profitability. Andrew previously worked for both PriceWaterhouseCoopers Consulting and IBM Business Consulting Services and has an International MBA in Logistics and Marketing.

Andrew Miller
President
ACM Consulting
Toronto, ON Canada
Contact Phone: 416-817-1336
Click to Contact from Web Site

GARY YAMAMOTO -- PERFORMANCE IMPROVEMENT EXPERT

Tuscon, AZ United States
www.GaryYamamoto.com

Gary Yamamoto is a professional speaker sharing his unique multi-level framework for improving an individual's business performance and their own personal lives. He speaks to corporations, associations, and government agencies at their meetings and conventions to improve productivity and achieve bottom-line results. His management experiences include communications and nuclear weapons engineering for the federal government. Gary is the author of a business improvement book, "Professional Power, Personal Excellence." As the author of a book on dreams, "Creative Dream Analysis," he is an expert on dream analysis, which he has done for audiences and on both radio and television.

Andrea Gold
Gold Stars Speakers Bureau
Tuscon, AZ United States
Contact Phone: 520-742-4384
Contact Main Phone: 520-742-4384
Cell: 520-730-4356
Click to Contact from Web Site

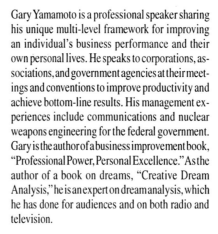

ALLEN B. FALCON -- CUMULUS GLOBAL

Boston, MA United States
www.cumulusglobal.com

Allen has assisted large, mid-size, and small businesses with strategic technology planning, management, and operations. Allen has led efforts to improve the quality and efficiency of information services for internal and external customers. Bringing his experience and expertise to small and mid-size organizations, Allen has served as a part-time CIO for businesses in multiple industries. He has planned and managed technology projects that directly support business goals and bottom lines. Most recently, Allen has focused on helping SMBs benefit from cloud-computing solutions. Horizon Info Services offers best-of-breed solutions to SMBs with full integration and support services.

Allen B. Falcon
CEO
Cumulus Global
Westborough, MA United States
Contact Phone: 508-948-4071
Contact Main Phone: 866-356-1202
Cell: 508-989-4792
Click to Contact from Web Site

Cloud Computing
Allen B. Falcon

Allen Falcon, CEO and Founder of Horizon Info Services, helps small and mid-size businesses use cloud computing and other managed IT services to lower costs, increase productivity, and improve profitability. Allen is a recognized expert in Software-as-a-Service applications and Google Apps, in particular.

Previously, Allen co-founded and was President of Horizon Information Group. Consulting to corporate CIOs, Allen has led efforts to improve the quality and efficiency of information services for internal and external customers. He has helped clients develop effective service definitions and operating models for IS organizations; realize measurable improvements in problem and change management procedures; and implement financial modeling tools for budgeting and technology investment analysis.

Allen has served as a part-time CIO for businesses in multiple industries, planning and managing technology projects that directly support business goals and bottom lines. Beyond improving day-to-day operations, Allen has defined and led critical business application and infrastructure projects designed to improve and enable new business opportunities.

Prior to co-founding Horizon Information Group, Allen held positions in consulting and in network systems development, specializing in large systems analysis and design. Allen has published several articles on technology issues for smaller businesses and has served on advisory boards for industry conferences and trade events. Allen holds an Honors Bachelor of Science degree in Computer and Communication Sciences from the University of Michigan.

Allen B. Falcon
President
Horizon Info Services, LLC

CONTACT INFO:

T: 1-866-356-1202 / 508-948-4071

F: 1-866-329-7604 / 508-948-4073

WEB: http://www.HorizonInfoServices.com

TWT: http://www.Twitter.com/allenfalcon

BLOG: http://horizoninfoservices.com/blog

CALENDAR: http://tungle.me/allenfalcon

Horizon Info Services, LLC

www.HorizonInfoServices.com

JIM MATHIS, CSP -- REINVENTION SPEAKER

Atlanta, GA United States
http://www.jimmathis.com

World markets are on a roller coaster from global economic events that are changing and with that the stomachs of many of the world business economic leaders. Business leader and Reinvention Strategist Jim Mathis, isn't surprised. "We've got to realize that things are coming back, but in a different way than they used to be and adapt accordingly." Mathis says that business leaders need to reinvent! Reinvention Made Easy is about how business leaders can adjust themselves in a world of higher expectations and constant change. Change Your Strategy; Change the Outcome.

Jim Mathis, CSP
The Reinvention Strategist
The Mathis Group
Lexington, SC United States
Contact Phone: 803-829-8067
Contact Main Phone: 800-688-0220
Cell: 803-261-0220
Click to Contact from Web Site

ADICIO -- POWERING MEDIA COMPANIES

San Diego, CA United States
http://www.adicio.com/

Adicio develops interactive classified advertising software solutions for the careers, motors and real estate markets, which serve the Internet's leading media companies and web portals. With its award-winning technology and enterprise-class software platforms, domain expertise, and customer service, Adicio delivers a private-label application that seamlessly integrates within online classified advertising offerings, enabling clients to generate revenue and retain their brand while building and managing their online classified efforts. Clients can deploy Adicio's software as a turnkey solution or customize Adicio's application to leverage existing brand strategy and support online sales and marketing objectives.

Steve Dahl
Vice President, Marketing
Adicio
Carlsbad, CA United States
Contact Phone: 760-602-9502
Click to Contact from Web Site

ADAM ARMBRUSTER -- TELEVISION ADVERTISING EXPERT

Sarasota, FL United States
www.esacompany.com

Adam Armbruster is a television advertising expert, author and a senior partner with ESA Company, the nation's largest retail and broadcasting consulting company, located in Red Bank, New Jersey. At ESA Company, Armbruster consults advertisers seeking to create financially successful television and web-based campaigns. He has also served as the director of retail marketing with the ABC/Disney Corporation Television Station Division. Armbruster appears regularly in 'America's Nightly Scorecard' on the Fox Business Network, The Wall Street Journal, NPR Radio, US Weekly, NBC International, TV Week Magazine, Ward's Dealer magazine, Advertising Age Magazine and more.

Adam Armbruster
Sarasota, FL United States
Contact Phone: 941 928 7192
Click to Contact from Web Site

Media Marketing

There's More Than One Expert for You at Adicio

Adicio, Inc., is well known for its user friendly, technologically advanced job board solutions. With the job board technology at its foundation, the company develops interactive classified advertising software solutions for the careers, real estate and motors markets. Its award-winning technology and enterprise-class software platforms fuels Adicio's ability to deliver a private-label application that seamlessly integrates within online classified advertising offerings, enabling clients to generate revenue and retain their brand while building and managing their online classified efforts.

Clients can deploy Adicio's job board software, real estate platform or motors platform as a turnkey solution. Clients can easily customize Adicio's application to leverage existing brand strategy and support online sales and marketing objectives. Adicio also powers the award winning, Best-of-The-Web job search portal CareerCast.com and JobsRated.com, where 200 jobs across North America are ranked based on detailed analysis of specific careers factors.

Adicio's CareerCast Niche Networks Include:

CareerCast Diversity & Bilingual Network
CareerCast Healthcare Network
CareerCast Nursing Network
CareerCast Green Network

POWERING MEDIA COMPANIES

Innovative Technology / Exceptional Support

www.Adicio.com   www.CareerCast.com   www.JobsRated.com

Contact Steve Dahl, VP marketing
800-276-1332

MEDIA FINANCIAL MANAGEMENT ASSOCIATION
Northfield, IL United States
http://www.mediafinance.org

Media Financial Management Association (MFM) provides education, networking, information, and signature products to meet the diverse needs of financial and business professionals in the media industry throughout the U.S. and Canada. More information about MFM is available on its web site: http://www.mediafinance.org. MFM's media credit reporting subsidiary - BCCA - provides revenue management services, including professional development programs and credit reports on national and local media advertisers. More information about BCCA is available at http://www.bccacredit.com.

Andy Holdgate
Media Financial Management Association
Northfield, IL United States
Contact Phone: 720.270.1325
Click to Contact from Web Site

JEFF SIEGEL -- ADVANCED TELEVISION ADVERTISING EXPERT
Boston, MA United States
www.RoviCorp.com
NASDQ ROVI

Jeff Siegel -- Senior Vice President, Worldwide Advertising -- Areas of Expertise: Smart TV, Interactive TV and In-App Guide Advertising, Next Generation Entertainment Advertising --- Second Screen, New Ad Ecosystem - Brands, Agencies, Content Owners, Broadcasters, App Developers and CE Makers. Trends: The monetization of advertising and integration with over-the-top (OTT) services, video-on-demand (VoD) offerings and interactive TV applications. How connected devices such as SmartTVs are impacting traditional advertising, The future of next-generation advertising and its effect on consumer viewing habits.

Allison Yochim
Finn Partners
San Francisco, CA United States
Contact Phone: 415-348-2724
Click to Contact from Web Site

STOMPERNET -- SEARCH ENGINE OPTIMIZATION EXPERTS
Atlanta, GA United States
www.stompernet.com/

Join the thousands of online entrepreneurs and small business owners who have already discovered the most actionable, most distilled Internet marketing journal available anywhere presented by the best online educators in the world! The Net Effect will strip away all the noise and confusion about what works and what doesn't with Internet marketing. Take your business to the next level today!

Andrea Warner
StomperNet.com
Sandy, UT United States
Contact Phone: 801-769-6624
Click to Contact from Web Site

BILL THOMPSON -- TV, INC. -- INFOMERCIAL MARKETING COMPANY
Clearwater, FL United States
www.tvinc.com

Infomercial Marketing Expert -- Bill Thompson and TV Inc., a major force in the marketing of products, services, political agendas, cause marketing and image development, has been in business for over 30 years. We have provided our clients immediate access to the marketplace using innovative marketing strategies that are both effective and economical. We are available: On a fee basis; As your Joint Venture partner; As the Underwriter, Manager & Implementer. With offices in California, Florida and New York City we are available to serve your needs worldwide. For our international division, please go to www.Global-Promise.com.

Bill Thompson
CEO
TV, Inc.
Clearwater, FL United States
Contact Phone: 800-326-5661
Contact Main Phone: 310-985-1229
Cell: 310.985.1229
Click to Contact from Web Site

EVANA MAGGIORE -- FASHION FENG SHUI INTERNATIONAL
Boston, MA United States
http://www.fashionfengshui.com

Evana Maggiore, AICI, CIP, President of Fashion Feng Shui International, is an award winning professional image consultant, internationally-recognized feng shui practitioner and environmental healer. The world's foremost expert on the feng shui of personal appearance; she is a pioneer of the holistic lifestyle movement. Feng Shui is a three thousand year old body of knowledge that links environment with empowerment. Evana's groundbreaking concept of Fashion Feng Shui™ teaches that clothing is the body's most intimate environment, and therefore, as influential on the wearer's life as feng shui purports one's home and business decors to be.

Evana Maggiore
President
Fashion Feng Shui International
Woburn, MA United States
Contact Phone: 781 569-0599
Cell: 781 718 2003
Click to Contact from Web Site

ANNIE PANE -- EAST COAST FENG SHUI
Richmond, VA United States
www.AnniePane.com

Annie Pane is a nationally recognized expert on the ancient practice of Feng Shui. she grew up in the Northern Neck of Virginia on a farm. And, although, she came from a meager background, she's a highly successful and respected business woman. After launching her company East Coast Feng Shui in 1998, she quickly rose to the top of her field for three reasons: first, she's the only Feng Shui educator and advisor to help people learn this ancient science from a Christian worldview. second, she showed enthusiasts how to reap the physical, mental AND spiritual benefits of Feng Shui. Another first! And, third, she intuitively meets people where they are. In other words, she modifies their physical environments to empower them in living a balanced life. Whatever they need is what Annie addresses. . .be it more money, love, happiness, health or getting rid of clutter.

Annie Pane
Woodbridge, VA United States
Contact Phone: 703-508-8617
Contact Main Phone: 703-508-8617
Click to Contact from Web Site

LILLIAN TOO -- FENG SHUI EXPERT
Los Angeles, CA United States
www.Lillian-Too.com

Lillian Too is the world's most prolific and highest selling author of books on Feng Shui. Since publishing her first book on the subject in 1995 in Malaysia, she has written over a hundred books and sold over ten million copies to a worldwide audience of readers. Her books have been translated into 31 languages and whole sections of bookstores in capital cities of the world carry shelves of her books on feng shui, astrology and Chinese divination methods. She is the world's #1 selling writer on Feng Shui. She is also its most eloquent advocate and each January she addresses capacity crowds of thousands at her Feng Shui Extravaganza Road Shows.

Lily Noon
Noon Books
Danville, CA United States
Contact Phone: 925-736-6696
Cell: 925-323-9110
Click to Contact from Web Site

ANGI MA WONG -- FENG SHUI EXPERT
Palos Verdes Estates, CA United States
www.angimawong.com

Feng Shui Lady ® Angi Ma Wong is an award-winning author, intercultural consultant, entrepreneur, health advocate and motivational speaker, who has been on OPRAH, CBS Sunday Morning, CNN Headline News, TIME, Redbook, and over 600+ other Internet, broadcast and print features. Since 1989, Ms. Wong has conducted sales and marketing seminars for businesses, bridging cultures for productivity and profitability between Asians and non-Asians, entrepreneurship, inspirational, motivational and stress management. She has authored over 27 titles, including 15 on feng shui, the best-selling Feng Shui Dos and Taboos series, as well as Mom's Choice and Pinnacle Achievement Award-winners: Barack Obama: Historymaker (ages 10-adult) with speech excerpts, index & timeline; Meet President Obama: America's 44th President (ages 4-8), Bitter Roots: A Gum Saan Odyssey and her latest, a multiple MCA winner, A Survivor's Secrets to Health and Happiness, crammed with simple strategies, advice and inspiration from this 23-year, 5-time breast cancer survivor.

Angi Ma Wong
Author/Publisher
Pacific Heritage Ent., Inc.
Palos Verdes Estates, CA United States
Contact Phone: 310-541-8818
Cell: 310-213-2898
Click to Contact from Web Site

MARIE DUBUQUE --SOCIAL MEDIA ETIQUETTE EXPERT AND LIFE COACH
St. Louis, MO United States
http://www.youtube.com/MannersByMarie

This popular author, radio and YouTube host examines how to navigate the tricky waters of social media. What do you say to someone who blocks you on Facebook? How do you politely reject someone's friend request? How many tweets a day is too many on Twitter? Could you be on too many social media sites? When is it time to back off? How do you do damage control when you've just offended someone online and didn't mean it? Social media etiquette expert Marie Dubuque also talks about tricky social situations in real life too!

Marie Dubuque
Saint Louis, MO United States
Contact Phone:
Contact Main Phone: Prefers e-mail
Click to Contact from Web Site

BOB ELSTER -- SPEAKER -- BUSINESS AND LIFE COACH
Boston, MA United States
www.FullofPotential.com

Bob has been studying and empowering people for more than 15 years. Unlike many speakers and coaches Bob truly understands people, with a background in social work and years of experience working with people in numerous settings. Bob's passion and focus is seeing real results. Although Bob is entertaining, humorous and a powerful speaker he strives to leave people always with practical content and tools that they can immediately apply. He's not looking for an empty feel good motivational display that makes no lasting change. Too many speakers are actors that entertain but make no lasting impact or give great information but leave you wondering what to do with it. You will not experience this with Bob.

Bob Elster
Bellingham, MA United States
Contact Phone: 508-207-5042
Click to Contact from Web Site

INTERNATIONAL SOCIETY OF PROTOCOL AND ETIQUETTE PROFESSIONALS
Washington, DC United States
http://www.ispep.org

International Society of Protocol & Etiquette Professionals is the professional association for protocol, etiquette and communications consultants and trainers serving business and community. ISPEP offers the only internationally recognized professional certification by examination in the fields of etiquette and protocol.

Cynthia W. Lett
Executive Director
International Society of Protocol and Etiquette Professionals
Silver Spring, MD United States
Contact Phone: 301-946-5265
Click to Contact from Web Site

THE LETT GROUP -- BUSINESS ETIQUETTE
Silver Spring, MD United States
www.lettgroup.com

Cynthia Lett CPP, CEP is respected worldwide for her knowledge of American and international etiquette and protocol. Clients include offices of protocol, executives and professionals at all levels. Quoted in Entrepreneur, Robb Report, Newsweek, Success, Washington Post, Forbes, CNN.com, Washington Business Journal, CFO, CIO, TellerVision, Esquire and dozens more print and broadcast sources, Cynthia often comments live on Fox News and CNN. Her book, That's So Annoying: An Etiquette Expert's Take On The World's Most Irritating Habits And What To Do About Them was released July, 2009. Her talkshow, It's Apropos! airs on the Success Talk Channel on Internet.

Cynthia Lett CPP CEP
Director
The Lett Group
ISPEP
Silver Spring, MD United States
Contact Phone: 301-946-8208
Contact Main Phone: 301-946-8208
Cell: 240-893-9469
Click to Contact from Web Site

SHANNON SMITH -- MANNERS AND ETIQUETTE CONSULTANT

Toronto, Ontario Canada
www.premiereimageintl.com
Ontario

SHANNON SMITH is a leading image strategist and founder of Premi [e87265] Image International, the foremost provider of personal brand training. Since 1983, Shannon and her team of experts have taken companies and individuals from unnoticed to unforgettable, bringing about transformations that lead straight to success.

Shannon Smith
Premiere Image International
Toronto, ON Canada
Contact Phone: 416.324.8955
Click to Contact from Web Site

GLORIA STARR -- IMAGE ETIQUETTE -- COMMUNICATION AND LEADERSHIP

Charlotte, NC United States
http://www.gloriastarr.com

Gloria Starr is the leading international provider of Impression Management, Etiquette, Communication and Leadership seminars and training programs. Ms. Starr has worked in more than 60 countries world-wide. She is the author of nine books. She received Board Approval for Excellence by The Society for the Advancement of Consulting and is recognized by the United States Government as the leader in Impression Management, Etiquette and Communications. Ms. Gloria Starr is the Preferred Training Partner of the United States Pentagon and the Strategic Alliance Partner - Velosi and the Qatar Learning Resource Center.

Gloria Starr
Master Image, Etiquette, Communication Coach
Charlotte, NC United States
Contact Phone: 704-596-9866
Cell: 704-941-0578
Click to Contact from Web Site

BARBARA PACHTER - BUSINESS ETIQUETTE EXPERT

Cherry Hill, NJ United States
www.pachter.com

Barbara Pachter is an internationally renowned business etiquette and communications speaker, coach and author. She has delivered more than 2,100 seminars throughout the world, including the first-ever seminar for businesswomen in Kuwait. In 2010, NJ Biz named her one of the 'Best 50 Women in Business' in New Jersey. Pachter is the author of nine books including GREET, EAT, TWEET, NewRules@Work, When The Little Things Count and The Power of Positive Confrontation. Her books have been translated into 11 languages. Her client list boasts many of today's top organizations, including Microsoft, Chrysler, Pfizer, Inc.,and Con Edison

Barbara Pachter
President
Pachter and Associates
Cherry Hill, NJ United States
Contact Phone: 856-751-6141
Click to Contact from Web Site

EXECSENSE WEBINARS - THE LEADING PUBLISHER OF EXECUTIVE WEBINARS
San Rafael, CA United States
www.ExecSense.com

ExecSense is the world's largest publisher of webinars led by top business executives, legal executives, and industry experts, producing over 1,200 new webinars every year, and replaying thousands of others from our vast library of webinar-based thought leadership. ExecSense enables executives to be in-the-know on the most important topics, skills, contracts and technologies that impact their specific profession, in a schedule-friendly format that is easily viewable on their computer, mobile phone, iPod, iPad, Kindle, or even printed out.

Chris Beaver
ExecSense Webinars
San Rafael, CA United States
Contact Phone: 855-ExecSense
Cell: 415-578-2080
Click to Contact from Web Site

JEFFREY HANSLER, CSP -- SALES PRESENTATION TRAINING
Los Angeles, CA United States
www.oxfordco.com

Jeffrey Hansler, CSP, author of Sell Little Red Hen! Sell! is an expert trainer, motivator and educator with over 100 articles published. A specialist in sales, negotiation, influence, and persuasion, he focuses on the dynamics and interaction in business while inspiring audiences with his unique ability to translate organizational objectives into entertaining, absorbable and memorable programs. He is eager to serve those who are excited about their future, and what they have learned.

Jeffrey Hansler, CSP
Speaker, Trainer, Author, Consultant
Oxford Company
Huntington Beach, CA United States
Contact Phone: 714-960-7461
Contact Main Phone: 714-960-7461
Cell: 714-225-7461
Click to Contact from Web Site

GRANVILLE TOOGOOD ASSOCIATES, INC.
Darien, CT United States
http://toogoodassoc.com

Granville Toogood is America's top leadership communications coach. Clients include more than half the Fortune 500 CEOs, political candidates, and business leaders throughout the 'new' economy. He is best-selling author, lecturer, executive and political coach, seminar leader, keynote speaker and author of three best-selling books, 'The New Articulate Executive-- Look, Act and Sound Like a Leader'; 'The Articulate Executive in Action--How the Best Leaders Get Things Done'; 'The Creative Executive--How Business Leaders Innovate by Stimulating Passion, Intuition and Creativity.'

Granville Toogood Associates
Darien, CT United States
Contact Phone: 203-655-5155
Cell: 914.414.8773
Click to Contact from Web Site

MITCHELL P. DAVIS -- EDITOR AND PUBLISHER OF WWW.EXPERTCLICK.COM
Washington, DC United States
http://www.linkedin.com/in/expertclick

Broadcast Interview Source, Inc., was started in 1984 by Mitchell P. Davis, a recent Georgetown University graduate. His e-mail is ExpertClick@ Gmail.com. The Yearbook has been reviewed in The Sunday New York Times Magazine.

Mitchell P. Davis
Editor
Broadcast Interview Source, Inc.
Washington, DC United States
Contact Phone: 202-333-4904
Contact Main Phone: 202-333-5000
Click to Contact from Web Site

DANIEL J. KNIGHT
Washington, DC United States
www.HPStrategy.Com

Dan founded and heads HP Strategy Associates, LLC which serves leaders in government, small to medium sized businesses and Fortune 500 companies. He helps leaders develop their strategic thinking and create innovative improvement and growth strategies. And he delivers these services through research, interactive seminars, coaching and consulting. He also is an award winning writer and a contributing editor for Strategy and Leadership, a leading business strategy journal. He wrote, Leveraging Intellectual Capital with Knowledge-Based Management, the American Management Association, New York, NY 1997.

Daniel J. Knight
High Performance Strategy
Alexandria, VA United States
Contact Phone: 703-971-5235
Click to Contact from Web Site

RHONDA L. SHER -- TWO MINUTE NETWORKER
Thousand Oaks, CA United States
http://www.2minutenetworker.com

Rhonda Sher is a recognized expert on how to create a powerful 30 second marketing message, identify your target market, the secrets to developing strategic alliances and networking at tradeshows to get solid leads and a high return on your investment. Rhonda's programs are ideal for corporate meetings, conferences, conventions as well as chambers of commerce, and associations. Rhonda provides innovative ideas for taking any business to the next level using the power of networking.

Rhonda L. Sher
Murrieta, CA United States
Contact Phone: 805-279-7295
Click to Contact from Web Site

Granville Toogood
A S S O C I A T E S

*"Three minutes in front of the right audience
can be worth more than a year at your desk."*
--Granville Toogood

Granville Toogood is America's most successful executive communications coach. Clients include most of the Fortune 100, as well as dozens of startups in the "new" economy. He is a lecturer, personal coach, seminar leader, keynote speaker and author of three best-selling books, "The Articulate Executive--Learn to Look, Act and Sound Like a Leader"; "The Inspired Executive-- The Art of Leadership in the Age of Knowledge"; "The Creative Executive--How Business Leaders Innovate by Stimulating Passion, Intuition and Creativity."

He has appeared on CNN, CNBC, the Business Channel, Fox TV and many more. Since 1981, he has helped thousands of executives and CEOs to position themselves, and their companies, as leaders in their industries. *The Wall Street Journal* calls Granville Toogood America's greatest executive communications coach.

Do you want to be a world-class leader able to command any audience? Do you want to advance rapidly through the ranks? Do you want your company to have a signature voice? Do you want employees, shareholders, customers and Wall Street to see you in a whole new light? Do you want to turn heads, influence investors, impress new clients, even move markets?

CONTACT:
Granville Toogood
5 Salem Straits
Darien, CT 06820
(203) 655-5155
fax (203) 655-6423
toog5155@aol.com
www.toogoodassoc.com

"A superb executive coach." --Arthur Martinez, Chairman/CEO, Sears, Roebuck and Co.

"The master coach." --Mike Szymansck, President, Philip Morris USA

"What an impact Granville Toogood has had on the art of leadership and communication. What a great teacher!" --Bob Johnson, COO, Honeywell Aerospace

"Granville Toogood's work with clients is like a lifeline to good communication." --Charlotte Beers, Chairman, WJN Thomson Worldwide

"Toogood is a real expert and the advice he gives is indispensable." --Charles Lee, CEO, GTE Corp.

"Granville Toogood is the best in the business." --Allen Wheat, Chairman, CS First Boston

"Granville Toogood understands that you simply can't be a leader without being a good communicator." --Bill Lane, General Electric Company

"Granville Toogood is not only the best executive coach I know, he is an absolute must for business leaders who want to get the most out of themselves and their people." --Arnie Pollard, CEO, Chief Executive Magazine

"Granville Toogood can show you how to get the most out of yourself and your employees." --Elizabeth Baltz, Sr. VP, Mastercard Int'l

"Granville Toogood makes the capable business person more capable, more successful and definitely more self-confident." --Martha Stewart

HARMONY TENNEY -- SALES PERFORMANCE CONSULTANT
Richmond, VA United States
www.businessempowerment.com

International Business Empowerment Consultants, Inc. www.BusinessEmpowerment.com What if your organization could have sales certainty, rather than 'guess your best' ?? What if your marketing was actually a profitable investment, rather than 'hope we get some calls' ?? IBEC, Inc brings performance to the equation, catalyzing desired outcomes and benchmarks. It brings concrete experience to each team member for maximum value contribution, and accountability for continued achievement. Harmony Tenney IBEC, Inc.

Harmony Tenney
International Business Empowerment
Consultants, Inc.
Staunton, VA United States
Contact Phone: 540-255-5686
Click to Contact from Web Site

DR. JOACHIM DE POSADA -- BILINGUAL MOTIVATIONAL SPEAKER
Miami, FL United States
www.jdeposada.com

Dr. Posada's best seller Don't Eat the Marshmallow Yet is about the most important factor for success: Self discipline. The ability to delay gratification. As an international speaker with over 30 years of experience in over 60 countries he has had the opportunity to work with international companies, associations and professional and olympic teams. He delivers inspirational, transformational and unforgetable speeches that will radically change the way participants think about success, failure and change. He is an expert on human behavior, leadership, change and psychological persuasion applied in business, specially in consultative sales. He has been in numerous television shows, radio, internet, and print. His unique perspective of business and world affairs points to a lively and interesting interview.

Dr. Joachim de Posada
International speaker and author
Miami, FL United States
Contact Phone: 305-220-8398
Cell: 787 317 7970
Click to Contact from Web Site

ARNOLD SANOW -- THE BUSINESS SOURCE
Vienna, VA United States
www.arnoldsanow.com

Arnold Sanow, MBA, CSP (Certified Speaking Professional) is the author/co-author of 5 books to inclde, 'Get Along with Anyone, Anytime, Anywhere...8 keys to creating enduring connections with customers, co-workers - even kids'. His keynotes and seminars focus on getting along, building positive workplace relationships, people skills-,dealing with and managing change, and how to build instant rapport, relationships and connect. He has been on numerous televison and radio shows as well as in the print media. Shows include the CBS evening news, ABC world morning news, USA Today, and others. He is a regular guest talking about relationship and people skills issues on Sirrus Radio and Family Net Television.

Arnold Sanow, MBA, CSP
Speaker, Seminar Leader, Facilitator
The Business Source
Vienna, VA United States
Contact Phone: 703-255-3133
Cell: 703-869-1881
Click to Contact from Web Site

The Five Star Decision Making System

Colonel Dan Knight
Strategic Decision Making Expert

Are you struggling with details in making important decisions? Is your team battling over which steps to take to finalize your important projects? Do you waste time in trying to decide the best approach in dealing with problems?

What if you were given a clear and direct approach to problem solving that saved you time, money, and team disruptions?

Lt. Colonel Dan Knight, U.S. Army, Retired, a renowned leadership expert for corporate and government agencies, has developed the "Five Star Decision Making System" that streamlines all critical decision making and implementation processes for leaders.

This system provides a simple and effective understanding of how the "best of the best" make tough decisions and make them stick.

It offers leaders a fully developed and researched system to overcome frustrations and roadblocks that hinder decision-making and stifle productivity.

Don't get bogged down again in struggling over complexities in your decision-making and waste precious time and resources.

☆ **Assessment**

☆ **Deliberate Step-by-Step Process & Tools**

☆ **Creative & Innovative Mindset**

☆ **Influence & Persuasion**

☆ **Strategy, Execution & Measurement**

Call Dan Knight and let him show you the system that works every time. He delivers his "Five Star Decision Making System" through leading-edge keynote addresses, seminars, publications and coaching.

Dan Knight
703-971-5235
dan@hpstrategy.com
www.FiveStarDecisionInstitute.com

JERRY CAHN, PH.D., J.D. - ADVISOR, COACH TO LEADERS - PRESENTERS
New York, NY United States
www.presentationexcellence.com/

Jerry Cahn is a leader who provides practical information to connect and inspire audiences to unleash their potential for success. He is a powerful speaker, "trusted advisor" to C-level executives, and media resource. An attorney and psychologist (who teaches Management for CUNY), he taps his experiences and thought-leadership to educate and guide people. He's worked on Capitol Hill, turned around a public company, and built Brilliant Image which helped 5000+ clients produce winning sales, marketing and investor presentations. He heads Presentation Excellence, providing strategic and leadership related consulting and training. See webinars on www.presentationexcellence.com; visit www.leaderconnections.com and www.vistagenewyork.com and www.poweryournetwork.com.

Jerry Cahn, Ph.D., J.D.
President & Managing Director
Presentation Excellence / Leader Connections
Vistage New York
New York City, NY United States
Contact Phone:
Contact Main Phone: 646-290-7664
Click to Contact from Web Site

PATRICIA FRIPP -- BUSINESS PRESENTATION EXPERT
San Francisco, CA United States
www.fripp.com

Why are so many executive presentations so darn boring? Perhaps it is because the poor speakers have not been Frippnotized! Hall of Fame speaker Patricia Fripp is THE executive speech coach, an expert in effective public speaking, business communications, and persuasive presentation skills. Patricia has a unique ability to simplify and demystify the process of designing and delivering important presentations. Patricia Fripp, CSP, CPAE is a professional who teaches as well as she speaks. For over 25 years corporations and associations have benefitted from her high-content speeches and entertaining style. At the same time audiences are delighted by her engaging delivery. Meetings and Conventions magazine called her 'One of the country's 10 most electrifying speakers.' Kiplinger's Personal Finance wrote 'Patricia Fripp's Speaking Skills seminar is the 6th best way to invest in you.'

Patricia Fripp, CSP, CPAE
President
Fripp & Associates
San Francisco, CA United States
Contact Phone: (415)753-6556
Cell: 415-637-4281
Click to Contact from Web Site

RENEE GRANT-WILLIAMS -- COMMUNICATION SKILL TRAINING EXPERT
Nashville, TN United States
http://www.morevoicepower.com

Renee Grant-Williams is a communication skill training expert, vocal coach, and author of Voice Power, (AMACOM, NY). Commentary and hot tips: Public speaking, voice mail, analysis of politicians voices, customer service and sales. Created a public speaking course for the Barnes & Noble Online University. Coached Faith Hill, Tim McGraw, Dixie Chicks, Huey Lewis, Linda Ronstadt, Quoted in Cosmopolitan, BusinessWeek, Southern Living, TV Guide, UP/AP, Chicago Tribune, Boston Globe. Appearances on ABC, CBS, NBC, FOX, PBS, BRAVO, BLOOMBERG, MTV, GAC, BBC, NPR.

Elaine Collins
Office Manager
ProVoice
United States
Contact Phone: 615-259-4900
Click to Contact from Web Site

Empowering organizations to harvest market potential

Sales and marketing are the lifeblood of any successful organization. International Business Empowerment Consultants, Inc., is a consulting organization dedicated to identifying and implementing improvement strategies for your business's customer acquisition and retention endeavors, increasing cash flow to your business both immediately and in the long term.

IBEC, Inc., specializes in:

■ **improving** the performance of sales persons, their managers and the internal structures and systems in which they operate;

■ **fueling** individual and enterprise leadership for maximum value contribution of the organization to all of its dependents;

■ **managing** the systematic change and conflict inherent in benchmarking, continuing performance improvement and ongoing accountability

Drawing from more than 25 years of experience in sales, with an emphasis in the wireless sales and radio marketing industries, as well as having consulted with businesses of all sizes and industries, IBEC, Inc., provides your business with the foundation, resources and abilities to "reap the lion's share" in your market.

Harmony Tenney
International Business Empowerment Consultants, Inc.
511 Robin Street
Staunton, Virginia 24401

Phone: (540) 255-5686
Fax: (540) 886-2433

Harmony
@BusinessEmpowerment.com

CHERYL STEPHENS -- PLAIN LANGUAGE EXPERT

Vancouver, British Columbia Canada
www.plainlanguage.com

Cheryl Stephens has been a plain language champion for over two decades, consulting to businesses, legal organizations, and government. She has mentored business people, attorneys, other professionals, and students in the art of clear communication. Her lively, informative seminars and her no-nonsense consulting approach can help anyone create clearer, more client-friendly documents and processes.

Cheryl Stephens
Vancouver, BC Canada
Contact Phone: 1-604-739-6884
Click to Contact from Web Site

PATTI WOOD -- COMMUNICATION DYNAMICS

Decatur, GA United States
http://www.pattiwood.net

Patti Wood, MA, CSP -- the Body Language Lady -- a dynamic speaker and trainer. She is an expert on Body Language, Public Speaking, Customer Service and Dealing with Difficult People, delivers keynote speeches, workshops and convention seminars, nationally recognized college teacher, books on body language, public speaking, first impressions and other topics, and private coaching.

Patti Wood
President
Communication Dynamics
Decatur, GA United States
Contact Phone: 404-371-8228
Click to Contact from Web Site

JOEL RUSSELL -- A COMBAT MARINE'S LIFE STORY

Seattle, WA United States
http://www.EscapingDeathsSting.com
AL

A lot of soldiers face death in a foxhole and make promises to God about what they would do if their life was spared. But when Marine Joel Lee Russell was introduced to death in Vietnam and made a promise, he kept that promise after returning home - by writing a book. The story of Russell's near-mortal wound and journey of faith that followed is told in Escaping Death's Sting: A Combat Marine's Life Story (ISBN: 978-1-60911-019-2,

Scott Lorenz
Westwind Communications
Plymouth, MI United States
Contact Phone: 734-667-2090
Click to Contact from Web Site

Get Along With Anyone, Anytime, Anywhere

Communications/ People Skills Expert
Arnold Sanow

Arnold Sanow, MBA, CSP (Certified Speaking Professional) will share with your audience what it takes to build rapport, relationships and connect with others.

Arnold has delivered over 2,500 paid presentations to more than 500 different companies, government agencies and associations. He is the author of 5 books, including "Get Along with Anyone, Anytime, Anywhere," the "Charisma Card Deck" and "Marketing Boot Camp."

He is a frequent guest in the media (USA Today, ABC Morning News, the Wall Street Journal and CBS Evening News) and a former adjunct professor at Georgetown University.

If you need an entertaining, interesting, informative and easy-to-understand communications/people skills/get along expert to deliver a presentation or to interview, contact Arnold anytime at:

www.arnoldsanow.com
www.speakingcoach.com
speaker@arnoldsanow.com

703-255-3133

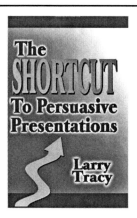

Barbara Hemphill
America's Productivity Specialist
'Taming the Paper Tiger'

LARRY TRACY -- EXPERT PRESENTATION COACH
Alexandria, VA United States
www.Tracy-presentation.com

President Ronald Reagan described Larry Tracy as 'an extraordinarily effective speaker' due to his hundreds of successful presentations before demanding audiences. He has converted this real world experience into a highly-acclaimed communications coaching program, in either English or Spanish, providing time-pressed executives a short cut system to deliver persuasive presentations. His Web page is in the number one position on the Google, MSN and Yahoo! search engines under Presentation skills training for executives.

Larry Tracy
Tracy Presentation Skills
Alexandria, VA United States
Contact Phone: 703-360-3222
Click to Contact from Web Site

BARBARA HEMPHILL, CPO -- PRODUCTIVE ENVIRONMENT INSTITUTE
Raleigh, NC United States
www.BarbaraHemphill.com

Author of Kiplinger's Taming the Paper Tiger book series and a revolutionary software program by the same name. As CEO of Hemphill Productivity Institute, Barbara is the founder of the PTAC program - Productivity Trainers and Authorized Consultants in the US and Canada who assist clients to create and sustain a productive environment so they can accomplish their work and enjoy their lives. Clients include corporations, government, non-profits and small businesses, as well as individuals.

Barbara Hemphill, CPO
Founder & CEO
Hemphill Productivity Institute
Raleigh, NC United States
Contact Phone: 919-773-0722
Contact Main Phone: 800-427-0237
Cell: 919-349-9247
Click to Contact from Web Site

OTHNIEL DENIS, MBA -- MICROSOFT EXCEL EXPERT
Brooklyn, NY United States
www.ExcellentOnes.com

Othniel Denis, is Principal of Excellent Ones Consulting LLC. A company called one of the 'hopeful' stories by the Wall Street Journal. He has authored white papers 'The Hidden Gems in Microsoft Excel', 'Paper! The Arch Nemesis of Automation' and '17 Common Spreadsheet Mistakes' to name a few. His white papers have been downloaded thousands of times from the company website. Find out how Microsoft Excel can help businesses grow, households manage and governments balance.

Othniel Denis, MBA
Excellent Ones Consulting LLC
Brooklyn, NY United States
Contact Phone: 347-763-1035
Click to Contact from Web Site

If you are looking for an expert in public speaking, stop here.
Being perceived as a dynamic, inspiring public speaker
is no longer a nice skill to have; it is a matter of business life and death.
Sales are lost because of pathetic sales presentation skills.

Patricia Fripp, CSP, CPAE

Expert in Business Communications

"Patricia Fripp is the best speech coach an executive could ask for! She turns executives into business rock stars!"
– *Scott Bajtos, Group Vice President, Business Objects*

"Patricia Fripp builds leaders and transforms sales teams through her expert speech coaching and sales presentation techniques."
– *Dan Maddux, Executive Director, American Payroll Association*

"In my 10 years in sales and marketing, Patricia Fripp is the most dynamic, charismatic and knowledgeable sales trainer and coach I know."
– *Bill Lewis, Director of Sales and Marketing, North America, Unitech*

Ask Patricia about . . .

■ **What are the major mistakes sales people make?**

■ **Why are most executives such dull presenters?**

■ **How does a good public speaker go from good to great?**

"My partner Robin and I have spent our entire careers in advertising. Our agency is known for putting Aflac on the map. What the creative minds of The Kaplan Thaler Group do for a 30-second commercial, Fripp does for a 60-minute convention speech. If you want THE executive speech coach, **call Fripp."** – *Linda Kaplan Thaler, CEO, The Kaplan Thaler Group*

Patricia Fripp is THE executive speech coach for executives, successful professional speakers and sales teams. They benefit from her unique ability to simplify and demystify the process of designing and delivering important presentations.

Patricia is a *Hall of Fame* keynote speaker who has *Meetings and Conventions* magazine calling her "One of the country's 10 most electrifying speakers."

Kiplinger's Personal Finance wrote "Patricia Fripp's Speaking Skills seminar is the 6th best way to invest in you."

Author of *Get What You Want!* and *Make It, So You Don't Have to Fake It!* Co-author of *Speaking Secrets of the Masters, Speakers Edge* and *Insights into Excellence.*

www.ExecutiveSpeechCoach.com
415-753-6556 ■ PFripp@ix.netcom.com
www.Fripp.com

EVERYTHING IN ITS PLACE -- PRODUCTIVITY EXPERT
Scottsdale, AZ United States
http://www.everythinginitsplace.net

Eileen Roth is a national speaker and the author of Organizing For Dummies. Eileen shows people how to put everything in its P-L-A-C-E. Her simple organizing secrets are easy to remember and implement immediately. Best of all, maintenance is minutes a day to stay that way! Eileen's organizing principles will reduce your stress, and save you time and money. Eileen has appeared on the Today Show and Oprah. She is a national speaker and consultant on all aspects of organization including Office Organization, Time Management, Home Organization and Student Organization.

Eileen Roth
Your Tour Guide for Success
Everything in its Place ®
Scottsdale, AZ United States
Contact Phone: 480-551-3445
Click to Contact from Web Site

JAN YAGER, PH.D. -- SPEAKER, AUTHOR AND CONSULTANT
Stamford, CT United States
www.JanYager.com

A dynamic speaker, workshop leader, consultant, and prolific author praised for her extensive original research, Dr. Yager is a member of the National Speakers Association, NAPO (National Association of Professional Organizers), ASJA (American Society of Journalists and Authors), and the American Sociological Association. She is often interviewed on national television and radio, or quoted in print, including the Associated Press, USA Today, People, The Wall Street Journal, The New Yorker, New York Times, The Oprah Winfrey Show, Good Morning, America, The Today Show, CBS This Morning, CNN, ABC Radio, National Public Radio, and CBS Radio. Her preferred form of contact except for urgent matters is email: jyager@aol.com

Jan Yager, Ph.D.
Stamford, CT United States
Contact Phone: 203-968-8098
Click to Contact from Web Site

ADVOCATES FOR WORLD HEALTH
Tampa, FL United States
awhealth.org

Overview - Advocates for World Health(AWH) is a 501(c)3 corporation that recovers surplus medical products and distributes them to relief agencies working in developing nations, thus assisting underserved patients and reducing medical waste. This mitigates against directing large amounts of unused medical products into landfills and incinerators while also supporting better access to healthcare to patients in impoverished communities abroad.

Ryan Kania
Advocates for World Health
Tampa, FL United States
Contact Phone: 352-263-4219
Click to Contact from Web Site

Barbara Hemphill

America's Productivity Specialist
'Taming the Paper Tiger'

Are you taking advantage of the best time in history to help businesses get organized and increase productivity?

Attention, Organizing & Productivity Consultants:
Equip yourself to create a thriving and profitable organizing business by joining the world-class team of Paper Tiger Authorized Consultants. There's no need to reinvent the wheel. Barbara Hemphill has been refining it for 30 years.

If you ...
...want to own your own business, but don't want to re-invent the wheel;
...are an organizing professional and see the huge earning potential of adding market-proven products and services to your existing business;
...want to have a business that will enable you to make more money with less effort and that can sustain you and grow in profits each year;
...want to become part of a community of world-class organizing professionals;
...want to leverage time and resources to grow your business exponentially instead of trying to do it alone, then contact us now!

Barbara Hemphill is author of "Kiplinger's Taming the Paper Tiger at Home" and "Taming the Paper Tiger At Work." She is also co-author of "Love It or Lose It: Living Clutter Free Forever," launched on the Home Shopping Network. Organizational principles, featured in Kiplinger's Taming the Paper Tiger software, promise to "find anything in your office in five seconds or less."

As CEO of the Paper Tiger Productivity Institute, she is the founder of the PTAC program -- a group of productivity trainers and authorized consultants, whose mission is to assist clients to create and sustain a productive environment so they can accomplish their work and enjoy their life.

Hemphill has been a featured guest on TV shows, such as NBC's Today Show, ABC's Good Morning America, CNBC, CBS Nightly News, HGTV and The View.

www.PaperTigerConsultant.com
www.PaperTigerInstitute.com
888-380-6799
support@papertigerinstitute.com

Barbara Hemphill, CEO, Paper Tiger Productivity Institute, Raleigh, North Carolina

DR. ELIZABETH CARLL -- STRESS AND TRAUMA EXPERT

Huntington, NY United States
http://www.DrElizabethCarll.com

An internationally recognized clinical and consulting psychologist, author and speaker, Dr. Elizabeth Carll is an expert on stress and post-traumatic stress, crisis management in relationship to life events and violence, including family, workplace, youth and media violence. She is the author and editor of a variety of publications, including Trauma Psychology: Issues in Violence, Disaster, Health and Illness, Two Volumes. (Vol. 1: Violence and Disaster; Vol. 2: Health and Illness.) She is also an authority on the mind-body connection to health/illness, body image, eating disorders, self-injury behavior, family relationships and media. Dr. Carll has responded to numerous disasters and crises and served on the American Psychological Association's National Disaster Response Advisory Task Force for seven years and founded the New York State Psychological Association Disaster/Crisis Response Network, the first statewide volunteer disaster response network in the nation, which she coordinated for ten years. Frequently interviewed by national television, print and radio, Dr. Carll is a past president of the Media Psychology Division of the American Psychological Association and also chairs its News Media, Public Education, and Public Policy Committee.

Elizabeth Carll, Ph.D.
PsychResources, Inc.
Huntington, Long Island, NY United States
Contact Phone: 917-941-5400
Contact Main Phone: 631-754-2424
Click to Contact from Web Site

DR. MARC HALPERN -- AYURVEDA EXPERT

Sacramento, CA United States
http://www.ayurvedacollege.com/college/halpern.php

Dr. Marc Halpern is an expert in the fields of Ayurveda, Yoga and Self-Healing. He is the President of the California College of Ayurveda, Cofounder of the National Ayurvedic Medical Association and the author of Healing Your Life; Lesson's on the Path of Ayurveda. An inspiring public speaker and educator, Dr. Halpern is a pillar of the Ayurvedic and Yoga communities. He has been on CBS's 60 minutes and is featured in the Ricky Williams biographic film Run Ricky Run.

Dr. Marc Halpern
California College of Ayurveda
Nevada City, CA United States
Contact Phone: 530-478-9100
Click to Contact from Web Site

MELLANIE TRUE HILLS -- HEALTH AND PRODUCTIVITY EXPERT -- STOPAFIB

Dallas, TX United States
http://www.mellaniehills.com/

This best-selling author is your internationally-recognized expert on heart disease, wellness, workplace productivity, stress, life balance, and women's business success. As founder of the American Foundation for Women's Health, she saves lives by sharing her near-death experiences with heart disease and stroke and launched www.StopAfib.org to advocate for patients with atrial fibrillation, a life-threatening irregular heartbeat. Her successful track record as transformation agent includes being a high-tech executive and an Internet pioneer (Dell, Cisco, JCPenney).

Mellanie True Hills
CEO
StopAfib.org, American Foundation for Women's Health
Greenwood, TX United States
Contact Phone: 940-466-9898
Cell: 940-399-3010
Click to Contact from Web Site

Stress and Trauma Expert

Dr. Elizabeth Carll

An internationally recognized clinical and consulting psychologist, author and speaker, Dr. Elizabeth Carll is an expert on stress and post-traumatic stress, crisis management in relationship to life events and violence, including family, workplace, youth and media violence.

She is the author and editor of a variety of publications, the most recent (2007) being **Trauma Psychology: Issues in Violence, Disaster, Health and Illness**, Two Volumes. (Vol. 1: Violence and Disaster; Vol. 2: Health and Illness.) She is also an authority on the mind-body connection to health/illness, body image, eating disorders, self-injury behavior, family relationships and media.

Dr. Carll has responded to numerous disasters and crises and served on the American Psychological Association's National Disaster Response Advisory Task Force for seven years and founded the New York State Psychological Association Disaster/Crisis Response Network, the first statewide volunteer disaster response network in the nation, which she coordinated for ten years.

Frequently interviewed by national television, print and radio, Dr. Carll is a past president of the Media Psychology Division of the American Psychological Association and also chairs its News Media, Public Education, and Public Policy Committee and the Interactive Media Committee.

She edited a special issue of the *American Behavioral Scientist*, "Psychology, News Media, and Public Policy: Promoting Social Change" and chairs the Media/ICT Working Group for the United Nations NGO Committee on Mental Health, New York. She is also a representative to the United Nations from the International Society for Traumatic Stress Studies.

Elizabeth Carll, Ph.D.

PsychResources, Inc.
Huntington,
Long Island, N.Y.

Main Phone:
631-754-2424
Contact Phone:
917-941-5400

ECarll@optonline.net

DrCarll.com

JOHN IAMS, M.A., P.T. -- PAIN MANAGEMENT EXPERT

Poway, CA United States
http://www.theprrt.com

John was born in San Diego , CA and continued living in San Diego until he was accepted into the Physical Therapy Program at the University of California School of Medicine in San Francisco . Upon graduation, he was commissioned an ensign in the U.S. Navy and served 3 years as a physical therapist during the Vietnam War. He also married Vonnie Hardesty at that time and continues to be married to her to this day. They have 3 sons who've graduated from school and done very well in their careers.

John Iams, M.A., P.T.
Primal Reflex Release Technique™ (PRRT™)
Poway, CA United States
Contact Phone: 1-858-487-3700
Click to Contact from Web Site

DEBORAH KING -- HEALTH AND WELLNESS EXPERT

Los Angeles, CA United States
www.deborahkingcenter.com

Deborah King is a Master Healer and New York Times best-selling health & wellness author of 'Be Your Own Shaman,' which takes you on a one-of-a-kind journey into the powerful esoteric world of healing. Featured regularly on Huffington Post and Psychology Today, Deborah also makes frequent appearances on national TV, where she comments with both wisdom and humor on the issues of the day.

Scott Hartley
Director
Deborah King Center
Malibu, CA United States
Contact Phone: (310) 266-3594
Click to Contact from Web Site

DR. TONI LEONETTI, PH.D., L.M.F.T -- HUMAN POTENTIAL INTERNATIONAL

Los Angeles, CA United States
http://www.drtonileonetti.net/

Dr. Toni Leonetti, Ph.D., L.M.F.T., Founder of Human Potential International, is a Media Psychology Expert and Licensed Psychotherapist dedicated to the study and communication of cutting edge discoveries which maximize happiness, excellence, and self-actualization. Knowledge acquired from years of research and private practice are revealed in her upcoming book The Ten Traits of Happy People. Dr. Leonetti has consulted for the United States Navy, corporations and colleges.

Dr. Toni Leonetti
Psychotherapist, Founder
Human Potential International
Camarillo, CA United States
Contact Phone: 805-484-7868, Ext.43
Cell: 310-951-6015
Click to Contact from Web Site

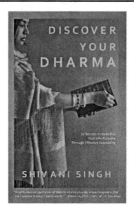

LESLIE NOLEN -- HEALTH, WELLNESS AND HEALTHCARE TREND EXPERT
Dallas, TX United States
http://www.radialgroup.com/about.htm

Leslie Nolen authors The Health and Wellness Trend Report (4th ed.) and is a nationally-consulted expert on business trends across the entire health and wellness spectrum. Her refreshing perspective cuts across the traditional industry silos of fitness, nutrition, yoga , conventional healthcare, complementary and alternative medicine, diabetes, obesity, aging and longevity. The Radial Group's president, she's an insightful, highly-rated industry speaker and source for national media including The New York Times and The Wall Street Journal. Previously CFO & COO for start-ups and Fortune 500 companies, she's a CPA with master's degrees from Northwestern University and DePaul University.

Leslie Nolen
President
The Radial Group
Dallas, TX United States
Contact Phone: (877) 851-0098
Click to Contact from Web Site

RENEE PASER-PAULL -- RAPE AND SEXUAL ASSAULT RECOVERY EXPERT
Buffalo, NY United States

Rape and Sexual Assault == Renee Paser-Paull, M.S. is an expert on UnVictimizing. As a Speaker, Trainer and Consultant, Renee specializes in helping to UnVictimize those who have been affected by rape and other forms of sexual assault, to regain control of their life. Renee acquired her expertise in this area through raw, painful and almost deadly personal experience. She is a living example of her message of resilience, recovery, and renewal. Renee has degrees in Elementary and Adult Education, is a former teacher and skilled professional speaker. She is a certified instructor of the Creative Problem Solving Process. Renee's first book will be published in 2012.

Renee Paser-Paull, M.S.
Soaring Pathways
Medina, NY United States
Contact Phone: 716-913-9891
Click to Contact from Web Site

SHIVANI SINGH -- DHARMA EXPRESS
San Diego, CA United States
DharmaExpress.com/

Founded by Shivani Singh, author of the award-winning book, Discover Your Dharma: 10 Secrets to Redefine Your Life Purpose Through Effective Journaling, Dharma Express provides a fresh new perspective on discovering and living your dharma now. Through experiential programs and products designed for the savvy and sophisticated urbanite, Dharma Express incorporates tools and media to empower those with a vision, with a fire in their belly, and a deep sense of urgency that pushes them beyond the conventional route to happiness.

Shivani Singh
Dharma Express
Carlsbad, CA United States
Contact Phone: 858 754 9838
Click to Contact from Web Site

NORMA ROTH -- AGING GRACEFULLY WITH DIGNITY AND SPUNK INTACT
Lincoln, NH United States

Norma Roth is the author of Aging Gracefully With Dignity and Spunk Intact: Aging Defiantly; and the poetry books Fear, Trembling and Renewal: Poems to Age With. In her new book, Aging Gracefully - Aging Defiantly, Ms. Roth asserts: while science is predicting that members of the Silver Generation and Baby Boomers face unlimited possibilities, societal pressures push them out to pasture. Roth says, 'Stop! Don't Panic! You're definitely not over the hill!' Discover the freedom to go beyond the limits imposed by our world. Her book is a roadmap to a larger landscape of unlimited opportunities for the dynamic

Brad Butler
Account Executive
Promotion in Motion
Hollywood, CA United States
Contact Phone: 323-461-3921
Click to Contact from Web Site

ERIC R. BRAVERMAN, M.D. -- ANTI-AGING EXPERT
New York, NY United States
http://www.pathmed.com/

The Place for Achieving Total Health, PATH Medical, is a patient care center for complete health care devoted to body and mind wellness. We offer complete primary care, and treat neurological, psychiatric, cardio logical, gastroenterological, pulmonary, gynecological, and hematological disorders. PATH is a general medical and nutritional practice, offering comprehensive diagnostic and therapeutic service for children and adults.

Donna Ruth
Media Relations
PATH Medical
New York, NY United States
Contact Phone: 2122136155
Click to Contact from Web Site

SILVER PLANET -- TRUSTED SENIOR RESOURCE
Bainbridge Island, WA United States
www.silverplanet.com

Silver Planet® empowers boomers and seniors to make informed decisions about where and how to live. Providing rich content, personal advice, and access to trusted services, Silver Planet helps make aging with choice a reality.

Karen Klein
Bainbridge Island, WA United States
Contact Phone: 206.498.4594
Click to Contact from Web Site

MARK SINGER -- RETIREMENT EXPERT
Boston, MA United States
YourRetirementJourney.com

Mark Singer is a CERTIFIED FINANCIAL PLANNER™ professional and the author of The Changing Landscape of Retirement—What You Don't Know Could Hurt You. He has been The Retirement Guide to thousands of investors for close to 25 years and is the creator of the Retirement Roadmap and the Financial Organizer System, both of which contribute to a solution to investors' greatest concerns—properly coordinating their financial affairs. These systems have become a primary resource for the people who have worked with Mark over the years.

Mark Singer
Boston, MA United States
Contact Phone: 781-599-5009
Click to Contact from Web Site

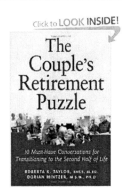

**DR. DAVID J. DEMKO -
GERONTOLOGIST CREATOR OF
ZOOMER -1998-**
Boca Raton, FL United States
http://www.demko.com

**THE COUPLE'S RETIREMENT
PUZZLE -- DORIAN MINTZER &
ROBERTA TAYLOR**
Boston, MA United States
CouplesRetirementPuzzle.com

Dorian Mintzer and Roberta Taylor, co-authors of
The Couple's Retirement Puzzle: 10 Must-Have
Conversations for Transitioning to the Second Half
of Life, are relationship therapists and retirement
coaches who have found that when couples are able
to communicate effectively and know how to com-
promise and negotiate, they are less likely to avoid
the often difficult and uncomfortable issues related to retirement transition. Mintzer and Taylor
are both members of the National Speakers Association and the Life Planning Network.

Dr. Dorian Mintzer
Co-Author
The Couple's Retirement Puzzle
Brookine, MA United States
Contact Phone: 617-267-0585
Click to Contact from Web Site

ZOOMER magazine, a publication of AGEVEN-
TURE news service, is celebrating a decade (1998-
2008) of service to the 50-plus population.
ZOOMER creator, Dr. David J. Demko, professor
of gerontology believes today's boomers are determined to age and retire on their own terms. They
aspire to be ZOOMERS, awesomely ageless
boomers.

Dr. David J. Demko
Gerontologist
ZOOMER magazine
www.AgeVentureNewsService.com
Boca Raton, FL United States
Contact Phone: 561-866-8251
Cell: query via email 1st
Click to Contact from Web Site

**LOUIS LEVY -- SUCCESS IN
RETIREMENT**
Washington, DC United States
www.LouisLevy.com

Louis Levy breathes new life into the word 'retirement.' He is an award-winning Voiceover expert,
and an accomplished actor who has performed on
Broadway, in regional theater and in numerous
films. Louis is also a captivating cabaret singer and
songwriter. A member of SAG and AFTRA, the
Toastmasters Hall of Fame and the National Speakers Association, Louis is also co-founder and co-
sponsor of the Jewish Film Festival in his hometown of Louisville, Kentucky. Louis knows the
secrets of how to savor life's 'second chance' in
retirement. He will empower your 'Over 50' viewers with passionate, sage advice spiced with humor

Louis Levy
Alexandria, VA United States
Contact Phone: 703-739-0077
Cell: 240-463-0388
Click to Contact from Web Site

BARBARA MORRIS - PHARMACIST - AGING MANAGEMENT COACH FOR BOOMERS
Escondido, CA United States
http://www.NoMoreLittleOldLadies.com

Barbara Morris, R.Ph., is an 81-year-old pharmacist and expert on unique anti-aging strategies. Author of Put Old on Hold, and her new book No More Little Old Ladies!, her message is for Boomers and younger women who want to feel and function as as well or better than they do now for another 25 years or more.

Barbara Morris, R. Ph.
Image F/X Publications
Escondido, CA United States
Contact Phone: 760-480-2710
Click to Contact from Web Site

CYNTHIA SHELBY-LANE, M.D. -- LAUGHTER IS GOOD MEDICINE
Detroit, MI United States
shelbylanemd.com

Getting Things Done...Keys to a Well Balanced Life' is the latest book co-authored by the dynamic Dr. Cynthia Shelby-Lane, MD. Physician, world-renowned speaker and webinar host, celebrated writer, producer, comedienne, mother, and now television talk-show host. . . Dr. Lane is a board-certified anti-aging expert. Dr. Lane's proven approaches to whole body healing reached worldwide demand, leading her to become THE 'Internet Doctor', answering questions for patients through her website service 'Diagnose Me'. Radio, television or the internet, Dr. Lane's mission is to confront heart disease, weight loss, stress reduction, and cancer. As a certified professional health coach, she provides an effective blend of lifestyle management and medical technique to healing benefit of her patients and clients. 'Laughter is Good Medicine' is the motto of Dr. Cynthia Shelby-Lane, MD. And through her latest entertaining and informative tele-seminars, she educates the public about Anti-Aging, and the choices to lead a happy & healthy life.

Cynthia Shelby-Lane, M.D.
Second Opinion
Southfield, MI United States
Contact Phone: 800-584-4926
Contact Main Phone: 800-584-4926
Click to Contact from Web Site

TOTAL MRO PROTECTION
New Haven, CT United States
www.TotalMroProtection.com

Your complete resource for medical, research and occupational supplies: Extensive inventory, If we don't have what you're looking for, we'll find it, Unmatched personal service and reliability, All at great prices, Total MRO delivers the high-quality personal, material and environmental protection supplies your facility needs to operating safely and efficiently. We're committed to ensuring your total satisfaction.

Lowri Foyle
Total MRO Protection, LLC
Guilford, CT United States
Contact Phone: 203-453-3088
Click to Contact from Web Site

Cynthia Shelby-Lane, M.D.
"Laughter is Good Medicine"

"Laughter is Good Medicine," says Cynthia Shelby-Lane, M.D., a doctor, speaker, comedienne and talk show host, who loves to laugh.

Do you know a doctor, who stops to save a life, then gets up on stage to make you laugh . . . at life . . . at yourself . . . and at herself?

Well, Shelby-Lane, M.D., is that kind of doctor. Known as "the ageless doctor," Shelby-Lane is a graduate of the University of Michigan Medical School. She trained as a surgeon at the University of Texas in Houston and committed herself to saving lives as an emergency physician in Detroit. She then re-invented herself and is now a board-certified, anti-aging specialist, keeping people young and healthy from the inside out.

Her practice, Elan Anti-Aging & Longevity Center, incorporates alternative and complementary therapies to promote optimal health and youthful aging. She also expanded her practice to the Internet as "THE Internet Doctor," answering questions for patients worldwide through a detailed Internet evaluation. The doctor is also a certified, professional health coach, helping people make difficult health and life choices and create changes for optimum health and wellness.

Seen on national radio and television, discussing issues such as anti-aging, heart disease, weight loss, stress reduction and cancer, Shelby-Lane speaks nationwide and is also a certified professional health coach. She tackles tough social issues through community work and took thousands of dollars worth of drugs and medical supplies to the victims of Katrina on a solo mission in 2005.

This graduate of Second City Comedy School in Chicago and student at UCLA Motion Picture and Television Program produces TV shows and produces a "live" comedy show called, "Laugh Attack": Stopping the #1 Killer -- Heart Disease. Appearances on the Oprah Winfrey Show and featured articles in the *New York Times*, *Ebony* and *Jet* magazines and *Women's Health Style* magazine have given her expert status as the anti-aging and comedy doc.

She can cook, too. She's no Emeril or Rachel Ray, but Dr. Shelby-Lane is now the host of her new food show, "What's Cookin', Doc?"

Trading in her stethoscope for an apron, her food show features "food remedies and foods that heal." So, if "Laughter is Good Medicine," then "great food is the cure."

Cynthia Shelby-Lane, M.D.
Second Opinion
Southfield, Michigan

Contact Phone: 1-800-584-4926
Main Phone: 313-492-0427
E-mail: agelessdoctor@aol.com

DELORES PRESSLEY -- THE BORN SUCCESSFUL INSTITUTE
Canton, OH United States
www.delorespressley.com

DeLores Pressley is an international keynote speaker, author and life coach. She is one of the most respected and sought-after experts on success, motivation and confidence in the workplace. She is the founder and principal of the BornSuccessful Institute, a professional and personal development company. Having spent 27 years teaching elementary school students, DeLores knows about inspiring others to achieve their potential. During her teaching tenure, she also founded a successful modeling agency for plus-sized women. DeLores is a frequent media guest and has been interviewed on every major network -- ABC, NBC, CBS and Fox -- including America's top rated shows, The Oprah Winfrey Show and Entertainment Tonight. Her national magazine features include People, Glamour, Ebony, Essence, First for Women, Success and Marie Claire. She has been quoted as a success and confidence expert in the New York Daily News, Chicago Tribune, Black Enterprise and the Washington Post.

DeLores Pressley
Founder
DeLores Pressley Worldwide
Canton, OH United States
Contact Phone: 330-649-9809
Cell: 330-327-7477
Click to Contact from Web Site

DIANNE M. DANIELS, AICI
Norwich, CT United States
http://www.imageandcolor.com

A Total Image Consultant, Dianne's advice on subjects including visual appearance, vocal presentation and verbal excellence helps clients increase their self-esteem and self-confidence, and reach new levels of success. Dianne's vibrant and charismatic personal presence is sure to interest readers and audiences of all sexes, ages and backgrounds. Call Image & Color Services at 866 618-8735 -- to book this exciting and easy-to-work-with guest.

Dianne M. Daniels, AICI
CEO
Image & Color Services
Norwich, CT United States
Contact Phone: 866-618-8735
Contact Main Phone: 866-618-8735
Click to Contact from Web Site

YASMIN ANDERSON-SMITH, AICI CIP, CPBS -- IMAGE CONSULTANT
Washington, DC United States
www.kymsimage.com

Yasmin Anderson-Smith is a certified image, personal branding and civility, trainer, author and radio talk show host. Yasmin empowering emerging business women and professionals for higher achievement by aligning their image and personal brand with civility principles and values. Often misunderstood, civility is essential to building the trust and respect needed for harmonious relationships. A creative, passionate and dynamic high achiever, Yasmin successfully rebranded herself in 2006 after completing image management and professional development training with the London Image institute. Her consulting firm KYMS Image International offers professional development, 360 personal brand assessments and civility workplace skills training.

Yasmin Anderson-Smith
Image, Personal Branding and civility trainer
K.Y.M.S Image International, LLC
Bowie, MD United States
Contact Phone: 301-792-2276
Pager: 20007-4132
Cell: 301-792-2276
Click to Contact from Web Site

What do Oprah, Saks Fifth Avenue and Entertainment Tonight have in common?
They all featured keynote speaker . . .

DeLores Pressley
Personal Power Expert
"Helping People Live a Life of Significance"

DeLores Pressley, Motivational Speaker, is founder and principal of The Born Successful Institute, a personal and professional development company. DeLores's credentials and experiences speak for themselves and her empowering and motivational keynotes inspire and motivate the most diverse audiences to realize their potential, be energized and live a significant life.

She doesn't just teach success, she teaches significance.

■ Featured expert in . . .

People
Entertainment Tonight
New York Daily News
Glamour
Essence
Success
Inside Business
Chicago Sun Times
Oprah Winfrey Show

■ Presenting for such companies as Procter & Gamble, First Energy and Roche Pharmaceuticals

■ Founder, Dimensions Plus Model Agency

■ Creator, Plus USA National Beauty Pageant and Convention

■ Author of *Clean out the Closets of Your Life, Believe in the Power of You,* and *How to Grow From No*

"DeLores can do the job!"
-- Maury Povich, Maury Povich Show

"Your presentation will be the topic of discussion for some time."
-- B. Clugh, FirstEnergy Corporation

"DeLores . . . that's great, that's great!"
-- Oprah, The Oprah Winfrey Show

BORN SUCCESSFUL
Where Inborn Potential is Released™

551 36th Street, N.W.
Canton, Ohio 44709

Voice: (330) 649-9809
Fax: (330) 649-9309

info@bornsuccessful.com

www.BornSuccessful.com

DEBORAH BOLAND -- IMAGE -- ETIQUETTE -- COMMUNICATIONS

Toronto, Ontario Canada
www.deborahboland.com

Deborah Boland is a leading Image, Etiquette & Communications coach who grooms executive leaders, entrepreneurs, authors, speakers and celebrities for success. With over 2 decades of experience in television and personal development coaching Deborah understands how to help give professionals stepping into the spotlight the competitive edge. Under Deborah's guidance her clients experience a surge in confidence, an increase in image impact, and greater success both in their professional and personal lives. Deborah is the expert to call to upgrade your image, boost your confidence and skyrocket your success.. Deborah is a certified by AICI -The Association of Image Consultants International.

Deborah Boland
Image, Etiquette and Communications Coach
Deborah Boland Image Consulting
Toronto, ON Canada
Contact Phone: 905 466-4406
Click to Contact from Web Site

SANDY DUMONT -- THE IMAGE ARCHITECT

Hampton Roads, VA United States
http://www.theimagearchitect.com

Sandy Dumont, The Image Architect, is a sought-after speaker and expert on the subject of image. She's lectured, coached and has been interviewed throughout the U.S., Europe and Asia. When firms want to get rid of 'corporate casualty', she's their source; when they need Branding for People®, she's top on their list. Sandy Dumont's skill sets apply to the areas of corporate and political image, branding, risk communications, executive management media interactions, and situations of litigation. Ms. Dumont provides the necessary actions and training required in an environment where perceptions drive motivations, performance and marketplace position.

Sandy Dumont
President
THE Image Architect
Norfolk, VA United States
Contact Phone: 757/627-6669
Click to Contact from Web Site

HEBA AL FAZARI -- EXECUTIVE IMAGE - ETIQUETTE AND COMMUNICATION COACH

Abu Dhabi, United Arab Emirates
www.hebaalfazari.com

Recognized expert in the field of international etiquette and protocol services, Heba Fazari is the Director of Heba AL Fazari International. With a decade of operational protocol experience, Ms. Al Fazari brings in-depth knowledge and skill to the protocol, etiquette, communication and leadership. She has actively pursued additional etiquette and finishing training in Dubai, United Arab Emirates and the United Sates including international protocol training. She has worked in a diverse number of global cities for major multinational firms where she built up her credentials in corporate etiquette, VIPs and Diplomats social etiquette, international protocol, and communication.

Heba AL Fazari
Executive Image, Etiquette and Communication Coach
Abu Dhabi, United Arab Emirates
Contact Phone: 0501119634
Cell: 0501119634
Click to Contact from Web Site

CAROL KINSEY GOMAN, PH.D. -- BODY LANGUAGE IN THE WORKPLACE
Berkeley, CA United States
www.silentlanguageofleaders.com

Carol Kinsey Goman, Ph.D. is the leading expert on body language in the workplace. Her books include The Silent Language of Leaders: How Body Language Can Help - or Hurt - How You Lead and The Nonverbal Advantage: Secrets and Science of Body Language at Work. Carol is a leadership blogger for Forbes.com, a business body language columnist for 'The Market' magazine, and a panelist for The Washington Post's 'On Leadership' column. Carol's interview topics include: The Silent Language of Leaders, Body Language Traps and Tips for Women Leaders, How to Spot a Liar, and Check Your Curb Appeal!

Carol Kinsey Goman, Ph.D.
President
Kinsey Consulting Services
Berkeley, CA United States
Contact Phone: 510-526-1727
Cell: 510-206-4085
Click to Contact from Web Site

JANICE HURLEY-TRAILOR -- THE IMAGE EXPERT
Scottsdale, AZ United States
JaniceHurleyTrailor.com

Janice Hurley-Trailor is The Image Expert. Her clients seek out her coaching to ensure that every aspect of their professional presence is used as a tool for success. She is a top-rated coach on improving 'The Visual, The Verbal and the Body Language' necessary in presenting your very best. 'YOU'RE NEVER STUCK' is the message which her keynotes resonate. Increased excitement, confidence and clarity are the results from her one-on-one coaching and corporate workshops.

Janice Hurley-Trailor
Scottsdale, AZ United States
Contact Phone: 480-219-3860
Cell: 559-972-0489
Click to Contact from Web Site

JEN MUELLER - INSPIRING CONVERSATION - CONFIDENCE THROUGH SPORTS
Seattle, WA United States
http://www.talksportytome.com/

Jen Mueller, America's Expert Talker, is rarely at a loss for words. She pursued a career in sports broadcasting after repeated comments of 'talks too much' from teachers and family members. She's honed her speaking skills as a sports broadcaster and sideline reporter. Jen launched Talk Sporty To Me in 2009 after identifying a communication void in the workplace that could be filled with sports conversations. Jen provides a practical game plan to productive conversations. Her techniques and insights help business professionals level the playing field at work and understand the value of sports conversations as winning business strategy.

Timothy J. Lorang
Media Consultant
Image Media Partners
Seattle, WA United States
Contact Phone: 206-201-2517
Cell: 206-947-4001
Click to Contact from Web Site

Associated Bodywork & Massage Professionals

JENNIFER MAXWELL PARKINSON --
LOOK CONSULTING INTERNATIONAL
Glencoe, IL United States

As a pioneer in the field of image consulting, Jennifer Maxwell Parkinson has helped clients -- individuals and corporations -- fine-tune their public personas. Because of the results she has delivered, she has been invited by many major corporations to speak to their employees about how they can use the same principles. As founding president of the Association of Image Consultants International (AICI), she helped put image consulting on the professional map.

Jennifer Maxwell Parkinson
President
Look Consulting International
Glencoe, IL United States
Contact Phone: 914-629-9180
Click to Contact from Web Site

CAROLYN FINCH -- BODY LANGUAGE EXPERT
Danbury, CT United States
www.CarolynFinch.com

Carolyn Finch, MS, SLP, is an internationally recognized body language expert and an authority on speech and interpersonal communication. From princesses to presidents and the infamous to the everyday, Carolyn brings both professional and entertaining Body Language insight into the media's hot topics. She combines her experiences from the business, educational and medical worlds to analyze leaders, politicians and celebrities as well as employees, coworkers and potential clients. Carolyn's focus is to make her audience aware of nonverbal communication and its significance. Carolyn works as a private coach and with business and associations as a motivational/keynote speaker. Her clients include: Aflac, Duracell, IBM, MENSA, NY State Bankers Association, Intermountain Hospital, Norman Vincent Peale Center, and more. Carolyn is a frequent contributor to First for Women magazine and Bizymoms.com. She has also been quoted in TV Guide, Cosmopolitan, and a variety of national and international newspapers. Carolyn has appeared on NBC,

Carolyn Finch
Electrific Solutions
Danbury, CT United States
Contact Phone: 203-791-2756
Click to Contact from Web Site

ASSOCIATED BODYWORK AND
MASSAGE PROFESSIONALS
Golden, CO United States
www.massagetherapy.com

Associated Bodywork & Massage Professionals (ABMP) is the nation's largest massage membership organization. Founded in 1987, it is the most authoritative online resource for health, lifestyle and business media needing up-to-date, fact-filled reference tools and background on the massage therapy industry. ABMP is the media's guide to consumer trends, economics and legislation affecting massage practice. Among the features on the Media Corner at www.massagetherapy.com are: a glossary explaining more than 250 types of massage and bodywork practiced in the United States, free downloadable photography, a searchable archive of more than 1,000 articles on everything from Acupressure to Zen (reprints permitted with attribution), fact sheets, press releases and comprehensive statistical information on the massage therapy profession.

Carrie Patrick
Public Relations Specialist
Associated Bodywork and Massage
Professionals
Golden, CO United States
Contact Phone: 800-458-2267
Click to Contact from Web Site

America's *Premier* Body Language Expert
Carolyn Finch M.S. SLP

Motivating Others to Motivate Themselves

Carolyn's focus is to make your audience aware of non-verbal communication and it's significance.
Look out, she may read your body language too!
Carolyn works as a private coach with individuals and as a motivational/keynote speaker with organizations and associations.

Featured in "Yearbook of Experts & Authorities" for 25 Years
also seen on:

www.CarolynFinch.com
Danbury, Connecticut, 06811 U.S.A.
203-791-2756   carolyn@carolynfinch.com

JOE LORENZ --- BODYBUILDING PRE WORKOUT SUPPLEMENTS
Detroit, MI United States
www.TheNewRealDeal.com

Joe Lorenz is the founder of Real Sports Labs which produces The Real Deal http://www.The-NewRealDeal.com a powerful performance enhancement supplement that helps improve endurance, energy, strength and mental focus whether biking, swimming, running, body building or weight training. Lorenz has also released a new smartphone app called "Suppa Time." This app was created to help fitness enthusiasts in their training routines by planning out and reminding them when to eat, exercise, and take their supplements. "It's especially good for contest prep for N.P.C Figure, Fitness, Bikini and Bodybuilding Competitors," says Lorenz

Scott Lorenz
Publicist
Westwind Communications
www.westwindcos.com
Plymouth, MI United States
Contact Phone: 734-667-2090
Contact Main Phone: 734-667-2090
Cell: 734-667-2090
Click to Contact from Web Site

BRIDGES TO CROSS
Oakland, CA United States
www.bridgestocross.org

Bridges to Cross is the vision of artist, educator, and health advocate, Michael Grbich. He is committed to promoting good health and healthy living by tap dancing across historic bridges across the country. His campaign began soon after his triumphant crossing of The Golden Gate Bridge on November 18, 2007 to celebrate his 75th birthday. On November 26, 2008, Michael tap danced across The Brooklyn Bridge

Corinne Innis
Bridges to Cross
New York, NY United States
Contact Phone: (516) 902-5640
Click to Contact from Web Site

LYNN FISCHER'S HEALTHY LIVING. INC.
Lakeland, FL United States
www.lynnfischer.com

Nutrition Expert for TV, Radio and Print - Author of seven healthy cookbooks, three best sellers, 1,000,000 books in print, Lynn Fischer has hosted and produced hundreds of her own television shows including, 'The Low Cholesterol Gourmet' on The Discovery Channel, which ran for five years nationwide, 'Lynn Fischer's Healthy Indulgences,' which ran for three on Public Broadcasting years (both in the early to late 1990's). Lynn Fischer wrote: 'Low Fat Cooking for Dummies', 'Quick & Healthy Cooking for Dummies', 'Fabulous Fat Free cooking', and 'The Better Sex Diet,' etc. She speaks on several nutrition subjects such as 'How To Have Fun With Your Hated Diet.' Lynn Fischer was always anti-Atkins and pro complex carbohydrates, but she is not a vegetarian.

Lynn Fischer
Lynn Fischer's Healthy Living, Inc.
Lakeland, FL United States
Contact Phone:
Contact Main Phone: 863-644-1383
Cell: 863-838-5886
Click to Contact from Web Site

Massage Therapy/Bodywork Experts

Associated Bodywork & Massage Professionals (ABMP) is the nation's largest massage membership organization and is the most authoritative resource for health, lifestyle and business media needing up-to-date, fact-filled reference tools and background on the growing massage therapy industry. ABMP is the media's guide to consumer trends, economics and legislation affecting massage practice.

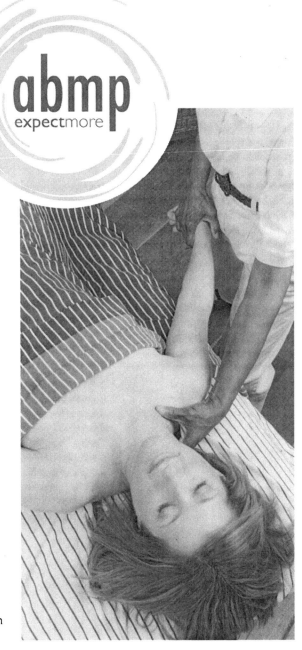

The Media Corner at
www.massagetherapy.com features:

Reference

- Glossary explaining more than 250 types of massage and bodywork practiced in the United States
- Free downloadable photography, hi- and lo-res
- Searchable archive of more than 1,000 informative articles, available for reprint with proper attribution
- Fact sheets and press releases, including results of national consumer research
- Massage therapist referral service for identifying local practitioners
- Demographic snapshot of today's massage therapist
- Trends in massage therapy training

Consumer Perspective

- Why Americans seek massage, what they spend
- Benefits of massage – research and resources
- Massage therapy as complementary/alternative medicine
- What to expect from a massage therapy session
- Consumer protections
- Insurance coverage for massage

Public Policy & Licensing

- Analysis of regulatory and licensing issues
- Links to all state agencies regulating massage
- Editorials on key issues facing the massage therapy profession

---

Media Contact:

Carrie Patrick
Public Relations Specialist

Associated Bodywork & Massage Professionals

25188 Genesee Trail Road, Suite 200

Golden, Colorado 80401

carrie@abmp.com
800-458-2267, ext. 647
8:30 a.m. to 5 p.m. MST

We will always respond promptly, but if you are on a tight deadline please let us know when you call or email.

www.massagetherapy.com

CONNIE BENNETT, CHC, CPC, SUGAR FREEDOM COACH, AUTHOR: SUGAR SHOCK BOOK
San Francisco, CA United States
www.sugarshockblog.com

Connie Bennett, CHC, CPC, ACC, is a sugar expert and author of the book, SUGAR SHOCK!: How Sweets and Simple Carbs Can Derail Your Life--And How You Can Get Back on Track (Penguin Group), with Stephen Sinatra, M.D. Connie is a certified life coach, certified health coach, experienced journalist, and sugar addiction expert, who now helps people worldwide release their sugar habit. In 1998, she quit sweets on doctor's orders and boosted her energy, concentration, moods, and more. Her next book, The Beyond Sugar Shock Diet, comes out next year by Hay House.

Connie Bennett, CHC, CPC
Stop SUGAR SHOCK!
San Francisco, CA United States
Contact Phone: 1-866-542-5784
Contact Main Phone: 1-866-KICK-SUGAR
Click to Contact from Web Site

The American Society of Bariatric Physicians
To advance and support the physicians' role in treating overweight patients.

AMERICAN SOCIETY OF BARIATRIC PHYSICIANS
Denver, CO United States
http://www.asbp.org

Professional society of weight management physicians offering patients specialized programs in the medical treatment of overweight, obesity and their associated conditions. Provides reliable physician spokespersons who can knowledgeably address medical complications of overweight and obesity, plus available treatments and protocols. The first medical society to advocate for classifying obesity as a chronic disease. Responsible for the exposure of numerous weight loss scams and fraudulent products. Established and maintains bariatric practice guidelines and provides medical education.

Beth Little Shelly, CAE
Executive Director
American Society of Bariatric Physicians
Denver, CO United States
Contact Phone: 303-770-2526
Contact Main Phone: 303-770-2526
Cell: 303-995-8652
Click to Contact from Web Site

DR. DAVE E. DAVID - BOSTON VASER LIPO DOCTOR
Norfolk, MA United States
www.drdavedavid.com

Media Physician/Medical Broadcaster and Product Spokesperson: Dr. David has been appearing on national television for over 20 years. You may recognize him from his appearances on CNN, Fox News Channel, or as Medical News Analyst, appearing live at the news desk regularly on NECN, having appeared as a guest on countless national and local talk shows and producing and hosting the TV talk show: 'There's a Doctor In the House' and appearing with Joan Rivers, Farrah Fawcett, Marilu Henner, Gloria Loring, Leeza and many others, Dr. David is know across the country as an educator. Additionally, he has acted as a spokesperson.

Dave E. David, M.D.
Medical Consulting Services, Inc.
Norfolk, MA United States
Contact Phone: 781-764-4747
Click to Contact from Web Site

SUZANNE ARMBRUSTER -- FEMALE FINE HAIR REPLACEMENT
Sarasota, FL United States
www.remaneyourself.com

Suzanne Armbruster is a leading resource for issues for sudden women's hair loss due to Alopecia Areata, chemotherapy, and female pattern baldness. She has served as a regional president of several of the National Alopecia Areata Foundation support groups, and attended many NAAF conventions and events. Suzanne has an 'inside track' on the latest in medical hair treatments, wig styles, and wig manufacturer advancements. She also speaks routinely on the social implications of sudden hair loss of women and how it affects their intimate relationships, their work peers, and normal daily life activities.

Suzanne Armbruster
RemaneYourself.com - Female Fine Hair Replacement
sarasota, FL United States
Contact Phone: 9419282124
Click to Contact from Web Site

BILLY LOWE -- CELEBRITY STYLIST AND BEAUTY EXPERT
Los Angeles, CA United States
www.billylowe.com/

Celebrity hairstylist & beauty expert Billy Lowe has worked with the hottest names in Hollywood on and off the red carpet. He is reponsible for creating extraordinary beauty behind the scenes of Hollywood, as well as in his private hair studio. His work has been featured on shows such as Extreme Makeover, MTV's Made, TLC's 10 Years Younger and countless others, and he is a guest speaker at countless trade shows nationwide on beauty trends and tips. You'll find his beauty tips and techniques in magazines and news articles around the world, as well as his hot beauty blog.

Billy Lowe
Billy Lowe Hair Studio
Los Angeles, CA United States
Contact Phone: 310-430-4045
Click to Contact from Web Site

DAVE E. DAVID, M.D. -- BOTOX EXPERT
Boston, MA United States
medfacebody.com

Dave E. David, M.D. specializes in VASER Liposuction, wide-awake minimally invasive lipo, not reuqiring general anesthesia, with quick recovery, low risk and minimal pain. Dr. David also specializes in Botox injection and the use of facial fillers, such as Restylane, Radiesse and Juvederm, which can make wrinkles disappear immediately, while turning back the clock in the appearance of faces. Dr. David believes that 'less is more,' when it comes to facial procedures, giving a natural and youthful appearance.

Dave E. David, MD
Medical Director
Medical Face & Body Aesthetics
Dedham, MA United States
Contact Phone: 508.520.9872
Cell: 508.404.3669
Click to Contact from Web Site

Dr. Christine Anderson's
DYNAMIC
Prenatal Yoga

For All Fitness Levels

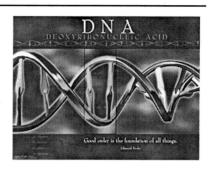

HOWARD BIRNBERG
Carmel, CA United States

Geneticist Catherine Fox and archaeologist Paul Butler are remarkable individuals; attractive, accomplished, ethical and widely acclaimed. Their world of the mid-21st century is not unlike our own. Political, religious and scientific institutions are attempting to cope with rapid medical advancements that allow the great potential of our own genomes to be unlocked.

Howard Birnberg
Birnberg & Associates
Carmel, CA United States
Contact Phone: 312-664-2300
Click to Contact from Web Site

CHRISTINE ANDERSON - A DOCTOR OF CHIROPRACTIC
Los Angeles, CA United States
http://www.kidchiropractic.com/

Christine Anderson, a Doctor of Chiropractic, has been practicing in Hollywood since graduating Summa Cum Laude from Cleveland Chiropractic College(CCC-LA)in Los Angeles in 1989. As an intern, Dr. Anderson was on the faculty at CCC-LA and also assisted the head of the radiology department in the clinic. Dr. Anderson completed a 3 year post graduate program which gives her diplomate status and Board Certification in Chiropractic Pediatrics and Pregnancy (DICCP).

Brad Butler
Promotion In Motion
Hollywood, CA United States
Contact Phone: 323-461-3921
Click to Contact from Web Site

AMERICAN MASSAGE THERAPY ASSOCIATION (AMTA)
Evanston, IL United States
http://www.amtamassage.org

American Massage Therapy Association, (AMTA®), has over 57,000 member-massage therapists and massage schools, with chapters in every state. Founded in 1943, AMTA promotes standards for the profession, a code of ethics and has an active Government Relations program. The best resource for information about: choosing and finding a professional massage therapist, massage as a complement to conventional medicine, state regulation of massage therapy, consumer views of massage, consumer usage of massage therapy, research confirming benefits of massage, National Massage Therapy Awareness Week® each October.

Ronald Precht
Communications Manager
American Massage Therapy Association (AMTA)
Evanston, IL United States
Contact Phone: 847-905-1649
Contact Main Phone: 877-905-2700
Click to Contact from Web Site

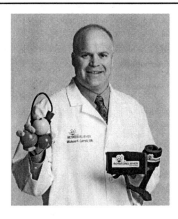

DR. MICHAEL F. CARROLL -- SHOULDER PAIN EXPERT
Traverse City, MI United States
www.rotatoreliever.com

Dr. Michael Carroll suffered from a common complaint — shoulder pain caused by problems with his rotator cuff. The doctor had trouble sleeping because of the pain. One sleepless night about six years ago, he took his arm, held it down and noticed it felt better. 'It was my 'Eureka' moment,' Carroll said. Dr. Carroll fashioned a makeshift traction device out of bandages to keep his shoulder and arm in position. Within days of using the system, Carroll said his pain practically vanished. After perfecting the brace, Carroll added a highly-functional exercise component, calling the system ROTATORELIEVER ™.

Scott Lorenz
Westwind Communications Medical Marketing
Plymouth, MI United States
Contact Phone: 734-667-2090
Click to Contact from Web Site

MARTINE EHRENCLOU, MA -- PATIENT ADVOCATE
Los Angeles, CA United States
www.thetakechargepatient.com

Martine Ehrenclou, M.A., is an award-winning author, patient advocate and speaker. Her first book, Critical Conditions: The Essential Hospital Guide To Get Your Loved One Out Alive received 15 book awards. In her newest health book, The Take-Charge Patient, Martine empowers readers to become proactive and effective participants in their own health care. Her mission is to bring to light the importance of being an advocate for others and for ourselves. Through her books, media interviews, les, blog, and lectures, Martine Ehrenclou reveals insider information on how to interact effectively with medical professionals and navigate the health care system.

Martine Ehrenclou
Los Angeles, CA United States
Contact Phone: 310 502 5244
Click to Contact from Web Site

BEATRICE C. ENGSTRAND, M.D., F.A.A.N. -- NEW YORK CITY NEUROLOGIST
New York, NY United States
www.doctorengstrand.com

Beatrice C. Engstrand, M.D., is a board-certified neurologist, ethicist and geriatrician. She is a licenced physian and published author and has hosted a radio show Neurology with Dr. Engstrand weekly on WOR Radio for seven years, taking callers and interacting with the audience. Listed at top of PodJockey.com, she is versatile with additional expertise in animal care, wildlife rehabilitation and legal matters. Of note, Engstrand is a single adoptive parent of two Russian children. She has travelled extensively throughout the world and has knowledge of several languages. She has spoken at the Diabetic Association, the Epilepsy Foundation, N.Y. Marathon, Canyon Ranch and other venues. She has a well-rounded compassionate concern for total well-being. Her listeners remain faithful and trust her advice. As a recipient of many honors -- Woman of Distinction, White House National Finalist and Honorary Doctorate from Lehigh University -- Engstrand provides an expansive insight which adds to entertaining, expansive dialogue.

Beatrice C. Engstrand, M.D.
Huntington, NY United States
Contact Phone: 631-423-2100
Cell: 631-300-8575
Click to Contact from Web Site

DR. EDWARD LAMADRID -- ACUPUNCTURIST, HERBALIST, MASSAGE THERAPIST

Chicago, IL United States
www.integrativehealthstudio.com

Dr. Edward Lamadrid, licensed acupuncturist, massage therapist, and board certified herbalist, has over 25 years of bodywork experience. He has a Masters and Doctorate Degree in Acupuncture and Herbal Medicine from Pacific College of Oriental Medicine. He is preapring his weight loss research study for publication. He is the Chief Operating Officer and Campus Director at Pacific College of Oriental Medicine in Chicago, as well as a member of their teaching faculty. Ed specializes in the treatment of sports injuries, musculoskeletal pain and internal medicine.

Dr. Edward Lamadrid, DAOM L.Ac.
NY United States
Contact Phone: 917-741-7419
Click to Contact from Web Site

DR. BURTON S. SCHULER, FOOT DOCTOR PODIATRIST, MORTONS TOE EXPERT

Lynn Haven, FL United States
http://www.footcare4u.com/

Dr. Burton S. Schuler, Podiatrist, Foot Doctor, of Panama City, Fl is this country's leading expert on the painful medical problem know as the Morton's Toe He is the author of the new book Why You Really Hurt: It All Starts In The Foot, which is the story of how the Morton's Toe can cause pain thru out the whole body. Dr. Schuler is a 1975 graduate of the New York College of Podiatric Medicine. He has also written the 1982 The Agony Of De-Feet, A Podiatrist's Guide To Foot Care, His articles about the foot, have appeared in the leading podiatric journals and publications. He has been interviewed by such varied publications as the New York Times, Cosmopolitan Magazine, and First for Women. During his 37 year career he has appeared on hundreds of radio stations to give his expert opinion regarding the Morton's Toe and other foot

Michelle Matisons, Ph.D.
Administrative Assistant
The La Luz Press
Panama City, FL United States
Contact Phone: 850-763-3333
Click to Contact from Web Site

DR. DOUGLAS SEA -- DC MENTORS -- CHIROPRACTIC

Sioux Falls, SD United States
www.DCMentors.com

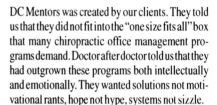

DC Mentors was created by our clients. They told us that they did not fit into the "one size fits all" box that many chiropractic office management programs demand. Doctor after doctor told us that they had outgrown these programs both intellectually and emotionally. They wanted solutions not motivational rants, hope not hype, systems not sizzle.

Jeremy D. Brown
Throne Publishing Group
Sioux Falls, SD United States
Contact Phone: 605-610-8326
Click to Contact from Web Site

L. ERIK WESTERLUND, M.D., FACS
Atlanta, GA United States
www.TopDoctorsLabs.com

Dr. L. Erik Westerlund, M.D. is a board-certified orthopedic surgeon, fellowship trained in reconstructive spinal surgery. Dr. Westerlund is a Fellow of the American Academy of Orthopedic Surgeons, the American College of Surgeons, an active member of the North American Spine Society and appointed faculty member in Spine Surgery with the highly regarded AO North America organization. Dr. Westerlund is an experienced and dynamic speaker that has regularly worked in academic settings, with private industry and public media. He speaks and travels frequently and has the rare gift of scientific brilliance coupled with the ability to be understandable and engaging

Curtis Farber
Top Doctors Labs
Columbus, GA United States
Contact Phone: 706-507-7314
Contact Main Phone: 706-507-7314
Cell: 858-775-0161
Click to Contact from Web Site

DR. AIHAN KUHN -- CHINESE MEDICINE FOR HEALTH
Boston, MA United States
www.DrAihanKuhn.com

Dr. Aihan Kuhn, an expert in Natural healing and prevention provides you with exciting and eye opening information and amazing healing wisdom. You will gain extensive knowledge and practical tools to build a stress free life, to maintain a healthy immune system and energy level, optimize your weight, and keep your brain sharp and creative. With her extensive knowledge and experience on women's health, cancer prevention and healing, children's health, anti-aging education, you get a wider insight into healing. Participants describe her as "The best teacher I ever had". Her slogan: Quality, Truthful, Natural, Effective

Dr. Aihan Kuhn
Director
Chinese Medicine for Health
Holliston, MA United States
Contact Phone: 508-380-0449
Contact Main Phone: 508-429-3895
Cell: 508-380-0449
Click to Contact from Web Site

DENNIS MAHONEY -- HEALTHCARE CONSULTANT
Boston, MA United States
http://www.DennisMahoney.org

Dennis enthusiastically entered the health care industry as a licensed respiratory therapist. He was blessed with the opportunities of being involved in a number of pioneer innovations in managing critical and emergency care patients. In the hospital setting, he quickly moved into leadership, management and teaching roles.

Dennis Mahoney
Boston, MA United States
Contact Phone: 617-298-0699
Click to Contact from Web Site

AMERICAN ASSOCIATION FOR LONG-TERM CARE INSURANCE
Los Angeles, CA United States
www.aaltci.org

Jesse Slome is one of the nation's leading long-term care insurance experts. Executive Director of the American Association for Long-Term Care Insurance (www.aaltci.org), the industry trade group, Slome is the author of 20 books, booklets and consumer guides on the subject of long term care planning. Slome directs annual LTC insurance research studies which are published in the Association's annual Long-Term Care Insurance Sourcebook. Slome is also director of the recently formed American Association for Critical Illness Insurance (www.aacii.org).

Jesse Slome
Executive Director
American Association for Long-Term Care Insurance
Westlake Village, CA United States
Contact Phone: 818-597-3227
Contact Main Phone: 818-597-3227
Click to Contact from Web Site

JAKE POORE -- INTEGRATED LOYALTY SYSTEMS
Orlando, FL United States
www.wecreateloyalty.com

Healthcare is facing an uncertain future and everyone is searching for answers about what healthcare will look like tomorrow. Jake Poore is busy creating that future today. Jake is one of the most in-demand and highly rated speakers in healthcare, sharing his practical insights. Jake spent over two decades with Disney, before founding his own consulting organization, where for the past ten years he and his team have successfully adapted proven strategies from Disney and other world-class organizations to healthcare. A polished and respected expert and storyteller, Jake's passion for improving patient experiences shines through in every speech, article and media interview.

Jenna Kinkade
Integrated Loyalty Systems, Inc.
Orlando, FL United States
Contact Phone: 407-859-2826
Click to Contact from Web Site

DR. GABY CORA -- LEADERSHIP & WELL-BEING CONSULTANT & SPEAKER
Miami, FL United States
www.DrGabyCora.com

Gabriela Cora, MD, MBA. Dr. Gaby Cora works with leaders who need to hit the ground running while they lead under pressure and strive to experience peace of mind. She works with C-level executives, entrepreneurs, and their executive teams as they make the most critical business and strategic decisions affecting their success and well-being as well as the success and well-being of the companies they serve. She's the author of ExecutiveHealth.com's Leading Under Pressure (Career Press, 2010). Dr. Gaby is the Wellness Doctor and Coach™ on A Lifetime's Health & Wellness Makeover™ at Balancing Act on Lifetime Television.

Gabriela Cora, MD, MBA
Executive Health and Wealth Institute, Inc.
Miami, FL United States
Contact Phone: 305-762-7632
Click to Contact from Web Site

AMERICAN ASSOCIATION OF PHARMACEUTICAL SCIENTISTS
Arlington, VA United States
http://www.aapspharmaceutica.com

The American Association of Pharmaceutical Scientists (AAPS) is a professional, scientific society of approximately 12,000 individual members employed in academia, industry, government, and other research institutions worldwide. Founded in 1986, AAPS provides a dynamic international forum for the exchange of knowledge among scientists to enhance their contributions to public health. Call AAPS for expertise in the areas of drug discovery, design, development, analysis, production, quality control, clinical evaluation, and manufacturing.

Joseph Catapano
Communications Specialist
American Association of Pharmaceutical Scientists
Arlington, VA United States
Contact Phone: 703-248-4772
Click to Contact from Web Site

LOUIS B. CADY, M.D.
NEUROPSYCHIATRIST AND WELLNESS EXPERT
Evansville, IN United States
www.indianatms-cadywellness.com

Dr. Louis Cady straddles the world between science and art. Trained first as a classical pianist, he went on to obtain two degrees, with honors, from the Conservatory of Music of the University of Missouri at Kansas City, before obtaining his medical degree in 1989 from the University of Texas Medical Branch in Galveston, Texas. He then trained in psychiatry at the world-famous Mayo Clinic, beginning his practice of child, adolescent, adult, and forensic psychiatry in Evansville, Indiana in 1993. In addition to his conventional medical training in medicine and psychiatry, Dr. Cady has subsequently received additional training in Age Management Medicine from the Cenegenics Medical Institute in Las Vegas, Nevada, adding that modality into his practice.

Louis. B. Cady, M.D.
CEO, Founder
Cady Wellness Institute
Newburgh, IN United States
Contact Phone: 812-429-0772
Contact Main Phone: 812-429-0772
Pager: call cell
Cell: 812-760-5385
Click to Contact from Web Site

STEPHEN D. FORMAN, LTCI SPECIALIST
Seattle, WA United States
www.ltc-associates.com

Tracing our roots to 1974, LTCA is one of America's pioneering firms in the long-term care insurance field. Our Specialists rank in the Top 1% of agents nationally, according to AALTCI, our industry trade. My expertise has been sought by the Congressional Research Service (reporting on the CLASS ACT), by Kiplinger's, and by LifeHealthPro. I've been quoted in National Underwriter, and contribute regularly to both ProducersWEB and Producers eSource, where I am resident 'LTCI Expert'. LTCA received a 2012 Best of the Web Finalist Award, and was named a Top 10 Most Influential Insurance Account to Follow, with over 130k Followers @ltcassociates.

Stephen D. Forman
Senior Vice-President
Long Term Care Associates, Inc.
Bellevue, WA United States
Contact Phone: 425-462-9500
Contact Main Phone: 800-742-9444
Cell: 206-972-1777
Click to Contact from Web Site

DAN FRIESLAND -- DOCTORS WITH DINGS™ INC
Salem, VA United States
http://DoctorsWithDings.com/

Career assistance for Doctors with blemishes on their record. The blemish in the file has been following you for some time now and the credentialing process uncovers every detail, including that one. Where do you go, what do you do and how do you plan for career growth opportunities you have worked so hard for? Doctors With Dings™, Inc. was formed to provide a platform for Doctors to set their employment record straight. At Doctors With Dings™, Inc we are a catalyst for change. We are here to make it a better transition through the growing stages of your career.

Dan Friesland
Founder-President
Doctors With Dings™, Inc
Salem, VA United States
Contact Phone: 540-444-2623
Contact Main Phone: 540-444-2623
Cell: 540-293-3496
Click to Contact from Web Site

CAROL A. HARNETT -- HEALTH AND DISABILITY EXPERT
Hartford, CT United States
www.linkedin.com/in/carolharnett

Carol Harnett is a health and disability expert who consults with employers, insurance companies and employee benefits brokers on benefits design and workplace-based health and wellness programs. She is a regular on the speakers' circuit and writes a popular benefits column for Human Resource Executive Online. Carol's focus is on innovation in employee health, productivity and performance. She takes a no-nonsense approach by focusing on what works, what doesn't work and what might work in maintaining and improving employee health. Carol is also a clinical physiologist with broad experience in sports medicine, physical medicine and industrial rehabilitation.

Carol A. Harnett
Health & Disability Expert
Simsbury, CT United States
Contact Phone: 860-416-9347
Click to Contact from Web Site

CATHIE LIPPMAN, MD -- ENVIRONMENTAL AND PREVENTIVE MEDICINE
Beverly Hills, CA United States
http://www.cathielippmanmd.com/

Beverly Hills' own environmental doctor presents the health tips she has been giving her patients for years. Now available in her booklet: STAYING HEALTHY IN A CHALLENGING WORLD A HANDBOOK.

Cathie Lippman, MD
Medical Doctor
The Lippman Center for Optimal Health
Beverly Hills, CA United States
Contact Phone: 310-289-8430
Click to Contact from Web Site

Cathie-Ann Lippman, M.D.
Beverly Hills Environmental Doctor
"Creating Vibrant Health in a Toxic World"

As a member of the American Academy of Environmental Medicine since the early 1980s, Dr. Cathie Lippman has been one of the pioneers in alternative medicine. Her message, "Create Vibrant Health in a Toxic World," resonates with audiences who are concerned about how the environment affects their health.

Dr. Lippman received her M.D. in 1973 from the University of Chicago Pritzker School of Medicine. After a pediatric internship at L.A. County-U.S.C. Medical Center, she studied adult and child psychiatry at U.C.L.A. and was board certified in each specialty in 1980.

Dr. Lippman became dissatisfied with the limitations of a psychiatric focus. She changed her practice from psychiatry to alternative medicine in order to address the whole individual. Dr. Lippman's extensive knowledge and understanding of the whole person, including psychological, nutritional, and physiological influences, as well as environmental factors, make her uniquely qualified to examine how these various influences affect the patient.

Thousands of patients over the years have consulted and trusted Dr. Lippman. Now, she is generously sharing her special knowledge with audiences and listeners throughout the United States.

As one satisfied listener commented, "Who would think: a lecture by a doctor who educates as well as treats." (Susan R., R.N.) Another comment: "Because you are a leading expert in the field of alternative medicine, my expectations were high. You delivered! I learned so much from just one lecture. You made me aware of everyday exposures that are affecting my health. Thanks very much." (Andy K.) Lastly: "Dr. Lippman gave sound and thoughtful answers to my questions. I have never been able to understand a doctor so easily as I could with her."

- Toxins in our water
- Poisons in our air
- Metals in our seafood
- Pesticides in our fruits and vegetables
- Dangerous ingredients in our snacks
- Chemicals in our cosmetics

What is a person to do?
Dr. Lippman has answers.

Read Cathie Lippman, M.D.'s blog, "Staying Healthy in a Challenging World":
http://cathielippman.wordpress.com/

291 S. La Cienega Blvd., Suite 409 ■ Beverly Hills , Calif. 90211
310.289.8430 (telephone) ■ 310.289.8165 (fax)
doclipp@gmail.com

www.CathieLippmanMD.com

LONG TERM CARE LEARNING INSTITUTE -- MARILEE DRISCOLL
Plymouth, MA United States
http://www.LongTermCareLearning.com

Marilee Driscoll is the leading objective authority on all the ways to plan for and pay for long-term care. Author of 'The Complete Idiot's Guide to Long-term Care Planning,' she has been interviewed on CBS Early Show, NPR, and quoted several times in the Wall Street Journal, NY Times, Money Magazine and Kiplinger's Personal Finance Magazine. She founded Long-term Care Planning Month (October) to encourage everyone to make this planning part of their personal retirement planning.

Marilee Driscoll
Long Term Care Learning Institute
Plymouth, MA United States
Contact Phone: 508-830-9975
Cell: 508-830-9975
Click to Contact from Web Site

LTC TREE -- LONG TERM CARE INSURANCE
Atlanta, GA United States
www.longtermcareinsurancetree.com

Long Term Care Insurance is more than just retirement planning. It removes the worry of having to earmark your nest egg for the uncertainty of needing Long Term Care so you can enjoy doing the things you like. We provide Long Term Care Insurance quotes from all top-rated companies, company financial ratings, comparisons and reviews that will help with your decision and save you money.

Drew Nichols
LTC Tree
Atlanta, GA United States
Contact Phone: 1-800-800-6139
Click to Contact from Web Site

NATIONAL LTC NETWORK -- LONG TERM CARE INSURANCE
Kansas City, MO United States
www.NLTCN.com

The National LTC Network is an alliance of leading distributors of long term care insurance. Network members work with multiple insurers and are dedicated to marketing long term care insurance with knowledge, ethics and excellence. Founded in November 1994, members of our alliance include some of the largest and most-respected distributors in the nation.

Terry Truesdell
President and CEo
The National LTC Network
KS United States
Contact Phone: 913-385-7899
Click to Contact from Web Site

NATIONAL TOXIC ENCEPHALOPATHY FOUNDATION
Las Vegas, NV United States
www.NTEF-USA.Org

NTEF's core purposes are to provide education and services to the growing segment of the population who are adversely affected by everyday chemicals and toxins in our environment, primarily neurotoxicity. It has been proven that chemicals/radiation have a direct effect upon the brain whether during pregnancy, childhood or in adults. Chemicals such as pesticides, cleaning/disinfectant products, building materials, vaccine preservatives, perfumes, air fresheners, fragranced products, mold, along with EMF/RF smart meters are most likely causing harm to your health and/or to the health of those around you. Our experts are available to assist in litigation or for personal consultations.

Angel De Fazio
President
NTEF
Las Vegas, NV United States
Contact Phone: 702.490.9677
Click to Contact from Web Site

VICKI RACKNER MD FACS -- DOCTOR CAREGIVER
Seattle, WA United States
www.drvickirackner.com

Dr. Vicki Rackner is a former surgeon who now helps build strong heathy caregiving families that reap more love, more joy and more satisfaction. She brings common sense to caregiving. A decade ago this board-certified surgeon and former faculty member of the University of Washington School of Medicine left the operating room to help patients, caregivers and health care professionals work towards their shared goals. Her books include 'Caregiving Without Regrets,' 'The Biggest Skeleton in Your Doctor's Closet,' 'The Personal Health Journal' and 'Chicken Soup for the Soul Healthy Living Series: Heart Disease.' She is regularly quoted in the national media including The Wall Street Journal, CNN.com, USA Today, Time and AARP, to name a few.

Vicki Rackner MD FACS
caregiving Expert, Author and Speaker
Mercer Island, WA United States
Contact Phone: 425-451-3777
Click to Contact from Web Site

ADVANCED BIOMEDICAL CONSULTING, ABC, LLC
St. Petersburg, FL United States
www.abcforfda.com

Advanced Biomedical Consulting (ABC), LLC is a "hands-on" consulting organization that provides a full range of services for Food and Drug Administration (FDA) and state food and drug regulated industries such as medical device manufacturers, pharmaceutical distributors, cosmetic product marketers, food packagers, and developers of dietary supplements. Whether it be vendor audits, expert witness, state board of pharmacy licensing, software validation, regulatory submissions, or mock FDA inspection services, all of ABC's solutions are designed to be cost-effective, fully compliant, and sustainable. For additional information, please go to www.abcforfda.com or contact us directly at info@advancedbiomedical-consulting.com.

Jonathan Lewis
Principal
Advanced Biomedical Consulting, LLC
St. Petersburg, FL United States
Contact Phone: 727-641-6175
Cell: 727-641-6175
Click to Contact from Web Site

UT SOUTHWESTERN MEDICAL CENTER
Dallas, TX United States
www.utsouthwestern.edu/home/news/index.
html
TX

The University of Texas Southwestern Medical Center is one of the nation's leading academic medical centers, specializing in Alzheimer's and other neurological disorders; cancer care; heart, lung and vascular issues; pediatric illnesses, birth defects and inherited disorders; urology; neurosurgery; infectious diseases and immunology; and basic genetic and molecular research, computational biology and biotechnology; as well as many other clinical and research specialties. UT Southwestern, a component of The University of Texas System, includes a medical school, graduate biomedical sciences school, school of health professions, university hospitals, research centers and outpatient clinics.

Michael Berman
Director
UT Southwestern Medical Center
University News Bureau
Dallas, TX United States
Contact Phone: 214-648-3404
Contact Main Phone: 214-648-3404
Click to Contact from Web Site

SEYMOUR M. WEAVER, III, M.D., BOARD CERTIFIED DERMATOLOGIST
Houston, TX United States
www.DrSeymourWeaver.com/dermatology-blog

Board Certified Dermatologist with 30 years of experience with medical, surgical, and cosmetic dermatology. Manufacturer of supplements for weight loss, author of information products on hair and scalp diseases and publisher of Healthy 365 e-newsletter

Seymour M. Weaver, III, M.D.
Board Certified Dermatologist
Katy, TX United States
Contact Phone: 281 395-7770
Click to Contact from Web Site

AMERICAN ACADEMY OF COSMETIC DENTISTRY
Madison, WI United States
www.AACD.com

Photo is of: John Sullivan, DDS -- The American Academy of Cosmetic Dentistry® (AACD) is dedicated to advancing excellence in the art and science of cosmetic dentistry and encouraging the highest standards of ethical conduct and responsible patient care. The AACD fulfills its mission by: offering superior educational opportunities; promoting and supporting a respected Accreditation credential; serving as a user-friendly and inviting forum for the creative exchange of knowledge and ideas; and providing accurate and useful information to the public and the profession.

Kristina Hoffman
PR Director
Vibe Communications
Oconomowoc, WI United States
Contact Phone: 262-468-6798
Click to Contact from Web Site

Chronic Pain Management Expert

Creating " 'All Better' Mommy Magic"

Dr. Vicki Rackner, M.D., is a former surgeon who now helps families find more love, more joy and more hope -- even in the face of chronic pain.

Some describe her Pain Stompers system as "the 7 Habits of Highly Effective People meets Emotional CPR." This simple set of steps empowers people with no medical training to comfort a loved one in pain.

She also empowers health care professionals to coach families members to a caregiving success.

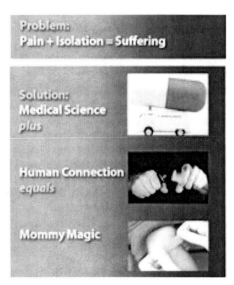

Problem:
Pain + Isolation = Suffering

Solution:
Medical Science plus

Human Connection equals

Mommy Magic

Dr. Vicki Rackner works with:
- Family caregivers
- Health care professionals
- Eldercare providers
- Hospice staff and volunteers

Her services include:
- Speaking engagements
- Coaching
- Pain Stompers training
- Books and Practical Guides
- The Caregiver Club eNewsletter
- Pain Stompers Pearls
  -- short daily pearls of wisdom

Dr. Vicki Rackner has been on all sides of hospital bed -- as a patient with a life-threatening emergency, the surgeon and the family caregiver. After treating tens of thousands of patients and serving as a clinical faculty at the University of Washington School of Medicine, she is now a full-time author and speaker with the mission of building strong healthy families -- no matter what.

YouTube video:
www.youtube.com/watch?v=JOez6KTMlng

Go to
PainStompers.com
to sign up
for daily
inspirational tips
delivered to
your smart phone.

Her Books

Chapters in

Quoted in

DrVickiRackner.com
425-451-3777
8441 SE 68TH #298
Mercer Island,
Washington 98040

DrRackner
@MedicalBridges.com

AMERICAN ASSOCIATION OF ORTHODONTISTS
St. Louis, MO United States
http://www.braces.org

The American Association of Orthodontists (AAO) is the voice of orthodontics. Its 17,000 members in the U.S., Canada and abroad are dentistry's orthodontic specialists. Orthodontists' extensive specialty education qualifies them to treat patients of all ages. AAO spokespersons are uniquely qualified to discuss the relationship of orthodontic health and whole body health, the trend of more adult patients, why the first orthodontic exam should occur no later than age 7, benefits of treatment and research.

Pam Paladin
Marketing and Member/Consumer Relations Manager
American Association of Orthodontists
St. Louis, MO United States
Contact Phone: 314-993-1700
Contact Main Phone: 314-993-1700
Click to Contact from Web Site

GENTLE DENTAL
Fort Lauderdale, FL United States
www.GentleDentalGroup.com

Why Choose Gentle Dental? General Cosmetic Dentistry & More At Its Finest. You say 'why choose Gentle Dental?' We say 'for every reason.' Gentle Dental is the leading provider of dental health services in South Florida. If you're looking for an affordable dentist in the tri-county area, you'll find them at Gentle Dental. . . and so much more. We are equipped to meet all of your dental needs or wants under one roof whether you're looking for general or cosmetic dentistry specialists such as orthodontic care specialists, oral surgeons, endodontists, pediatric, periodontists or prosthodontists.

Michael Sherman
Big Couch Media Group
Boca Raton, FL United States
Contact Phone: 954-254-1650
Click to Contact from Web Site

TIMOTHY KOSINSKI DDS -- ESTHETIC DENTISTRY
Detroit, MI United States
http://www.SmileCreator.net

Dr. Timothy Kosinski is an Adjunct Assistant Professor at the University of Detroit Mercy School of Dentistry and serves on the editorial review board of Reality, the information source for esthetic dentistry, Contemporary Esthetics and Clinical Advisors, and became the editor of the Michigan Academy of General Dentistry. Dr. Kosinski received his DDS from the University of Detroit Mercy Dental School and his Mastership in Biochemistry from Wayne State University School of Medicine. He is a Diplomat of the American Board of Oral Implantology/Implant Dentistry, the International Congress of Oral Implantologists and the American Society of Osseointegration.

Scott Lorenz
Westwind Communications Medical Marketing
Plymouth, MI United States
Contact Phone: 734-667-2090
Click to Contact from Web Site

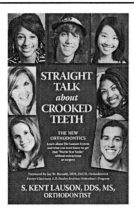

S KENT LAUSON, DDS, MS
Denver, MI United States
Www.StraightTalkaboutCrookedTeeth.org

The best way to learn the straight facts about crooked teeth is to read a new book about a revolutionary, holistic and pace-setting treatment that prevents unnecessary extractions, surgeries, and teeth-straightening braces. That book by Kent Lauson, DDS, is Straight Talk About Crooked Teeth ISBN 978-0-9839629-0-7, Greenleaf Book Group, 2012, 246 pages, $27.95, http://www. StraightTalkAboutCrookedTeeth.org - 'This is the book every mother should read before choosing an orthodontist for her family,' says Michael Gelb, DDS, and Clinical Professor at the NYU College of Dentistry. 'Most practitioners doing orthodontics don't pay enough attention to the airway and TMJ. The nine keys to lower facial harmony should be part of every graduate orthodontic curriculum. Why not have a more beautiful smile while opening the airway, alleviating headaches and clicking jaws, and improving posture? A must read for every parent, dentist and orthodontist.'

Scott Lorenz
Westwind Communications
Plymouth, MI United States
Contact Phone: 248-705-2214
Click to Contact from Web Site

JOAN MAJORS - DENTISTRY BY CHOICE
College Station, TX United States
http://www.joanmajors.com

JoAn Majors is a professional speaker. She is a member of the National Speakers Association and the Global Speakers Network, a two-time business founder and a three-time author. JoAn's newest book, EncourageMentors: 16 Attitude Steps to Building Your Business, Family and Future is available for orders now. Often referred to as a "team member who's temporarily left the office," she brings systems for encouragement, achievement and results oriented communication to the workplace and home. Her highly sought-after presentations are known for their authenticity, humor and engagement. Visit her website at www.joanmajors.com.

Jeannie Russell
Seminar Coordinator
Dentistry by Choice
Caldwell, TX United States
Contact Phone: 979-567-4452
Click to Contact from Web Site

DR. JOE PELERIN -- FAMILY DENTIST
Detroit, MI United States
www.GrindGuardN.com

Dr. Joe Pelerin of Lake Orion, Michigan who has practiced family dentistry for three decades, says teeth grinding and clenching not only damages teeth and fillings and leads to receding gums and root canals, but also can be the cause of migraine headaches and pain in the shoulders, neck, back and ears. That's why Pelerin invented Grind-GuardN www.GrindGuardN.com, a newly patented, FDA-approved mouth guard that is far more effective than other solutions and costs only $50. Says Pelerin, 'I've invented some 10 products but I take the greatest pleasure from inventing Grind-GuardN because of the terrific, life-changing results that patients experience.'

Scott Lorenz
Publicist
Westwind Communications Medical Marketing
Plymouth, MI United States
Contact Phone: 734-667-2090
Contact Main Phone: 7346672090
Cell: 7346672090
Click to Contact from Web Site

DR GARTH D PETTIT
Campbelltown, SA, Australia
http://www.PaintYourMouth.com

In July 1996 my granddaughter developed tooth decay. I embarked on a mission: Prevent Oral Disease in Children. In January 1997 I returned to dentistry to research and create educational resources for children's parents and educators. Currently, April 2012, there are a total of 86 books listed in Amazon for Dr Garth Pettit: Two adult paperbacks, six adult eBooks and the remainder are children's eBooks I set out to create. How Do I Look After My Kids Teeth? 1 of 12 to 12 of 12 and 1 thru 12 are published in six languages: English, French, German, Italian, Portuguese and Spanish.

Dr Garth D Pettit
Sole Proprietor
4 Your Smile 2 Shine Pty Ltd
Campbelltown, South Australia Australia
Contact Phone: 61 08-8365-1889
Click to Contact from Web Site

DAVE E. DAVID, M.D. --- DOCTOR SPOKESPERSON
Norfolk, MA United States
http://www.DrDaveDavid.com

Dave E. David, M.D. is an experienced host, guest and dynamic lecturer, whose personality and naturally-inquisitive nature make him an exciting interviewer, guest or spokesperson. Dr. David, a Board Certified Obstetrician and Gynecologist as well as a weight loss specialist and cosmetic surgeon is a physician with over 30 years of experience. He is Harvard-trained and former teaching faculty at Harvard University. Dr. David is available to appear as a TV or radio guest or host, or as a spokesperson for health/fitness/nutritional/medical products that he believes in. His areas of expertise include women's health, weight loss, fitness, nutrition and Cosmetic Surgery. He can comment or act as medical news analyst for a whole host of medical topics. Dr. David is also an international caregiver, having led emergency medical and surgical teams into Haiti after the devastating 2010 earthquake and into Sri Lanka after the massive tsunami of 2004.

Dave E. David, M.D.
Norfolk, MA United States
Contact Phone: 508.520.9872
Contact Main Phone: 781-764-4747
Cell: 508.404.3669
Click to Contact from Web Site

NATIONAL HEADACHE FOUNDATION
Chicago, IL United States
www.headaches.org

Established in 1970, NHF is the premier educational and information resource for headache sufferers, their families and the healthcare providers who treat them by offering: breaking news; access to headache specialists; access to support groups; award-winning publications and Web site; cutting edge research grants. A nationwide network of physician experts specializing in headache is available to comment on research findings, translate medical data into lay language and offer patients for interviews.

Suzanne E. Simons
Executive Director
National Headache Foundation
Chicago, IL United States
Contact Phone: 888-643-5552
Click to Contact from Web Site

DAVE E. DAVID, M.D.

Do You Need a Physician As a Product Endorser, TV Spokesperson,

Host or Speaker? Look no further than Dave E. David, M.D.:

- ■ *Obstetrician, gynecologist and weight loss/fitness specialist*
- ■ *Can represent all types of health, fitness or medical products*

If you have a medical product, pharmaceutical product or health/fitness product that could use an endorsement by a prominent, well-known medical doctor, consider Dave E. David, M.D.

Dr. David has a warm nature and is very charismatic on camera and in person. As an experienced host and dynamic lecturer, his personality and naturally inquisitive nature make him an exciting interviewer.

Dr. David is a physician with more than 20 years of experience, treating patients and serving as assistant clinical professor at a major medical school. Harvard-trained and formerly on the teaching faculty at Harvard University, Dr. David is available to appear on television infomercials and commercials and as a spokesperson in several different venues for products he believes in.

Twenty years of media experience includes medical analyst/commentator for CNN, FOX News Channel and New England Cable News, host of his own weekly television show ("There's a Doctor in the House") and radio talk show, creator and host of "Making Womb for Baby "(full-length videotape on pregnancy and childbirth) and "Secrets to a Slimmer You" (audiotape program).

Dr. David is a SAG/AFTRA member, well-versed with teleprompter, earprompter and well-trained in commercial and dramatic acting. His appearances include infomercials with prominent celebrities and as a guest on dozens of television talk shows and extensive national exposure and recognition.

Featured on the cover of *Woman's World Magazine* and with publications in countless lay magazines and prestigious medical journals, Dr. David has treated members of the U.S. Olympic team and has acted as a medical consultant to personal fitness trainers in southern California.

As a board-certified obstetrician and gynecologist and as a weight loss specialist, Dr. David has expertise in women's health, weight loss, fitness, nutrition and herbal remedies.

DAVE E. DAVID, M.D.

NORFOLK, MASSACHUSETTS

MAIN PHONE:

800-326-4789

CONTACT PHONE:

781-764-4747

PAGER: 781-764-4747

WWW.DRDAVEDAVID.COM

AMERICAN LUNG ASSOCIATION IN GREATER CHICAGO
Chicago, IL United States
http://www.lungil.org

AMERICAN SOCIETY FOR RADIATION ONCOLOGY
Washington, DC United States
http://www.astro.org

THE UNION OF MEDICAL MARIJUANA PATIENTS
Los Angeles, CA United States
www.unionmmp.org

The Union of Medical Marijuana Patients (UMMP) is a not-for-profit civil rights organization based in Los Angeles, CA. Through aggressive legal and political action in association with education and counseling on compliance with state law, the Union is devoted to defending and asserting the rights of medical cannabis patients. With a philosophy of personal growth and responsibility, the Union supports patients, their member organizations, and the cause of freedom across our country.

Sophie Jacobson
Public Relations Director
The Union of Medical Marijuana Patients
Los Angeles, CA United States
Contact Phone: (310)663-6682
Cell: (843)801-3901
Click to Contact from Web Site

Now in its second century, the American Lung Association is the leading organization working to save lives by improving lung health and preventing lung disease. With the generous support of donors, the American Lung Association is "Fighting for Air" through research, education and advocacy. Our Lung HelpLine and Illinois Tobacco Quitline provide callers convenient access to our registered nurses, respiratory therapists, and tobacco cessation specialists. Both toll-free services grant callers the time and attention needed for asking complex medical questions, in a non-threatening environment. Call 1.800.LUNGUSA for more information or visit www.lungil.org

Katie Lorenz
American Lung Association in Greater Chicago
Chicago, IL United States
Contact Phone: 312-445-2513
Click to Contact from Web Site

The American Society for Radiation Oncology is the largest radiation oncology society in the world, with more than 10,000 members who specialize in treating patients with radiation therapies. As the leading organization in radiation oncology, biology and physics, ASTRO's mission is to advance the practice of radiation oncology by promoting excellence in patient care, providing opportunities for educational and professional development, promoting research and representing radiation oncology in a rapidly evolving socioeconomic health care environment. For more information on radiation therapy, visit www.rtanswers.org. For more information on ASTRO, visit www.astro. org.

Beth Bukata
Director of Communications
American Society for Radiation Oncology
Fairfax, VA United States
Contact Phone: 703-839-7332
Contact Main Phone: 1-800-962-7876
Click to Contact from Web Site

CureSearch
National Childhood Cancer Foundation

CURESEARCH FOR CHILDREN'S CANCER
Bethesda, MD United States
http://www.curesearch.org

CureSearch for Children's Cancer funds the life-saving, collaborative research of the Children's Oncology Group, the largest, cooperative pediatric cancer research program in the world who treats more than 90% of all children with cancer at more than 230 hospitals. Through collaborative research, the Children's Oncology Group has improved cure rates for children's cancer at a pace much faster than any one individual or single institution could accomplish alone. The Children's Oncology Group research has turned cancer from a virtually incurable disease 40 years ago to one with an overall cure rate of 78%. Our goal is 100% cure rate.

Erica Neufeld
V.P. Communications
CureSearch for Children's Cancer
Bethesda, MD United States
Contact Phone: 240-235-2205
Contact Main Phone: 800-458-6223
Click to Contact from Web Site

AMELIA FRAHM -- CANCER BOOKS AUTHOR
Raleigh, NC United States
www.nutcrackerpublishing.com

Amelia Frahm is the author the contentious award-winning children's picture book 'Nuclear Power: How a Nuclear Power Plant Really Works!' and the award-winning 'Tickles Tabitha's Cancertankerous Mommy.' She helped pioneer resources for children affected by cancer and was the first cancer survivor to create an elementary program about cancer. But the first school program she created was about nuclear power plants. She's the owner of Nutcracker Publishing Company, a contributor to the inspirational book 'How We Became Breast Cancer Thrivers' and creator of Crack Open a Book! education programs.

Amelia Frahm
Executive Director
Apex, NC United States
Contact Phone: 919-924-2058
Cell: 919-924-2058
Click to Contact from Web Site

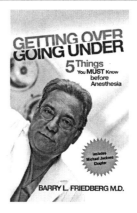

DR. BARRY FRIEDBERG -- BOARD CERTIFIED ANESTHESIOLOGIST
Los Angeles, CA United States
www.drbarryfriedberg.com

A board certified anesthesiologist for more than three decades, Dr. Friedberg is author of Anesthesia in Cosmetic Surgery as well as Getting Over Going Under. He developed The Friedberg Method of administering anesthesia in 1992 and the Goldilocks Anesthesia protocol in 1997. Dr. Friedberg was awarded a US Congressional award for applying his methods on wounded soldiers in Afghanistan and Iraq. The founder of the Goldilocks Foundation, Dr. Friedberg has been published and cited in several medical journals and textbooks.

Scott Lorenz
Westwind Communications
Plymouth, MI United States
Contact Phone: 734-667-2090
Click to Contact from Web Site

STOPAFIB.ORG AMERICAN FOUNDATION FOR WOMEN'S HEALTH
Dallas, TX United States
www.stopafib.org

Five million Americans suffer from atrial fibrillation, a frightening irregular heartbeat that can lead to stroke, congestive heart failure, or death. Mellanie True Hills is now cured of afib and created StopAfib.org to provide patients with information about living with and curing afib. StopAfib.org features an Atrial Fibrillation Services Directory for locating hospitals and physicians to help. StopAfib.org—by patients, for patients—one of the most trusted resources for atrial fibrillation patients.

Mellanie True Hills
CEO
StopAfib.org
Amer Foundation for Women's Heath
Greenwood, TX United States
Contact Phone: 940-466-9898
Click to Contact from Web Site

MAYER EISENSTEIN, M.D., J.D., M.P.H. -- HOMEFIRST HEALTH SERVICES
Chicago, IL United States
http://www.homefirst.com/

Dr. Mayer Eisenstein is a graduate of the University of Illinois Medical School, the Medical College of Wisconsin School of Public Health, and the John Marshall Law School. In his 33 years in medicine, he and his practice have cared for over 75,000 parents, grandparents and children. He is the author of: Give Birth at Home With The Home Birth Advantage, Safer Medicine, Don't Vaccinate Before You Educate, Unavoidably Dangerous - Medical Hazards of HRT and Unlocking Nature's Pharmacy. His medical film "Primum Non Nocere" (Above All Do No Harm), a documentary on home birth, was an award winner at

Brad Butler
Promotion In Motion
re: Mayer Eisenstein, M.D., J.D.
Hollywood, CA United States
Contact Phone: 323-461-3921
Click to Contact from Web Site

MEG JORDAN, PHD., RN, CWP -- GLOBAL MEDICINE HUNTER®
San Francisco, CA United States
www.MegJordan.com

USA Today describes Meg Jordan, PhD, RN, CWP as a 'health trendspotter'. She is a medical anthropologist, an international health journalist, radio personality, editor and founder of American Fitness Magazine, and the Global Medicine Hunter. She is Department Chair and Professor of Integrative Health Studies and Somatic Psychology at the California Institute of Integral Studies in San Francisco and has presented keynote addresses internationally. Dr. Jordan is a behavioral medicine clinician at Health Medicine Center in northern California. She is the author of five books including The Fitness Instinct, (Rodale Reach 1999).

Meg Jordan, PhD., RN, CWP
Global Health Media
San Mateo, CA United States
Contact Phone: 415 599-5523
Click to Contact from Web Site

PATRICK REYNOLDS -- TOBACCOFREE.ORG

Los Angeles, CA United States
www.TobaccoFree.org

Patrick Reynolds, grandson of RJ Reynolds and anti-smoking advocate, was the first tobacco industry figure to speak out against the industry, after his father died from smoking. Today he speaks internationally to youth and adults about tobacco issues and advocates pending legislation. Good Morning America called him 'an articulate and formidable guest.' CNN commented, 'Reynolds' knowledge and insights made it easier for audiences to understand complex issues.' In 2011, TobaccoFree.Org released 'The Truth About Tobacco,' an acclaimed educational video of his live talk for grades 7-12. He's author of 'The Gilded Leaf'. His bio is posted at www.TobaccoFree.org/bio and /news

Christine Hou
Office Manager
TobaccoFree.org
Los Angeles, CA United States
Contact Phone: 310-577-9828
Contact Main Phone: 800-541-7741
Cell: 310-880-1111
Click to Contact from Web Site

DR. GARY KAPLAN -- INTEGRATIVE MEDICINE

McLean, VA United States
www.KaplanClinic.com

Gary Kaplan, D.O., is the founder and medical director of The Kaplan Center for Integrative Medicine. A pioneer and leader in the field of integrative medicine, Dr. Kaplan is one of only 19 physicians in the country board-certified in both family medicine and pain medicine. He is also board-certified in Medical Acupuncture and is a fellow of the American Board of Medical Acupuncture.

Nancy Rose Senich
McLean, VA United States
Contact Phone: 703-442-0080
Cell: 202-262-6996
Click to Contact from Web Site

BOB BARE--ENTREPRENEURIAL EXPERT

Dallas, TX United States
www.bobbare.com

Bob Bare has been creating new businesses and marketing concepts since his teenage years. Mr. Bare not only originates new business ideas, he does it often, and he takes action and implements them. Mr. Bare is a force of experience when it comes to launching and bootstrapping new businesses. He is a speaker for conventions and continuing education seminars.

Bob Bare
Visionary ~ Entrepreneur
SEGR Enterprises
Irving, TX United States
Contact Phone: (972(600-2320
Contact Main Phone: (888) 556-7347
Click to Contact from Web Site

ENABLEMART - YOUR NUMBER ONE SOURCE FOR ASSISTIVE TECHNOLOGY
Salt Lake City, UT United States
http://www.enablemart.com

EnableMart is the worldwide leader in assistive technology distribution. With customers in all 50 states and over 45 foreign countries, EnableMart provides over 3,000 assistive technology and assistive living devices from over 200 manufacturers. EnableMart is inspired to continually seek out and provide the best assistive technology products at the most affordable costs and remains steadfast in their mission to change the lives of individuals with disabilities by eliminating barriers and paving the way to independent living.

Michele Paley
Marketing / Product Manager
EnableMart
Salt Lake City, UT United States
Contact Phone: 801-281-7664
Contact Main Phone: 866-640-1999
Cell: 801-719-8351
Click to Contact from Web Site

SUZAN STIRLING
Crestwood, KY United States
www.SuzanStirling.com

Suzan Stirling is a fulltime author living in Kentucky. Stirling has been published in several magazines through the U.S. and world. Besides The Silence of Mercy Bleu, she has two other novels in progress. A fundraiser, advocate and writer for the Glaser Pediatric AIDS Foundation, Stirling also is a supporter and volunteer with amFar and The National AIDS Memorial Grove and has appeared as a speaker for several AIDS organizations. She volunteers with Trikes for Tikes to donate bikes to needy children. She studied under Pulitzer-nominated author Lee Pennington at Jefferson Community College.

Scott Lorenz
Westwind Communications Book Marketing
Plymouth, MI United States
Contact Phone: 248-705-2214
Click to Contact from Web Site

DR. HANS J. KUGLER, PHD -- ANTI-AGING MEDICINE EXPERT
Los Angeles, CA United States
www.antiagingforme.com

Dr. Hans J. Kugler, PhD: a) Author of (e-book) Dr. Kugler's Ultimate Anti-Aging Factor: Applied Anti-Aging in Action; longer, stronger, shapelier, sexier, brainier." For key topics click on book cover at http://www.antiagingforme.com. b) President, International Academy of Anti-Aging Medicine, Calif. 501-C non-profit educational organization, Physiology, U. Munich Med. School under Nobel Laureate Butenandt, PhD, SUNY Stony Brook, NY, professor of chemistry - longevity studies with cancer-prone animals - at Roosevelt U, Chicago. Lecturer at medical meetings and available as keynote speaker. Click on picture at website above. c) President of "HK Stem Cell Research." Making person-specific embryonic stem cells via nuclear transfer. http://www.antiagingforme.com/html/stemcells.html

Dr. Hans Kugler, PhD
President
International Academy of Anti-Aging Medicine
Redondo Beach, CA United States
Contact Phone: 310-634-2478
Click to Contact from Web Site

TWILIGHT WISH -- CELEBRATING SENIORS AND MAKING DREAMS COME TRUE
Doylestown, PA United States
www.TwilightWish.org

Twilight Wish Foundation, founded in 2003 in Bucks County, Pennsylvania, is a 501(c)(3) non-profit charitable organization that grants wishes to economically-disadvantaged seniors age 68 and older who cannot make their own dreams come true. Our mission is to honor and enrich the lives of deserving elders through wish granting celebrations that connect generations. Our vision is to make the world a nicer place to age, one wish at a time.

Cass Forkin
Twilight Wish
Doylestown, PA United States
Contact Phone: 215-230-8777
Click to Contact from Web Site

DR. GAYLE CARSON - MIDLIFE CRISIS COACH
Miami, FL United States
www.spunkyoldbroad.com

Dr. Gayle Carson's program "Healthy, Wealthy and Fabulous: The 9 Secrets to Living Regret Free and Feeling Alive at Any Age" is designed for anyone wanting a happier and healthier lifestyle. Known as the S.O.B., Spunky Old Broad, Dr. Carson has appeared on ABC, CBS, NBC and Fox and in the Wall Street Journal, Newsweek, USA Today and the Larry King radio show as the premier expert in the boomer market. A fitness enthusiast, business woman for over 5 decades and a great-grandmother, she has the energy of someone half her age. A three time breast cancer survivor and the champion of 16 surgeries, she's appeared on CBS, NBC, ABC, Fox and WSJ, Newsweek, USA Today and Larry King Radio show.

Dr. Gayle Carson
Spunky Old Broad
Miami Beach, FL United States
Contact Phone: 800-541-8846
Click to Contact from Web Site

BRAD BLANTON, PH.D., RADICAL HONESTY
Stanley, VA United States
www.radicalhonesty.com

Dr. Brad Blanton, psychotherapist, seminar facilitator, author of six books about Radical Honesty teaches that the primary cause of stress, depression and anger is living in a story and trying to maintain it by lying, and that we are all doing it to some degree all the time. Brad's media appearances include 20/20, Roseanne, Dateline-NBC, CNN, Montel Williams, Iyanla, NPR and others. Articles in Cosmopolitan, Family Circle, Inner Self, Men's Health, The Chicago Herald-Tribune, The Washington Post, The London Times, Esquire, and others all over the world. His newest book, The Korporate Kannibal Kookbook has just been released. (Dec, 2010)

Brad Blanton
Radical Honesty Enterprisess, Inc.
Stanley, VA United States
Contact Phone: 540-778-1336
Cell: 540-244-8392
Click to Contact from Web Site

DR. PATRICIA A. FARRELL -- PSYCHOLOGIST
Englewood Cliffs, NJ United States
http://www.drfarrell.net

Dr. Farrell is author of 'How to Be Your Own Therapist' and 'It's Not All in Your Head.' TV appearances include Today Show, Good Morning America, AC360, The O'Reilly Factor, Court TV, MSNBC News, The View, VH1, Maury, ABC World News, FOX News. Farrell has written articles on health, child abuse, medical illness, and managing stress, is listed in Who's Who in the World and is the Moderator, WebMD's Anxiety/Panic Board. Website: http://www.drfarrell.net where you can find links to video of TV appearances. Dr. Farrell's Twitter account is @drpatfarrell.

Dr. Patricia A. Farrell, Ph.D.
Licensed Psychologist
Dr. Patricia A. Farrell, Ph.D., LLC
Fort Lee, NJ United States
Contact Phone:
Cell: 201-417-1827
Click to Contact from Web Site

SUSAN FLETCHER, PH.D.
Plano, TX United States
fletcherphd.com

Susan Fletcher, Ph.D. is a psychologist, author and speaker who specializes in helping individuals, professionals and organizations apply strategies for fast improvement. Her Smart Zone strategies provide ways to be a top performer at work and home. She is a quoted expert on AD/HD, emotional intelligence, stress, work/life balance, communication, trust and parenting.

Zan Jones
Smart Zone Solutions
Plano, TX United States
Contact Phone: 214-536-6666
Click to Contact from Web Site

DR. JEAN CIRILLO, PSYCHOLOGIST
Huntington, NY United States
http://drjeantv.net

Meet the psychologist who appeals to younger audiences. Dr. Jean Cirillo has been seen on hundreds of national talk shows as an expert guest and staff psychologist. She has screened contestants for reality shows on MTV, Vh1 and BET. As the author of 'The Complete Idiot's Guide to Self-Testing Your IQ' (Penguin Books), Dr. Cirillo has been featured on The History Channel demonstrating the effect of hypnosis on the brain. Her specialties include women's issues, teens, self-esteem and relationships. Dr. Cirillo is affiliated with several self-help groups and can being guests willing to discuss personal issues.

Dr. Jean Cirillo
Psychologist
Huntington, NY United States
Contact Phone: 516-795-0631
Click to Contact from Web Site

Mid-Life Crisis Coach
GAYLE CARSON

Dr. Gayle Carson, also known as the "Wiz of Biz," has written a new book especially for women over 50. Gayle knows how to handle questions about mid-life and beyond.

"How to Be an S.O.B.: A Spunky Old Broad Who Kicks Butt" teaches the nine secrets of a regret-free life and offers 13 key tips to living a more productive and fulfilled life. Gayle offers short, easy-to-follow advice to achieve health and fitness, open your own business, invest in real estate or do whatever else your SOB heart desires.

Celebrating more than 47 years in business, the "Wiz of Biz" heads up a radio show for Entrepreneur Magazine – "Women in Business" – which celebrates women who embody success in many different ways, giving its audience valuable life lessons.

An expert advisor and coach to CEOs and entrepreneurs, Gayle is also a CSP (certified speaking professional) and CMC (certified management consultant), who has been named to many "Who's Who" books, and whose media exposure ranges from USA Today to the Larry King Radio Show.

Gayle Carson, S.O.B.

2957 Flamingo Drive, Miami Beach, Florida 33140-3916

305-534-8846 Phone   305-532-8826 Fax

gayle@spunkyoldbroad.com

www.SpunkyOldBroad.com

CARLTON DAVIS -- ARTIST, AUTHOR, ARCHITECT AND PUBLIC SPEAKER

Los Angeles, CA United States
http://www.bipolarbarebook.com/meet-carlton-davis

Carlton Davis, is an author, artist, architect, life coach, and public speaker. Mr. Davis is a graduate of Yale University and the University of London. His book, Bipolar Bare, chronicles his thirty year struggle to overcome mental illness. His art and architecture career make him an expert in creativity and bipolar disorder. Mr. Davis speaks to the public about his experience and issues with bipolar disorder, creativity and mental illness, and the two minded self. Mr. Davis has a new website that shows a different aspect of his writing and expertise. This website www.artdock.net is about a drive-by art gallery in LA from 1981-1986. The Art Dockuments chronicle the tales, often hilarious, of this experimental art gallery in a loading dock. Carlton Davis is an expert in comtemporary art in Los Angeles. See his website www.carlton-davisart.com for a view of his artistic skill.

Carlton Davis, AIA, CDT
Principal
The Art Dock
Tanzmann/Davis Architects
Pasadena, CA United States
Contact Phone: 626-840-7997
Cell: 626-840-7997
Click to Contact from Web Site

DR. RAYMOND H. HAMDEN -- CLINICAL AND FORENSIC PSYCHOLOGIST

Dubai City, United Arab Emirates
http://www.hridubai.com

Dr. Hamden has consulted in Psychology of Terrorists Profiling, Critical Incident Debriefing, and Emergency Planning as well as Trauma Situation and Identification and Political Psychology in Middle East and Africa, Europs, Asia, North America, and more than 25 other international nations. For professional distinction, Dr. Hamden was awarded Fellow status in the American College of Forensic Examiners International. He also serves on the Board of Advisors (since 2004) and Chair, American Board of Psychological Specialties (Since 2010). He is also a Member of the American Academy of Forensic Sciences (2011). Published in peer reviewed journals and books, he has presented globally to various professional bodies. He is credentialed, content, and connected with the matters-in-question. Available world-wide, Dr. Raymond H. Hamden can be contacted via dr.raymond.hamden@hridubai.com and +(971-50) 651-8837, an international mobile for consultation in Clinical & Forensic and Political Psychology.

Dr. Raymond H. Hamden
Clinical & Forensic Psychologist
Human Relations Institute
Dubai, United Arab Emirates
Contact Phone:
Contact Main Phone: +1 (202) 262-8800
Cell: + (971-50) 651-8837
Click to Contact from Web Site

CAROLE LIEBERMAN, M.D., M.P.H. MEDIA PSYCHIATRIST

Beverly Hills, CA United States
http://www.drcarole.com

Internationally renowned, Dr. Carole Lieberman is the psychiatrist the world turns to for help coping with today's times. Hundreds of interviews include Oprah, Larry King, the Today Show, Good Morning America, O'Reilly Factor, ET, Court TV, the N.Y. Times & USA Today. She is the author of Coping With Terrorism: Dreams Interrupted, and Bad Boys: Why We Love Them, How to Live with Them, and When to Leave Them. A multiple Emmy-award winner for her TV work, she is also the host of 'Dr. Carole's Couch', an Internet radio show on voiceamerica.com. The news/entertainment industry relies upon Dr. Carole for her uncanny ability to jump in, deliver and excel in any position for which she is needed: TV/radio host, commentator or regular guest; author; trial analyst; reality show therapist; and much more. If it's breaking news... she's on it. Dr. Lieberman has a high-profile clinical and forensic practice, and is on the Clinical Faculty of UCLA's Neuropsychiatric Institute.

Carole Lieberman, M.D., M.P.H.
Psychiatrist
Beverly Hills, CA United States
Contact Phone: 310-278-5433
Cell: 310-251-2866
Click to Contact from Web Site

Dr. Jean Cirillo
Psychologist

Appealing to younger audiences, Dr. Jean Cirillo has been seen on hundreds of national talk shows as an expert guest and staff psychologist. Her specialties include women's issues, teens, abuse, self-esteem and relationships. Dr. Cirillo is affiliated with several self-help groups, including AA and NA, Al-Anon, Parents in Crisis, Father's Rights and Children with Attention Deficit Disorder (CHADD). She can bring guests, willing to discuss personal experiences with such problems as living with alcohol or substance

abusers, seriously disturbed teens or children, domestic violence and divorce and custody issues. She is past president of the New York State Psychological Association Division on Women's Issues.

Top: Dr. Jean performs hypnosis on the History Channel. Second from top: Telepictures' reality show pilot, "The Perfect Dorm." Third from top: Dr. Jean's book, "The Complete Idiot's Guide to Self-Testing Your IQ," Penguin, USA. Above: Dr. Jean on MSNBC Live.

Since she began her training at Columbia University, Dr. Jean Cirillo has been a published author, speaker, professional association officer, practitioner, consultant to reality shows and media commentator.

Dr. Cirillo is available to discuss psychological aspects of current events or breaking news related to women's issues, children and teens, violence, relationships, divorce, addictions, brain functioning and health.

516-795-0631 ■ 516-532-3625
1-800-499-WELL (N.Y. only)
27 Fairview St., Huntington, New York 11743

Video clips at **www.DrJean.tv ■ JeanCirillo@aol.com**

**DR. DEBORAH SERANI -- AUTHOR OF
'LIVING WITH DEPRESSION'**
New York, NY United States
www.deborahserani.com

DR. DEBORAH SERANI is a go-to expert on the subject of depression. What makes her perspective unique is that she specializes in the treatment of depression *and* also personally lives with depression. Serani's interviews can be found in ABC News, Newsday, Psychology Today, The Chicago Sun Times, Glamour Magazine, The Associated Press, Dr. Oz's ShareCare and affiliate radio station programs at CBS and NPR, just to name a few. SPECIALTIES: Expert Psychologist for print, radio or television: Celebrity Self-Disclosure of Mental Illness, Depression, Mental Health, Psychotherapy, Resilience, Sexual Assault, Stigma, Trauma.

Deborah Serani, Psy.D.
Psychologist
Author of 'Living with Depression'
Smithtown, NY United States
Contact Phone: 1.631.366.4674
Click to Contact from Web Site

MICHAEL S. BRODER, PH.D.
Philadelphia, PA United States
http://www.DrMichaelBroder.com

Michael S. Broder, Ph.D. is a renowned psychologist, executive coach, bestselling author, continuing education seminar leader, and popular speaker. He is an acclaimed expert in cognitive behavioral therapy, specializing in high achievers and relationship issues. His work centers on bringing about major change in the shortest time possible. A sought-after media guest, he has appeared on Oprah and The Today Show as well as making more than a thousand other TV and radio appearances. For many years, Dr. Broder also hosted the radio program Psychologically Speaking with Dr Michael Broder. He has been featured in the New York Times, the Wall Street Journal, TIME, Newsweek, and hundreds of other publications. Dr. Broder's latest book is Stage Climbing: The Shortest Path to Your Highest Potential, strongly endorsed by Deepak Chopra, Stephen Covey and dozens of other luminaries.

Michael S. Broder, Ph.D.
Philadelphia, PA United States
Contact Phone: 215-545-7000
Click to Contact from Web Site

**DR. FRANK FARLEY -- HUMAN
BEHAVIOR EXPERT**
Philadelphia, PA United States

Internationally recognized authority in psychology and human behavior. Former president, American Psychological Association (160,000 members). Articulate and experienced in working with the media, including Time, Newsweek, U.S. News, New York Times, Wall Street Journal, USA Today, Business Week, Today Show, 20/20, Good Morning America, 48 Hours, CNN, FOX, PBS Newshour, Discovery, A & E, NPR, Leeza, and others.

Dr. Frank Farley
Psychology
Temple University
Philadelphia, PA United States
Contact Phone: 215-204-6024
Cell: 215-668-7581
Click to Contact from Web Site

Artist, Author, Architect, Public Speaker

Carlton Davis

**Pasadena, California
626-840-7997
zelapolarbear@earthlink.net**

Carlton Davis, AIA, CDT, is an author, artist, architect, life coach and public speaker. A graduate of Yale University and the University of London, Davis speaks to the public about his experience and issues with bipolar disorder, creativity and mental illness -- and the two-minded self.

His book, "Bipolar Bare," chronicles his 30-year struggle to overcome mental illness.

Resolution of the conflict between these two selves constitute his recovery. Davis speaks on how he recovered through therapy, medication and meditation. His art and architecture career make him an expert in creativity and bipolar disorder.

www.BipolarBareBook.com

NIELS C NIELSEN -- PROFESSOR OF PHILOSOPHY AND RELIGIOUS THOUGHT EMERITUS

Houston, TX United States

Niels C. Nielsen is Professor of Philosophy and Religious Thought emeritus at Rice University. B.A. Pepperdine University, Ph.D Yale. Before coming to Texas he taught in Yale College. He was the founding chairman of Rice's Department of Religious Studies. Some of his books have had German, Swedish, Dutch and Chinese translations: Religions of the World is a widely used textbook. Nielsen's research on religion in Eastern Europe is the basis for Solzhenitzyn's Religion and Religion After Communism. God in the Obama Era, Presidents' Religion and Ethics from George Washington to Barack Obama will be published in the summer of 2009.

Niels C Nielsen Ph.D
Professor emeritus
Rice University
Houston, TX United States
Contact Phone: 713-667-0783
Cell: 713-865-0440
Click to Contact from Web Site

WILMA TAYLOR -- WILMA TAYLOR MINISTRIES

Chicago, IL United States
www.WilmaTaylorMinistries.org

Dr. Taylor is a great motivational speaker with a message to inspire and assist you in understanding how to deal with life issues. She appeals to audiences that are dealing with relationship issues. She it the voice of the broadcast (HELP) Her Elevated Level of Potential, while will begin to air on radio station (WILD) Mobil, AL; (WBXR) Huntsville AL; (KLNG); Omaha, NE; and (WNVY) Pensacola, FL. She is a registered nurse, minister, trainer, evangelist, and conference speaker. She has a stimulating and exciting message with an unusual way of reaching people. She has traveled throughout the United States speaking and changing lives. She serves the Church of God in Christ as Supervisor of Women in Guyana, South America, where her focus is to build a clinic and train workers for the clinic.

Wilma Taylor
Wilma Taylor Ministries
Chicago, IL United States
Contact Phone: 773-336-5790
Click to Contact from Web Site

RANDY ROLFE - PARENTING, FAMILY AND LIFESTYLE AUTHOR AND SPEAKER

West Chester, PA United States
www.randyrolfe.com

The author of seven popular books on family life and weekly radio host of Family First on the Voice America Health Channel, family therapist, attorney, theologian, and clinical nutritionist Randy Rolfe offers timely advice and a broad perspective on the challenges facing today's families. A traveler in 29 countries before age 20, Randy practiced law with a top Philadelphia law firm before she and her husband moved to an old farmstead in upstate New York to live off the land and begin their family. When they returned to Pennsylvania, Randy founded the Institute for Creative Solutions to help families thrive. A World Ambassador for Family, she became a popular media personality, appearing on 100s of radio shows and 50 top network talkshows, including repeatedly on Sally, Geraldo, Montel, Maury, and Ricki. Her topics include positive parenting, college success, happy marriage, work-life balance, setting boundaries, homeschooling, and natural living.

Randy Rolfe
President
Institute for Creative Solutions
West Chester, PA United States
Contact Phone: 610-429-5869
Click to Contact from Web Site

Consultant in Political Psychology
Expert on Terrorism and the Middle East

Dr. Raymond H. Hamden
Clinical & Forensic Psychologist

United States of America   ❖   United Arab Emirates

Dr. Raymond H. Hamden has performed clinical and forensic consultations in Baghdad, Iraq, Kabul Afghanistan, the Kingdom of Saudi Arabia, Syria, Algeria and other locations throughout the Middle East, Europe, Africa and North America.

Born in the United States, Hamden has practiced psychology in Washington, D.C., since 1979. His diverse cross-cultural services are in clinical, forensic, organizational and international consultation: critical incident debriefings, training and development programs, emergency response planning, employee selection and placement, homeland security and medical investigation consulting.

He holds a Ph.D. in psychology and continued post-graduate studies in modern psychoanalysis. At the University of Maryland in 1986, Dr. Hamden was a visiting fellow at the Center for International Development and Conflict Management. His research and consulting was in political psychology – the psychology of terrorists and hostage situations. He coined the term "The Retributional Terrorist – Type 4."

He is director of the Human Relations Institute in Dubai Knowledge Village and International Consulting via the Washington, D.C., location. Dr. Hamden is a life member in the Association of Psychological Sciences, International Society of Political Psychology, International Council of Psychologists and American College of Forensic Examiners International.

Dr. Hamden has appeared as an expert in international media: Al Jazeera International, CNN, the BBC, Al Arabiya, Canada AM, National Public Radio and many others. Local networks have regularly called on his professional analysis and testimony in various topics on psychological profiling and critical incidents.

Available for radio, television, newsprint, workshops, seminars, lecturers, conferences and conventions. Dr. Hamden is informative and entertaining. His public speaking style is spicy, yet tasteful.

Dr. Raymond H. Hamden is an independent clinical and forensic psychologist with offices in Washington, D.C., and Dubai, United Arab Emirates
+ (971-50) 651-8837

rhhamden@gmail.com

Topics -- which Dr. Hamden has addressed as a consultant to media, government, industry and academia -- include:

Political Psychology		International Relations and Conflict Resolution
Psychology of Terrorists	Lebanon and Its War Problems	
Fundamentalist Thinking	Middle East and Vulnerability	Expatriates in the Arab Gulf
Hostage Situations	People of War	Cross-Culture Issues

MACHE SEIBEL, MD -- HEALTHROCK
Newton, MA United States
www.doctorseibel.com/

DocRock™ - Dr. Mache Seibel is a real doctor who sees patients. But when he's not doing the usual doctor stuff, he is DocRock, singing fun music about health and speaking to audiences so everyone can learn how to stay healthy. DocRock's music is called HealthRock®. Come listen to songs about nutrition, hygiene, smoking, obesity, healthy living and much more or invite DocRock to make a HouseCall™ to your next event. The doctor is in!

Mache Seibel, MD
Founder
HealthRock
Newton, MA United States
Contact Phone: 617-916-1880
Click to Contact from Web Site

NANCY BOYD -- BRIGHT WINGS INC.
Briarcliff Manor, NY United States
http://www.brightwings.com

Bright Wings, Inc. generates ideas, products, and programs for individuals, families, groups, and small businesses ~ to foster healthy personal growth and self development, profitable enterprises, and satisfying lives. Nancy Boyd, its founder, has three super-powers: 1) She is an Idea Machine. She generates ideas lighting-fast. 2) She gets you at a soul level ~ where the work begins. 3) She understands meta-context. You need to know more than just surface data, in a rapidly changing world.

Nancy Boyd
Bright Wings, Inc.
Briarcliff Manor, NY United States
Contact Phone: 800-914-2975
Contact Main Phone: 800-914-2975
Click to Contact from Web Site

COMPULSIVE GAMBLING FOUNDATION
Lake Worth, NJ United States

Mission Statement of the Compulsive Gambling Foundation. The mission of the Compulsive Gambling Foundation (CGF) is to provide education, awareness, prevention and assistance to those persons and family members, suffering from Compulsive Gambling. We will provide speakers, literature and outreach, as well as financial assistance to those in need of legal and treatment services in the form of scholarships. If you are interested in obtaining a speaker or literature about the legal needs and treatment of compulsive gambling, or are in need of financial assistance for the treatment of a compulsive gambling addiction, please contact us.

Sheila Wexler
Compulsive Gambling Foundation
Lake Worth, NJ United States
Contact Phone: 561-249-0922
Cell: 954-501-5270
Click to Contact from Web Site

Learning to Be Healthy Through Music

DocRock, creator of HealthRock® (www.healthrock.com), is a renowned doctor and award-winning educator who teaches health through original music and entertainment. His core belief is "It's better to stay well than to get well."

DocRock offers chicken soup in the form of catchy songs with meaningful lyrics and educational patter to teach the "hows" and "whys" of key health issues.

DocRock can:

- Entertain or speak on health using music for meetings, corporate events, educational venues;
- License existing songs;
- Create new works for your audience.

DocRock™
aka Mache Seibel, M.D.

health educator, speaker, entertainer

Dr. Seibel has been featured or quoted in: The Today Show, ABC, Fox, NPR, PBS, NECN, Inside Edition, People Magazine, Vogue, the New York Times, Wall Street Journal, Boston Globe, Washington Post, L.A. Times and others

Available for interview with media

MSeibelMD@HealthRock.com
Newton, Massachusetts
617-916-1880
www.MSeibelMD.com
www.HealthRock.com

ROSE LEE ARCHER M.S. -- DISABILITY ADVOCATE FOR SOCIAL EQUALITY

Palm Beach County, FL United States
http://www.roseleearchershow.com

Elevate your career from an unknown to a distinguished expert through: How to be a Media Magnet. Discover Rose Lee's Award Winning approach to a dynamic interview. Reveal your talents and skills to light up the airwaves to create a lasting impression: Documented research reports that the delivery of a television interview impacts an audience based on 7% content, 38% voice, and 55% body language.

Rose Lee Archer
TV Producer & Host
Rose Lee Productions
Archer Disability Foundation
Boca Raton, FL United States
Contact Phone: 561-241-7987
Click to Contact from Web Site

MARILYN REDMOND, BA, CHT, IBRT-- HEALING AND SPIRITUAL GROWTH

Edgewood, WA United States
http://www.angelicasgifts.com

Professional Speaker and consultant focuses on Therapeutic Hypnotherapy/ Holistic Counseling. In Manchester's 'Who's Who' for her pioneering work in healing the causes of trauma and illness. Inspirational and knowledgeable presentations from personal understanding and study. Addresses all addictions, illness, domestic violence, rape, relationships, health, healing and educational issues. Shares over fifty years of teaching school, college, and research for solutions. Award-winning international writer, speaker, consultant, counselor, minister and member of The International Board for Regression Therapy (IBRT), American Board of Hypnotherapy (ABH), life member of Edgar Cacye's Association for Research and Enlightenment (ARE) and lifetime member of the National Education Association (NEA).

Rev. Marilyn Redmond
Marilyn Redmond, BA, CHT, IBRT
Edgewood, WA United States
Contact Phone: 253-845-4907
Click to Contact from Web Site

DR. MICHAEL LEVITTAN -- ANGER MANAGEMENT SPECIALIST

Los Angeles, CA United States
www.michaellevittan.com

Dr. Levittan: psychotherapist, professor, expert witness, media person for television/radio. He consults for L.A. Times, Dallas Morning Herald, Inside Edition, In-Touch Magazine, Orlando Sentinel, L.A. Times Magazine, Golf Magazine, Riverside Press, etc. Dr. Michael has appeared on the 'Tyra Banks Show', 'Montel Williams Show', NBC-TV's 'Starting Over', 'The Bad Girls Club', 'Hollywood 411,' and the 'Michelle Tafoya Show'. He is a noted Anger Management expert, and has been published in Workplace Violence Prevention Reporter, CA. Batterers Intervention Newsletter, and upcoming work on 'Infanticide'. Dr. Michael teaches courses and seminars on Domestic Violence, Child Abuse, Post-Traumatic Stress, Anger Management at UCLA, etc.

Dr. Michael Levittan
Psychotherapist/Media Spokesperson
Michael Levittan, Ph.D.
Los Angeles, CA United States
Contact Phone: 310-820-4111
Cell: 818-618-9785
Click to Contact from Web Site

Marilyn Redmond, BA, CHT, IBRT

International Speaker & Consultant

Areas of Expertise Include:

- Holistic Health and Healing
- Complimentary Medicine
- Counseling / Therapeutic Hypnosis
- Regression Therapy
- Empowerment / Self-Esteem
- Relationships
- Domestic Violence
- Addictions and the Family
- Educational Issues
- Spiritual/Metaphysical
- Inspirational

Marilyn Redmond's journey reveals the secrets to life and living, imparting reality to all areas of our lives in health, wholeness, happiness and prosperity; it is available to everyone. Experiencing addictions, mental illness, childhood and adult domestic violence are a few of the problems that became Marilyn's laboratory to understand the dynamics of life and living.

She shares this wisdom throughout her more than 25 years of speaking, writing, and counseling. In addition, her 50 years in education -- acquired through years of teaching elementary through college students -- offers solutions to educational problems.

An international lecturer, award-winning author and columnist, she appears at universities, schools, seminars, retreats and conventions. Marilyn's first book, "Roses Have Thorns," along with her videos on Empowerment & Domestic Violence, are available. Marilyn hosted and produced her own radio show and appears on radio and television.

Marilyn Redmond is an international board-certified regressionist and counselor, holds a bachelor of arts in education and has completed three years of graduate work toward a doctor of science. An ordained minister, she has been inducted into "Manchester's Who's Who" for pioneering work in restoring traumatic lives, healing emotional causes of illness and releasing negative energy.

Here are a few testimonials:

"She understands addictions better than most doctors," asserts psychiatrist Dr. George Zerr, M.D.

"I very much enjoyed the real life stories and examples," says Corrine Thompson, Association for Research and Enlightenment Program. "Marilyn is an excellent speaker and down-to-earth."

AVAILABLE FOR YOUR NEXT EVENT:

Book her expertise
Transform your life

Marilyn Redmond

253-845-4907

marilyn@angelicasgifts.com

www.angelicasgifts.com

SUSAN MAXWELL, MA., MFT.
Los Angeles, CA United States

Susan Maxwell is a psychotherapist and nationally recognized expert on the psychological issues surrounding money, sex and power. A media source on 'the psychology behind the news,' Ms. Maxwell is known for her insightful commentary on the current trends and topics in today's news. A knowledgeable and articulate speaker, she also lectures, conducts seminars and has a private practice in West Los Angeles. She is a clinical member of the American Association for Marriage and Family Therapy.

Susan Maxwell, MA., MFT.
Psychotherapist
Los Angeles, CA United States
Contact Phone: 310-475-6547
Cell: 310-990-1430
Click to Contact from Web Site

Dr. Diana

DIANA KIRSCHNER, PH.D. - DATING AND LOVE EXPERT
New York, NY United States
http://www.dianakirschner.com

Diana Kirschner, Ph.D., psychologist and frequent relationship expert on NBC's Today Show, appeared on Oprah and ran the 90-Day Love Challenge on The Morning Show with Mike & Juliet. Her acclaimed new book, 'Love in 90 Days, is the basis for her one-woman PBS Pledge Special, 'Finding Your Own True Love.' Dr. Diana has completed more than 1,000 radio and print interviews. Her reel is available at www.DianaKirschner. com, and her video blog and articles are at www. lovein90days.com.

Diana Kirschner, Ph.D.
New York, NY United States
Contact Phone: 212-420-8079
Cell: (917) 749-7791
Click to Contact from Web Site

MICHAEL J. MAYER -- LICENSED PSYCHOLOGIST - CONSULTANT
Columbia, MO United States
http://www.mikemayer.com

Psychologist, consultant to businesses and professionals, coach and personal guide. Offers professional perspectives to a variety of business settings that increases profit, reduces absenteeism and promotes good morale. Author of four books, the latest being, 'Choose a Better Road: Tips for Life's Traffic Jams'. Partner in a psychological practice and consultant to many businesses. Presenter at state/national workshops on a variety of topics. Individualized training, retreats and workshops available. Presents live radio programs on the radio every two weeks and some television interviews. Focus is on helping people resolve work and home issues thus bringing positive meaning to their lives and to those they influence. Challenging informative and motivating. Likes media presentations. Answers questions relating to work and personal relationships, conflicts at home and office, employee selection, professional and executive insight into effective problem resolution and other personal and work related issues. Dr. Mayer has good and effective answers. Call him.

Michael J. Mayer
Psychologist/Consultant
Michael J. Mayer -- Licensed Psychologist/ Consultant
Columbia, MO United States
Contact Phone: 573-443-1177
Click to Contact from Web Site

LOVE EXPERT
Diana Kirschner, Ph.D.

Dr. Diana explains to Montel how to keep marital love hot.

A Proven Performer

Who Connects, Entertains and Inspires

Psychologist and bestselling author, Diana Kirschner, Ph.D., is the guest TV shows call when they want ratings. She is a recurring relationship expert on the **Today Show** and has appeared on **Oprah**, **Good Morning America**, **Nightline**, **World News With Charles Gibson** and **Access Hollywood**. Dr. Diana hosted a field segment on **Montel**, was featured as the Love Specialist on **The Simple Life** and starred as the love coach in **Love in 90 Days Boot Camp**, a reality pilot that was an Official Selection of

Dr. Diana as the Love Specialist with Paris Hilton and Nicole Ritchie in "The Simple Life."

the New York TV Festival. She is the author of the hot new book, ***Love in 90 Days: The Essential Guide to Finding Your Own True Love***. Dr. Diana's topics include: *balancing love and work, relationships, sex, recovering from affairs, divorce, singles, on-line dating and finding love in 90 days*. Dr. Diana leads with her heart and never fails to connect, entertain and deliver her inspiring roadmap for success.

Kirschner debunks urban love legends on the Today Show.

Diana Kirschner, Ph.D.
See her reel at **www.dianakirschner.com** and her Web site: **lovein90days.com**.
To reach Dr. Diana for an interview or speaking engagement, call her at **212-420-8079**, or e-mail **drdiana@dianakirschner.com**.

JACQUELINE SIDMAN, PH.D. -- STRESS AND ANXIETY SOLUTIONS
Orange County, CA United States
www.sidmansolution.com

The Sidman Solution Tackles Problems Quickly, Creates Resolve, Boosts Careers, and Illuminates Relationships. The Sidman Solution helps people break through barriers, making them more effective and self confident. Whether it is fear of failure, fear of success or fear of the unknown, The Sidman Solution has been proven to rapidly identify and resolve the source of that fear, eliminating it as a life-limiting issue. The result is a happier, more productive and more successful person. That's what Jacqueline Sidman can talk about live on the air, and she welcomes telephone interviews.

Brad Butler
Promotion In Motion
Hollywood, CA United States
Contact Phone: 323-461-3921
Click to Contact from Web Site

JILL B. CODY, M.A. -- TRANSFORMING PERSPECTIVES
Frederick, MD United States
www.jillcody.com

CHEAT the Losing Mentality ! Win Your Weight War! The struggle with the "Battle of the Bulge" is filled with temptations pushing you to a higher weight. Enhance 'Will-power' with 'Won't-power' as you learn winning strategies to help you weigh what you want. Losing is a negative term that means it's something to avoid. 'Winning' is a powerful motivator. It requires that you set a goal in your mind, want it with all your heart, and generate the courage (or guts) to achieve it. Create your own compelling future. Enjoy the live Seminars, Webinars, Book, CD, or E-zine.

Jill B. Cody, M.A.
Transforming Perspectives
Win the Weight War
Frederick, MD United States
Contact Phone: 301-662-2266
Cell: 301-639-2645
Click to Contact from Web Site

SIMA COHEN -- FAST FAT LOSS THAT LASTS
Los Angeles, CA United States
www.MeetSima.com

4.5% of all 'eating out' that's done in the U.S. is fast food, and in 2004 Americans spent nearly $150 billion on it. If you don't believe there's a connection between fast food and obesity, you need to get real. Check out the calorie counts of some popular value meals from a few of our most popular fast food chains:

Sima Cohen
Sherman Oaks, CA United States
Contact Phone: Prefers E-mail
Click to Contact from Web Site

SUSAN BATTLEY, PSYD., PH.D. -
LEADERSHIP PSYCHOLOGIST AND
AUTHOR
Stony Brook, NY United States
www.battleyinc.com/

Susan Battley, PsyD, PhD, is an internationally
recognized leadership psychologist and CEO ad-
viser. She is an authority on leader behavior, strategic change and talent management, and global
career and workplace trends. Her book, 'Coached
to Lead: How to Achieve Extraordinary Results
with an Executive Coach,' is the first consumer's
guide to executive coaching. (Jossey-Bass, 2006)
She is regularly featured as an expert commentator on leader effectiveness and workplace trends in
top-tier media outlets, such as CNBC, CNBC, and
NPR, and in top-tier business publications.

Susan Battley, PsyD, PhD
Battley Performance Consulting, Inc.
Stony Brook, NY United States
Contact Phone: 631-751-6282
Click to Contact from Web Site

LOVE AND LOGIC INSTITUTE, INC.
Denver, CO United States
www.loveandlogic.com

Jim Fay, Dr. Charles Fay, and all the experts at the
Love and Logic Institute can provide you with important and practical insights and suggestions regarding parenting, teaching, and positive discipline techniques, such as how to: make parenting
fun and rewarding; effectively use choices, conse-
quences, and empathy; end temper tantrums, bullying and sibling rivalry; get the most out of parent/
teachers relationships; and deal with specific
issues facing toddlers, children, and teenagers. Jim
& Charles have appeared on PBS, Good Morning
America, 20/20 and in the Wall Street Journal.

Kelly Borden
Operations Manager
Love and Logic Institute, Inc.
Golden, CO United States
Contact Phone: 800-338-4065
Click to Contact from Web Site

JILL B. CODY -- TRANSFORMING
PERSPECTIVES
Washington, DC United States
www.JillCody.com

Jill is a psychotherapist/coach with 35 years experience in presenting informational and entertaining keynotes, workshops, and seminars. A professional member of the National Speakers
Association, she is the author of 'Winning the
Weight War', focused on successful strategies to
reach your weight goals. She can help you utilize
dynamic, effective strategies to transform limiting
perspectives into empowering ones which tap into
your unique, internal resources to improve the
quality of your life.

Jill Cody
Transforming Perspectives
Frederick, MD United States
Contact Phone: 800-287-5866
Click to Contact from Web Site

THOMAS LIOTTA - CREATING CHAMPIONS FOR LIFE

Seattle, WA United States
http://www.90daychallengeforlife.com

Thomas Liotta is a Master Coach, Trainer and a 4th Degree Black Belt in Tae Kwan Do. He is an author, international public speaker and the creator of an award-winning philosophy for child rearing. Thomas holds six University Degrees including Early Childhood Development & Early Childhood Development For School Age kids, along with studies in Psychology. He has studied and trained all over the globe including Egypt, Korea, China and North America.

Thomas Liotta
FLS
Seattle, WA United States
Contact Phone: (877)249-0352
Click to Contact from Web Site

GARY M UNRUH -- PARENTING EXPERT

Colorado Springs, CO United States
Unleashingparentallove.com

Are you seeking parenting advice from a professional with years of both counseling and personal experience? And is it important that this professional present advice in a step-by-step, easy-to-use-right-away fashion with useful childhood development information that explains your child's behavior? You've just described Gary M. Unruh, MSW LCSW. He has been a child and family mental health counselor for nearly forty years. During that time he and his wife, Betty, have been blessed to raise four beautiful children, and he is a very proud 'papa' of seven terrific grandchildren. For two years, he learned a lot about what kind of care clients respond to best when he was the CEO of a mental-health managed-care company for Colorado Blue Cross and Blue Shield.

Gary M Unruh
Lighthouse Love Productions LLC
Colorado Srpings, CO United States
Contact Phone: 719-660-0253
Click to Contact from Web Site

ARTHUR MURRAY INTERNATIONAL

Coral Gables, FL United States
www.arthurmurray.com

As America's second oldest franchise organization, Arthur Murray International, Inc. is known around the world as a prominent entertainment company with franchises located throughout North and South America, Caribbean, Europe, the Middle-East, Africa, Australia & Asia. Today, the Arthur Murray Franchised Dance Studios continue a tradition of more than 100 years of teaching the world to dance.

Shari Peyser
PR Director
Poller & Jordan Advertising Agency
NY United States
Contact Phone: (631) 595-7150
Contact Main Phone: 305-470-8005
Click to Contact from Web Site

LISSA COFFEY -- LIFESTYLE AND RELATIONSHIP EXPERT
Los Angeles, CA United States
http://www.coffeytalk.com

Lissa Coffey is a lifestyle and relationship expert who mixes up an inspiring blend of ancient wisdom and modern style! Her bestselling book, 'What's Your Dosha, Baby? Discover the Vedic Way for Compatibility in Life and Love,' is endorsed by her mentor, Dr. Deepak Chopra. Bright, fun, and super media-friendly, Lissa is a frequent contributor to The Today Show. Streaming video in the pressroom on www.coffeytalk.com. Twitter: @coffeytalk Huffington Post Blogger: http://www.huffingtonpost.com/lissa-coffey, Spokesperson: The Better Sleep Council YouTube: http://www.youtube.com/coffeytalk

Lissa Coffey
President
Bright Ideas Productions
Westlake Village, CA United States
Contact Phone: 818-707-7127
Cell: 818-370-9025
Click to Contact from Web Site

MARK HANSEN --- SUCCESS FOR TEENS
Ft. Lauderdale, FL United States
www.success101forteens.com/

Mark Hansen has an extensive entrepreneurial background with his first speech given back in 1991 to a group of middle school students. Since then, Mark has given over 1,300 seminars, appeared on radio and television programs and written a book entitled "An Ark for Learning" which was used in many middle schools as a learning guide for students and teachers.

Mark Hansen
Success for Teens
Parkland, FL United States
Contact Phone: 561-213-2616
Click to Contact from Web Site

STEVEN RIZNYK -- RELATIONSHIPS AUTHOR AND EXPERT
San Diego, CA United States
www.Relationships901.com

Steven Riznyk authored, produced, and directed a 5-1/2 hour DVD on making relationships work using negotiation strategy. With 20 improv actors, this educational, yet entertaining presentation outlines a very fast and effective method of solving some of the toughest problems in relationships within a week or less. This groundbreaking work took 2-1/2 years of research into relationships and is extremely effective. Steven has been a high-level negotiator since 1988, successfully dealing with many complex and difficult marital issues as well as extortion, blackmail, career destruction, and international kidnapping for a number of high-profile people in the United States.

Steven Riznyk
Lead Negotiator
Relationships901
San Diego, CA United States
Contact Phone: 310-779-0188
Contact Main Phone: 619-793-4827
Cell: 310-779-0188
Click to Contact from Web Site

ROGER FRAME -- PARENTING EXPERT
Denver, CO United States
Frameworks4learning.com

Don't Carve the Turkey with a Chainsaw: Resolving Family Conflict provides powerful tips to resolve communication disputes and develop your relationship and family life. The Conflict Whisperer teaches how to parent to minimize clashes and feuds to improve parent and child relationships. He describes why conflict and power struggles increase during the teen and adolescent years, and provides practical conflict resolution tips that enhance any conflict management program. These include marriage relationships and family relationships. He provides strategies that develop harmonious relationships and reduce strife, contention, and antagonism. He uses fly-fishing as a metaphor for positive conflict management strategies.

Roger Frame
author, speaker
PineStar Publishing
Centennial, CO United States
Contact Phone: 303-796-9656
Cell: 720-556-9515
Click to Contact from Web Site

DR. CARON GOODE, NCC, ACADEMY FOR COACHING PARENTS INTERNATIONAL
Lake Elsinore, CA United States
www.AcademyForCoachingParents.com

Dr. Caron Goode is the founder of the HeartWise coaching & relationship strategies of the Academy for Coaching Parents International, where professionals and parents become ACPI Certified Parenting Coaches and use HeartWise coaching with their clients and in their business. The Academy for Coaching Parents International (ACPI) offers Professional Parenting Coaching, an exclusive certification program uniquely positioned as the global leader. In addition Dr. Goode trains and certifies Intuitive Consultants who bring HeartWise strategies into their professional business or practice. HeartWise Parenting strategies offer connection and responsiveness to meet our children's needs and encourage their core strengths for well-rounded living.

Dr. Caron Goode, NCC
Founder
Academy for Coaching Parents Inernational
Lake Elsinore, CA United States
Contact Phone: 682-351-0328
Click to Contact from Web Site

EILEEN KENNEDY-MOORE PHD - CHILD PSYCHOLOGIST, PARENTING EXPERT
Princeton, NJ United States
www.EileenKennedyMoore.com

Eileen Kennedy-Moore, PhD, is a psychologist, speaker, and award-winning author of books about parenting and children's feelings and friendships. She's a lively, informative guest who offers practical tips on topics such as: Competitive parenting; Mom melt-downs; Helping children make friends; Sibling rivalry; Struggles that make kids stronger; Talking with kids about disaster. Dr. Kennedy-Moore has been featured on many high-arbitron and nationally syndicated radio shows and quoted in numerous magazines and newspapers, including Parents, Parenting, Family Circle, and The Chicago Tribune. She frequently speaks at schools and conferences. Books: SMART PARENTING FOR SMART KIDS (Jossey-Bass); THE UNWRITTEN RULES OF FRIENDSHIP (Little, Brown); WHAT ABOUT ME? 12 Ways to Get Your Parents' Attention WITHOUT Hitting Your Sister (Parenting Press). Website: http://www.EileenKennedyMoore.com, Blog: Http://www.psychologytoday.com/blog/Growing-Friendships, Media demo video: http://www.EileenKennedyMoore.com/wp/?p=1157, Speaker demo video: http://www.EileenKennedyMoore.com/speaking_info.html. *** Dr. Kennedy-Moore has a private practice in Princeton, NJ (lic. # 35SI00425400), commuting distance from New York City and Philadelphia, PA. ***

Eileen Kennedy-Moore, PhD
Psychologist, Author, Speaker
(NJ licensed psychologist #435SI00425400)
Princeton, NJ United States
Contact Phone: 609-655-2010
Click to Contact from Web Site

Eileen Kennedy-Moore, PhD
Child Psychologist and Parenting Expert

A lively and informative guest, Eileen Kennedy-Moore, PhD, is a psychologist who specializes in parenting and children's feelings and friendships. Drawing from research as well as her clinical experience, she'll offer your audience practical strategies for addressing their most pressing parenting concerns.

Dr. Kennedy-Moore has been a featured guest on many high-arbitron and nationally syndicated radio shows, and she has been quoted in numerous magazines and newspapers, including *Parents, Parenting, Family Circle*, and *The Chicago Tribune*. She frequently speaks at schools and conferences. Dr. Kennedy-Moore has a private practice in Princeton, New Jersey (lic. #35SI00425400), commuting distance from New York City and Philadelphia.

Sample Media Topics
- Competitive parenting;
- Mom melt-downs;
- Helping children make friends;
- Sibling rivalry;
- Struggles that make kids stronger;
- Talking with kids about disaster.

Books by Dr. Kennedy-Moore
- *Smart Parenting for Smart Kids* (Jossey-Bass/Wiley);
- *The Unwritten Rules of Friendship* (Little, Brown);
- *What About Me? 12 Ways to Get Your Parents' Attention Without Hitting Your Sister* (Parenting Press);
- *Expressing Emotion* (Guilford Press).

CONTACT: 609.655.2010 or ekm@EileenKennedyMoore.com

www.EileenKennedyMoore.com

BLOG: www.psychologytoday.com/blog/Growing-Friendships

VIDEO DEMO: www.EileenKennedyMoore.com/wp/?p=1157

EXPERTCLICK MEDIA PAGE: www.expertclick.com/19-4196

AMY KOSSOFF SMITH -- MOMTINI LOUNGE
Rockville, MD United States
www.momtinilounge.com

The MomTini Lounge is an internationally recognized parenting website (www.MomTiniLounge.com), and its founder, Amy Kossoff Smith, has been featured on The Today Show and is a frequent guest on FOX and CBS News, as well as on radio, online, and in print media. A national wire columnist, Amy reports on parenting topics, is published in newspapers nationwide and has a successful public speaking platform. In addition, she authored an essay in Knowing Pains: Women on Love, Sex and Work in our '40s. Smith's professional memberships include of WOMMA (Word of Mouth Marketing Association), PR Consultants Group, Social Moms, and more.

Amy Smith
MomTini Lounge
Rockville, MD United States
Contact Phone: 301-367-2200
Click to Contact from Web Site

MARK BROOKS -- INTERNET DATING CONSULTANT
New York, NY United States
http://www.onlinepersonalswatch.com

Courtland Brooks exclusively serves Internet Dating services, and companies that want to talk to them. Media Relations -- We provide media relations services to help you shape your messaging and deliver compelling stories for maximum impact and credibility with the press. We help the press discover your story, monitor your reputation and amplify and quantify your press hits. Business Development -- We guide your business development strategy so you identify sustainable revenue channels and we help you find and negotiate good deals with the right partners. Product and Marketing Strategy -- We help get product and marketing strategy right first time, so you make efficient ad spends, generate word-of-mouth exposure and build long term user trust and reputation

Mark Brooks
Courtland Brooks
Valrico, FL United States
Contact Phone: 212-444-1636
Click to Contact from Web Site

DR. AVA CADELL -- LOVE AND RELATIONSHIP EXPERT
Los Angeles, CA United States
www.AvaCadell.com

World-renowned love and relationship expert Dr. Ava Cadell says, 'The meaning of life is learning how to give and receive love.' Founder and president of Loveology University, a veteran media therapist, public speaker and author of seven books, Dr. Ava's mission is to promote the benefits of healthy love and intimacy around the globe. Dr. Ava has appeared on numerous TV shows as an expert including, Good Morning America, Extra, Montel Williams, Anderson Cooper and various reality shows on MTV, VH1, Discovery, Lifetime, TLC, A & E and E! For a full press kit, visit Dr. Ava's website at www.avacadell.com. To view the list of love lesson courses on Loveology University®, visit www.loveologyuniversity.com.

Dr. Ava Cadell
Kudos, Inc.
Los Angeles, CA United States
Contact Phone: 310-882-5438
Contact Main Phone: 877-405-6838
Cell: 310-780-0919
Click to Contact from Web Site

ELOVE -- PAUL FAZONE
Boston, MA United States
www.eLove.com

At eLove, we see true love happen every day. Singles that make finding someone special a priority in their lives and come in with an open mind and heart are the most successful. eLove Matchmaking is a great alternative to online dating or other online personal dating sites.

Paul A. Falzone
Elove
Norwell, MA United States
Contact Phone: 781-982-4522
Click to Contact from Web Site

FRAN GREENE, LCSWR -- FLIRTING - DATING - RELATIONSHIP COACH
Commack, NY United States
www.FranGreene.com

Nationally recognized, sought after expert on flirting, dating and relationships. Author of The Flirting Bible, (Fair Winds Press). Greene has appeared on Dateline NBC, The Today Show, Wingman, and The Travel Channel, national and international radio, and has been featured in the New York Times, Seventeen, Cleo, Self, Cosmopolitan and Princess Cruises. Fran Greene is a well known energetic, popular and inspiring speaker. Her humor and charisma make her workshops a sell out. Former Director of Flirting and Dating at Match.com, the Internet's premiere matchmaking service. Personal consultations are available. Her insight, compassion and practical strategies are her trademarks. A rare find!

Fran Greene, LCSWR
Flirting, Dating, and Relationship Coach
Commack, NY United States
Contact Phone: 516-317-5818
Pager: 3
Cell: 631-265-5683
Click to Contact from Web Site

CORINNE INNIS --PENN FLEMING MATCHMAKING SERVICE
New York, NY United States
www.pennfleming.com

Penn Fleming is a confidential matchmaking service catering to singles who are committed to finding a soul mate. Matches are made based on compatibility. Every effort is made to assist clients in presenting their most attractive attributes to prospective dates. Referrals may be made to assist with style and self-image when necessary. e emphasize customer service and small-town hospitality. Our goal is to support mature adults on their journey to find an ideal soul mate. They will receive continuous follow-up, support, and encouragement.

Corinne Innis
Penn Fleming Matchmaking Service
New York, NY United States
Contact Phone: (516) 902-5640
Click to Contact from Web Site

TOMMY DANGER KIM -- JUST CALL HER
New York, NY United States
www.JustCallHer.com

Hi! Hope you're enjoying this goofy labor of love (in more ways than one). As for myself, I'm usually single, in my early 30s, a Korean-American, originally from Los Angeles and now living in New York City. Can someone show me how to walk faster here? So, as you can see, I've been on my share of dates, good ones and bad ones and straight-up weird ones. It seems I have knack for dissecting what's really going on a date, but also the keen ability to forget important tips when on a date. It's only natural I need a blog for awkward myself. If you have any questions or comments, you can drop me a line on my Facebook page or at danger_at_justcallher.com. You should see the victory dance I do whenever I get emails. Much obliged for your readership. Looking forward to share more with you! Tommy Danger

Tommy Danger Kim
Just Call Her
New York, NY United States
Contact Phone: 646-504-0612
Click to Contact from Web Site

MARC LESNICK -- INTERNET DATING INDUSTRY EXPERT
New York, NY United States
www.InternetDatingConference.com/

The Internet Dating Super Conference is the largest convention and trade show. iDate is attended by senior business executives from internet dating, social networking, mobile dating, matchmaking, date coaching and affiliate marketing industries. The event covers management of an internet dating and social media business. Topics covered include: new technologies, business strategies, mobile technologies, advanced marketing methods, venture capital, partnerships, legal issues, affiliate marketing and payments.

Marc Lesnick
President
Ticonderoga Ventures, Inc.
New York, NY United States
Contact Phone: 212 722-1744
Contact Main Phone: 212 722-1744
Click to Contact from Web Site

AMY SCHOEN, MBA, CPCC -- DATING AND RELATIONSHIP EXPERT
Washington, DC United States
www.heartmindconnection.com

Amy Schoen, MBA, CPCC is a certified professional life coach and a dating and relationship expert who coaches singles to attract the right relationship into their lives and couples to create the relationships of their dreams. She speaks professionally to adult learning classes, professional organizations and social groups. Amy, author of 'Get It Right This Time- How to Find and Keep Your Ideal Romantic Relationship' and 'Motivated to Marry- Now There's a Better Method to Dating and Relationships', has been featured in the Washington Post newspaper, the Washington Examiner, as well as, interviewed on TV, radio and online magazines.

Amy Schoen, MBA, CPCC
HeartMmind Connection
Rockville, MD United States
Contact Phone: 240-498-7803
Click to Contact from Web Site

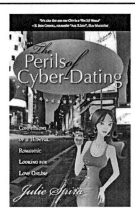

JULIE SPIRA -- ONLINE DATING EXPERT
Los Angeles, CA United States
www.CyberDatingExpert.com

Julie Spira is a worldwide expert in online dating. She's the author of the bestseller, 'The Perils of Cyber-Dating: Confessions of a Hopeful Romantic Looking for Love Online.' Julie has appeared on over 250 media outlets for her expertise in online dating and social media including ABC News, BBC, CBS, CNET, Cosmo Radio, FOX, Glamour, iVillage, Los Angeles Times, Men's Health, New York Times, Psychology Today, Wired, and Woman's Day. Julie creates irresistible online dating profiles for singles on the dating scene. She is writing her second book, 'The Rules of Netiquette: How to Mind Your Manners on the Web.'

Julie Spira
CEO
Cyber-Dating Expert
Marina del Rey, CA United States
Contact Phone: 310-433-7786
Click to Contact from Web Site

ALINE ZOLDBROD PH.D. - SEXUALITY AND RELATIONSHIP EXPERT
Boston, MA United States
www.sexsmart.com

Dr. Aline Zoldbrod (aka 'Dr. Z') is a nationally and internationally acknowledged authority in sexuality and relationships. Besides being a psychologist with thirty years worth of clinical experience, insight, and fascinating stories, she is a lecturer, commentator, three time author, and was IVillage's expert on Mismatched Libidos message board. Acknowledged as the originator of the interpersonal theory of sexual development, The Milestones of Sexual Development, Zoldbrod's theory explains how non-sexual aspects of family life profoundly define sexual personality, the development (or not) of sexual pleasure, and sexual functioning.

Zoldbrod, Aline Ph.D.
Lexington, MA United States
Contact Phone: 781-863-1877
Click to Contact from Web Site

MARILYN ANDERSON -- DATING AND RELATIONSHIP EXPERT
Los Angeles, CA United States
www.neverkissafrog.com/press1.html

MARILYN ANDERSON is a relationship coach and author of NEVER KISS A FROG: A Girl's Guide to Creatures from the Dating Swamp. She was the Dating, Flirting & Kissing Coach on TV's Extreme Makeover. Marilyn has appeared on over 250 radio and TV shows and has been featured in newspapers & magazines nationwide. She writes humorous relationship articles for various venues as well as travel & entertainment articles. Marilyn is the creator and writer of the Never Kiss a Frog web series featuring dating situations that people everywhere relate to and enjoy.

Marilyn Anderson
Never Kiss a Frog
Marina Del Rey, CA United States
Contact Phone: 310-502-4047
Cell: 310-502-4047
Click to Contact from Web Site

TWOOLOGY.COM
Boulder, CO United States
www.Twoology.com

VALENTINE DMITRIEV, PH.D
Hackettstown, NJ United States
http://www.ValentineDmitriev.com

NICHOLAS KHO -- REAL SOCIAL DYNAMICS
Los Angeles, CA United States
http://www.howtoattract.com

Real Social Dynamics (RSD) is the world's largest dating coaching company. With dating coaches based in Los Angeles, New York, London, Sydney, and San Francisco, programs are conducted in major metropolitan English-speaking cities throughout North America, Europe, Central America, Asia, South America, and Australia. RSD hosts live programs in 70 countries and 270 cities through approximately 1000 live programs annually for over 40,000 clients. Through its LIVE world tours, Real Social Dynamics conducts Bootcamps and Superconferences, that have trained thousands of clients, including a diverse variety of individuals ranging from Fortune 100 executives, royalty, celebrities, college students, and professionals from over 70 different countries. RSD specializes in dating advice, image consultation, public representation, and integrating clients into social scenes. Initially, live programs were offered solely through word of mouth via private clients. However, now, top-tier dating coaching is made available for the public via the Internet and direct phone contact. www.HowToAttract.com and RSDNation.com

Nicholas Kho
Co-Founder
Real Social Dynamics
West Hollywood, CA United States
Contact Phone: 310-402-7863
Contact Main Phone: 310-652-0137
Cell: 310-402-7863
Click to Contact from Web Site

Exclusively designed to be a 1-stop, has everything for any couple resource! Performs like your own relationship personal assistant. Forgets nothing and does everything to keep you together! Find fun things to do. Romantically guides you to keep passionately in touch. Saves time. Saves money. Saves your relationship. Makes sense. Scientifically sound, personalized, easy to use. Gets smarter with use. Anything you need. Always ready. All in one place.

Jeff Ullman
Tunomi Unlimited Incorporated
Superior, CO United States
Contact Phone: 720-310-0167
Click to Contact from Web Site

Born in Shanghai, China in 1918, Dmitriev moved with her family to Vancouver, Canada, and as an adult settled in Seattle, Washington. Dr. Dmitriev, was a pioneer in infant learning and early intervention for special needs children and received national recognition for her Model Preschool Program for young children with Down Syndrome and other disabilities. Over a period of 15 years she traveled widely giving lectures and workshops in 40 cities in America and 11 foreign countries including Australia, England, Indonesia, Italy, Japan, Russia and Spain. Dmitriev has written numerous professional articles, seven books on parenting, education and child development

Scott Lorenz
Westwind Communications
Plymouth, MI United States
Contact Phone: 734-667-2090
Click to Contact from Web Site

RUTH HOUSTON - INFIDELITY EXPERT
New York, NY United States
www.InfidelityAdvice.com

Infidelity expert, Ruth Houston is the author of Is He Cheating on You? - 829 Telltale Signs and founder of InfidelityAdvice.com. Frequently called on by the media to comment on infidelity issues in the news, Ruth has been quoted in the New York Times, Cosmopolitan, the Wall Street Journal, the Los Angeles Times, USA Today, the New York Post, and numerous other print and on-line media. Ruth has appeared on The Today Show, Good Morning America, CNN, and over 500+ TV and radio talk shows worldwide.

Ruth Houston
Elmhurst, NY United States
Contact Phone: 718 592-6039
Click to Contact from Web Site

DR. NANCY KALISH -- LOST LOVERS EXPERT
Sacramento, CA United States
www.LostLovers.com

Psychologist Nancy Kalish, Ph.D. is the international expert on rekindled romance. Her landmark survey of 3000 reunited couples, and nearly two decades of consulting with reunited couples worldwide, catapulted Dr. Kalish into the limelight as the leading source for print & broadcast media stories on lost love, reunions, teen romance, Internet dating, marriage and affairs, and Baby Boomer relationships. Dr. Kalish has authored two books on rekindled romances and welcomes interviews.

Dr. Nancy Kalish
Sacramento, CA United States
Contact Phone: 916-453-0777
Click to Contact from Web Site

**ANNE NORDHAUS-BIKE --
SPIRITUALITY EXPERT**
Chicago, IL United States
http://www.anbcommunications.com/

Spirituality expert, astrologer, artist, writer, performer, and time management expert Anne Nordhaus-Bike offers practical, creative advice using sound business principles, mysticism, and spirituality to help one live life in harmony and balance. Anne's book, Follow the Sun: A Simple Way to Use Astrology for Living in Harmony, was published in 2011. Follow the Sun offers a timeless, annual guide for living in harmony with yourself, others, and nature. Her free monthly e-newsletter, Living in Harmony, reviews the current month's planetary influences from a spiritual and mystical perspective.

Anne Nordhaus-Bike
President
ANB Communications
Chicago, IL United States
Contact Phone: 773-229-0024
Click to Contact from Web Site

Geographic Index

San Jose
Nina Amir - Human Potential Speaker, 97

San Rafael
ExecSense Webinars - The Leading Publisher of Executive Webinars, 299

Santa Barbara
Patricia Bragg -- Vegatarian Health Recipies, 141
Lois Clark McCoy -- National Institute for Urban Search and Rescue, 131
Dan Poynter -- Book Publishing Industry Expert, 177

Santa Paula
Robert A. Gardner, CPP -- Security, Crime Prevention Advisor, 118

Thousand Oaks
Rhonda L. Sher -- Two Minute Networker, 300

Valencia
Craig Duswalt -- RockStar System for Success, 200

Colorado

Boulder
Institute for Social Internet Public Policy, 213
Room 214 - Social Media Agency, 184
Twoology.com, 376

Colorado Springs
Gary M Unruh -- Parenting Expert, 368

Denver
American Society of Bariatric Physicians, 328
Judith Lee Berg -- Human Resource Communication, 105
Buddy Beds -- Orthopedic Memory Foam Dog Beds, 138
John Fischer - StickerGiant.com - Sticker Sociologist, 185
Roger Frame -- Parenting Expert, 370
Linda Jeschofnig - Science Lab Kit - Online Lab Kit- Biology Lab, 136
Love and Logic Institute, Inc., 367
MobileHomeUniversity.com, 146
Gary Rosenzweig -- Game Developer - Apple Expert, 213
Karen Susman -- Karen Susman and Associates, 237
tw telecom inc., 170
Dray Wharton -- Management Consultant, 264

Golden
Associated Bodywork and Massage Professionals, 324

Lakewood
Maggie Holben -- Public Relations Expert Resource, 186

Pueblo
EllynAnne Geisel -- Apron Expert, 159

Connecticut

Danbury
Carolyn Finch -- Body Language Expert, 324

Darien
Granville Toogood Associates, Inc., 299

Hartford
Carol A. Harnett -- Health and Disability Expert, 336
Brian Jud -- Book Marketing Expert, 176

New Haven
Discount Watch Store, 164
Total MRO Protection, 318

Norwich
Dianne M. Daniels, AICI, 320

Stamford
The Baby Boomers Retirement Network (BBRN) -- Richard Roll, 220
Jan Yager, Ph.D. -- Speaker, Author and Consultant, 310

Westport
Susan Filan -- MSNBC Senior Legal Analyst, 116

District of Columbia

Washington
Jennifer Abernethy-- Social Media Marketing, 206
Alliance to Save Energy, 132
American Foreign Service Association, 125
American Public Transportation Association, 149
American Society for Radiation Oncology, 346
Yasmin Anderson-Smith, AICI CIP, CPBS -- Image consultant, 320
Glen Boyls -- Risk Management - Business Continuity Expert, 258
Building Owners and Managers Association (BOMA) International, 143
Patrina M. Clark, HCS, SPHR - Pivotal Practices Consulting LLC, 257
Jill B. Cody -- Transforming Perspectives, 367
Carolyn A. Cook -- United 4 Equality, LLC, 92
The Council of Independent Colleges, 82
Francie Dalton -- Certified Managment Consultant, 251
Mitchell P. Davis -- Editor and Publisher of www.ExpertClick.com, 300
DEET Education Program, 137
Omekongo Dibinga -- The UPstander, 92
Angela Dingle -- Ex Nihilo Management, LLC, 274
Ann Dolin -- Educational Consultant, 82
DriveLab, 152
FUTUREtakes.Org International Futurist Magazine, 190
Global Academy Online, Inc., 80
Steven Roy Goodman, M.S., J.D. -- College Admissions Expert, 83

Maj. Brian Hampton, Publisher, VETERANS VISION, 125
Sylvia Henderson - Interpersonal Skills Expert, 238
Andrew Horn-- Dreams for Kids - Wash DC, 84
Institute for Gilgit Baltistan Studies, 128
Institute of Management Consultants USA. Inc., 260
Integrity Research Institute -- Researching Scientific Integrity, 134
International Society of Protocol and Etiquette Professionals, 297
Daniel J. Knight, 300
Larry LaRose -- Performance Coach, 266
Louis Levy -- Success in Retirement, 317
Mark N. Lewellen -- Unmanned Aircraft Systems (UAS) Instructor, 153
Douglas M. McCabe, Ph.D. -- Employee Relations Expert, 242
David Morey -- The Underdog Advantage, 270
National Association of Letter Carriers, AFL-CIO, 244
National Association of Military Moms and Spouses, 124
National Immigration Forum, 129
The Newseum, 172
Nordlinger Associates, Inc. -- Politics and Public Affairs, 102
Pet Food Institute, 138
Laura B. Poindexter, 176
Zoe Rastegar -- Talk Show Host, 128
Amy Schoen, MBA, CPCC -- Dating and Relationship Expert, 374
Search for Common Ground, 101
Michael D. Shaw -- Air Quality Expert, 135
John M. Snyder -- Gun Law Expert, 106
Specialized Information Publishers Association, formerly NEPA, 169
Debbie Weil -- Corporate Blogging Expert, 210
Wharton School Club of Washington, 100
World Future Society, 192
World Government Of World Citizens --World Citizen Government, 129
Young Marines of the Marine Corps League, 125
Kate Zabriskie - Training Seminars, Workshops and Keynotes, 241

Florida

Boca Raton
Dr. David J. Demko - Gerontologist Creator of Zoomer -1998-, 317

Clearwater
Bill Thompson -- TV, Inc. -- Infomercial Marketing Company, 295

Coral Gables
Arthur Murray International, 368

Georgia

Hawaii

Idaho

Illinois

Indiana

Bloomington
Sheryl Woodhouse-Keese --
Eco-friendly Invitations &
Celebrations, 185
Evansville
Louis B. Cady, M.D. Neuropsychiatrist
and Wellness Expert, 335
Indianapolis
121five.com -- Aviation Industry News,
Tim Kern, 153
indianapolis
Mike McCarty -- Safe Hiring Solutions,
123
Indianapolis
National Association of Mutual
Insurance Companies, 224
Society of Professional Journalists, 168

Kansas

Kansas City
Vernon Jacobs, CPA -- President,
Offshore Press, Inc., 101
Manhattan
Kansas State University, 79
Wichita
Chuck Gumbert -- Aerospace and
Aviation Consultant, 154
Ford Saeks - Business Growth - Internet
Marketing - Marketing, 214

Kentucky

Crestwood
Suzan Stirling, 350
Lexington
Tom Clark -- Executive Coaching, 251

Louisiana

New Orleans
Irv Schwary -- ZENTIREMENT, 215
Carl Van -- Employee and Management
Performance, 268

Maine

Kennebunkport
Lifesaving Resources, LLC, 131

Maryland

Annapolis
Judge Monty Ahalt (Ret)
VirtualCourthouse Online
Mediation Expert, 108
John Collard -- Turnaround Interim
Management Expert, 254
John P. Dentico Leadership and
Simulation Expert, 228
Jim Jenkins - Applied Technology
Institute, 154

Baltimore
Kathryn Seifert, Ph.D., Trauma and
Violence Expert, 87
Bethesda
CureSearch for Children's Cancer, 347
Columbia
Carolyn Long -- Angels Over America,
105
Frederick
Aircraft Owners and Pilots Association
-- AOPA, 154
Jill B. Cody, M.A. -- Transforming
Perspectives, 366
Rockville
Goodwill Industries International, Inc.,
93
Amy Kossoff Smith -- MomTini
Lounge, 372
Silver Spring
The Lett Group -- Business Etiquette,
297
Upper Marlboro
Sharon B. Jones -- Personal Finance
Expert, 218

Massachusetts

Boston
Eric Bloom -- Market Research, 283
Mike Bonacorsi, CFP® -- Certified
Financial Planner ™, 223
Dennis Charles -- Career Expert, 228
The Couple's Retirement Puzzle --
Dorian Mintzer & Roberta Taylor,
317
Dave E. David, M.D. -- Botox Expert,
329
David M. Rich -- Experience
Marketing, 210
David W. DeLong -- Future Workforce
Skills, 236
John Doehring -- Management
Consulting, 268
William E. Donoghue -- The Father of
Safe Money Investing, 216
eLove -- Paul Fazone, 373
Bob Elster -- Speaker -- Business and
Life Coach, 297
Allen B. Falcon -- Cumulus Global, 290
Claudia Gere -- Publishing Expert, 174
Paige Stover Hague -- Content
Development Expert, 175
Margaret Innis -- Home Staging &
Color Expert, 145
Kathleen Burns Kingsbury, Wealth
Psychology Expert, 222
Dr. Aihan Kuhn -- Chinese Medicine
for Health, 333
Lincoln Institute of Land Policy, 94
Evana Maggiore -- Fashion Feng Shui
International, 295
Dennis Mahoney -- Healthcare
Consultant, 333
Amy Beth O'Brien -- Speaker - Author
- Coach, 256
Suzanne O'Connor -- Quality
Improvement Expert, 266
OPTIMIZE International- Optimizing
the Results of Executive Teams, 246

Belinda Rosenblum -- Own Your
Money LLC, 218
scHammond Advisors, 224
Robert Siciliano -- Identity Theft
Expert, 120
Jeff Siegel -- Advanced Television
Advertising Expert, 294
Mark Singer -- Retirement Expert, 316
Carol Ann Small -- Laughter With A
Lesson.com, 202
Society for Advancement of
Consulting, LLC, 258
Aline Zoldbrod Ph.D. - Sexuality and
Relationship Expert, 375
Cambridge
Dr. Rob Moir -- Ocean River Institute,
135
Successful Transition Planning
Institute, 256
Hanson
The Art and Creative Materials
Institute, Inc., 80
Nantucket
Marsha Egan -- Workplace Productivity
Coach and E-mail Expert, 252
Newton
Mache Seibel, MD -- HealthRock, 360
Norfolk
Dave E. David, M.D. --- Doctor
Spokesperson, 344
Dr. Dave E. David - Boston Vaser Lipo
Doctor, 328
Plymouth
Long Term Care Learning Institute --
Marilee Driscoll, 338
Springfield
Shel Horowitz, Marketing Consultant -
Green And Profitable, 230
TALKERS Magazine --- Talk Radio
Magazine, 168
Stow
Stephen R. Balzac, Leadership
Development Expert, 286
Wayland
Chris DeVany -- Pinnacle Performance
Improvement Worldwide, 257

Michigan

Denver
S Kent Lauson, DDS, MS, 343
Detriot
Ian Lyngklip -- Consumer Law Firm,
110
Detroit
Mark Accettura --- Inheritance Expert,
112
Cochran, Foley and Associates Personal
Injury Lawyers, 115
Employee Involvement Association,
283
Giant Motorcycle Swap Meet, 152
Hilco Industrial. LLC -- Experts in
Industrial Machinery Auctions, 212
Timothy Kosinski DDS -- Esthetic
Dentistry, 342
Joe Lorenz --- Bodybuilding Pre
Workout Supplements, 326

Eric R. Braverman, M.D. -- Anti-aging Expert, 316

Mark Brooks -- Internet Dating Consultant, 372

Jerry Cahn, Ph.D., J.D. - Advisor, Coach to Leaders - Presenters, 304

Ziggy Chau -- Next Media Animation LLC, 172

Congress of Racial Equality -- CORE, 92

John Cruz -- World Banking World Fraud, 120

Stephanie Diamond -- Marketing Message Expert, 213

Beatrice C. Engstrand, M.D., F.A.A.N. -- New York City Neurologist, 331

EPM Communications -- Research On Consumer Behavior & Licensing, 283

Fidelifacts -- Background Investigations, 122

Food Allergy Initiative, 141

Eugenia Foxworth, CIPS, NYRS, Broker Foxworth Realty, 146

Valerie Geller -- Talk Radio Consultant, 166

Richard Gottlieb -- Toy Industry Expert, 159

Kent Gustavson, PhD Blooming Twig Books., 175

Ruth Houston - Infidelity Expert, 377

In-motion Courier Service, 152

Corinne Innis -- Artist, 160

Corinne Innis -- Penn Fleming Public Relations, 185

Corinne Innis --Penn Fleming Matchmaking Service, 373

Andrew P. Johnson -- Immigration Author -- Expert -- Attorney, 130

Ron Karr -- CSP -- Sales Leadership Expert, 284

Michael G. Kessler, President and CEO of Kessler International, 122

Tommy Danger Kim -- Just Call Her, 374

Diana Kirschner, Ph.D. - Dating and Love Expert, 364

D.E. Lamont - Fiction and Health & Self Improvement Author-Writer, 178

Marc Lesnick -- Internet Dating Industry Expert, 374

Roger H. Madon -- Labor Arbitrator - Labor Attorney, 242

Susan Mangiero, Ph.D., CFA, FRM AIFA -- Business Consultant, 222

Jerry Mintz -- Alternative Education Resource Organization, 80

National Cartoonists Society, 173

Chika Onyeani -- Africa Affairs Expert, 127

Ovations International Inc. -- Matthew Cossolotto, 248

PartyLine - Public Relations Media Newsletter, 180

Bob Rankin -- Tech Support Expert, 211

The Research Department -- Focus Groups and Qualitative Market Research, 284

Dr. Deborah Serani -- Author of 'Living with Depression', 356

Shoplet.com -- Discount Office Supplies, 163

Dr. Julia Sloan -- Global Strategic Thinking Expert, 272

Penfield

Grant Langdon -- Land Ownership Expert History, 113

Scarsdale

Jonathan M. Bergman, CFP, EA - Financial Advisor, 223

Mompreneurs, 241

Stony Brook

Susan Battley, PsyD., Ph.D. - Leadership Psychologist and Author, 367

Troy

Michelle Pyan -- Commercial Investigations LLC, 123

Yorktown Heights

Larry Eidelman - Emergency Management Expert, 130

North Carolina

Boone

Noel Jameson -- Famous Quotes, 194

Carrboro

Jeff Cobb -- Lifelong Learning, 79

Charlotte

Audri G. Lanford, Ph.D. -- Going Paperless -- Productivity Expert, 124

Edie Raether Enterprises and Wings for Wishes Institute, 87

Gloria Starr -- Image Etiquette -- Communication and Leadership, 298

Raleigh

Amelia Frahm -- Cancer Books Author, 347

Barbara Hemphill, CPO -- Productive Environment Institute, 308

David King -- Wikipedia Expert, 169

Wilmington

Dr. Howard Rasheed -- Idea Accelerator Technologies, 249

Ohio

Akron

Timothy A. Dimoff -- High Risk Security Expert, 118

Berea

Harry J. Bury -- An Emerging Worldview to the Third Millennium., 190

Canton

DeLores Pressley -- The Born Successful Institute, 320

Cincinnati

Mark Faust -- Management Consultant, 258

Melvin J. Gravely II Ph.D. - Institute For Entrepreneurial Thinking, LTD., 270

Cleveland

Benjamin Y. Clark, PhD -- Public Budgeting Expert, 94

Jeff Hurt -- Velvet Chainsaw -- Midcourse Corrections, 196

National School Safety and Security Services -- Ken Trump, 119

Dublin

Jim Camp - Negotiation Expert, 265

Findlay

Shelley Hitz -- Self Publishing Coach, 175

Hilliard

Personal Best Consulting -- Dr. Leif H. Smith, 225

Toledo

National Child Abuse Defense and Resource Center, 86

Oklahoma

Oklahoma City

Amy Jo Garner Ministries, 99

Greg Womack -- Certified Financial Planner, 219

Tulsa

Nathan R Mitchell--Small Business Expert, 276

Oregon

Ashland

Dr. Rick Kirschner -- Communication Skills Expert, 188

Beaverton

Ateba Crocker -- Shoe Revolt, 84

Portland

Senator Don Benton -- Political Expert, 102

Brendon Burchard, 200

Kevin Savetz -- Free Printables, 214

Redmond

Gail Kingsbury -- Speaker Resource Connection, 194

Pennsylvania

Allentown

Dr. Henry Borenson -- Algebra Problems Expert, 80

Altoona

Tamira Ci Thayne -- Humane Treatment for Dogs, 137

Carlisle

U.S. Army War College, 126

Doylestown

Twilight Wish -- Celebrating Seniors and Making Dreams Come True, 351

Gibsonia
Craig Conroy, Conroy Research Group, 184

Philadelphia
Michael S. Broder, Ph.D., 356
Dr. Frank Farley -- Human Behavior Expert, 356
Denny Hatch -- Direct Mail Expert, 282
InfoCommerce Group -- Specialized Business Information Publishing Expert, 169
National Adoption Center, 83
TeamChildren -Youth Charity, 90
Sam Waltz, 188

Pittsburgh
Technolytics -- Strategic Issues, 211

Punxsutawney
Scott Anthony - Pizza Marketing Expert, 142

Waynesboro
Mike Cermak -- Tech Support Guy, 193

West Chester
Randy Rolfe - Parenting, Family and Lifestyle Author and Speaker, 358

PR

Vieques Island
Sandy Malone -- Owner of Weddings in Vieques - Culebra, 162

Rhode Island

Block Island
Holland Cooke, 168

East Greenwich
Summit Consulting Group, Inc. -- Alan Weiss, Ph.D., 264

Newport
Subscription Site Insider -- How to Create Membership Sites, 169

South Carolina

Charleston
JK Harris and Company, LLC -- Tax Problems and Solutions, 219

Greenville
Dr. Ira Williams, A Better Health Care Delivery System expert, 110

York
Jeff Harris -- Independent Pension Consultant, 218

South Dakota

Sioux Falls
Dr. Douglas Sea -- DC Mentors -- Chiropractic, 332

Tennessee

Chattanooga
Katie Schwartz -- Business Speech Improvement, 187

Knoxville
Greg Maciolek - Speaker, Author, Business Consultant, 250
Dan Stockdale -- Adventures in Leadership, 138

Memphis
Robin L. Graham -- InnerActive Consulting Group Inc., 240
Voss W. Graham -- InnerActive Consulting, 230
Mahaffey Fabric Structures, 145
Mahaffey Tent and Party Rentals, 145

Nashville
Christopher Bauer, Ph.D. -- Business Ethics Training, 100
Renee Grant-Williams -- Communication Skill Training Expert, 304
Carol M. Swain -- Vanderbilt University Law School, 93

Texas

Austin
The Herman Group -- Strategic Business Futurists, 190
Dave Klivans -- FirePit Ceramics, 162
Donald McLachlan -- Strategic Planning Expert, 262
Nettie Reynolds, 99

College Station
JoAn Majors - Dentistry By Choice, 343

Dallas
Bob Bare--Entrepreneurial Expert, 349
Mellanie True Hills -- Health and Productivity Expert -- StopAfib, 312
Leslie Nolen -- Health, Wellness and Healthcare Trend Expert, 315
Sandra A. Shelton, 237
StopAfib.org American Foundation for Women's Health, 348
Dr. Joyce Willard Teal, 81
Trinity Foundation, Inc -- Religion Fraud Detectives, 99
UT Southwestern Medical Center, 340

Ft. Worth
Mary Murcott -- Customer Service Expert, 203

Hempstead
Tobi Kosanke -- Crazy K Farm Pet and Poultry Products, LLC, 140

Houston
D. Kevin Berchelmann - Speaker -- Strategist -- Executive Facilit, 273
Krista Fabregas -- KidSmartLiving.com, 88
Niels C Nielsen -- Professor of Philosophy and Religious Thought Emeritus, 358
Chaplain Dr. Keith Robinson -- PTSD Media Consultants, LLC, 167
Seymour M. Weaver, III, M.D., Board Certified Dermatologist, 340

Plano
Susan Fletcher, Ph.D., 352

San Antonio
American Payroll Association, 238

Mark Dankof's America, 104
D. Anthony Miles, Ph.D., MCP, RBA, CMA, MBC, 262

Utah

Salt Lake City
EnableMart - Your Number One Source for Assistive Technology, 350
Danny Quintana, 130

Vermont

Woodstock
Antoinette Matlins -- Professional Gemologist, 162

Virginia

Alexandria
Jack Marshall -- ProEthics, Ltd., 100
National Taxpayers Union, 96
Eugene A. Razzetti -- Certified Management Consultant, 263
Larry Tracy -- Expert Presentation Coach, 308

Arlington
American Association of Pharmaceutical Scientists, 335
The American Waterways Operators, 149
Geoff Drucker--Dispute Resolution, 242
Rick Maurer -- Change Management Expert, 270
National Rural Electric Cooperative Association, 135

Fairfax
Jason R. Hanson -- Concealed Carry Academy, 106
Marketing Solutions -- Professional Business Of Beauty, 282

Falls Church
Circle of Friends for American Veterans, 126
National Association of Government Communicators, 104

Glen Allen
eAtlasAmericaInsurance.com --- Atlas America Travel Insurance, 224

Hampton
Rick Frishman -- Morgan James Publishing, 174

Hampton Roads
Sandy Dumont -- The Image Architect, 322

Leesburg
Skills USA-VICA, 93

McLean
Dr. Gary Kaplan -- Integrative Medicine, 349
National Automobile Dealers Association, 150

Monterey
Americans for Immigration Control, Inc., 129

Washington

Wisconsin

Canada

United Kingdom

Participant Index

What do journalists say about the Yearbook of Experts® & ExpertClick.com?

"An invaluable tool."
-- *CNN*

"Dial-an-Expert."
-- *The New York Times*

"... an encyclopedia of sources."
-- *The Associated Press*

"... internet dating service of PR"
-- *PRWeek*

"The type of tool great stories are made of."
-- *Chicago Tribune*

"Something every talk show host must have."
-- *Larry King Show*

"If your clients include experts, you should make sure they are included."
-- *Public Relations Quarterly*

"... it will make your group the central point for interviews in your field."
-- *Association Trends*

"An impressive directory that produces results."
-- *Book Marketing Update*

Broadcast Interview Source, Inc.
Washington, DC
(202) 333-5000
www.ExpertClick.com

Yearbook of Experts®
Volume XXXVIII, No. I
ISBN:0-934333-81-5
ISSN # 1051-4058
Printed Edition: $9.95

CPSIA information can be obtained at www.ICGtesting.com
Printed in the USA
BVOW05s0843060114

340851BV00005B/23/P